First Footprints

First Footprints

Scott Cane

The epic story of the First Australians

ALLEN&UNWIN
SYDNEY • MELBOURNE • AUCKLAND • LONDON

First published in 2013

Allen & Unwin
83 Alexander Street
Crows Nest NSW 2065
Australia
Phone: (61 2) 8425 0100
Email: info@allenandunwin.com
Web: www.allenandunwin.com

Cataloguing-in-Publication details are available
from the National Library of Australia
www.trove.nla.gov.au

ISBN 978 1 74331 493 7

Internal design by Nada Backovic
Maps by Janet Hunt
Illustrations by Alissa Dinallo
Index by Trevor Matthews
Set in 12.2/15.2 pt Bell MT by Post Pre-press Group, Australia
Printed and bound in China by Everbest Printing Co Ltd

Photograph on p. i: Signatory image of the Australian nomad: dreadlocks tied back with twine woven from human hair.
Photograph on p. ii: This magnificent vision conveys a subliminal truth: human frailty in command of the most marginal permanently inhabited environment on earth (Mann Range, far northwest of South Australia).

10 9 8 7 6 5 4 3 2

CONTENTS

First Footprints is based on the four-part documentary series of the same name. It was written, produced and directed by Bentley Dean and Martin Butler, and first screened on ABC TV in 2013. The book includes many stills from the documentary series.

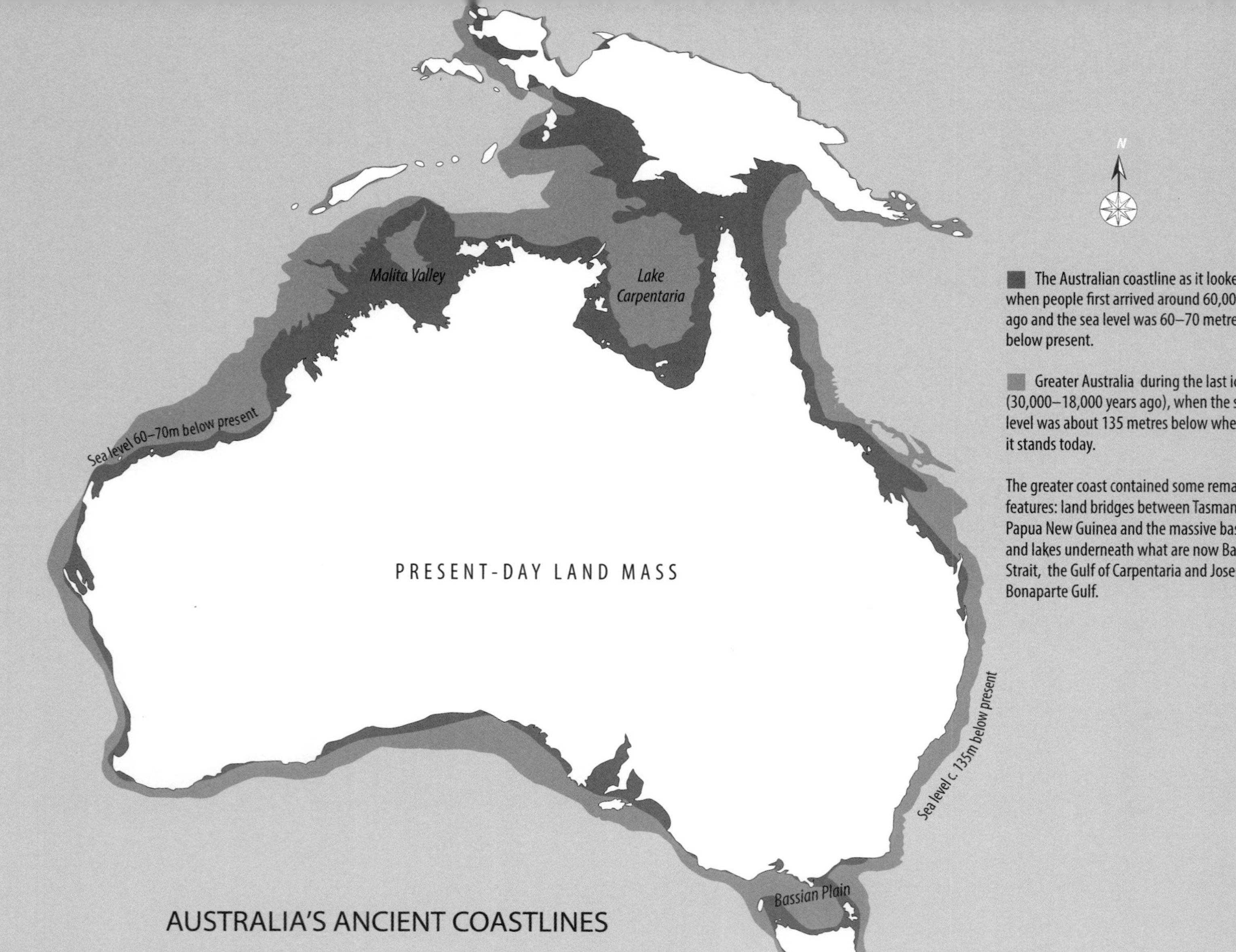
N
Malita Valley
Lake Carpentaria
PRESENT-DAY LAND MASS
Sea level 60–70m below present
Sea level c. 135m below present
Bassian Plain
The Australian coastline as it looked when people first arrived around 60,000 years ago and the sea level was 60–70 metres below present.
Greater Australia during the last ice age (30,000–18,000 years ago), when the sea level was about 135 metres below where it stands today.
The greater coast contained some remarkable features: land bridges between Tasmania and Papua New Guinea and the massive basins and lakes underneath what are now Bass Strait, the Gulf of Carpentaria and Joseph Bonaparte Gulf.
AUSTRALIA'S ANCIENT COASTLINES

TIMOR
Coburg Peninsula
Possession Island
Cape York
PAPUA NEW GUINEA
Bobongara
Ivane Valley
INDIAN OCEAN
Ashmore Reef
Joseph Bonaparte Gulf
Malakunanja
Nauwalabila and Deaf Adder Gorge
Nawarla Gabarnmang
ARNHEM LAND
Groote Eylandt
Cape Keerweer
Gulf of Carpentaria
Buccaneer Archipelago
Koolan and High Cliffy Islands
Widgingarri rock shelter
THE KIMBERLEY
Ingalaadi
Early Man site
Sandy Creek
Magnificent Gallery
Ngarabullgan
NORTH WEST SHELF
Carpenter's Gap
Riwi Cave
TANAMI DESERT
Colless Creek
GRE8
Coral Sea
GREAT SANDY DESERT
Paraku (Lake Gregory)
Yiripanta Range
Nara Inlet
Noala Cave
Karrku mesa
Jansz site
THE PILBARA
Mandu Mandu rock shelter
Djadjiling rock shelter
Puritjarra rock shelter
Kulpi Mara Cave
GIBSON DESERT
PACIFIC OCEAN
Keppel Islands
Serpents' Glen
SIMPSON DESERT
Shark Bay
Silver Dollar site
Wilgie Mia quarry
Wallen Wallen Creek
Mirramirratjara soak
Lake Eyre
GREAT VICTORIA DESERT
Anna Creek quarry
MURRAY–DARLING BASIN
North Creek midden
Hookina Creek
Yantara
Cuddie Springs
Wombah midden
NULLARBOR PLAIN
Ooldea soak
Koonalda Cave
Allen's Cave
FLINDERS RGS
Sturts Meadow
Lime Springs
Rottnest Is.
Upper Swan River
Long Beach
Dempsey's Lagoon
Wadla Wadlyu Quarry
Clybucca midden complex
Birubi Point
Devil's Lair
Tunnel Cave
Mammoth Cave
Cheetup Cave
Great Australian Bight
Lake Nitchie
Lakes Menindee and Tandou
Willandra Lakes (Lake Mungo)
BLUE MTS
Kangaroo Is.
Roonka Flat
Lake George
SNOWY MTS
Currarong
Murray River
Burrill Lake
Seton site
Toolondo
INDIAN OCEAN
Wyrie Swamp
Lancefield Swamp
Cape Howe
Spring Creek
N
King Is.
Bass Strait
Flinders Is.
LOCATIONS MENTIONED IN THE BOOK
TASMANIA
Cave Bay Cave
Rocky Cape
Rushy Lagoon
West Point
Nelson Bay
Greens Creek
Sundown Point
Temma
Parmerpar Meethaner Cave
Warragarra rock shelter
Derwent R.
Warreen Cave
Nunamira Cave
Ballawinnie Cave
Wargata Mina Cave
Carlton Beach

TIMELINE

YEARS AGO	EVENT	SETTING
74,000	*Near extinction*	*Mt Toba explodes in central Sumatra.*
	First ocean crossing	The first people to settle Australia arrive by boat. They make the first oceanic water crossing in world history.
	Increased burning	There is a dramatic increase in charcoal at locations throughout Australia between 73,000 and 60,000 years ago. The increase in firing may have been natural—but it may also be explained by the arrival of people in Australia and their settlement of the country with firesticks in their hands.
60,000	*Super-nomads*	
	Settlement of northern Australia	Artefacts appear for the first time at Malakunanja and Nauwalabila, Arnhem Land.
51,000	Settlement of southeastern Australia	Artefacts in the ancient Willandra Lakes system date between 45,000 and 52,000 years ago.
50,000	People penetrate the Australian desert	One stone artefact is found at Paraku (Lake Gregory) on the northern margin of the Great Sandy Desert.
47,000	Occupation of the far corners of Australia	People were living at Devil's Lair in southwestern Australia.
46,000	Hafted axes	Axes found on an ancient terrace on the Huon Peninsula, Papua New Guinea, are dated to around 46,000 years but may be as old as 61,000 years. Some axes contain traces of starch and are associated with charred nuts that may be 49,000 years old.
45,000	People occupy the arid heartlands Megafauna die out	Artefacts and ochre at Puritjarra, in the Cleland Hills, central Australia. The last of Australia's megafauna become extinct, due to hunting, burning and the effects of climate change.
44,000	Occupation of glacial Tasmania	People occupied caves and hunted wallabies at Parmerpar Meethaner and many other caves across southwestern Tasmania in sub-Antarctic conditions.
42,000	Human burial Human cremation	The complete skeleton of a man is found in the Willandra Lakes. The nature of his burial suggests an early belief in the afterlife. The burial is perhaps the first of its kind on earth. The cremated remains of a small woman were found in the Willandra Lakes—the world's first known cremation.

40,000	Art	Ochre is found coating a slab of limestone at Carpenter's Gap, in the Kimberley—the oldest evidence of art in the world.
36,000	Pre-agricultural activity	New technology, environmental management and food procurement in the New Guinea Highlands suggests pre-agricultural activity at least 15,000 years before anywhere else on earth.
35,000	Ground-edged axes	Fragments of a ground-edged axe are located at Nawarla Gabarnmang, western Arnhem Land.
33,000	Seed grinding	There is variable evidence for the processing and consumption of grass and succulent seeds 10,000 years before anywhere else on earth in the Willandra Lakes and the Kimberley.
32,000	Shell beads	Shell beads have been found at Carpenter's Gap and Riwi in the Kimberley, as well as Mandu Mandu rock shelter on North West Cape. These beads are among the oldest evidence for jewellery in the world and date between 30,000 and 32,000 years ago.
30,000	***The great drought***	
	Glacial drought begins	Australia entered a major ice age 30,000 years ago. The sea levels dropped, temperatures cooled and much of the country was subjected to an extreme drought that lasted 10,000 years.
28,000	Drawing	A charcoal drawing is found on a fragment of rock at Nawarla Gabarnmang.
27,000	Art	Some of the oldest art in the world has been found in southeastern Cape York.
25,000	Facial representations	The first depictions of the human face appear throughout arid Australia. The faces are part of a widespread artistic tradition known as the Panaramitee, thought to be between 10,000 and 25,000 years old.
22,000	Unique footprints	Over 560 footprints representing the tracks of 23 people were left as they hunted and walked in the Willandra Lakes.
21,000	Occupation of the emerging coasts	As the sea began to fall, people occupied the emerging continental shelf. They were living, for example, on the plains now beneath Bass Strait 22,000 years ago and out on the North West Shelf over 30,000 years ago.
20,000	Emergence of dramatic descriptive art	The ancient Gwion and 'Dynamic' art of the Kimberley and Arnhem Land appears. It has been dated to between 16,000 and 23,000 years ago, and displays elaborate personal decoration and technology.

18,000	*The great flood*	
	Ice age ends	The climate begins to warm, the coasts of greater Australia flood and the climate becomes wetter, windier and more unpredictable.
13,000	Conflict	Artistic representations across northern Australia suggest increasing territorial conflict, possibly in response to rising seas and proportional competition for land and resources.
10,000	Regional inundation	Bass Strait and the Gulf of Carpentaria are inundated by rising floodwaters. Thousands of islands are formed around the coast. Populations remaining on Flinders and Kangaroo islands will die out as a consequence.
	Boomerangs	10,000-year-old boomerangs found in a swamp in southeastern Australia—the oldest found.
9000	More efficient tools	A more diverse and efficient range of tools develop, including small 'backed' blades, spear-throwers and composite spears.
6000	Environmental impact	Estuaries around Australia choke with sediments resulting from erosion caused by burning and rainfall, creating enormous mangrove swamps that grow into flood plains over the next 1500 years.
5000	New arrivals	The arrival of the dingo 4500 years ago indicates new arrivals in Australia. A previous migration also seems to have occurred 7000 years ago.
4000	Anatomical drawings	The famous X-Ray art of Arnhem Land emerges, portraying both human and animal anatomy.
3000	Increased territoriality	Evidence for territorial demarcation and conflict, in response to increased population. Economies specialise and there is intense use of coastal resources in southeastern Australia. Sea levels peak and climate becomes increasingly unpredictable (and drier).
2000	Consolidated settlement	Villages emerge across southeastern Australia. People use watercraft. Aquaculture develops and there is evidence for gardening. Complex social and religious systems develop.
1000	Trade and exchange	Extensive trade routes develop across the country for the distribution of precious resources (narcotics and ochre) and tools (boomerangs, grindstones, axes).
300	New arrivals	Indonesian fishers visit and trade on the northern coasts. Portuguese, Dutch and British sailors explore the Australian coastline. British colonists settle.

Introduction

My grandfather had a bag of 'flints'. The bag was made of calico, the sort used in banks to carry small amounts of cash. The flints were (I would eventually discover) not in fact flint but stone artefacts made on 'cherty hornfels'—itself a rather curious name for ancient mudstones that had been cooked hard by equally ancient lava. The material had an appealing fine-grained texture, enriched by the scalloped fractures on the stone made by the people who used it. The artefacts fascinated me as a child, and I would look at them and touch them at every chance. My interest was subliminal, almost tangible but as yet unformed. The aesthetic appeal of the artefacts drew me to some mysterious human place I could neither understand nor stop longing for—where had they come from, who had made them and what were they for?

My grandfather was crippled after being shot in the hip during World War I. In the 1960s he was old and could no longer walk easily. He lived as a hermit in an old wooden army hut among the sand dunes on what was then a remote windswept beach—Clifton Beach, in southern Tasmania. He was a large man with a powerful frame, a formidable personality and a swaying limp that stopped conversations when he entered a room. He had presence, and most people were frightened of him. I was terrified. So I never asked about the flints, how he came by them, or what they were, what they meant or who they once belonged to. My parents told me they belonged to people who lived here before us, a long time ago. Where had they gone? Who were they? Where did they live? No one seemed to know. And so the flints were all the more mysterious.

As a child I would walk through the dunes on my grandfather's windswept beach and look for more flints, imagining the people who made them (who I was sure were watching me) and seeking the places they lived. I found them in vast carpets of shells and stone split across open dunes. And I found them in layers within sand dunes, trapped underneath sand that, I intuited, meant they were underneath the ground on which I walked and so belonged to a time before time. The revelation told me, in an untutored way, there was something about the island I lived on that I didn't understand: there was another human experience in the places I loved, that I could see and feel but could not quite grasp.

So, in time I began to look further, in other places, within theses, histories, microfiche and explorers' journals. I discovered there were people who lived in Tasmania when all of Tasmania looked like the remote parts I loved most. And I discovered that these people lived in comparative peace for a staggeringly long period of time before my great grandparents arrived to live there as well. These were people who lived in Tasmania without destroying its natural beauty or degrading its natural bounty. Their Tasmania was a different Tasmania, and theirs was a unique story of a remarkable society of great antiquity, which survived ice ages and walked with strange now-extinct animals through changing environments I could only imagine. The Tasmania of my experience was little more than a veneer on a rich and ancient history. It was history in need of appreciation in a country not quite understood.

Yet, in my youth, the story of Australia before Europeans was not told. At that time there was no school curriculum dedicated to the true social history of Australia, and the matter of Aboriginal prehistory was only (newly) taught at one Australian university.

While Australians generally learnt about the British Empire and 'first settlement' from atlases coloured pink, a revolution in archaeological investigation was revealing that first settlement was in fact 60,000 years earlier and that the first settlers were black not white. The first settlers, archaeologists were discovering, had in fact made the first oceanic crossing in the history of humankind, performed the oldest human cremations on earth, revered the afterlife before anyone else, dug the oldest mines in continuous use, painted the largest art galleries on the planet, and were the first to recognise and depict the human face, paint battle scenes, make axes and invent the returning boomerang. Australia's first settlers recall the longest oral histories and belong to the oldest continuing culture on earth.

Much of this was known 40 years ago and all of it was known 20 years ago, but it is still possible to ask any Australian—as I did of my taxi driver from the airport last night—about that history and be greeted with the same blank stare and the same shrug of the shoulders. The original Australian story remains one of the world's greatest unknown human narratives. But it is, by decades and degrees, a story that appears ever more frequently in school curricula and university courses, in social commentary and political discourse. There are now over 1000 Australian archaeologists, and the Aboriginal voice, gifted with emotive political nuance, speaks loud in proportion to its constituent base. Aboriginal heritage is quite big business. There is, as well, a growing national empathy for an Australian Aboriginality, that is as intuitive as it is informed (more and more people seem to know that 'Aboriginal people have been here for 40,000 years', even though they have actually been here much longer) and there is an increasing urban awareness of something greater, yet to be understood, about the country we live in and the people who occupied it before European settlement.

It is in this emergent social context that documentary filmmakers Martin Butler and Bentley Dean sat with archaeologist Peter Veth during the making of their award-winning documentary *Contact*,[1] in 2009, and discussed his idea of telling this great story to an Australian TV audience. The story had not been previously told in this way and its fabric (from first settlement to European settlement, and across vast landscapes which changed dramatically through immeasurable time), enriched by modern archaeology and the science of dating and genetics, might lend itself to epic and informed viewing.

Thus *First Footprints* began—a story about the people who made the first footprints on Australian sands, and a distant answer to the questions I had asked of my grandfather's 'flints' almost 50 years before. *First Footprints* is a story of and by Aboriginal people and archaeologists, told through oral history, art, ethnography, science and intuition via contemporary film, archival footage and computer-generated imagery.

This book is a product of that documentary, a companion that seeks to capture its imagery and elaborate its themes. The book is some 70,000 words long and, in appreciation of the story about to unfold, the reader might imagine that each word read is equivalent to one year of time lived. This is the greatest Australian story, one of enormous antiquity and remarkable diversity, a story of monumental events and incredible environments, and of the people who came first, settled and stayed. It is about events leading up to the first settlement of Australia and the nature of settlement itself. It is about the character and consequences, mechanisms and means of continental colonisation in ancient times, and of ongoing human experience through distant millennia, across a great ice age and through a great flood. It is, in short, a story about the people and the cultural landscape that constitute the sunburnt country we call home.

Scott Cane
July 2013

In the desert, food is everywhere but nowhere to be seen. Here children dig for witchetty grubs. They will have enough food for the day in about two hours (Musgrave Ranges, northern South Australia).

1 Near Extinction

74,000–60,000 YEARS AGO

'Until we arrive in the Great Ocean where we are battled and tossed by the angry waves. Onward and onward.'

—David Unaipon, 'Narrinyeri Saying', *Native Legends*, 1929

Fire

The first footprints were running. They didn't run for long because the people making them died. Others followed as far as they could before they, too, died. Some were too scared to move. Others didn't have time. Children screamed, mothers ran to them, fathers strained in anxious desperation. But there was little to be done, for at that moment Mount Toba erupted.

Further away, across the lowlands of southern Sumatra, the earth moved with such force that people were thrown high and landed hard. Heat seared and wind tore through the whiplashed forest. A girl watched her brother fall broken from the treetop where he was collecting honey. She ran down the hill slope, stretching herself towards the camp. The stream was dry, blocked by an avalanche in its headwaters. The plains were empty, swept bare by the monstrous velocity of the tsunami. There was no life. Dead bodies. Mud. Fish. She staggered as others around her fell to their knees. Nothing was left. It started to rain, fine grey drops that washed the colour from the remnants of the forest.

Previous pages: The surprising thing about a dugout canoe is that it has a fast hull shape, is very stable and never sinks. The ancestors of these Arnhem Landers made the first ocean crossing to Australia over 60,000 years ago.

She found her father, but her mother and sisters were gone. The rain continued and the morning was cold. She felt empty, her grief compounded by the steady fall of ashen rain. Even the sun had fled from the ferocity of the earth's violence.

People clustered in the forested foothills. None cared to go higher. Small people lived there, and with them danger lurked. But hunger turned an organic wheel and some among them started to move. We must eat and we must shelter.

And we must go. Home is devastation. The coast is unsafe; the mountains explode. There are people who will harm us. We will travel the middle road, down from the mountains, up from the shore. Grief belongs to the shore. We must go south. We will travel south, away from the rain, as far from this place as we can go.

The great eruption

The Toba eruption is the largest volcanic eruption in the last 2.5 million years.[1] It occurred about 74,000 years ago,[2] and destroyed the central northern section of northern Sumatra—obliterating an area about half the size of Tasmania. By comparison, the eruption of Krakatoa in 1883, the most violent in recent history, blew 20 cubic kilometres of rock into the air, was heard over 4800 kilometres away and reverberated around the world seven times. Krakatoa was equal in force to 200 megatonnes of TNT—four times the size of the most powerful thermonuclear weapon ever detonated—and unleashed a 40-metre tidal wave that was even registered in the English Channel.[3] But the super-eruption at Toba was 20–40 times larger than Krakatoa: it blew *3000* cubic kilometres of volcanic rock into the air, beyond the world's atmosphere and at least 40 kilometres into space at a rate of about 10 million tonnes per second. Of that pyroclastic vastness, 800 cubic kilometres was ash[4]—surging up and then sweeping northwest and northeast 2500 kilometres with the trade winds and jet stream towards the Indian subcontinent and China. The ash covered some 5 million square kilometres—more recent assessments suggest 10 million square kilometres—over the Indian subcontinent, and south and west across the Indian Ocean, the Bay of Bengal and as far as the Arabian and East China Sea.[5] In Malaysia, 400 kilometres from Toba, ash fell in layers up to 3 metres thick. Much of India and Pakistan was also covered with up to 3 metres of ash.[6] By comparison, no ash travelled more than 200 kilometres from the source of Krakatoa.

The region around Mount Toba must have been shaking and erupting by degrees for decades prior to the eruption, and one might imagine that people living in the vicinity would have long since fled. But how do people anticipate the consequences of something that is beyond anticipation? How far is far enough from the inconceivable, the extreme in nature, that which is beyond cataclysmic and against which there is no human reference point for safe judgement. No one could have foreseen the consequences of the eruption, or what it would mean in human terms—who can imagine the near end of the human world? Even today our vocabulary is not adequate to convey the magnitude of the event and our science can only just describe it through expressions of magnitude. And so, in the absence of words of adequate physical and emotional force, the violence of the eruption is described in hyper-affected English—the eruption becomes a 'super-eruption' of 'mega-colossal' proportions. Measures of magnitude and intensity become 'exceptional', and exception itself begs enhancement to give it due measure. The compounding sense of tragedy, fear, awe and catastrophe are compartmentalised into statistical segments of earth quaking, tsunami and sound wave, set beyond empathy in the realm of descriptive science as conduit for arrested emotion and apprehension.

The eruption at Mount Toba lasted almost two weeks, after which an area of almost 30,000 square kilometres was devastated—covered with a layer of volcanic rock between 50 and 400 metres thick. The inferno of poisonous gas, lava, rock and ash moved across the tropical landscape like liquid fire at a rate of 1 million cubic metres per second at a temperature of 750 degrees Celsius (at the vent) and 550 degrees Celsius (when it came to rest). The heat must have remained for years, accompanied by months of explosions, secondary eruptions and magma flows.[7]

Then it was over. But what was left? Regional devastation set under a mushroom cloud filled with sulfuric acid aerosols and silica dust that stretched 20–40 kilometres into the sky. The paroxysm now spread as this ash, dust and gas blew across the northern hemisphere. The sky darkened, perhaps as light as an overcast day, perhaps as dark as night under a full moon. Leaves were coated with ash, and photosynthesis slowed, then stopped. Forests turned to grassland, animal populations declined, extinctions occurred, temperatures fell, aridity increased. The world was already in the grip of an emerging ice age, and much of eastern and southern Africa was experiencing a 'mega-drought'. Now the cooling and drying accelerated, and the changed atmospheric conditions created a volcanic winter that lasted for years: the atmospheric after-effects of Toba were comparable to a nuclear winter.[8]

This winter initiated 1000–1800 years of relentless cold, the first 200 years of which were aggravated by high concentrations of atmospheric dust from erosion, desiccating forests and sediments exposed by dropping sea levels. Recent estimates describe a period that was perhaps the coldest on earth over the last 125,000 years, accompanied by prolonged drought and semi-desert in vast areas of the Indian subcontinent and the Middle East.[9]

Reduced photosynthesis led to low environmental productivity that in turn led to famine. The consequences were devastating for humanity. Environmental and climatic diversity created human refuges within the disaster area, but the human population suffered horribly—reduced, perhaps, to a population of 50,000 people in which there were as few as 4000–10,000 breeding females. (There are 1 billion reproducing females on the planet today.)[10]

The scenario is, the reader might feel, too nightmarish to believe and impossible to accept in global human terms. No volcano could be *that* big. How could the human population be reduced so? Surely humans were able to adapt to the sudden environmental changes. If the population did reduce so dramatically how could it recover so fast in the subsequent millennia?

Ancient humans

My own feelings reverberate between the science (documenting the magnitude of the eruption) and my intuition (which has difficulty believing it). I find it hard to accept that such an event, as large as it was, had such a global consequence and could impact humankind so devastatingly. Other scientists have questioned the consequences accordingly, but the geological and genetic evidence seems to point to disaster: these were 'the most critical millennia in human history'. And it seems that it was then, after the catastrophe of Mount Toba, that modern humans emerged from Africa and expanded rapidly across the globe: 'When the modern African human diaspora passed through the prism of Toba's volcanic winter, a rainbow of difference appeared.'[11]

But what of those left behind? What about those who survived in refuges in the path of the firestorm? And what about those who sat in the lee of the great explosion? It is likely that all those living on the coast were killed by the largest tsunamis humankind has ever seen. The coast was then about 60 metres below its current level so all traces of that devastation and those people rest deep underwater. But in those inland areas where the explosions were heard and the earthquakes felt, but where oceanic surges could not reach, and the heat and ash did not penetrate, it is possible that life continued. Mammalian populations survived in an arc 350–1800 kilometres south and east of the eruption. One might infer that people did also.[12]

Ancient humans were living in the Indonesian archipelago before and after the super-volcanic eruption. *Homo erectus* has been living in Java for 1.8 million years and there is disputed evidence that they continued to do so until 27,000 years ago. Remains of *Homo erectus* found on Flores in Indonesia have been dated to 840,000 years ago and recent dates suggest a minimum age of over 1 million years—indicating, apart from that brilliant chronology, these ancient people travelled far and made numerous water crossings in ancient times.[13]

The small skeletons of *Homo floresiensis* have also been found in a cave called Liang Bua on Flores Island. They have an antiquity of possibly 74,000 years and survived to at least 38,000 if not 18,000 years ago. They made and left thousands of stone tools, and hunted komodo dragons and young pygmy elephants.[14] It is also apparent that an ancient people known as Denisovans were living in Indonesia before and after this time. They have genetic links with Australian nomads that point to dispersal into eastern Asia 62,000–75,000 years ago.[15] Modern humans (*Homo sapiens*) may also have been living in the archipelago in these ancient times, across the time of the Mount Toba eruption. There is, for example, tentative evidence for modern humans in Java 125,000 years ago as well as artefacts elsewhere in Java and Sulawesi indicating modern humans may have lived there 70,000–74,000 years ago.[16] The explosion at Mount Toba did not terminate these populations. Life, it would seem, went on in the eastern part of Indonesia, upwind from the volcanic catastrophe.

But what did it do to them in the short term? How did these ancient people respond to the violence of the eruption? What did the great explosion feel like and how did it sound? How much and how often did the archipelago shake as tectonic shocks, avalanches and tsunamis cascaded across the region before and after the eruption? What did people think as temperatures cooled, aridity increased and the volcanic winter encroached? Did they stay where they were and accept the cacophony and upheaval of their known world, or did they seek sanctuary from it? Could that super-eruption have encouraged *Homo floresiensis* to move south to Flores, perhaps finding safe refuge in the mountains? Could that cataclysm have encouraged people to move east along the Indonesian archipelago? Could it have triggered migration to Australia?[17]

Perhaps one has to have experienced earthquakes, volcanic eruptions and tsunamis to have a sense of what it must have been like. I have been in villages devastated by tsunamis, and have experienced half a dozen earthquakes, including one in which I was nearly killed, in Padang, 500 kilometres south of Lake Toba, in 2009. The magnitude of this quake was insignificant compared with Toba, but nonetheless registered a magnitude of 7.9, destroyed the homes and livelihoods of 1.25 million people and killed several thousand people in less than 20 seconds. The quake was felt in Jakarta, 900 kilometres away. The event itself was traumatising, but it was the psychological effects of repeated aftershocks—up to five or six a day for several months—that drove families to migrate into the hills away from the coast and built environments. The psychological toll was crippling—exhausted adults, fearing for their lives, the safety of their children and their livelihoods, were reduced to involuntary fits of tears, unable to see through the days, weeks, months to come.

Today, the frequency of tectonic movement in this part of the world is continual and distressing.[18] The mounting fear is subliminal, suppressed in the face of a known reality: that these are aftershocks from the 'Boxing Day Tsunami', west of the Andaman islands, on 26 December 2004, and, as tectonic pressures increase, the prospect of the predicted 'big one' moves ever closer.[19] The earthquake that triggered that devastating tsunami was the third largest ever recorded. It had a magnitude of 9.2 and lasted 10 minutes, generating a 30-metre high tsunami that killed over 240,000 people. It set off earthquakes as far away as Alaska and caused the earth to vibrate as much as 1 centimetre. The energy released was equivalent to 56 megatonnes of TNT—1500 times the size of the atomic bomb dropped on Hiroshima in World War II, but 53 times smaller than the Mount Toba eruption.

How difficult it must have been for those living in the eastern Indonesian archipelago to have stayed after Mount Toba erupted. People I know who live in this zone of distress today have adjusted to the threshold of tension and risk. They would move away from the daily tension if they could, only population levels are high and there is nowhere to go. In the past there were fewer people, and one might expect that, after something as horrific as Mount Toba, those who had not already gone would have moved as far away as they could. How far could they go?

Boat people

Movement south from Sumatra was comparatively easy 74,000 years ago: a cooler climate and sea levels some 60 metres below present levels created a land bridge between Sumatra and Java (the water today is only 20 metres deep at the narrowest crossing). It was possible to walk between Singapore and Java in those days. From here a number of water crossings were required to get further south, but none were insurmountable:[20] *Homo erectus* had already achieved them 840,000 years ago. Even today it is only 2 kilometres from Java to Bali, and just 22 kilometres from Bali to Lombok (via an island in the centre of the Lombok Strait). Lower sea levels at the time of Toba narrowed and decreased the number of crossings required, although the precipitous nature of Indonesian islands meant the distances did not change much with changes in sea level.[21] Today, six water crossings are required to get to Flores from Lombok: 74,000 years ago there were probably three or four crossings, with the widest sea a distance of no more than 15 kilometres and the shortest a mere 300 metres. From Flores there were another five short (less than 14-kilometre) crossings to Alor, and then a final 20-kilometre leap to Timor. Australia was the next stop.[22]

People had made a number of these crossings a long time ago—a long time before Mount Toba erupted. The evidence of *Homo erectus* in Flores makes that obvious. How these people made the voyages remains a mystery, but a number of options are self-evident. They may have swum, floated on bamboo or bamboo rafts, on trees, large logs, small logs, logs with bamboo stabilisers, or logs that had been levelled or hollowed for protection and seaworthiness. The inter-island seas of tropical Java and Sumatra are awash with floating logs and trees after standard tropical storms, such that it is dangerous to navigate at night. One might assume this was also the case in the past—floating debris was unlikely to have been hard to find. After the tsunamis and earthquakes associated

A staged photo taken at Mabuyag, Torres Strait, showing a craft equipped for down-wind sailing: a single hull, simple outriggers and natural sails.

with the Mount Toba eruption the surrounding seas must have been choked with driftwood.

The climate at the time of the explosion was similar to today's, perhaps cooler, with lower sea levels than today. Things would have deteriorated rapidly after the cataclysm, but otherwise one might reasonably expect there to have been as many suitable woods for craft construction in the tropical jungles then as there are now. I recall on one occasion on Sipora Island (in the Mentawai Islands, 500 kilometres southeast of Toba) hearing a relatively disconcerting chant coming from the upper headwaters of the remote river we were navigating. Voices are muffled in such jungles and distances are difficult to judge. On this occasion the distant voices turned out to be two river bends away and, before we had time to express the mounting concern we were feeling, 26 men rounded the corner alternately pushing and resting on a 15-metre tree trunk they had cut from the forest and were taking downriver to their village. All the men were either astride, pushing or hanging from the log—its flotation was readily apparent. Our surprised distress was their pleasure—for our small inflatable boat and 4 horsepower outboard soon became the donkey that dragged the trunk and its passengers the rest of the way back to the village. It was a lucky encounter for them. A large ceremonial feast waited, after which boat construction began. A tree trunk is clearly a rudimentary ship.

Whatever the craft used in the distant past, sea crossings cannot have been without hazard—but it is surprising how far the most flimsy craft can travel in the hands of a competent seaman. On another occasion, sailing along the western side of Java, we met and ate lunch with a man camped adjacent to a shallow anchorage on Nusa Barong (southeastern Java). His small dugout was drawn up on the beach, its triangular sail rolled down and its bamboo outrigger resting on the cobbles. The next day we sailed to an anchorage in Pujiharjo, 60 kilometres further north. The trade wind was strong, gusting around 27 knots, on a large swell. As we entered the bay, looking for an anchorage, we were surprised to see the same man from the previous day sailing towards us, waving enthusiastically and pointing us to safe anchorage. He had travelled the same 60 kilometres, in the same wind and swell, in an open boat, faster than us. (Perhaps he had left earlier?) The point is that this 60-kilometre sail was clearly nothing out of the ordinary for this man, in a vessel that I thought was largely unseaworthy and certainly too small for such a voyage. The moral of the story is that seamanship and endurance counterbalance the need for sophisticated watercraft and so, whatever the possible craft and whatever its possible means of propulsion (sticks, paddles, arms, sails of bark, broad leaf or woven mat), ancient inter-island navigation was probably easier (and may have been more frequent) than one might think it to have been.[23] There is a small postscript to this story: later that same day a 40-tonne Filipino fishing trawler came into the same anchorage and stayed for three days. The reason they had chosen safe-harbour was that the previous year their sister ship had rolled and sunk in similar wind and swell conditions. All hands were lost. We did not notice the severity of the conditions in our boat. Nor, apparently, did the Indonesian in his open dugout. But the large steel flat-bottomed trawler saw the conditions as life-threatening. Size and sophistication are not everything; seamanship and endurance count for more.

The example is not to underestimate the difficulty involved in making inter-island crossings, but it helps contextualise them. Risks existed, but they may have been no more or less than the risks on land—from disease, other predators and neighbours, not to mention earthquakes, volcanoes and tsunamis. The sea is a dangerous place, and the crossing between Bali and Lombok was probably the most dangerous, even though the islands can be seen from each other on a clear day. Here the current is diurnal and strengthened by the prevailing winds. It is among the strongest currents in the world, running at rates of up to 6 knots (11 kilometres an hour), with frightening overfalls, eddies and windborne turbulence.

Local currents, generally, can be surprisingly quick: in 1909 a boat off the south coast of Java reported a current drift of 130 kilometres in a day,[24] meaning, of course, that, in the past, a coastal sailor might make a long shore trip (perhaps an inter-island crossing) without even meaning to. Normally Indonesian currents are not as strong, although the normal surface currents still travel about 30 kilometres a day. The direction changes with the seasons so the movement is north along the islands during the dry season (June to August, concordant with the southeasterly trades), and south down the chain during the wet (December to February, concordant with the summer monsoon).[25] The transitional months are a bit of a mixture.

The inter-island currents decrease significantly as one moves east towards Timor and New Guinea—although the rates might be still as high as 3 knots (5 kilometres an hour), which translates to an average movement of 20–30 kilometres a day most of the time.[26] The South Equatorial Current to the south of Indonesia flows westward at a rate of about 1 knot (1.8 kilometres), raising the probability that, in the absence of opposing winds, any unfortunate person washed out to sea may be never seen again.

Other marine conditions are conducive to inter-island crossings: the southeasterly trades (which also blew 70,000 years ago) assist the sea surface currents and create a steady, reliable breeze for island hopping in the dry season. The summer monsoons do the same in reverse and provide a gentler southwesterly breeze, rarely more than 10 knots. This is an ideal wind for moving down the island chain and, in fact, as far as Australia. The gale frequency is less than 1 per cent across the archipelago throughout the year. It increases to the south—being as high (or as low, depending on your perspective) as 5–10 per cent towards the Kimberley Coast of Australia. Tropical storms are a threat but they are also rare. The average frequency of tropical storms across the ocean south of Timor is less than one a year.[27] They occur between January and April, and always veer southwest towards Australia. Water temperatures are between 26 and 28 degrees Celsius—allowing for a minimum survival time in seawater of at least a day, but much longer for a fit, robust individual (enough time for a current to take a person across a standard inter-island strait).

Archaic sea crossings were thus rather more possible than one might think, with or without sophisticated watercraft. The combination of abundant wood and bamboo, cooperative currents and winds, warm sea temperatures and long survival rates meant that both planned and accidental inter-island crossings were feasible—and perhaps frequent for any knowledgeable, committed individual. And, clearly, such crossings were made: ancient humans made them to Flores at least 840,000 years ago.[28] The juvenile pygmy elephants hunted by *Homo floresiensis* made the crossing as well, although they probably swam.[29] Sea travel was a reality.

Pleasant weather and favourable winds

The likelihood of ancient sea travel raises an obvious question: when did people cross to Australia? Did they do it a long, long time ago—well before any impetus from the Toba super-eruption? Given that *Homo erectus* had made water crossings almost 1 million years previously it is conceivable that they also crossed to Australia—or ended up there by accident: theoretically, a young pregnant female on a log could have been Australia's Eve.[30] An argument could be mounted that colonisation by castaways must have happened across that vastness of time. The necessary conditions—flotation, wind, current, sea level, endurance and bad luck—are likely to have coincided at least a few times over the hundreds and hundreds of thousands of years since people first took to the sea. The possibility has been discussed accordingly,[31] but as yet there is insufficient archaeological or genetic evidence to support it. And, apart from the factor of chance and bad luck, it is difficult to think of a motivation for making that last long sea voyage to the great southern land. Why would anyone do it? Post-Toba sentiments may have been different.

Then, as mentioned, the sea level was about 60, perhaps 80, metres below its present level (see the map on page vi).[32] This meant that much of the continental shelf along northern Australia was exposed. Ashmore Reef was then the tip of a long, attractively shaped peninsula rising about 10 metres above sea level.[33] Its distance was only 130 kilometres from Timor—about six times the largest distance humans had already crossed between islands. Another part of the continental shelf was exposed closer to Timor, forming a large plateau-like island (25 kilometres across), 18 kilometres northeast of Ashmore Peninsula and 90 kilometres from Timor—four times the inter-island sea miles already made good: still some distance, but notably shorter. Distance may not have been a relevant factor in any case, as it is unlikely that the first voyagers actually knew how far away Australia was. Given that the original seafarers were competent, the actual distance was only relevant in proportion to that competence. The critical elements, I would have thought, were knowledge (including seamanship), craft, provisions and timing.

Of knowledge, the primary consideration was an awareness that another landmass actually existed to the south. This was most likely known because the environment indicators are strong. Even today one can sense Australian aridity and see the end-of-dry-season haze when standing on the southwestern tip of Timor—and it is over 500 kilometres away today. The Australian continent influences the weather in Timor. It is hotter there than further north and the sky has a pastel orange haze. The sense of a large, hot landmass to the south is implicit even with 500 kilometres separating the two islands. In the past, with only 90 kilometres between Timor and Australia, it must have been possible to smell Australia. The glow of wild bushfires must have been visible at night, and large smoke-filled clouds during the day—dust from the southeast trades makes visibility poor across the Timor Sea even today. Violent thunderstorms may have been sighted although the land itself was too low to have been seen. Migratory birds would have also provided a clear indication of land to the south, and the occasional beach-washed derelict must have been food for thought—or, more likely, thought for food.[34]

Knowledge of the seasons, particularly the best time to sail, would have been beneficial: the dry season was less suitable because the winds and currents moved away from Australia. The wet season was more attractive, save for the risk of storms. At this time of year the winds and currents generally headed in the right direction—with the added likely bonus of accompanying rains (drinking water). Travel in this season also meant arriving in Australia when water was abundant. The climate of Timor and the southern Indonesian archipelago was like northern Australia—dry in the dry season and wet in the wet.

A number of scholars have speculated about the type of craft people may have used to make such a journey. Crafts made of bamboo are a possibility, although there is less sizeable bamboo in the southern latitudes of Indonesia.[35]

Bamboo does, however, create a handy storage container—the segmented structure of the great grass provides a perfect container for transporting water and food. Fishermen and coastal foragers in remote Indonesia use bamboo in this way today—typically carrying sweetened rice and water in its natural compartments. The mixture can be stored and steamed over fire within the bamboo, although often the mixture is carried already cooked: the world's first takeaway. In the past, treated rhizomes, nuts and palm sugar may have travelled just as well,[36] as would fresh shellfish such as the giant clam, or any unfortunate turtle kept upside down in the boat.

An alternative building material for sea-faring craft would, I imagine, have been tree trunks, modified or not, lashed or singular. Some sort of propulsion would have helped—rudimentary paddles, or sails of bark or various broad-leaf tropical leaves (single leaves, on branches, bound or matted). The windage of such natural, unmodified materials is surprisingly effective—people still use broad tropical leaves and palm fronds for downwind sailing with dugout canoes today in the remoter parts of Indonesia. Even the windage of a human body has surprising velocity—ask anyone who has recently tried to paddle a standup paddleboard into the wind.

The ocean itself in this part of the world is not demanding: 'ideal cruising' is how it is described today, with wind and sea conditions mild in comparison to a typical southern Australian sea breeze. The sea state was probably considerably calmer then—with currents, swell and wind reduced by the cooler climate.[37] Today the current across the Banda Sea, between the Moluccas and New Guinea, moves about 20 kilometres per day,[38] and this, with a favourable breeze, would transport people to land in three or four days. A current of just one knot would result in over 40 kilometres being made good a day. Thus the 90-kilometre ocean crossing between

Timor and Australia could have been a leisurely two to three day downwind sail (if undertaken in the wet season). The possibility is digestible—particularly as it appears that coastal foragers in those times were familiar with the sea and its resources. Excavations in southeastern Timor, for example, have revealed coastal fishers using sophisticated fishing technology, with fishermen capturing open ocean fish such as tuna 42,000 years ago.[39] Clearly these ancient people knew the sea.

There is oral history of a recent, accidental sea crossing between Timor and Australia that provides some insight into past possibilities and experiences. The story goes that nine generations ago (approximately 200 years ago), a vessel carrying a cargo of palm sugar was forced to run ahead of a storm for five days, after which it was in the open seas. The crew did not know where they were but saw seabirds and, thinking this indicated another country where they could seek help, followed the birds returning to land. As they followed they saw the green reflection on the clouds and so, with added confidence, sailed into the western end of what is now Ashmore Reef. The vessel had no compass, but the sailors were familiar with the night sky and used the Southern Cross as a back bearing to steer north and return home.[40]

There is considerable archaeological discussion about the route the original colonisers might have taken.[41] If they came around 70,000 years ago the sea level was low and the crossing from Timor was a possibility. If they came later, say around 50,000 years ago, when the sea level was possibly 20 metres higher[42] and the Ashmore Peninsula and its neighbouring islands were underwater, Australia would have been 200 kilometres away, in which case a northerly route from Sulawesi through the Moluccas to New Guinea might have been more likely.[43] The debate here is engaging and goes some way to helping us understand how people settled Australia, but it is unlikely to amount to more than preferred speculation, as the route and associated landfall(s) have been under at least 50 metres of water for the last 15,000 years. We will never know where, how or exactly when people arrived in Australia. What is known is that conditions around 70,000 years ago were conducive and the consequences of the Mount Toba eruption might have provided encouragement.

First settlement

Genetic research suggests that the founding population of Australia was in the order of 1000 people.[44] This is a surprising and intriguing figure. It is larger and more focused than one might intuitively expect. Colonisation seems to have been a simultaneous event—not, as one might expect, incremental, sporadic and over a long period of time. The founding population seems to have been a single migration composed of a number of separate, closely spaced events.[45] The landing parties were likely to have contained between five and ten women, and thus about 10–20 people each. The craft must have been quite large or the number of boats considerable (at least 50 boats if each carried just 20 people). Why did they come, and why did they come all at once? How many actually emigrated if some were presumably lost on the journey? What were they thinking, and what were they expecting to find?

Genetic evidence provides a link, directly or indirectly, between the catastrophic events at Mount Toba and colonisation: the estimated antiquity of common (maternal) genetic ancestors of all living Aboriginal people is similar to the date of the Toba explosion.[46] But the temporal window is wide, with research indicating that Australia may have been colonised anytime between 45,000 and 75,000 years ago—the primigenial conclusion being that over 70,000 years have passed since the most recent common female ancestor of Aboriginal people. The estimated antiquity of common (maternal) genetic ancestors of all living Aboriginal people is similar to the date of the Toba explosion.[47]

Were their ancestors already in Indonesia at the time of the Toba catastrophe? Or did they come afterwards? The available

After surviving the perilous sea crossing, Australia's first arrivals faced many new threats. *Megalania prisca*, which grew up to 7 metres in length, was both fast and carnivorous.

evidence allows for both possibilities but increasingly suggests that they were already there. There is, as already mentioned, some evidence that modern humans were in India and southeastern Asia over 70,000 years ago and genetic evidence that the ancestors of the first Australians were in Asia 62,000–75,000 years ago.[48] If they were there, and they survived the eruption, they may well have migrated east and, perhaps, moved on to Australia. If they were not there, then others soon were.

Something dramatic happened to human culture and demography in Africa around the same time, circa 75,000 years ago.[49] This spark period saw a cultural explosion, accelerated human evolution and rapid global colonisation—so rapid that people occupied every continent from Africa to Australia in no time at all, perhaps over a period as little as 3000 years.[50] If the colonisers followed a southern coastal route around the Indian subcontinent to Southeast Asia then they travelled and settled at least 20,000 kilometres of coast—at the staggering rate of 6 kilometres per year. In Asia the entire 4500-kilometre northern arc could have been accomplished within a millennium, equalling a colonisation rate of 4.5 kilometres a year.[51]

That figure is fast, so fast one might be forgiven for thinking that it relates to a plague of locusts rather than human beings. It implies a momentum that must have tested the fundamental sociability and inter-communal dependencies that define humanity and on which the process itself was dependent. The inferred rate of colonisation allows little time for social development, the establishment and transmission of tradition, and the cultural and material adaptation required to meet the diverse environmental needs and social challenges they would have encountered along the way[52] (such as the 'mega-drought' in eastern Africa, the extreme aridity of the Middle East and possibly encounters with other entrenched and defensive refuge populations en route).

This period of time is thought to have been associated with key structural shifts in human social evolution. It is likely that regional social systems and networks evolved with 'social structure dominated by resource ownership, defense and control'.[53] People are thought to have been 'accustomed to maintaining connections with others over long distances, to which ideas of reciprocity and exchanging information were routine'; they 'were at one with their surroundings, no longer another predator among predators, but true human beings'.[54] This social archaeological portrayal begs a question: how were social networks maintained, and resources controlled, in such a transient, expansive social state?

Social nomadism necessarily includes extended travel and communication over vast distances, but it is also dependent on defined territory.[55] Exchange, cooperation, social engagement, intermarriage, and many other shared and learnt experiences are features of established nomadic society and stand in contrast to the instability implied by rapid colonisation. Mobility without acculturated territory is not consistent with human behaviour and its distinctive adaptive social structure: kinship, community, and society, defined and maintained by established tradition. Extreme nomadism allows for such attribution within the context of known country, but less so in the context of a population on the run.

From a human perspective it makes sense for more time to be factored into the colonising process. But even with more time, a further question emerges for reflection. What social and economic motivators drove the expansion? If the population numbers in African refuges were as small as they are said to have been after the eruption, what drove people to colonise—let alone colonise with such momentum? Why did so few travel so far so fast—across devastated environments in partial recovery? The answer here does not add up. Rapid population growth is given as an explanation but is hampered by a general scarcity of archaeological evidence to demonstrate it. That scarcity is in turn explained by low population numbers—and so invalidates the assumption of high population that is said to give rise to it in the first place, as the motivation for colonisation.[56]

It is possible that the colonisers moved around the ancient coasts and evidence of their settlement is now underwater. Sea levels were rising through the period of colonisation so the archaeology of such coastal settlement may have been drowned. But coastal colonisation, as a total colonising experience, seems unnecessarily limiting in the context of global settlement: such a vast human experience is likely to have left evidence in other places as well. Furthermore, destruction of coastal archaeological evidence by sea level rise seems less likely in the Indonesian region where, as already noted, the islands are generally steep and minimally affected by encroaching seas. In any case, the earliest evidence for people in Indonesia that might be associated with such migration is both coastal and inland.

On the island of Sarawak, Borneo, for example, archaeological materials, terrestrial food remains and a modern human skull have been found in Niah Cave, 15 kilometres inland. The sea was considerably further away at the time of occupation. The skull was originally dated to 40,000 years and is set within stratigraphy and other

This child, from the Great Sandy Desert, is waiting to eat emu eggs that are baking in coals nearby.

archaeological material dated between 34,000 and 46,000 years ago.[57] Equally, there are archaeological material and marine foods dated to 42,000 years ago at a site called Jerimalai on the southeastern coast of Timor.[58]

These sites are, despite their age, concurrent with, or younger than, the antiquity of people in Greater Australia[59] and so add little chronological and demographic clarity to the question of colonisation that is not already implicit in Australian archaeology, as described in the next chapter.

Clearly the genetic and the archaeological research have a way to go before we understand how the world was occupied both before and after Mount Toba erupted. That understanding is easier, and the nature of colonisation better assimilated, if the ancestors of the first Australians were already in Indonesia by the time Mount Toba blew up.

Did the super-eruption of Mount Toba, the subsequent volcanic winter and emergent ice age push a resident Southeast Asian human population to Australia (about 70,000 years ago)? Or was the global human population so decimated after the catastrophe that none save those in isolated refuges in Africa survived? Did they then expand rapidly across the globe, pushing through Indonesia and settling Australia (about 50,000 years ago)? Could those who survived Toba in eastern Indonesia have stayed, without migration, only to encounter a tsunami of modern humans migrating from Africa soon after the volcanic dust settled? Did that push the population over the top and move people to Australia (between 70,000 and 50,000 years ago)? Would the long and complex human experience of survival, resettlement, evolution and expansion have been a simple case of one option or another? Can human evolution and colonisation be reduced to an either/or equation? Or perhaps the human experience, as human experience inclines, was a combination of all of the above: human presence, Toba eruption, survival, migration and African exodus, overpopulation and migration. Whatever the circumstance, or combination of circumstances, it seems likely that the colonisation of Australia started with a bang.

2
Super-Nomads

60,000–30,000 YEARS AGO

'She came from the north. She was carrying dilly bags, lots and lots of babies [in the bags]. She came when the sea was calm. Wind was calm. The sea calmed down. That's when she travelled. Then she came somewhere on the coast. She stopped. She put down one baby, the first one. She travelled far, putting all the babies [in the land].'

—Wilfred Nawirridja, Episode 1, *First Footprints* documentary, 2013

Land

The early dawn on the northern Australian coast is brimming. The warm air shimmers with sound, the effect strangely peaceful despite the constant noise and movement all around. The sudden bark of magpie geese punctuates the low hiss of nature, hinting at hidden encounters and feeding an underlying sense of unease.

The small boats drifted in the soft morning light. Land was visible through the storm during the night, but the westerly wind blew the small flotilla along the shore, separating the three tiny craft and keeping them away from the land they sought and upon which they were now afraid to land. So they listened and watched. Small children slept comfortably on their mothers' laps as the boats rocked gently, the men quietly poling them forward.

The crossing had been made with more ease than expected, but now the new land confronted them, relief turned to apprehension. Here it was, the sacred land of the sea-borne dead, where, in mythology, castaways found a last home and where those lost at sea were thought to rest. Was anyone watching out as they watched in? Were the dead waiting for them?

As the light increased, the low-lying coastline became clearer. The boats edged forward. The occupants surveyed the shore with the eyes of the endangered. The shoreline was packed with sea birds, the surrounding ocean full of turtles and dugong. A massive manta ray pulled slowly away. The

Previous pages: A posed image of men overlooking a broad floodplain in arid Australia, good country for hunting kangaroos. The central figure holds a broad spear in a spear-thrower. Broad-bladed spears are also used in punishment and fighting.

hull of the lead boat scraped on the sand and, while the men discussed how they should approach, a pregnant teenage girl stepped from the gunwale, her right foot dipping through the milky water onto the soft white sand. The first human footprint sank into the shore of Australia's northern coast, and just as quickly washed away as the boat rocked gently and regained its balance. Humans had arrived in Australia. Over 800 million years of isolated biological evolution had ended.

The small community gathered on the shore, taking in the abundance of wildlife and wondering at its indifference to their presence. Reptiles and birds intermingled. None moved with the arrival of the strangers. Some birds cast an inquisitive stare. The vegetation was lime green, some of it familiar in its stunted aridity but different in form. The sight of fat boab trees held the attention of the arrivals, and they intuitively assessed their worth as a resource for food, shelter, fibre and medicine.

The air smelt slightly of smoke. The morning sun was unexpectedly hot, but the pre-monsoon humidity was familiar. Not far away a stream flowed across a broad beach into the sea, and the small community moved slowly towards it. Camp was set in the lee of a headland, looking across the stream and the laden yellow beach sands. Fire was needed and the smell of smoke indicated it was not far away. The group did not stray far from their camp. Fresh water was abundant. Food was within reach.

Nature's gifts

The vision of ancient untouched abundance is nowhere matched today, and a traveller must go to the most remote locations in the world to catch a glimpse of anything like the environmental riches those first arrivals must have seen in Australia. The Galápagos Islands are perhaps such a location. Here, on the equatorial aridity of its volcanic shores, reptiles, sea birds and sea mammals lie compounded in their abundance—crawling and stepping over one another as they move between the sea and the shore, unconcerned by the inquiring visitors marching past them in their hundreds each day. The same vision arrests the visitor on the frigid shores of South Georgia Island: cold and hostile, infertile and seemingly uninhabitable, yet overlain with sea mammals and birds in such numbers that the visitor cannot move without infringing the territories of cantankerous seals or making slow headway through throngs of emperor penguins hundreds of thousands thick. Closer to home, Ashmore Reef conveys something of ancient Australia's shores. Despite centuries of fishing, the islands, reefs and surrounding sea are thick with sea birds, migratory birds, fish, crustaceans, dugong, turtles, sharks, stingrays and the greatest concentration of sea snakes in the world—40,000 of them, constituting 13 species.[1]

So it is not hard to imagine the northern coastline of Australia 70,000 years ago: vast abundances of animal life, heedless of humans and innocent to the risks of human predation. Even with tens of millennia of Aboriginal hunting and gathering, and centuries of European occupation, the natural resources of the Top End still astound. From the Kimberley to Cape York, there are over 5000 species of native plants (of which some 500 are only found there), 460 species of birds (over half the species in Australia), 110 species of mammals (one third of Australia's total) and 225 species of freshwater fish (75 per cent of the Australian tally). There are more species of fish in a single waterhole in Kakadu than in the entire Murray–Darling river system. Northern Australia also contains 65 per cent of all Australian butterflies and moths. The species of insects remain uncounted, although there are 161 species of grasshoppers in Kakadu alone, and over 1500 species of ants all told.[2] Add to that a giant suite of now extinct marsupials and reptiles, and a vast untapped marine fishery beyond an endless shoreline, and a picture of northern Australia as a grand environment of first settlement begins to emerge.

Australia then may have been as parts of Australia were not so long ago: full of abundant native food—as, for example, Kangaroo Island was when first visited by humans in the historic era. Here, Matthew Flinders recorded the 'extraordinary tameness' of kangaroos when he anchored there in 1802.[3] Docile wild animals are a rarity in Australia today, but may still be glimpsed in its untouched landscapes. I recall travelling through remote parts of the Great Sandy Desert in the mid 1980s, in areas never seen by non-Aboriginal people and not visited by Aboriginal people for over 30 years. The resident kangaroos and emus expressed no fear as they were approached and stood staring as they were shot. In 2011 I crossed a barren and remote part of the Great Victoria Desert that had not been visited for at least

Opposite: These men are investigating the nest of a wedge-tailed eagle—a rare encounter in the Great Sandy Desert. They are after its chick, but not for food. They want its down for ceremonial decoration.

80 years, and came across a female dingo and her pups. She stood, staring inquisitively as we drove past her and her family. She had clearly not seen a human (or a Toyota) in her lifetime. Last year I encountered a fresh generation of rabbits in a distant corner of the treeless Nullarbor Plain. No rabbits had been seen in this part of the Nullarbor since the release of the calicivirus in 1995. The new generation had never seen people or vehicles and showed no fear. There were hundreds and hundreds of rabbits—so many and so unaware that we had no choice but to run over them as they refused to budge from the path of our vehicles. Many were killed in this way and many more were shot at their warrens—while their neighbours sat watching,

Education is continual in the desert. These children have participated in the hunt for a bustard and are now enjoying plucking its feathers before it is baked (Thomas Peak, Great Sandy Desert).

unmoving, waiting to be shot in turn. Fear of predation is apparently a learnt behaviour: the kangaroos and emus in the Great Sandy Desert ran from the sight of a vehicle within a decade (the young clearly learning from the old), and likewise the Nullarbor rabbits would have soon become streetwise if another round of calicivirus had not decimated them the following year.[4]

So it is possible to imagine what Australia might have been like when its first visitors arrived: a land of naive wildlife and open abundance, but also a place that was reasonably familiar. The pioneering naturalist Alfred Russel Wallace noticed the biological similarity between Australia and southern Indonesia over 140 years ago.[5] The ancient mariners must have been equally discerning. One might anticipate the smallest adaptive leap in establishing a foraging and hunting routine in the new land. Excavations of human settlement in coastal Timor 40,000–42,000 years ago, for example, see people eating marine turtles, fish and shellfish as well as bats, mice, rats, birds, lizards and snakes.[6] All these species were present in spades along coastal northern Australia. In Flores there is evidence of people hunting komodo dragons and pygmy elephants. These animals were not present in Australia, but others were.

Gentle giants

The new arrivals had come from small islands where, as a general biogeographic rule, animals were also small—where elephants were, for example, pygmies. Australia is a large island and was then populated by large animals—very large animals in some cases. There were at least six genera and 50 species of animal that weighed as much as, and frequently more than, the new arrivals did.[7] Coming from a land where there were no flightless birds, the settlers were now confronted by species that were not only flightless but frighteningly large—and animals that hopped, and animals that carried their babies in small pouches and mammals that laid eggs.

It is a fact, although a surprisingly little known one, that Australia was then inhabited by giant animals in much the same way that Africa is inhabited by them today: mammals with pouches here; mammals without there. These animals would, in time, become extinct, never to be beheld by European eyes, but the eyes of the first settlers were surely fixed upon them.[8] Some species of marsupials and birds survived from that archaic era and they allow some appreciation of these past wonders. The red kangaroo and the emu are such examples, and provide a wondrous glimpse into the past—striking in size and in the originality of their look, manner and gait, they are smaller versions of their greater ancestors.

For anyone who has taken a good look at an emu or cassowary—or, better still, been chased by one—it is perhaps possible to imagine the large flightless bird *Genyornis*, which weighed over 200 kilograms (an average emu weighs 35 kilograms), and had massive legs, big toes and short stubby wings. It lived in the arid zone and had salt glands in its nose, suggesting it could tolerate saline water. Perhaps more closely resembling a giant goose than a big emu, it had a big wedge-shaped head, a large, deep lower jaw with a beak that was 30 centimetres long, and it laid eggs that weighed 1.5 kilograms each.[9]

Or imagine a modern-day red kangaroo, which weighs about 60 kilograms, and then try to conceptualise its ancestor, the giant kangaroo, grandly named *Macropus giganteus titan*, which weighed around 200 kilograms and stood hip to shoulder with the new settlers, looking down on them from a height of almost 3 metres. Or the ancient kangaroo-like marsupial *Procoptodon goliah*, which weighed 300 kilograms, stood over 3 metres tall, and had long arms and two very long fingers for reaching up and grasping branches for food. *Procoptodon*, the largest kangaroo to have ever evolved, was five times heavier than a large red kangaroo, and could lift its arms above its head like a human, something modern kangaroos cannot do. Their long arms probably helped them walk on four legs, even though the animal also hopped like a kangaroo. *Procoptodon* had broad, short, hoof-like feet with well-developed side toes, and an elastic ligament between the toe bones that gave them bounce—although they probably hopped rather slowly. Their tails were short and thick, and they had a pot-belly, a very short neck and a very large head (short and broad, rather like a human's). Hopping must have been a difficult experience with such a large head—and an ungainly sight. *Procoptodon* was one of 17 species of *Sthenurine*s that inhabited the open woodlands of northern Australia. One of these species, *Simosthenurus occidentalis*, was a heavy wallaby-like creature which weighed about 200 kilograms and had, like *Procoptodon*, distinctive feet, with a large fourth toe and greatly reduced side toes. They seem to have lived in the drier regions of Australia, browsing on salt bush and blue bush (chenopods).[10]

The ancient fauna also included euros (wallaroos) that were 20 per cent larger than those living today, and a giant rat-kangaroo (*Propleopus*), which was about the size of a female grey kangaroo (about 40 kilograms in weight). *Propleopus* lived in eastern Australia and seems to have eaten insects, nuts and fruit as well as eggs and small marsupials. It probably filled the ecological niche that small bears occupied in other countries and, in that sense, was our marsupial equivalent. There was also a long-nosed echidna (*Zaglossus*) that weighed 30 kilograms, and a terrestrial turtle (*Meiolania*) that was the size of a VW car. It weighed 200 kilograms and had feet like an elephant. It could not retract its head, but instead had two large horns protruding from its skull for protection. Its tail was armoured, and terminated in a bony club covered with blunt spikes.[11]

Ancient wombats (*Phascolonus*) grew up to eight times the size of modern ones. They weighed as much as 500 kilograms, and dug burrows large enough for humans to stoop and walk into (making *Phascolonus* easy prey). But the most remarkable was perhaps a wombat-like marsupial called *Diprotodon*. It was a mixed feeder and lived all over Australia, with a preference for the semi-arid lands. It was the size of a hippopotamus, weighed over 2500 kilograms and bore its weight on four pillar-like limbs. It was a huge slow-moving beast, up to 4 metres long with a heavy head measuring 1 metre in length. It had a large bony projection on its face that may have supported a large nose pad, like a koala. Interestingly, the back of the skull was wafer thin and hollow inside, perhaps to lighten the large head while also providing bone to attach muscles for its large jaws.[12] The animal's brain case was tiny, indicating a slow, dumb animal, with a thin skull, making it easy prey for the new arrivals.

Zygomaturus, often called the marsupial rhinoceros, was another remarkable animal. It weighed half a tonne, was about 2 metres long, and stood at least 1 metre high—about the height of a bullock—at the shoulder. Its body was the shape of a *Diprotodon* but its head was different. It had a pinched face with a steep forehead, forward-facing eyes, and a roughened patch of bone on either side of its nose that might have supported horns. *Zygomaturus* lived in the wetlands, scooping up reeds and sedges with two fork-like incisors.

Palorchestes was an even more curious beast. It was the size of a bull, walked on four legs and had a short trunk—like a tapir. It had massive and extraordinarily strong forearms, and paws with long (10-centimetre), sharp claws. Its elbow joints locked into a semi-flexed position, the anatomical composite creating a giant sloth-like animal—compact, hugely strong and almost mechanical in its ability to fell trees and strip branches for food. The morphology of its jaw indicates the animal had a long, slender tongue, suggesting it may have also eaten insects.[13]

These giants were generally harmless, although an encounter with a threatened and defensive bull *Diprotodon* might not have been so. Other ancient marsupials were more dangerous. When humans first arrived in Australia, the Tasmanian tiger or thylacine (*Thylacinus cynocephalus*), and the Tasmanian devil were widespread across the continent. They scavenged and hunted small animals, and presented no threat to humans. This was not the case with *Thylacoleo carnifex*, the 'marsupial lion', which was carnivorous, about the size of a leopard, and may have lived in trees. It was a strong, slow animal whose claws were adapted for climbing as well as ripping and pulling. Its teeth were designed for piercing, stabbing and slicing. *Thylacoleo* seems to have hunted from above, attacking from trees, leaping down onto its prey. The prey was then dragged to an arboreal lair for consumption, in a manner similar to a leopard's. *Thylacoleo* was widely distributed, with possibly one animal lurking in a tree every 100 square kilometres.[14]

Thylacoleo was the top marsupial predator. But there were other predators as well. The first settlers may have expected to encounter crocodiles, as these lived in the coasts and estuaries of Indonesia, but they are unlikely to have anticipated the enormous riverine crocodile *Pallimnarchus* or its smaller relation *Quinkana*, in addition to our extant 3-metre freshwater and 5-metre saltwater crocodiles.[15] The coasts and estuaries weren't likely to have been safe from crocodiles[16]—and nor was the land. *Quinkana* was probably a terrestrial crocodile—its remains have been found in cave deposits with other terrestrial fauna, a long way from water.[17] It weighed around 200 kilograms and had blade-like serrated teeth resembling those of a carnivorous dinosaur. Its feet were hoof-like (rather than webbed) on disproportionately long legs, suggesting it was a fast runner.[18] But speed was not a crocodile's chief weapon. Their method of attack was surprise and ambush, so the survival of the early occupants in the unknown continent must have been dependent upon precarious vigilance. *Pallimnarchus* added to the threat. It was an enormous crocodile resembling the largest living saltwater crocodile today. It had a broad, short snout and was thought to prey on larger mammals feeding at the water's edge.[19] But nowhere was really safe, as the ancient crocodiles patrolled the entire continent through the vast water catchment between northern Australia and Lake Eyre. During wet times, crocodiles could, potentially, move from the southern parts of central Australia to the Gulf of Carpentaria and the Arafura Sea.[20]

And on the riverbanks and near waterholes everywhere were snakes. Many snakes—snakes as we know them today and snakes like we have never seen. The extinct *Wonambi* was a 50-kilogram snake living in southern Australia. It grew to at least 5 metres in length, was a bulky 30 centimetres in diameter, and had a head the size of a shovel, flat and broad.[21] It was a giant, and implicitly terrifying. While it was possibly a constrictor, its mouth also had hundreds of tiny teeth; it may not have been able to disarticulate its jaws, making it less of a constrictor and more of a biter. *Wonambi* was possibly an aquatic snake living on fish and other water-borne prey, or an ambush predator, waiting by waterholes or along animal pathways in rocky areas.[22] But its remains have also been found in cave deposits in southern Australia, along with other faunal remains, suggesting it may have also lived away from water. Perhaps the caves provided an ambient temperature and sufficient shelter for survival: giant caves for giant snakes, in the same way that rabbit holes shelter snakes today.

In addition to giant crocodiles and giant snakes, ancient Australia was also blessed with giant lizards. The largest lizard living in Australia today is the perentie (*Varanus giganteus*), averaging some 1.6 metres in length; its ancestral relation, *Megalania prisca*, measured up to 7 metres in length. *Megalania* was a giant carnivore that weighed almost 2 tonnes. It had a bulky body and a short, thick tail. Its teeth were curved, chunky and serrated on one side like a steak knife.[23] *Megalania* was related to the komodo dragon,[24] which hunts in packs and both hamstrings and eviscerates its prey. The komodo dragon is fast, with the ability to run at speeds of 20 kilometres an hour, and its saliva contains particularly virulent strains of *E. coli* and *Staphylococcus* bacteria which, when transferred to its prey, ensure its ultimate death. Modern-day goannas also contain oral bacteria and it is suspected that *Megalania* did as well.[25] Komodo dragons are known to have attacked humans, yet they are only about 2.5 metres long with an average weight of about 80 kilograms. *Megalania* was, in comparison, three times larger and, it might be assumed, considerably faster and more deadly. I have never seen an Aboriginal person outrun a perentie (although I have seen a few try), and can scarcely imagine the futile difficulty of trying to outrun *Megalania*. They are thought to have been able to hunt *Diprotodon*, making human prey a breeze. *Megalania* had an estimated population density of about one per every 200 square kilometres. It favoured an aquatic habitat, lying dangerously hidden in the high grasses of the tropical savannah.[26]

Dreamtime animals

What did the first people in Australia think of these extraordinary creatures? How were they configured in their new cosmology? In addition to extant oral traditions that allow us to reflect upon what they might have thought, fragmentary remnants of ancient art allow us to imagine what they saw. Fortunately, tradition is embedded in art as art is embedded in stone across the continent. This stone tapestry contains some of the oldest art in the world; these captured images of ancient animals transcend time and give us a secular appreciation of the environmental, emotional and spiritual cognisance of Australia's first people. There are at least 6000 rock art sites in the Arnhem Land Plateau in northern Australia, for example, and in 126 of them are records of animals long past.[27] Some of the paintings must be between 40,000 and 50,000 years old, and are thus the oldest paintings in the world.[28] That they have survived at all is a gift beyond measure.

The ancient artists had an eye for natural details and, in washed combinations of ochre and pigment (oxides of iron applied and diffused in quartzite rock faces now encased in silica) skilfully painted emotive testaments to antediluvian animals we are at least 45,000 years too late to see. These rare works of art present as deceptively loose representations of fantastical animals, but confidence in their reality comes with an appreciation of the detail fixed within them. A thylacine, for example, is immediately distinguished from a dingo by the details of the depiction: the long, slender body; the tapered head; the accentuated length of the tail, re-curved, tapering and bent backward and down (and about one-third the length of the body); the obvious stripes across the rump; and the marsupial genitalia, with the scrotum above the penis, the latter bearing backwards, projecting beneath the base of the tail.[29] The painter is both artist and naturalist: one representation captures a reproductive rarity, a female with four young suckling in its rear-facing pouch.[30] Sketches of Tasmanian devils are equally distinctive, one painting showing the animal followed by a hunter with a boomerang, about to strike. But these animals disappeared from the Australian mainland quite recently: the tiger by about 3000 years ago, and the devil just 400 years ago.[31]

Other older, unearthly and equally marvellous animals have been similarly depicted in the galleries of Arnhem Land. A full-scale drawing of the extinct giant *Genyornis* is unmistakable—massive legs, tailless rump, and large, heavy feet with three rounded toes (unlike the pointed toes of an emu). The painting was sketched in outline and then in-filled with ochre wash, and the outline was repainted some time later. The pose is heavy, over-weighted towards the head, as if the artist was attempting to portray the solid, monumental appearance of the bird—the head shape, the blunt beak, its long neck, boldly apparent for others to revere. The legs and neck seem to have been striped and, unlike an emu or cassowary, the bird appears to have had a crop.[32]

A representation of the extinct giant long-beaked echidna (*Zaglossus*) is similarly distinctive: a long, narrow, tapering down-curved head; marked curvature of the back; and broad, ventrally directed tail.[33] Two paintings of the marsupial lion (*Thylacoleo*) reveal particular attention to detail within the guise of informal artistic expression. One depiction appears lifeless, with the animal lying motionless on the rock panel, its limbs seeming to hang, its feet pointing down as if the sketch has been made from a dead animal—from an actual animal laid out for inspection. The study goes beyond the art it creates and speaks of a concurrent social experience: the hunt, the carriage and the depiction; of an animal tracked, surrounded and killed—the dead body carried back to the cave and placed for inspection and discussion. Through the art we almost see hunter and artist combined as an expression of planning, predation and painting. Their artistry adds to our knowledge of this extraordinary animal known otherwise only through fragmentary skeletal remains: the aquiline head; a hairy tuft on the end of its tail; long, stiff hairs around its eyebrows, chin and nose; vertical markings resembling fur on its body; long legs, elongated five-fingered paws, surprisingly cute short round ears; a rump abruptly terminating at the base of its tail.

Another painting of *Thylacoleo* is located in the Kimberley,[34] a tiny but detailed masterpiece in ochre. The animal appears striped, and is very large compared to the person painted beneath it. It has a long tail, and massive forelegs and shoulders, as if to emphasise the epic proportion and deadly purpose of its forequarter. The person is spearing the animal: perhaps he is hunting, perhaps he is fending off an attack. He clasps the spear in both hands. The spear is barbed. There is no spear-thrower. The person appears to be jumping, the spear bending as if the person is lunging up at the beast as it leaps down from above.

There is also an extraordinary painting of a large bull-like animal thought to be the giant tapir, *Palorchestes.* The marvellous representation was executed in considerable detail and reveals an animal with an earless head directed upwards, a line suggesting a mouth, tongue projecting (small leaves or insects seem to be drawn adjacent to it), short legs with notable claws and angled heel joints, representations of a shoulder mane or shaggy long hair, long coarse hair on the back (represented by concentrations of dots) and a short, broad tail. There is, remarkably, a smaller version of the same animal painted adjacent to it. The second drawing could be a joey, a pouch-young *Palorchestes.* It is a refinement of the larger, its placement suggesting it is part of a deliberate composition. Both appear lifeless, as if they, like the subject of the *Thylacoleo* painting, are also trophies, intended documents of natural wonder—studies in nature drawn as still life.[35]

Paintings of these wonders are tangible first-hand accounts. A depiction has a form, the form has components, and the components conform to known particulars. Art becomes evidence, evidence engages understanding across the span of human experience. This is not the case with oral tradition. The meaning of mythology is open to interpretation, the interpretation open to dispute, the meaning lost in translation and rationalisation. Art is a subjective representation of biology (at the time) and oral tradition is a metaphysical interpretation of that biology (over a long period of time). But even so, perhaps such narratives are both a means for understanding and a mechanism of history. Perhaps the religious narratives of first settlement are more than sacred mysticism, but historical memory encapsulated in ritualised tradition.[36] The ancestral accounts of first settlement, for example, consistently recorded a familiar story: in Queensland, 'gales brought us here'; in New South Wales, 'ancestors came from a land beyond the sea'; in coastal Arnhem Land, 'great Djankawu came from an island far across the sea . . . in his canoe with two sisters'; and in Kakadu, 'the lightning man . . . entered the land on the northern coast'.[37] Stripped of their ritual enhancements they are, in effect, stories of colonisation—the arrival of people from across the sea, followed by settlement, occupation, population growth, regional expansion and diversification—a sacred account of the scientific, echoing the mantra of equivalent statistical conjecture and models of human colonisation.

So, one might reflect on religious belief as faithful tradition and encapsulated history held 'true' through the vastness of time: mythology in action where the traditional story embodies natural phenomena of supernatural dimensions. Western religious tradition provides an instructive parallel. Christianity is also an oral tradition held true over a lesser vastness of time. Its sacred elaborations are embedded in ancient Judaic tradition and based on a Mediterranean Jewish peasant called Jesus. Religious elaboration is drawn from him, as oral tradition from parables subsequent to fact. The tradition is embellished through the mythology without diminishing the fundamental truth of the historical experience from which it is drawn.[38]

Thus the nature of oral tradition does not deny the foundation behind the mythology it conveys. Nor, necessarily, does the passage of time. One might see in ancient Aboriginal mythology seeds of historical truth and be mindful of its mystical illumination. The universality of mythology relating to a giant snake makes the general point, whether it is the Rainbow Serpent of the north or the Wanampi of the desert (and after which the giant snake *Wonambi* acquired its Latin name). In Arnhem Land its artistic representations date to at least 8000 years ago, the most recent being painted in 1965.[39] The being central to this ancient oral tradition is there for the looking—one painting is 6.5 metres long—and open to elaboration through time.[40] The serpent is a symbol of fertility measured through propagation, progeny and precipitation. Danger lurks there as well and, stripped of visual imagery, rhetoric and ritual, the mythology in the desert is always and everywhere the same—about a large dangerous snake that lives in waterholes and caves, and punishes transgressors, among whom children are typically at most risk. The account presents as both superstition (in regard to every permanent and ephemeral waterhole I have ever encountered) and as integrated religious narrative across vast tracts of country: from the Kimberley to the Great Australian Bight, where the deep cave systems are, among other things, home to this subterranean monster, the penultimate refuge of Wanampi after being pursued by two great mythological figures (the Wati Kutjara, literally 'Two Men', but anthropomorphic sand goannas) to re-emerge in the central southeast of western Australia and present as the Waugle of Nyoongar mythology in the Swan River.

The most secret and most sacred religious narrative in the southern deserts relates to a giant goanna, reminiscent (to say the least) of *Megalania*. This being is at the core of the famous Red Ochre Dreaming of the greater Australian arid zone. The particular religious narrative (Tjukurrpa) is so significant and the ritual objects associated with it are so precious that they are transmitted from community to community with great care, deliberation, reluctance and ceremonial duty. The ceremonial expression moves, cyclically, around the desert in the slowest manner imaginable; the ritual cycle may take 20–30 years to complete.[41] The ceremonies went through

Milpatjunanyi is the desert version of make-believe families. Homely features are drawn on the ground with sticks while imagined mums, dads and children are made from leaves and twigs (Pukatja soak in the Everard Ranges, northern South Australia).

the Everard Ranges area in 1968 and have only cycled the desert once since then.

Within this broader symmetry of meaning is a myth that speaks of central Australia as a once fertile, well-watered place in which a monster, Kadimarkara, dwelt in the treetops. The story describes the drying of the landscape, the demise of the monster, and the accumulation of its bones in marshes around the lake[42] (where the bones of *Thylacoleo* and other megafauna are found in abundance today). The narrative may be young enough to interpret these extant fossil deposits or old enough to explain them.

The greatest and perhaps most defining religious narrative of Australia's arid zone relates to a giant transformative kangaroo,

Wati Marlu. The story is told from the eastern Kimberley, across the southern deserts, to the margin of the Pilbara, the edge of the Nullarbor, and through the central ranges towards Lake Eyre, where it encounters another signatory myth about another giant and fearful kangaroo. The people of the Lachlan and Murrumbidgee rivers also mythologised giant kangaroos as well as a giant bird (possibly *Genyornis*).[43] Another signatory myth of the southern deserts relates to a 'giant' emu, and in the Keep River district of the Northern Territory there are extraordinary engravings of the tracks of giant flightless birds, remarkably similar to those of *Genyornis*, that are thought to be a recent visualisation of ancient Aboriginal thoughts.[44]

Might there be some reality behind the mythical accounts of colonisation, reptilian monsters and marsupial giants? Is it possible that the suite of giant and frightening animals captured in Aboriginal mythology is an expression of natural history, or is it simply an extraordinary coincidence? Is the conjunction between mystical palaeo ontology and scientific palaeontology coincidence or chronicle? The possibility must be recognised, at least to the extent that it is as logical to accept the suggestive link between the nature of the past and the mysticism of the present as it is to assert there is no link at all. It would seem reasonable to allow that the experiences of the past in this unique, primaeval land had great and lasting social, psychological and spiritual effects on the people of the time.[45] It seems entirely possible that the biological and psychological effects of first settlement resonated in the social psychology and spirituality of subsequent tradition. One might expect, in such extraordinary circumstances, the unearthly narrative (and artistic representations) to have earthly referents. The rest is, essentially, elaboration.

Imagining country

The footprints of the settlers that first landed on this strange and foreign land would soon be lost in the vastness of time and environmental change. For the shores on which they alighted are now under water and some 200 kilometres from the present coast. That ancient coastal plain was then 1.6 million square kilometres in area, extending from the western Kimberley to Torres Strait, and continuing for another 2000 kilometres from the Gulf of Papua to north Fraser Island. Before it was flooded by rising seas 10,000 years ago, the sea was some 70 metres below current levels, and the coastline the settlers advanced along was a diverse subtropical plain vegetated with pristine rainforest, grassland, woodland and savannah.[46]

Between 70,000 and 60,000 years ago, the world was cool, sea levels were dropping and the land continued to dry. Then, about 60,000 years ago, the world started to warm again and the sea started to rise. The next 10,000 years saw two cycles of global warming and cooling, with an overall trend towards global cooling and increased aridity: the world was getting colder and drier despite cyclic ameliorations to this more general trend. By 50,000 years ago, the world was cool and dry again with sea levels 70–80 metres below present. The climate continued to oscillate over the next ten millennia, covering two more cycles of cooling and warming, with more arid conditions after 45,000–40,000 years ago. This vastness of time encompassed two environmental stages: the first from 70,000 to 60,000 years ago, which saw the start of colder glacial conditions, with sea levels about 70 metres below those of today; and the second, from 60,000 until around 18,000 years ago, when the world (and greater Australia) was exposed to vast periods of increasing aridity and increasing cold. The overall pattern was one of gradual cooling and gradual drying. The last time the Australian environment and climate looked and felt like it does today was almost 120,000 years ago.

Archaeologists will never know where or when the first Australians landed, but it is likely that, wherever they landed, they settled near water on a reasonably soft shoreline. It is not difficult or unreasonable to imagine them on a peninsula similar to the Cobourg Peninsula today, but they may have landed anywhere along the now submerged coastal plain: beside a river mouth, blown up against a precarious rocky promontory, perched uncomfortably in a mangrove forest, or stranded bewilderingly on a broad, long open beach. But regardless of where it was they first landed, the coastal hinterland was much the same as it is today: wide seaward-sloping valleys, subdued plains and broad river systems. It was an accepting environment.

The first settlers may have arrived in the far north, within the west-facing arm of Irian Jaya and Papua New Guinea's cordillera. It's possible they may have moved inland, along rivers and into the mountains, but intuition leans more easily to a coastal route where the topography would direct them towards a broad land bridge joining Cape York with Papua New Guinea. Today the sea is shallow here, just 12 metres deep, and Torres Plain (now Strait) would then have been 40–50 metres above the ocean. Some channels cut through the land—to depths of 120 metres—and would have provided estuarine and sea channels along which hunting and gathering must have been rewarding. Crossing south over the Torres Plain would have taken the colonisers to a huge embayment surrounding what is now the Coral Sea. They could have walked to the very margin of the (now) Great Barrier Reef and foraged within the lace-like network of ridges and canyons upon which the reef now anchors.

Or they may have explored west, drawn by the open plains and abundant river systems into the lakes and lands of Carpentaria. Between 70,000 and 50,000 years ago, the Gulf of Carpentaria was dry land and contained a vast lake. Among the largest ever lakes in the world, Lake Carpentaria was fed by 37 ancestral rivers[47] that carried 12,700 gigalitres of fresh water into the lake each year—Sydney Harbour, in comparison, holds just 560 gigalitres. The lake was 500 kilometres long and 250 kilometres wide, but shallow—just 15 metres deep on its eastern side.[48] As sea levels fluctuated so did the character of the lake. A channel existed that connected the lake to the Arafura Sea so that when the sea rose the environment changed from lake to embayment: Lake Carpentaria existed when the sea level was 75 metres below today's levels, but became a brackish swamp when the level rose another 15 metres (equalling about 60 metres below present-day levels). Another rise of 15 metres turned the swamp into a large bay fringed by numerous lakes.[49]

Lake Carpentaria must have been a perfect Eden-like environment in those times (except, of course, for the presence of giant crocodiles, goannas and snakes). Perhaps the ancient Australians were lucky enough to have landed there. Its location would certainly have been apparent to anyone at sea in the greater region: a clear indication of a major source of fresh water ahead would have been provided by sea birds and migratory birds, flood-washed vegetation, driftwood, and freshwater discharge and discolouration in the distant ocean.

Settlement here would have been close to ideal: abundant fresh water, and numerous rivers, tributaries, and small lakes around and upon which to live, hunt and gather shellfish, fish, dugongs and turtles, birds and terrestrial game. Analysis of pollen deposited over the last 40,000 years reveals black soil plains vegetated by eucalypts, bottlebrush and *Callitris* pines, with waterlilies, yams and bulrushes growing in the waterholes and lakes[50]—rather like Kakadu today. The settlers could easily have travelled south from this lake along the extensive river systems draining towards Lake Eyre Basin.[51] The continent was open, although the desert loomed, and expansion may have been sporadic, as cyclic climatic ameliorations allowed and regional weather patterns opportuned.

To the west of Lake Carpentaria lay the Arnhem Land coast and its magnificent escarpments. In those times the Alligator, Wildman, Mary and Adelaide rivers joined to form one deeply incised 'Arnhem Land river'. This flowed through a gentle valley between Cobourg Range (now Peninsula) and Melville Hill (now Island) onto the vast Arafura Plain (now Sea) before joining a giant 'Arafura river', which flowed south from Papua New Guinea and out to the Indian Ocean.[52] The Arnhem Land plateau itself was (and remains) a remarkable living environment, incised by small rivers, overhung with waterfalls, and skirted by fertile wetlands and savannah. The plateau is over 200 kilometres in diameter and rises 250 metres above the alluvial plains: the total environment was one of abundant food, water and shelter.

If the settlers had continued (or made landfall) west along the great northern coast they would have encountered the Ashmore Peninsula (now Reef) beside a huge basin central to the Joseph Bonaparte Gulf today. This basin also contained a large lake, 20,000 square kilometres in area, with a huge freshwater catchment covering some 350,000 square kilometres (Lake Argyle is 1000 square kilometres, by comparison). This lake was connected to the ocean by a relatively steep-sided valley, known as the sub-oceanic Malita Valley.[53] Tidal movements in this area today are massive and dangerous—and may have been so in the past as well. If so, the outpouring of water through the Malita Valley must have been something to see.

The lake itself, and associated embayments, are likely to have been rich living environments, with marine resources nearer the coast and freshwater resources inland (where monsoonal rains penetrated the great basin via great rivers). The descendants of these rivers are smaller today but nonetheless convey something of their past magnitude: the Mitchell, Drysdale and King Edward rivers, for example, are 117, 423 and 221 kilometres long with catchments of 2970, 8400 and 15,690 square kilometres respectively. They were long, fertile avenues of settlement and territorial expansion, leading colonisers towards the rugged plateaus of the Kimberley from where other larger freshwater arteries ran west and south, reconnecting with the sea and leading people towards the desert. The Fitzroy River, for example, skirts the Kimberley for 640 kilometres and draws on a massive catchment of 83,000 square kilometres. Anyone who followed it was led to the Sturt Creek and the dendritic channels of Tjurabalan (Milkwater), and to the large seasonal lake called Paraku (Lake Gregory) on the edge of the Great Sandy Desert.

Terra nullius

There is something mesmerising about the idea of ancient people living peacefully in quiet settlements in expansive fertile environments. Yet the shadow reality was the constant anxiety of living with the threat of the unknown and the savagery of the local reptilian wildlife. How did people make their way? How did they travel from the ancient shores, through the ancient escarpments and plateaus and into the remoter deserts? How conceivable was settlement across these diverse terrains and how might colonisation have progressed?

Ethnographic experience indicates that substantial cross-country journeys are possible for those with the nomadic know-how. I once knew a man well who made such a journey, from the Kimberley coast to the Great Sandy desert, alone and on foot. He was arrested in the late 1950s for stealing sheep on the northeastern margin of the desert. Europeans thought his name was Tjantjanu, but this was a nickname meaning 'to have (*tjanu*) chains (*tjan*)'. Tjantjanu and others were marched on foot, chained neck to neck, from the desert to Wyndam (on the Joseph Bonaparte Gulf). Here they were placed in jail, but Tjantjanu escaped:[54]

> He was hand-cuffed but his feet were not chained. He escaped when everyone was sleeping and walked from tree to tree. No one saw him. He sat on a big hill watching the road. He walked east, along the ridges, right around the back of the range to keep out of people's way. He used fire sticks to light a fire and caught a large goanna. He was hungry. He walked down Sturt Creek. He caught two pussycats, ate one and kept the other for later. He walked past Wolfs Creek Crater behind some granite tors. He watched there. He walked for two months. White people were all around and he climbed into the trees, and stood in the trees, hiding like a branch. He walked south around Lake Gregory and

Tjantjanu making fire in the Great Sandy Desert. He breaks and wets the end of the top stick (marnti, and male gender) before dipping it in sand and rubbing it between his palms to create burning friction in the base stick (tutju, female gender).

Tjantjanu firing the spinifex plains, Great Sandy Desert. The spinifex being held is alight and drops cinders, igniting a line of fire behind Tjantjanu as he walks.

> kept going until he got to the first sand dune. He walked through to the bottom of the lake and hid in a small cave. Countrymen found him. He was skinny and they hid him.

Tjantjanu's journey took him from the coast, over the eastern Kimberley, across the savannah, and along braided river channels to the desert. He walked for at least two months and travelled over 800 kilometres, alone and handcuffed. His story makes the prospect of ancient settlement look quite easy.

And he was not the only nomad to make an extraordinary journey through unknown lands. Another epic tale belongs to a man called Lantil. In 1957 he suffered severe burns to his neck and was sent from the Great Sandy Desert to Derby Hospital, 700 kilometres away. It was the first time he had left the desert, and within three days of arriving in hospital he absconded and disappeared. There was an extensive police and aerial search but he could not be found. Presumed dead, he turned up in the desert nine weeks later, fit and well.

His is another remarkable overland trip that says something about the endurance, skill and navigational aptitude of great nomads, and in whose tales of survival an understanding of ancient possibilities might be gained. Both Lantil and Tjantjanu survived alone for several months in foreign country, navigating their way home across 700–800 kilometres of hard unforgiving terrain, one in handcuffs, the other severely burnt. Both were men of enormous emotional strength and self-discipline, having acquired this (and an encyclopaedic knowledge of natural resources) from their experience of the demands of life in the desert. I had the pleasure of travelling through the desert with Tjantjanu on occasion, until his death in 1998. Lantil returned to the desert after escaping from hospital and, after his sighting nine weeks later, was never seen again. His descendants emerged from the desert in 1986.[55]

So the lessons of the present might inform our understanding of the past. Place those super-nomads in the pristine fertility of the northern Australia of the deep past, with its grand riverine conduits and abundant resources, and ancient colonisation exists as a self-evident consequence of successful settlement.

Ancient colonisation, it must be inferred, had a secure environmental foundation. The coastal environments of the north provided almost everything a nomadic hunter-gatherer could have dreamt of: fresh water, shelter, fire and food—fruits, nuts, tubers, shellfish, fish, birds, birds' eggs, reptiles and marsupials. The populations of marsupials, birds and reptiles were gargantuan, to say the least, and, save for the obvious risk of the people themselves becoming prey, the humans making those first tentative steps on Australian shores should have had an easy time of hunting and gathering. With the exception of cyclones, fires, floods and unduly hungry mega-reptiles, life on the new continent must have been reasonably free from danger. New hunting strategies and new food procurement and processing practices may have been required, but, by and large, existing subsistence strategies should have done the job: a sea turtle in Australia is no different to a sea turtle in Indonesia; sea birds' eggs are easy to collect wherever they are laid; a possum is no harder to kill than a monkey; plant tubers are harvested, processed and consumed in much the same way across the globe.

The experience of colonisation has, however, a concurrent social requirement—the ability to breed and, by implication, men's access to breeding females. Demographic simulations of colonising possibilities indicate that a population of 100 people may achieve a stable demographic state if they have one other social group of approximately the same number with which to exchange females.[56] Genetic indications are, as mentioned in the previous chapter, that Australia was colonised by a number of simultaneous landings—small groups constituting perhaps a total of 1000 people. The numbers were clearly sufficient for colonisation, breeding females were obviously available and, even with the likelihood of opportunistic incest, survival was predictably secure and proven on all counts.[57] History verifies this—these great nomads clearly survived, settled and stayed.

The first settlers confronted an open social and environmental horizon across which they needed only to adapt, breed, consolidate and move on. First settlement and continental colonisation might therefore have been quite fast. It is also worthy of reflection, however, that, at settlement, northern Australia was such a fertile environment that there may have been little need for nomadism at all. The fact that the country was both foreign and fertile may have been a significant disincentive to extreme nomadism, and may have instead encouraged the establishment of secure settlement in relatively small areas.

Equally, once a social group was secure there were few constraints to territorial expansion as the population grew and existing resources become scarce. So it is possible to envisage an ancient population growing steadily and expanding proportionally—never far from water and always within reach of its own social geographic traditions—in constant incremental pursuit of new country to live more easily in: a sinuous process of colonisation which, in the fullness of time, appears to have had a surprising agility.[58]

It is thus possible to picture a founding population growing and the country occupied by them becoming larger and larger, along the coasts, up river and across the savannah into the well-watered escarpments and hills. The original shores and hinterland upon which people first stepped was a landmass (now under water) greater than the Northern Territory today and twice the size of New South Wales. It was a large area and, intuitively, a tall order for the first settlers and their descendants to have colonised. But occupation may have taken less time than intuition inclines. If the founding population was 1000 settlers, and that population was composed of family groups of about 20 people with a territorial configuration similar to that of coastal Arnhem Land today, and the population grew at between 1 and 2.5 per cent per year, then the whole (now submerged) coastal plain could have been populated in 400 to 900 years.[59]

So if people arrived in Australia 50,000–70,000 years ago it is conceivable that they would have settled the entire (now submerged) coast within a period of time that was too short for even the best modern dating methods to detect: it would have been, in that sense, instantaneous. But people are social beings with a strong sense of place and, to the extent that people are dependent on their society and their society is dependent on the country to which it is attached, then the people themselves are partly contained geographically. The need for territorial expansion sits in tension with the need for social unification, a tension that is only broken under particular environmental conditions (such as a decline in resources or a prolonged drought) or changed social conditions (such as overpopulation), or

Women and children going to collect food near Mt Liebig in central Australia. They are not far from Puritjarra, where the ancestors also walked and gathered over 40,000 years ago. There are permanent springs in the hills behind and the dry plains are rich in reptiles, marsupials and witchetty grubs.

a convergence of the two (increased population and decreased environmental opportunity). Population growth is, therefore, difficult to predict, as it is bound by the pull of social cohesion and the push of environmental necessity, stabilised—at some point—by the relationship between the two in the context of indeterminate elements of time, environmental diversity, climatic variability and cultural evolution. The dynamic is active, the balance variable and the demographic consequence unpredictable. The fact that people did colonise Australia is obvious, but the rate and pattern of colonisation is less so. Colonisation may have been as rapid as demographic modelling suggests, or as slow as intuition supposes: tentative at first, incremental in form and comprehensive in time, always contextualised by human capacity, environmental constraints and climatic change through the millennia of occupation.

Antiquity

The population might have taken off, or crawled, risen exponentially or steadily, plateaued or declined—or all of the above at different times in different places. But even if it got off to a lazy start, gathered slow momentum and took five times longer than the hypothetical modelling suggests, coastal settlement 70,000 years ago (now submerged) might find indirect expression inland by 65,000 years ago. If people arrived 50,000 years ago their presence could be visible inland by 45,000 years ago. But the demographic possibilities are so vast it is hard to have confidence in any predictions about the timing of landfall and the timing of archaeological evidence that may relate to it. Plus there are so many destructive variables that it is hard to imagine anyone ever finding any trace of lives lived so long ago—whether they relate to landfall or not. What are the chances of a campsite, a small fire or a few artefacts accidently left behind 65,000 years ago being found in the 21st century? The negative probability is astronomical: 65,000 years of subsequent settlement and human disturbance, natural decay and erosion—almost too much wear and tear to think about, and certainly too much for ephemeral remains of human settlement to withstand. Even without the obvious risk of decay, erosion, disturbance and destruction, what are the chances of some ancient family leaving evidence of their lives at a small location somewhere in northern Australia and an archaeologist actually choosing to look at that same location *and* finding those remains 60,000 years later? Very old sites are very unlikely to have survived. Those on the ancient coast have now washed away anyway, or otherwise rest deep under water. Those inland that relate to the era of first settlement must be rare. But, remarkably, some have survived and, against the odds, have also been found.

A profound glimpse into the sands of time is found in a surprisingly small location, under the sheltered overhang of a sandstone outlier called Malakunanja, more recently known as Madjedbebe.[60] This outlier overlooks the floodplains of Magela Creek, a tributary of the East Alligator River in subtropical Arnhem Land—then cooler dry bushland. Malakunanja rests 50 kilometres from the present coast but was over 500 kilometres from the coast when Australia was first occupied. People had travelled some way over some time to get there—who knows how long it took them. Faded paintings cast an ancestral shadow across the shelter walls, and its floor contains histories of ages past. The sediments have been accumulating for over 105,000 years. There is no sign of human life in those distant years. Millennia pass—tens of millennia pass—and the sands remain empty of human life. And then, abruptly, people are there: there is evidence for the first time of human beings in the bush of inland greater Australia.[61]

Just a hundred or so artefacts represent these lives long past. The oldest artefacts have been dated to 61,000 years ago. Another 1500 artefacts were left at the camp over the next 15,000 years (contained within the next 30 centimetres of the deposit in the shelter). A date retrieved from the middle of this horizon of first occupation reveals an antiquity of 52,000 years. One of the occupants dug a small pit into the ground between 52,000 and 45,000 years ago. This fragile feature is just 20 centimetres deep and perhaps 40 centimetres wide—about the size of a typical oven used to roast goannas or bake tubers in earth pits today. Amazingly, the feature has not been disturbed or displaced through the vastness of time. There are artefacts within it. The sediments within the pit were last exposed to sunlight about 45,000 years ago (this indicates a minimum age for the pit and associated artefacts).[62]

Consistent with the ambivalence of time, these determinations of antiquity have a measure of statistical uncertainty about them. The oldest date of 61,000 years has a one in three chance of being 10,000 years younger, or 10,000 years older, meaning the antiquity of occupation at Malakunanja could be as old as 71,000 years or as young as 51,000 years old.[63] The older antiquity tallies with settlement as a consequence of the explosive impact of Mount Toba on human populations in Indonesia, while the younger date aligns with the broader antiquity of occupation so far discovered elsewhere in Australia.

These first people camped under the shelter of the overhang and left artefacts made of quartz and silcrete. They also left a grindstone and pieces of igneous rock they had carried to the shelter. Ground, use-striated crayons of haematite—a very high quality source of red ochre—were left at the camp, as were other fragments of red and yellow ochre as well as pieces of mica and chlorite.[64] Mica is perfectly laminated, sheeted silica. It has a sparkling crystalline quality—creating a magical sheen when rubbed into the skin. I have seen mica ground and mixed with ochre, and applied with dramatic effect in the most sacred of desert ceremonies. Chlorite also has a sparkling quality. It is soft and can be scratched with a fingernail. The resultant powder is green, with an oily feel.[65] What was the function of these minerals at this old site? The implied purpose is decoration and ceremony—either reason entailing self-awareness and consequential social consciousness. A conservative interpretation of the coloured crayons alludes to an ancient artistic tradition expressed (at least) as decoration: perhaps of the people's skin, or their hair, or their wooden artefacts and their valued possessions (bags, string, dishes and adornments). The possible association between ochre and ritual activity is equally obvious, and necessitates an acceptance of sophisticated social and political systems a long time ago.[66] Whatever the implied function of these minerals, their presence signifies creativity and aesthetic appreciation (as we might understand it) among ancient people at the very dawn of human settlement in Australia.

Antiquity and artistry seem to have been characteristics of the great past in Arnhem Land, and of archaeological discovery there. Just 70 kilometres from Malakunanja, for example, is another site called Nauwalabila. Here, early occupation is also associated with ground haematite.[67] This is a larger rock shelter formed when a giant boulder toppled off the adjacent escarpment. The shelter sits in a spectacular gorge, challengingly named Deaf Adder Gorge. The site was shown to archaeologists in early 1972 by two old men who once camped in it. Their ancestry goes deep, for the excavated deposit shows continuous occupation through time: over 30,000 artefacts, of which 230 sit within sand and interlocked gravel between 53,000 and 60,000 years old—with a one in three chance of being 48,000–67,000 years old.

A similar ancestral history is replicated at an extraordinary cave called Nawarla Gabarnmang in southwestern Arnhem Land. Two old Jawoyn men camped in the cave when they were children. They were the last people to sleep there—the first slept there at least 45,000 years earlier.[68] The cave has two entrances and about 2 metres of head space over a living area of at least 1500 square metres. The ceiling is flat, supported by 36 henge-like sandstone pillars. Each pillar has been painted, as has the ceiling throughout. The visual effect is stunning.[69] The pillars have formed by chemical weathering of softer sandstones between them—and by human modification. Rock has been removed to make the cavernous spaces even larger. The caverns link to create a labyrinth of interconnected space, and an effective balance between space, ventilation and insulation. The cave is, by dint of nature and human modification, a cool place to live.

Blocks that have fallen from the roof have been flaked for the production of stone tools. Other blocks have been reduced by flaking away their edges, and others still have been broken up and removed from the cave, clearing it for movement, comfort and accommodation. Large blocks have also been removed from the cave ceiling and can be matched to their original location: they have been taken intentionally, to make space, enlarge the cave and expose fresh unweathered surfaces for the application of new frescos. Nawarla Gabarnmang is an artefact of social and ritual endeavour: a cultural catacomb, a monument of structural engineering and an art gallery of unequalled magnificence. The physicality of the site and its cultural heritage exist as testament to tradition, community, social cohesion, artistic brilliance and ritual activity. It is a monolithic statement of human aesthetic achievement—a real stone henge, and a place of social, artistic and religious centrality that existed countless millennia before the first pillars of Stonehenge were erected in England.

In such grand style the bedrock of Arnhem Land asserts itself in the archaic tradition of Australia. From here a visitor might cast their arms wide in revelation. One arm might point west towards the Kimberley, the other balanced east, pointing towards Papua New Guinea. In either direction the history of old ages continues apace.

The reach to New Guinea finds ancient Australians camping on the coast and occupying the highlands about the same time people were grinding ochre and making stone tools in Arnhem Land. The climate then was perhaps 4 degrees Celsius cooler than today, and the tree line lower, with deciduous forests and savannah reaching the sea. Broad areas of dense rainforest covered the mountain valleys, but trees ceased growing above 3000 metres, and glaciers covered the mountains above 4200 metres.[70]

One ancient camp was located on the northeast coast of New Guinea, at Bobongara, on the Huon Peninsula. It was originally placed on a productive and hospitable shore vegetated with mangroves and

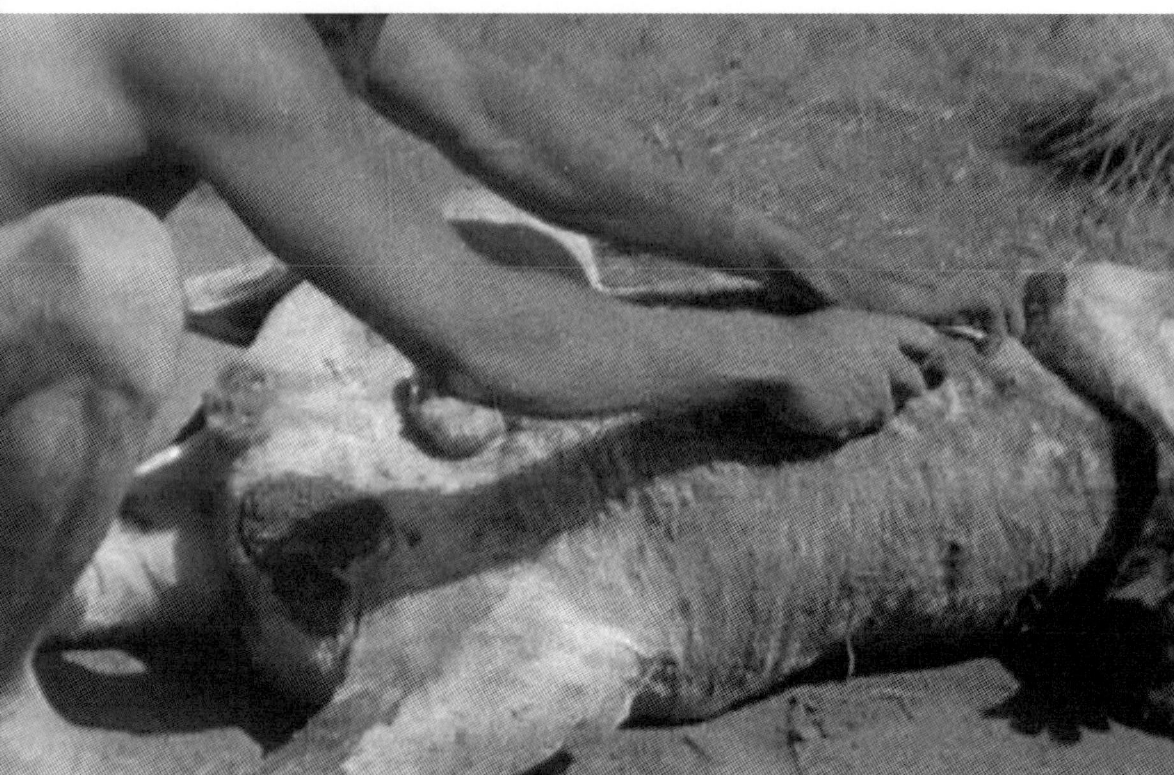

This red kangaroo is being cut open with a stone knife in the Warburton Ranges, Western Australia. The intestines will be removed, cleaned and eaten. Accumulated blood will be drunk and the intestinal fat will be cooked on the coals before the kangaroo is baked.

set among lagoons overlooking fringing reefs. The hinterland was forested. Yet a remarkable ongoing process of tectonic activity has now raised that coastline so the camp and the old shoreline now rest on a raised coral terrace about 400 metres above the sea.[71] There is a stream on the terrace and, adjacent to it, sealed beneath consolidated volcanic ash, are a number of stone axes. Hundreds more lie in the creek itself. These axes have been flaked and each has a notched groove chipped around its circumference. This groove creates a kind of 'waist' onto which a handle was once attached. These 'waisted axes' are at least 44,500 years old, and maybe as old as 61,000 years.[72] They are the oldest hafted axes anywhere in the world.

These 'waisted' axes indicate the coastal dwellers were utilising the forest, felling trees, and clearing areas for occupation and food collection. Nomads living in the mountains were also using them. People were living in the Ivane Valley, 2000 metres above sea level, at the same time people were living on the coast.[73] The ancient settlers of greater Australia had begun to tame the forests. The climate was cool and the valley was vegetated with beech trees. The settlers were people with an established forest tradition. The development of axes with fixed handles helped them clear the forest for hunting, gathering and living. They used axes to penetrate and exploit the forest, perhaps clearing trees, splitting wood, ring-barking trunks, trimming branches, clearing roots and opening the forest canopy. That allowed sunlight to penetrate the forest, and so encouraged the growth of useful plant foods (various bush bananas, vegetables and beans) and improved the production of fruit on *Pandanus* palms.[74]

Some of the artefacts recovered in this valley have microscopic starch grains still attached to them.[75] The grains reveal the harvesting, processing and consumption of *Dioscorea* yams. Charred *Pandanus* nuts have also been identified, indicating the consumption of both yams and nuts 49,000–44,000 years ago. At that time *Pandanus* grew abundantly in the local area but yams grew at lower altitudes, indicating either the large-scale territories over which the nomads gathered or that food was exchanged between people living in different altitudinal environments.

The vision of a colonising population felling forests is an arresting one—but perhaps not a surprising one. The first settlers came from tropical forested Southeast Asia and must have been familiar with the variety of potential foods—forest yams, taro, sago and *Pandanus* nuts. The ancient axe heads and the old organic remains are nonetheless testimony to the great ingenuity, environmental adaptation and social organisation of Australia's first settlers. The ancient sites in New Guinea demonstrate the penetration, modification, management, exploitation and successful occupation of high-altitude forest environments 40,000–60,000 years ago.

Across a sunburnt country

It is apparent that people had settled the coasts, the vast savannahs and the rainforests of greater northern Australia at least between 40,000 and 60,000 years ago. Settlement was clearly well established by that time, consisting of more than random nomadism, incipient settlement, and transient hunting and gathering. The first settlers had not only settled large parts of greater Australia but had established customs and traditions in relation to it. They were societies of allegiance and order, communication and cohesion, industry and artistry.

The forested environments in which these super-nomads lived covered the entirety of northern Australia, and the savannah extended from New Guinea to the Kimberley, sweeping across the Torres Strait land bridge, encircling the giant lake in the Gulf of Carpentaria and pointing south in a long arm into central New South Wales.[76] This expansive botanical conduit must have presented familiar and, in many respects, ideal settlement opportunities as populations grew and generations looked for new lands in which to settle. It is easy to imagine, therefore, the colonising population continuing through that familiar landscape east, west and south, and it is perhaps no surprise that there is evidence of human settlement south of the Gulf of Carpentaria and on Cape York around 40,000 years ago. The oldest camp in the gulf country, known as GRE8, is located near the Gregory River. It contains flaked stone tools and freshwater mussels, and is confidently dated to 39,900 years with the possibility of being between 37,460 and 42,300 years old.[77] The oldest camp in Cape York is in a large rock shelter that sits, interestingly, on top of a giant table-topped mountain, called Ngarabullgan (Mount Mulligan), 400 metres above the surrounding plain (and 10 kilometres west from Cairns). The site contains flaked artefacts and bone fragments that are 37,000 years old.[78]

Human occupation is even older in the Kimberley savannah. Here there is a site called Carpenter's Gap that was occupied 40,000–45,000 years ago.[79] It is located in the Napier Range, overlooking a beautiful valley cut by the Lennard River in the central southern part of the Kimberley. The mountains here are made of limestone, so the river has created echoing gorges, with broad riverine beaches backed against majestic cliffs. The Lennard River winds peacefully through the gorges in the winter dry season but, like every other river in the Kimberley, is a savage torrent in the summer wet season. Crocodiles are abundant in any season and, one might assume, were equally abundant in the distant past. It is a well-watered and attractive landscape today and was possibly even better when people first camped there. The climate was cooler and the rainfall lower, but reduced evaporation (as a consequence of the lower temperatures) may have meant parts of the area were slightly wetter and more fertile. Picture a softened semi-arid setting against ranges looking over plains interspersed with savannah and sand dunes. Sedges grew in open marshlands and tall tropical perennial grasslands covered the plains. Palms and fruiting trees grew in moister vine thickets and seasonal gullies.[80]

People camped in the lee of a limestone cliff and left large amounts of domestic materials for archaeologists to speculate upon. This vast array of organic remains survived from the earliest occupation because of the preserving effect of the alkaline limestone sediments in which they are located. Excavations have revealed small details of people's domestic and personal lives: abundant charcoal, small seeds, paperbark and wood shavings. These are the signs of domestic activity—life at camp, where food was prepared and cooked, and wooden tools repaired. People camped in the shelter of the overhang in the wet season (the remains of fruits that ripen at this time of year have survived at the camp). One of these (*Terminalia* sp.) is exceptionally rich in vitamin C. One can picture the occupants sheltered and warm, listening to the wet season storms, healthy and well fed.

The site also contains many fragments of grass from the base of the needle-like spinifex leaves (*Plectrachne*). The large quantity of this particular portion of the spinifex points to the production of a glue-like resin made from spinifex sap.[81] Spinifex resin is a remarkable adhesive and was used for many purposes in the past. It was frequently used to attach flaked stone tools to wooden handles and spears for woodworking, hunting and fighting. The resin was also attached to specially flaked stone blades to create a comfortable hand-hold—a kind of stone dagger—and was also an excellent sealant, used like putty to repair leaking wooden dishes. It had a decorative purpose as well, and was used as a foundation for attaching coloured beads and other attractive items to string made from human hair and natural fibres. Spinifex resin is a thermoplastic material: it softens with heat, and becomes hard, rock-like, when cool. I recall participating in an experimental test of the resin as a student and finding, to our surprise, that it proved to be harder and more resilient than the best equivalent glue (Tarzan's Grip, in those days).[82] Spinifex resin had the added advantage that it could be reheated, removed and reused without loss of strength or adhesive ability. It is a fascinating material to see produced. The spinifex is threshed and pounded, and the mixture is then winnowed and picked free of contaminants. The resulting material looks like grey dust. A firestick is moved gently across the dust so that it melts, coagulates and forms, as if by magic, globules of dark red resin. These are stuck together until a suitable sized ball is made. A ball of resin takes some time to accumulate, globule by globule, and has some value as a consequence. The material is treasured and traded. A lot of human behaviour can be read into 40,000-year-old fragments of spinifex grass.

And, indeed, there seems to have been a lot of human behaviour in the Kimberley at that time. Another fascinating component of the site is a slab of limestone coated with ochre.[83] The slab is at least 40,000 years old and, as intimated by the ancient ochre crayons at Malakunanja and Nauwalabila, and the paintings of ancient marsupials throughout Arnhem Land, points to extraordinarily old artistic activity and the emergence of artistic tradition in the earliest era of Australian occupation. Here we have a painted rock surface that has fallen from the roof onto an ancient camp floor 40,000 years ago.

What the artists were trying to paint remains unclear, but, regardless, they were members of a unique clique—the first painters in the world.

Two hundred kilometres south of Carpenter's Gap, on the southern edge of the Kimberley, is another old site that both demonstrates the great antiquity of human settlement in the Australian interior and implicitly confirms the ancient occupation of its original coastline. This site is located a fair way inland: along the Fitzroy River, facing the Great Sandy Desert, some 500 kilometres from the coast at the time it was occupied. The site is called Riwi. It is still used today and is located in a deep, high cave with a keyhole-shaped entrance. The cave is formed in a limestone cliff and overlooks wide plains vegetated by savannah woodland. Small creeks flow from the ranges and there are permanent pools of water in some of the caves nearby. People were living here over 40,000 years ago, possibly as long as 43,000–46,000 years ago.[84] This limestone has, once again, preserved organic remains, and one finds seeds, fragmented spinifex leaves and fragments of paperbark. Here the paperbark has traces of ochre attached to it—a tantalising hint at portable art, ancient aesthetic appreciation and, perhaps, ancient ritual. The traces possibly indicate ancient packaging of a particular kind. It is my experience that paperbark is typically used to wrap precious items such as bone points, special flaked points and traded shell. These are typically coated in ochre that then adheres to the paperbark wrapping. What ancient treasures might have been hidden in the paperbark found at Riwi Cave?

Desert people

The people of Riwi lived on the edge of the desert on the Fitzroy River. This great river leads to the Sturt Creek (Tjurabalan),[85] that in turn fills a vast freshwater lake, Lake Gregory (Paraku).[86] Paraku is an unusual desert lake. It becomes saline and sometimes dries after

Muwitja about to eat maku (witchetty grub), Musgrave Ranges, northern South Australia. There are about 418 kilojoules in an average witchetty grub—more than a fried egg and about the same as a small lamb chop. They have a nutty taste and are either roasted briefly or eaten raw.

periods of drought but, by and large, it is an extant freshwater lake on the edge of the desert. It was a mega-lake 300,000 years ago, covering some 6000 square kilometres, but has never been bigger than 1700 square kilometres in the historic period.[87] The last 40,000–60,000 years have seen oscillating periods of wet and dry including a period of increased fluvial activity and lake enlargement 50,000–45,000 years ago.[88] Conditions were cooler then and evaporation rates were lower. Today, summer temperatures are so high that the evaporation rate is over ten times the annual rainfall—the desert is continuously desiccating. But in the past the desert was cooler and, despite lower rainfall, the surface water stayed longer.

Paraku is still an attractive living environment today, and I know many people who have walked to it across vast distances in the past—across the desert heartland, casually journeying north for ceremonies held at the lake and enjoying the incidental pleasure of company, trade and food on the way.[89] After rains the lake supports large populations of breeding birds (even sea birds nest on the lake shores), mussels and small fish. Marsupials congregate around its fringes, and the floodplains and creeks are richly vegetated with high-quality bush foods such as tubers (*Vigna*), bush onions (*Cyperus*) and bush tomatoes (*Solanum centrale*).

It is easy to imagine why ancient nomads would have come to Paraku—and it is easy to imagine them staying there. It is less easy to find evidence of their occupation, but, remarkably, one ancient stone core flaked from an old river cobble has been found in lake sediments that are at least 45,000–50,000 years old.[90] It is a small find with big implications. It places people in the desert before almost any other geographic location in Australia. The artefact indicates that people were not just in the desert an extraordinarily long time ago but that the occupation of northern Australia, on the shorelines of first contact, must be considerably older—older even than the ancient sites so far found in northern Australia suggest.

The people I knew who had walked to Paraku followed a small number of traditional walking trails extending 350 kilometres

Bush tomatoes abound after fire and may be collected at rates equalling 70,000 kilojoules an hour (a day's food for eight people). They are easily stored and rich in vitamin C, although this species produces bad headaches if eaten in great quantities.

from Wilkinkarra (Lake Mackay) in the Great Sandy Desert. These trails followed the desert ranges and escarpments, fertile plains and large salt lakes that were once ancient river and lake systems themselves. The climate 40,000 years ago was, as mentioned, cooler and marginally wetter than it is today,[91] and it was probably easier for ancient people to access the desert from secure northern environments such as Paraku than it was for the people I knew who did so last century.

Water filling these ancient river systems after effective monsoonal rains is an irregular but impressive event now and must, by climatic implication, have been so in the ancient past. The old drainage systems turn into rivers and lakes after heavy rains, plainly apparent from satellite imagery and readily demonstrated by the floods of 2001, after which an inland sea remained over an area west of Wilkinkarra for three years. I was travelling through the desert after these rains, trying to make contact with nomads still living traditional lives in the area of the flood (local Pintupi Kukatja people were concerned about the welfare of these last nomads). The fresh water spread as far as the eye could see across the horizon and covered some 6700 square kilometres (and at least 12,500 square kilometres including Wilkinkarra itself)—greater than the ancient mega-lake of Paraku 300,000 years ago. The vast lake was intermittently studded with the tops of desert eucalypts, standing about 1 metre above the water. Swimming in this vast inland sea was a remarkable experience resonating with beauty and solitude, although my companions were unimpressed and stood on the dunes terrified for my safety, waiting for the giant snake, Wanampi, to consume me.

The experience evoked a vision of ancient people standing on similar dunes in antiquity. Major floods like this would take them deep into the desert and, over time, introduce them to the character of desert subsistence. The retreating floods would leave swamps, and the drying swamps would shrink to become soaks. And the soaks would sustain life. The great sand deserts are filled with such soaks and, as such, these deserts are not necessarily the barrier to human occupation they might superficially appear to be. But it is a deceptive landscape. Unlike almost every other environment in the world, what is needed for survival in the desert is hidden from view. It rests underground. Knowledge and skill are required to find it.

That knowledge is today contained in a body of lore called the Tjukurrpa. There are many Tjukurrpa, and some, such as the Wati Kutjara (Two Men), Minyma Tjuta (Many Women), Wati Marlu (Red Kangaroo) and Sand Goanna (the actual name being too sacred to present here) pass throughout the entire desert region and sometimes beyond (see Plate 27). Tjukurrpa is the core of desert tradition. It expresses the larger spiritual and social dimension of Aboriginal life. It is the dominant traditional concept, touches all parts of existence and imbues it with strong motivation and meaning. Tjukurrpa is, in essence, part religion, part history, and part moral and social charter. It is, in many respects, the conceptual vehicle through which people fulfil themselves, define their position and gain authority in society. Tjukurrpa provides an implicit prescription for environmental relations and explains the creation of the physical world. As such, Tjukurrpa is the intellectual and political basis by which people relate to the land. Tjukurrpa literally means 'to dream' and, in this metaphoric sense, equates the surreal and other-worldly experiences of religion with the experience of dreams.[92]

The Tjukurrpa is also a corpus of religious narratives—songlines—that create an iconography of the desert, explaining and defining its resources and the socio-political relationships of the people using them. Here two narratives come to mind, although there are hundreds within and across the desert region.[93] One is the history of the Two Men (Wati Kutjara), and the other is the history of the Red Kangaroo (Wati Marlu). The particular details of these two narratives need not be revealed, save to say that the former relates to the travels of Two Men from the very north (starting off as young uninitiated boys) to the south of the desert (by which time they are ancient heroic characters). They provide a kind of moral charter for desert society: prince-like characters that generally do well and inform social relationships and initiation procedures. The Red Kangaroo is rather more spectacular, transformative and magical. It travels in a cyclic manner through the desert, touching its very margins at each quadrant of the compass, and conveying much about landscape, kinship, initiation and sacred ritual.

The Tjukurrpa of the Two Men, Red Kangaroo and Many Women are the longest and most extensive Tjukurrpa that I am aware of in the arid zone. While it is probably too far-fetched to interpret these narratives as ancient maps of early occupation, they are nonetheless maps—iconic narratives that connect the best and most fertile parts of the desert in a manner that, if followed, allows the deserts of Australia to be traversed and occupied with comparative ease.

The skill of desert hunter-gatherers seems to know no bounds and never ceases to amaze, the appreciation of which assists those foreign to the landscape to understand how it might have been used. One only has to watch a woman track an echidna (with its perverse reverse footprints) for several kilometres, or watch a man intuitively extract a goanna from one of its many (real and false) burrows to appreciate this. Food is abundant in the desert if you have the skill to find it and, with seasonal qualification, is high in nutritional returns and low on labour. In my experience, for example, one person can collect enough goannas (*Varanus*) in an hour to feed themself. Bush tomatoes can be collected at rates that allow a family to eat for a day after an hour of picking. I have seen bush onions collected in just 20 minutes in such quantities that, on one occasion, 12 adults had enough (with plenty left over) to feed themselves. Wild sweet potatoes (*Ipomoea*) are so abundant in the northern deserts they appear domesticated—and indeed, in some senses, they are—snapped portions of the tubers are often reburied after harvesting to ensure there is a crop the following season. Sweet potatoes are likely to have been a major drawcard for early settlers as in a matter of hours they can be harvested in quantities that will feed a whole family.[94]

When I lived in the interior and recorded these subsistence returns the desert had been largely unoccupied for about 30 years. It was in a comparatively unexploited state and might be compared, with obvious caution, to the deserts of first settlement, being unoccupied with untapped resources: fields of grass seeds remained unharvested, hectares of tubers were not dug, and game was unaware of human predation. Subsistence returns were, therefore, likely to have been better than they might have been with a constant population and in a constant state of exploitation. Clearly the desert has bad seasons and not all parts of all deserts are equally rich in food and water, but it might be accepted that the desert was (and is) more attractive to human settlement than it might otherwise seem, and might therefore have more readily attracted settlement in the past than its contemporary aridity suggests. At least there were no giant crocodiles (*Pallimnarchus*), fewer man-eating goannas (*Megalania*) and considerably less chance of encountering a hungry possum lion (*Thylacoleo*) in landscapes that were dry, open and short on trees.

And thus, not surprisingly, the desert was occupied soon after people appeared at Paraku. The distance between Paraku and Wilkinkarra is 350 kilometres as the nomad walks or 250 kilometres as the crow flies. It is just another 250 kilometres again to the ranges of central Australia. To put these distances in perspective, two men I know, Napin and Nunyarangu, walked across the northern part of the treeless section of the Nullarbor Plain in the 1950s. The walk was conducted in the winter, but across appallingly harsh, rocky, waterless terrain. The distance covered was 260 kilometres and took over three days—walking at night and in the cool of the morning and evening. The men make no claims about the walk; one of them in fact walked back again several months later. It is simply what they did as bushmen—no demonstration of endurance or natural challenge to overcome, just a normal activity in the life of a desert nomad.

So, with nomadic perspective, it is not difficult to conceive of people settling, walking and occupying the country between Paraku and central Australia a long time ago, and there is in fact evidence for this occurring—several flakes, a core and a piece of red ochre—in Puritjarra rock shelter near the Cleland Hills, dating from approximately 45,000 years ago.[95] The cave was used more frequently over the next 10,000 years, so by 35,000 years ago occupation had become systematic, and a number of pieces of high-quality red and purple ochre were left in the cave. The ochre had come from an ochre quarry in a large mesa called Karrku (meaning 'ochre'), 125 kilometres out on the sand plains to the northwest and just 150 kilometres east of Wilkinkarra. This source is famous throughout the northern desert and is renowned for its high-quality and lustrous rouge-like texture and appearance.[96] It has particular ceremonial value and is treasured by senior Aboriginal religious leaders, and was traded extensively as a consequence. The ochre at Puritjarra is described as having been used for personal decoration and the creation of paintings in the cave, although I suspect a deeper religious significance and other mystical activities are secreted within the archaeological utilitarianism of painting and personal adornment.[97] The ochre clearly had great value then (as it does today), as people either walked over 250 kilometres to get it and bring it back, or traded commodities in exchange for it. That in itself is fascinating, not only raising the possibility of a system of desert trade 40,000 ago but indicating that ore extraction—mining—was taking place at Karrku an extraordinarily long time ago. The mine now extends some 80 metres underground and must be the oldest active mine site in the world.

The presence of the ochre at Puritjarra and the geographic relationship between that cave and Karrku indicates a certain adaptive genius, and a focused and resourceful socio-economic system among the first desert dwellers. It might be assumed that the ancient occupational strategies that enabled desert settlement so long ago were evolutionary in character and allowed (given the reliable food staples, flexible hunting and gathering strategies and the availability of water) long-term widespread desert occupation. Survival must have required extreme mobility to ensure access to necessary resources and implicitly required an inclusive social and economic network over a vast area. Today that network is articulated and maintained through the Tjukurrpa. Early settlement in the desert left a light footprint, but it is a footprint with a large personality: nomadic settlement and social cohesion that would, with minor elaboration, see people occupying every desert environment within the next 10,000 years, and which would continue to define society across the greater Australian arid zone until the historic period.[98]

The diversity and adaptability of human ecology in the desert is perhaps nowhere better demonstrated than through the ancient occupation of the most harsh and unappealing desert landscape in Australia—the Nullarbor Plain. The Nullarbor Plain is arid in every sense of the word. Trees are few and low, the ground is hopelessly porous and the nutritional base is limited. The limestone plain is so perforated and pockmarked with caves and tunnels, blowholes and dolines that it is dangerous to cross at night. Soils are thin and the ground immensely rocky—more closely resembling the surface of the moon than the Australian desert.

Palaeo-environmental indications are that the regional climate was drier 40,000 years ago than at present.[99] The 100-metre cliffs near the Bight were an escarpment then, overlooking a huge flat coastal plain—the coast was at least 70 kilometres further away. But people lived in, or at least visited, the inland plain all that time ago. Signs of human occupation 40,000 or possibly 43,000 years ago are found in a large rock shelter called Allen's Cave.[100] The shelter was formed after the roof of a larger cave collapsed 50,000–60,000 years ago. One metre of deposit built up over the next 10,000–20,000 years before the first person sheltered within it. The evidence for human presence is minimal but irrefutable, and consists of a small unmodified flake made of chalcedony and three pieces of flaked limestone. These artefacts were wedged between rocks and sealed beneath a thin layer of gravel, itself capped by a 7-centimetre band of laminated silts.[101] These silts have been dated to 39,850 years old (calibrated deviation of 36,750–42,950 years old), and the artefacts are clearly older still, as they lie beneath the silts. The silts are in turn overlain by an ancient hearth consisting of a thin layer of ash and two burnt rocks: the enclosed and compact association of the hearth and the artefacts, the laminated silts and the adjacent rocks gives this old site a secure antiquity of occupation.

A similar antiquity comes from an old cooking hearth found at Dempsey's Lagoon near Port Augusta in South Australia. The hearth is over 40,000 years old.[102] Port Augusta is, as the name suggests, a port, and the site is now near the water. It is dry today (receiving less than 250 millimetres of rain per year), but was even drier then, and was also further inland. Port Augusta sits at the northern end of a broad (flooded) plain, flanked by low cliffs. Forty thousand years ago that plain was flat and dry, and the sea was then at least

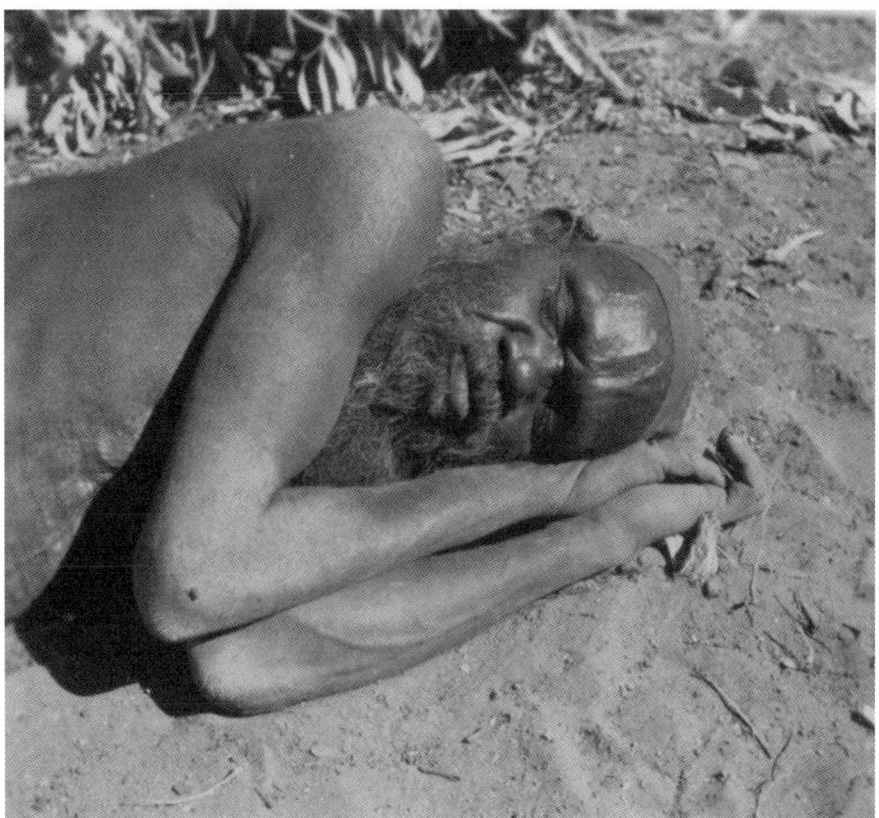

Hard ground is no impediment to sound sleep if you are tough enough.

Sleeping hollows and adjacent fires in the shelter of a windbreak are far warmer and more comfortable than they look. The open country surrounding the camp is the product of continual firing.

400 kilometres away, capping the ocean in the vicinity of Port Lincoln and the islands straddling the mouth of Spencer Gulf.

Such minimal archaeological evidence for desert occupation tells a major story of human adaptability and ingenuity in the history of Australian settlement. Three ancient pieces of flaked stone at Allen's

Cave, one flaked cobble at Paraku and a handful of flakes and ochre at Puritjarra see people settled in the very north, centre and south of Australian deserts 40,000–50,000 years ago. The archaeological account is small but its associated human history is great. Presumably people accessed the desert from more fertile lands via its semi-arid margins and, in the relative greatness of time, soon settled the core deserts, arid ranges and barren plains.

Ancient shores

Forty thousand years ago the desert extended west to the sea. That western desert was cooler than elsewhere, and ancient pollen records from the Pilbara indicate it was colder between 42,000 and 39,000 years ago than at any time in the last 100,000 years. The area appears to have been in a period of climatic transition, from cooler wetter to cooler drier, with an average of nine dry months a year, low rainfall and hardly any summer rain.[103] How people managed to settle this remote shoulder of the Australian continent remains an open question—but they did so nonetheless. Perhaps they occupied the Pilbara from the arid interior; perhaps they settled it from the coast. The archaeological evidence suggests both. Neither route was particularly easy as permanent rivers were (and continue to be) in short supply along its coastal seascape and its desert landscape.

South from the Kimberley, for example, the old coastline ran flat some 300 kilometres beyond its present shore and encompassed a vast fan of aridity extending west from the (now) Great Sandy Desert. There were no permanent rivers here. The largest rivers in the Pilbara itself are the Murchison, Gascoyne and Fortescue rivers. They are not permanent rivers, but they are long: the Fortescue River, for example, flows over 1000 kilometres from the desert to the sea. They also carry substantial amounts of water in the wet season and must have held permanent supplies of water in the past. The average flow of the Murchison River after wet season rains today is about 200 gigalitres, although it has been known to transport over 1800 gigalitres in extreme flood.[104] Wet season rains do to rivers in the Pilbara what they do to them in the Kimberley—create raging torrents in the wet and leave intermittent streams in the dry: rivers with subterranean water linked by freshwater pools; conduits for settlement between the desert and the sea and the sea and the desert.

So, perhaps it is no surprise to find sites of extreme antiquity on both sides of the Pilbara block: 39,400–41,700 years at Djadjiling in the Hamersley Plateau, and 39,000–41,300 at Jansz on Cape Range Peninsula.[105] Djadjiling is an interesting site as its early settlement is marked with some occupational intensity (compared, for example, to Allen's Cave). Here 664 artefacts have been left in the basal layers of the shelter and there is a small hearth. These artefacts account for over half the artefacts in the site, including all those left over the remaining millennia of occupation—giving some indication of settlement patterns and occupational intensity of the greater desert at this time.

A unique aspect of the early Pilbara living environment was that its shores are set against a steep continental shelf. This means that the coastline today is not unlike the coastline 40,000 years ago; in fact there is only 12 kilometres' difference. The Pilbara coast is thus perhaps the only coastline in Australia where we can glimpse life as it was so long ago. Everywhere else in Australia the rising seas have drowned old coastal occupation, but in the Pilbara sea level rise did not flood all the ancient coastal sites. They stood, so to speak, on a steeply sloping range just above the rising seas. So it is possible to discover ancient evidence of early coastal occupation, and, at a small cave called Jansz on Cape Range Peninsula, between Exmouth Gulf and the Indian Ocean, there is evidence of people living off both marine and terrestrial resources, hunting kangaroo, turtles and fish, as well as collecting emu eggs and shellfish 40,000 years ago. This site and others, like Mandu Mandu shelter just to the south, contain the oldest evidence of marine subsistence in Australia, in a mixed subsistence economy featuring bandicoots, bettongs and possums. Intriguingly, there are thylacine bones in the base of the site as well.[106]

The aridity of the Western Australian coast continues south of the Pilbara, and, again, there were no permanent rivers for over 1200 kilometres—until the Swan River is reached near Perth. Forty thousand years ago that river ran further west, across the coastal plain, beyond Rottnest Hill (now Island) and into a huge canyon. This canyon is now under water: it starts at the 50-metre contour and continues to a depth of over 2000 metres, 160 kilometres out to sea.[107] The underwater canyon is longer and deeper than the Grand Canyon, and must have been an intriguing natural feature and a wondrous source of marine food, with the coastal settlers emerging from the deep and feeding among the oceanic upwelling near the coast. Signs of life on this spectacular ancient coast are now also underwater, but evidence for it is implicit adjacent to it and further inland. Nearby, on what was then Rottnest Hill, there is provisional and indirect evidence for human occupation some 50,000 years ago.[108] Rottnest became an island 6500 years ago, but back then was a low hill on a broad plain, overlooking the vast oceanic canyon.

Further inland, up what is now the Swan River, is an old living floor strewn with artefacts. The artefacts are thought to be at least 38,000 years old, with the possibility that they are 40,200–46,900 years old.[109] A small number of those artefacts have been made from a fossiliferous chalcedony that comes from a source on the ancient coastal plain. The material is also found in other sites in southern Western Australia but disappears from the archaeological record 4600 years ago—by which time the rising seas had drowned the quarry and prevented people accessing the original source of the material. The presence of the fossiliferous chalcedony up the Swan River indicates that the people living there moved between the river and the coast to acquire the material.

The most southern part of Western Australia was dry 40,000 years ago, rather like today, except for a band of open forest across the hills and plains west of Albany and Bunbury. This forested area extended west 20 kilometres past the Naturaliste and Leeuwin hills (now capes) across a short coastal plain. This area was also settled an extraordinarily long time ago, as there is evidence for human occupation, in a limestone cave called Devil's Lair, that is 46,000–47,000 years old, with artefacts scattered at levels that are more likely 50,000 years old.[110] At the time of occupation the cave was about 25 kilometres from the archaic coastline. This ancient evidence for human occupation is reasonably sparse—four old fireplaces and 111 artefacts—suggesting infrequent short visits by small numbers of people. The occupants lived in semi darkness, ate possums and wallabies, and snakes, lizards, frogs, bats, birds and emu eggs—the eggs suggesting occupation of the site during the winter months. Bones of extinct giant marsupials, *Protemnodon, Sthenurus* and possibly *Thylacoleo,* have also been found at the site.[111] There are, interestingly, a surprisingly large number of bone tools in the cave—more than elsewhere in the country and among the oldest bone tools found in Australia. Some have been made into pointed awls by either splitting or grinding the bone. Some are small, suggesting needles used to puncture and sew animal skins together. The environment was cold then, and the cave perhaps provided a degree of subterranean warmth in the ancient winters, from which people ventured forth clothed in furs they had made there.

The occupation at Devil's Lair sees people living in a most southerly location, some 3000 kilometres from Arnhem Land. The remarkable antiquity of Devil's Lair might therefore be set against that of Malakunanja in Arnhem Land to convey the enormity and nature of settlement and adaptation across the continent. The timescale involved is immense, the terrain traversed colossal and the scale of human accomplishment difficult to comprehend. Comprehension finds corroboration through archaeological interpretations and physical chronologies that tell a human story of great social, geographic and chronological magnitude. Archaeological discoveries at Devil's Lair demonstrate that ancient people explored, established and expanded across a vast, dry continent in a manner that both absorbs and validates the oldest calibrated antiquities asserted for human settlement. Colonisation at such a grand

An interesting photograph of a child smoking a tree root, a tradition apparently independent of European influence (Musgrave Ranges, northern South Australia).

scale requires and gives proof to great uncontested antiquity, both documented and implied—through the establishment of regional societies of cohesion, order and engagement. Pan-Australian settlement was built on sequential regional occupation, and necessitated traditions of community and domesticity, creativity, self-awareness and resolute adaptability. It belongs to a greatness of time that is, by proof of the science required to define it, fundamentally beyond our intuitive grasp. Wherever one turns within palaeo-Australia there are great antiquities in landscapes embedded with innovation, artistry and adaptation: a land of seafarers, woodsmen, fishers, hunters and gatherers, adventurers, explorers and artists constituting a super-nomadic continental tradition at the very edge of measurable time.

Australia's oldest human remains

In the central southeast of Australia, it is possible, for the first time, to meet these ancient Australians. Here there was once an ancient system of large freshwater lakes that abounded with fish, birds, marsupials—and human life. The lake system is now called the Willandra Lakes and rests like a scalloped wing to the west of the Lachlan River, between the Murray–Darling Basin and the desert fringe. The lakes are dry now, but between 50,000 and 60,000 years ago they were full and fertile.[112] They were about 10 metres deep and covered some 1000 square kilometres. Aboriginal people took advantage of the lacustrine riches. They camped along the lakeshores and exploited the plentiful resources: frogs, fish, yabbies and shellfish. Burnt bone is rare around the lakes, but the pieces that have been found reveal the consumption of bettongs, bandicoots, quolls, wombats, possums, small wallabies, and the eastern grey and red kangaroos. Burnt-out wombat burrows are common around the lakes, indicating that burning or smoking wombats from their burrows was an ancient hunting technique.[113] The people also hunted emus and collected emu eggs, and starch residues on tools indicate they harvested and consumed sweet potato.[114] The first signs of settlement are slight but indicate the presence of people between 45,700 and 50,100 years ago (with a statistical variance meaning the lakes could have been occupied 43,400–52,500 years ago). Artefact densities increase and peak between 43,000 and 45,000 years ago, and it might be assumed that the human population similarly peaked at that time at these lakes.

One old man (popularly known as Mungo Man) died in this period and was buried in the sand dunes adjacent to the lake. His skeleton remained there undisturbed for at least 38,000–42,000 years. The man was about 50 when he died and was laid in a grave 80–100 centimetres deep, with his hands clasped and knees slightly bent. His head, chest and groin were covered with ochre—in such quantity that the surrounding sands are still stained with it. How the ochre was applied entreats haunting reflection. Was it rubbed onto the man's skin after he died? Was it sprinkled richly over him? Was it used as a decorative component of some kind of ancient shroud? Where did the ochre come from and what does its application mean in human terms?

There is no source of ochre in the regional riverine environment of the Willandra Lakes, and the likely source of the material is the Olary region in South Australia, some 200 kilometres to the northwest—so people either travelled some distance to mine it or traded goods for it. Either way the act suggests a degree of human effort and social organisation. Its generous application says something about human emotions and the status of the man covered by it. The ochre certainly implies some kind of ancient funeral rite, the decorative treatment suggesting consideration and compassion, care and respect, and perhaps even concern for the afterlife. If so, this is the first evidence in the world for emotive cognition and recognition of the metaphysical self. The burial thus speaks to us in human and spiritual terms: a loved one dead, his community grieving, a society responding with the acquisition of materials required for proper burial, his body adorned and respectfully buried, his ritual status recognised and his transfiguration anticipated through adornment. The sense of ritual attendance, the decorative consideration and careful placement of the corpse implies grief, communal concern and reverence. The importance of the burial is not simply that it is the first of its kind in the world, but that it presents us with recognisable

human emotions—and so creates an empathic link between us and this ancient community across more than 40,000 years of time.

The burial personalises the past and reveals beyond it a man who lived, had family and who died on the lakeshore among grieving family and friends. He was a real person. We can still look at his face. His features were androgynous: he was, perhaps, a refined, elegant-looking person. He had an infected arthritic elbow—perhaps worn and aggravated from throwing too many spears. The injury must have caused him considerable suffering in the later years of his life. His teeth were worn in a manner that looks like he used them for stripping plant fibres, perhaps for the construction of nets, baskets or dilly bags. I have seen people use their teeth to strip bark from herbaceous shrubs in the desert, to be used for making sandals for walking across hot sand in the summer. Perhaps this man made sandals for the hot Willandra dunes. The old man had also lost his two lower canine teeth. They seem to have been removed when he was young and perhaps indicate ancient initiation rituals (the first of their kind in the world).

The remains of a young woman are located nearby. The burials are not related, but she seems to have died around the same time. She was just 148 centimetres tall (4'10"), and lightly built. She had an oval head, a delicate, fine-featured face, and small teeth, the gracility suggesting she was rather pretty. Unlike the old man, this young woman was cremated. Her bones were then smashed and placed in a small burial pit. The burial practice is reminiscent of desert tradition where the dead are laid to rest, their spirit free to roam until past scores have been settled. Friends and family attempt to disguise themselves to avoid spiritual retribution. They shave their hair off and remove all physical attachment to the person's life, hoping to escape the attention of the wandering spirit. After a certain time the remains are exhumed, and the skeleton smashed and reburied—the spirit is now at rest, and the living can go about

Opposite: In some parts of Australia, body scarification is sacred. In others, such as the southern deserts, it is simply a form of body decoration—a means of enhancing one's sense of masculinity.

their daily business with ease. The present recollects the past, at least in so far as the contemporary ceremony makes us reflect on the meaning and emotion contained in the ancient ceremony. But, regardless of the meaning of this ancient woman's reburial, it is a fact that she is the first person known to have been cremated on the planet. And beyond that profundity is the reality of grief and the earliest traditions developed to deal with it: life and death at Willandra allows us to see the significance of the ancient human response and the application of ritual as people dealt with their loss through considered burial rites.

The final act of settlement

The temperate landscapes of southeastern Australia were cooler when people occupied the Willandra Lakes. That coolness turned to cold as latitude and altitude increased in the southern parts of temperate Australia, with glaciers covering large parts of the Snowy Mountains and southern ranges. In fact much of the globe was in the grip of a great ice age, and with so much water locked in ice, sea levels were substantially lower. By 43,000 years ago it was possible to walk to Tasmania.[115]

Tasmania was then a southern cape, joined to greater Australia by a land bridge—the Bassian Ridge (now underlying the shallow waters of Bass Strait), that itself was part of a massive continental plain that extends some 1.1 million square kilometres from Kangaroo Island to Cape Howe on the south coast of New South Wales.[116] The Bassian Ridge itself encompassed some 215,000 square kilometres—three times the size of Tasmania today. The ridge is under water now, but when humans were camped at the Willandra Lakes it was then just above sea level and rested as a broad, undulating plain pointing south towards Mount Flinders (now Flinders Island), 760 metres above it. It is hard to imagine the appearance of the long land bridge, but pollen records from central Tasmania suggest it was vegetated by grasses and daisies with small evergreen conifers and pockets of casuarina and eucalyptus. It was an open plain with alpine vegetation on hills and ranges over 400 metres high.[117] Emus and kangaroos grazed upon it, as did a number of extinct large marsupials—*Zygomaturus, Palorchestes, Protemnodon* and *Thylacoleo* among them. The climate was a little warmer than it had been in previous millennia, but the plain was still a cold, bitter place, swept by biting westerly winds. The westerly chill was sharpened as the winds blew across a massive freshwater lake that was 120 kilometres wide and 400 kilometres long, cupped by the Furneaux Ranges (now Islands) and Mount King (now Island) rising 200 metres above it. This vast lake would at times convert into a large embayment, but would nonetheless remain, until its inundation 14,000 years ago, a place of rewarding fertility: an environmental keystone in the southern march to Tasmania, a freshwater lake bigger than the size of Tasmania today. Thus one might imagine people in this bitter and almost forgotten plain moving south to the frozen heartland of sub-Antarctic Tasmania, one of the coldest known living environments then occupied on earth: a Tasmania that more closely resembled Macquarie Island than the picturesque holiday isle we know today.

The colonisers made that journey along the eastern side of the great lake, along the Bassian Ridge, past Mount Flinders and onto the ancient Tasmanian coast. From here they are likely to have occupied the hinterland and settled its rivers,[118] moved into its foothills and exploited the mountains of central and southwest Tasmania. These were covered with ice caps so that glaciers extended from the mountains into the upper Derwent Valley (in the south) and into the Forth and Mersey valleys (in the north). The beautiful forests of today's Tasmanian wilderness were largely absent, and grass, heath and shrubs covered most of the land. The high country between the grasslands and the glaciers was frigid—moorland vegetated with herb fields, button grass swamps and conifers. It was cold and wet with long winters, short summers and temperatures some 6 degrees Celsius below today's temperatures.[119]

Their journey ended in the coldest and most inaccessible regions of the known world, at the foot of Tasmania's glacial environment, in a number of limestone caves in the central highlands and the wild southwest. At Warreen Cave, on the Maxwell River, there is evidence of human occupation between 38,800 and 41,000 years ago. At Parmerpar Meethaner Cave, in the Forth River valley near Cradle Mountain, people camped within 3 kilometres of the glaciated highlands 44,200 years ago.[120] Humans settled here in periglacial conditions in the winter months as part of a seasonal strategy that moved from the highest, coldest altitudes in the summer to the lower altitudes during winter.[121]

The people visited the wild, frigid lands cyclically and targeted selected resources seasonally. The ice age settlers were mobile hunters, discerningly, intentionally and intelligently hunting easy prey in the glacial latitudes. They were after Bennett's wallabies (*Macropus rufogriseus*), a macropod that stands about 1.5 metres tall and weighs around 20 kilograms. The Tasmanian sub-species has longer, shaggier hair than its mainland relations and tends to flock on fertile patches of grassland in the tundra-like moors. The fertile patches were limited in the subalpine environment but were maintained by firing, so the wallabies were effectively tethered to them—creating a profitable localised hunting target.[122] The hunters attacked the wallabies selectively, generally killing the older and younger individuals so as, it would seem, not to unduly impact the breeding population and endanger the seasonal resource.[123] The cave dwellers had particular items of food in mind and returned specific body parts to the caves for consumption, systematically cracking skulls to eat the fat contained in the brain, and splitting long bones to extract the marrow contained in the limbs. The animals were also skinned, the winter pelts having the thickest and highest quality fur for warmth.[124]

These ice age hunters clearly knew what they were doing. Theirs was not a haphazard, opportunistic quest for survival. These were tough hunters with a particular hunting strategy in mind. They applied themselves to the hard and dangerous mountains and valleys in a manner that was scheduled, cooperative, coordinated and clever. These people had an obvious grasp of animal ecology, breeding patterns and population dynamics. They were not transient hunters struggling to make a living in a difficult environment, but skilled predators with cooperative strategies and advanced technology directed at profitable kills. It is worth pausing to reflecting that these hunters were living over 40,000 years ago. They were great hunters, impressive by any measure, but doubly so given they lived, walked and hunted in the chill of glaciers in the coldest and southern-most location then occupied in the world.

The settlement of the sub-Antarctic environments of Tasmania represents the final act of an epic that began some 70,000 years ago.[125] It represents the culmination of a great exodus that commenced and coincides, almost unbelievably, with a massive volcanic explosion in Asia and the near extinction of humankind across the globe. When populations recovered and expanded across the earth they travelled north and east, the long journey eastwards taking them to the rim of the Pacific, the shores of Australia and, ultimately, to the glaciers of southern Tasmania. The ancients left a record of their passing, an extraordinary material legacy of monumental achievement that saw occupation and settlement of the most remote corners and most diverse and difficult environments imaginable. It is testament to the enduring greatness of human ingenuity and adaptation. It is a story of a people who came, generation by generation, millennium by millennium, from Africa and Asia, via the distant tropical shores of northern Australia, through the savannah, into the highlands of Papua New Guinea, around Australia's massive coast, along its temperamental rivers and lakes, across its great deserts and down into its glaciated mountains, a great journey to the far ends of the earth.

3
The Great Drought

30,000–18,000 YEARS AGO

'We talked to them but they wanted to stay. So we left and walked far away. We stayed in a distant land but after a time we returned to our country. We travelled with people from that distant land. Together we walked. But when we returned the people who had stayed were dead. They were all gone. Then we stayed and the others stayed with us. But they did not like the desert. So they returned to their country. We stayed. We are the ones who stayed. And that is who we are and that is why we are here. We are the people of the spinifex plains.'

—De-sensitised version of the sacred tradition of the Spinifex People, from the Great Victoria Desert

Earth

She sat on a flat stone just inside the lip of the shelter. Her father had told her to move several times, but she liked sitting beside the stream of water that fell from the overhang of the cave. It created a fluid curtain that she watched, silver, ever changing. Occasionally she pushed her hand through the fluid sheen. It splashed her face and she flinched. Her father told her to stop doing it. But the falling water attracted her. She felt oddly secure, a hand's width from the torrential rain outside. The wet season was always like this, long days spent inside watching the rain pour across the valley below, waiting for it to stop. At least it was cool. Her grandparents said the rainy seasons were not as long as they used to be, but it did not feel that way to her. They said the world was changing. There were not as many cyclones. The dry seasons were getting longer. It was drier. The big animals were getting harder to find. The bush was different. But it looked the same to her.

She watched her father split a length of wood with a wooden hammer and a large flaked stone. He seemed to think the rain would stop and they would soon move back to the plains. He needed to fix his axe. She preferred the plains. Other families would be close, there were more places to play. Her father bound green bark around the wood, strapping it to the axe. His fingers left soft purple smears on the light-green fibre. She looked fleetingly, afraid to stare in case she was seen. The ochre captivated her. It was soft,

Previous pages: The great deserts of Australia grew by a third as the ice age arrived (Mann Range, northern South Australia).

purple-coloured, almost shiny. She wanted to touch it but would never dare. She knew her father would not remove the traces from his body. They would wear away, as life itself wore on, and the memory of its association faded. He had been in the upper escarpments for several days. She did not know why, and her grandmother said she could not know. It was secret, dangerous and important. She thought it had something to do with the changing weather. All the men went. The women waited. Sometimes she thought she heard hard chants in the darkness of the night. They frightened her and seemed to mix with the echoes of the storm, tumbling down the escarpment.

So she looked at him and felt safe. He was much bigger than her and had longer hair, twisted with feathers. Her hair was short and had been rubbed into tassels run through with small red beads. He wore a bracelet of brown seeds and a necklace of green and red shells. His hair hung loose as he worked and he called to her to lift it from his eyes. He bound the last lashings with his strong hands, but as he did so the handle of his axe caught his necklace and snapped it. The shell beads spilt into the sand. He swore, she bent and picked most of them up. Then she walked to the fire. It was still warm and she ate some small plums. She was sick of eating them, but that was all her mother seemed to collect at this time of year. Please, she thought, stop raining; I want someone to play with.

Along the base of the great cliffs

It rains a lot in Kakadu, and it is a place where a lot of people spent a lot of time inside, in rock shelters, sheltering from the summer storms. Eight of those shelters have been found in the escarpments. Each offers a peek into human life during the late Pleistocene. The people living there then, like the people living there in the recent past, occupied the upland valleys and escarpments during the wet season and fanned down over the plains in the dry season, living and hunting there, taking their implements with them.[1] The ancient population was well adapted to the local environment and used it intensively. People were burning the country as part of their subsistence activities and, as vegetation was cleared, sand washed from the escarpment and filled the plains below. The climate then was cooler and drier, and the bush thinned in the face of the frequent burning.[2]

The evidence of ancient human occupation is impressive in this part of the world—so impressive that it formed a crucial part of the scientific case for the establishment of Kakadu National Park and eventually its designation as one of Australia's World Heritage areas. The cultural record is truly outstanding—huge numbers of stone tools have been left in the caves and outliers across the escarpment: over 30,000 retrieved from excavations at Nauwalabila alone, at a density of over 12,000 flakes per cubic metre. The deposition reveals sequential periods of occupation, pulses of stone artefacts and charcoal suggesting seasonal settlement and seasonal religious relationships with favoured locations across the millennia.[3] The people living in these caves made stone tools of quartz and chert for woodworking and food preparation. They carried volcanic rocks to the shelters to grind stone axes. At Nauwalabila there are chips from ancient axes that are 30,000 years old. Other ground-edged axes are found elsewhere along the escarpment that are over 20,000 years old.[4] And there is also a fragment of ground-edged axe at Nawarla Gabarnmang in western Arnhem Land. It is 35,400 years old. These axes are the first ground stone axes in the world,[5] and tools like them would not appear in Europe until the New Stone Age, or Neolithic, 25,000 years later. Their invention and use in Australia was a material revolution: they were tools for felling trees and undertaking serious woodworking activities.[6]

The people in Arnhem Land were also grinding ochre on mobile grindstones and in cupolas in the sandstone bedrock. They also used ochre crayons 20,000–30,000 years ago as indirect signs of their artistic temperament.[7] The escarpments of Arnhem Land provide a wonderful canvas for artistic expression and there are thousands of galleries—art in every cavity, recess, shelter and cavern. Over 6000 galleries have been recorded to date, but the total has not yet been counted. In western Arnhem Land, counting continues: 923 galleries so far and over 44,000 individual works of art. The 'revolution' in Palaeolithic art in Western Europe pales into insignificance: just 275 sites with just over 10,000 individual representations, by comparison.[8]

The oldest drawing in Australia

The earliest known picture ever drawn in Australia is found in Nawarla Gabarnmang, in western Arnhem Land.[9] Here there is a small tabular rock measuring 2.8 by 3.5 centimetres that contains a charcoal drawing that has fallen from the roof of the cave. The drawing is difficult to describe but contains two crossed lines in which the longer axis is straight and one side of the shorter axis is curved. The curved part is bulbous and filled with a heavier (and darker) concentration of charcoal. The charcoal forming the rest of the design has faded with age. The fragment is between 15,600 and 45,600 years old, with a likely age of about 28,000 years.

A large ochre crayon with facetted surfaces has also been found in Nawarla Gabarnmang. The crayon is mulberry coloured and matches the hue of the 'Dynamic' figures painted on the cave walls. The crayon rests in sediments dating between 15,000 and 25,000 years old. Dynamic or 'Mimi' art (from the Mimi spirits who are thought to have made it) is an ancient form of art found throughout Arnhem Land. It is characterised by human-like figures in which movement is vibrantly expressed through pose and balance. The paintings are at once delicate and bellicose, depending, seemingly, on the mood of the viewer. The compositions effect a sensation of grace and agility through elongated limbs, refined body shape, alignment and contingent activity. The superb representation of form and balance creates an illusion of mystical momentum. The delicate beings are often adorned with armlets, necklaces, headdresses, tassels and feathers, enhancing the illusion of fluidity and creating a sense of ancient fantasy. The figures are usually in action—holding or throwing spears, a club, a boomerang or a hafted ground stone axe. Some hunt, others seem to dance. Some are in conflict.[10] They have great aesthetic appeal and convey much about human attributes.

Gwion figures in the Kimberley are probably over 15,000 years old and reveal the world's oldest boomerangs and rich personal adornment: tassels, armlets, fans, belts, bustles and elongated headdresses.

Men are most frequently portrayed. They have notable hairstyles and many wear long plaits. The male figures also wear elaborate headdresses, and have a hair belt with pubic apron and bustles over their buttocks. Penises are rarely seen (and when they are seen they are explicitly sexual in representation). The men wear necklaces, pendants, wristbands and armbands. Some have cicatrices—indicating body scarification and manipulated body image has a long history. Figures of women are infrequent, and are typically portrayed

The past in the present: richly decorated men holding spear-throwers and floral fans and wearing elaborate headdresses of Gwion ancestry, in the Kimberley.

running with a dilly bag and digging stick, and sometimes a firestick. They are mostly young women.

The paintings reveal people had single-barbed spears that were thrown by hand. (Spear-throwers had not yet been invented.) They also had boomerangs—the first boomerangs in the world. Their outlines are stencilled onto the rock face. Their forms are many: symmetrical, asymmetrical, hooked, large and small. Every kind of boomerang known in Australia is stencilled here—a complete aerial arsenal that could be as old as 16,000 years.[11] The paintings also represent a range of activities and emotions: one famous painting depicts an emu being speared by a hunter, both of whom emit some kind of exclamation (pain for the emu, success for the hunter).[12] The denotation of motion, voice and emotion is rare in art, and almost absent in ancient art, but common in this particularly old art; tracks, splatters and dashes are seen emanating from the figures, their feet and mouths providing perceptual clues to the sensory experience of the artist—sound and smell, speed and movement, fear and pain, shock and anxiety. The sensory past resonates in the present.

The Dynamic art of Arnhem Land finds its regional expression in the Gwion or Bradshaw paintings of the Kimberley. These have been dated to between 16,400 and 23,800 years old and overlie hand stencils that are clearly considerably older.[13] The Gwion are more solid than their northeastern counterparts but equally delicate and a little more elaborate. They reveal similar aspects of humanity and material culture (hand-thrown barbed spears, boomerangs) and dress (tassels, bustles, headdresses). They are part of a greater artistic tradition that is embedded in accretions of ochre across the northern arc of the ancient savannah lands of Australia. In the southeast of Cape York, for example, the people selected pigments from local weathered rock: red haematite, yellow goethite and white kaolinite clays which, after application to the local sandstone surfaces, impregnated the rock and left layers of ochre in fine mineral laminations. These creative zephyrs of artistry are 27,000 years old.[14] Artistic antiquity is astonishing across the north of Australia and takes its place among the first great art movements of the world.

Ancient jewellery

Artistic sentiment was established across the north of Australia in the late Pleistocene and, at Carpenter's Gap in the southern Kimberley, that artistry finds expression through the ancient hands of its local craftsmen. Here there are fragments of dentalium shell beads in the old Pleistocene layers of the site. 'Dentalium' comes from the Latin word *dentis*, or tooth, and these are tooth- or tusk-shaped shells that appear to have been strung as decorative necklaces. The shells are among the oldest shell beads in the world and are thus one of the world's ancient human treasures.[15] The shells are a startling discovery—all the more startling as Carpenter's Gap is currently 100 kilometres inland and was then over 400 kilometres from the sea. The owner of the necklace may have carried it that distance, perhaps travelling to and from the coast as part of a great nomadic seasonal journey, but it is more likely the shell beads were acquired through trade. That possibility is itself startling as it creates a social and geographic panorama, implying the existence of trade networks and established notions of material value, themselves necessitating inter-communal relationships, shared traditions, common law and custom—the content of which indicated the presence of established society over 30,000 years ago.

What were the shells used for? Perhaps they were items of ritual importance, or possibly personal charms, insignias of social identity, or aesthetic decorations. Did they belong to a man or a woman? Possibly a man, given the character of material adornment portrayed in art styles at the time. Either way, their presence is astonishing and points to aspects of ancient community (social organisation, identity, communal interaction, trade and exchange) and humanity (personal possession, aesthetic appreciation and self-awareness) that might not be expected among people living in Australia so long ago. Australia's first settlers had come a long way in both geographic and social terms—ancient art, industry and domesticity expressed in a manner that resonates comfortably with contemporary perceptions of sophistication and lifestyle—but long before these concepts, associated technology and human behaviours seem to exist elsewhere in the world.

The shell beads at Carpenter's Gap are quite something, but, even more surprising are the dentalium beads at Riwi, on the edge of the Kimberley facing the desert.[16] There are ten beads here that are 30,000 years old. They are associated with food material (freshwater mussels and bone) as well as stone artefacts and ochre. The beads are about 1 centimetre long and have been made by snapping and sawing the original shells. One bead is worn where it appears to have rubbed against a string thread, suggesting the beads were strung together. Astonishingly, almost impossibly, a small fragment of natural fibre has survived—and is still attached to one of the beads—a 30,000-year-old piece of string. Clearly the beads were worn as a decorative necklace or bracelet.

There is dark red and blackish residue on some of the beads, and this residue contains small amounts of blood—the beads thus appear to have been coloured with a mixture of ochre and blood. The only circumstance in which human blood is applied in decoration today is in the most important ceremonial rituals. The visual impact of ceremonial ochre is one thing; the emotional impact of the application of human blood is something else again. The existence of blood, human blood, in decorative form is in itself startling, but the fact that it has survived for so long is positively overwhelming. The evidence that people coloured these beads with ochre and blood, and then left them at Riwi 30,000 years ago, 500 kilometres from the coast, would seem to confirm that trade networks were both established and extensive, that social communication was open, artistry was fundamental, and ritual was complete in the context of common custom and traditions across the vastness of the settled lands in those ancient days. Human settlement seems to have been characterised by one people in one land a very long time ago.

More ancient beads have been discovered on the Pilbara coast at Mandu Mandu rock shelter. These beads are at least 32,000 years old. The discovery consists of 23 small cone shells (*Conus* sp.) selected, presumably, for their beautiful colour and intricate patterning. All but one of the shells has been deliberately modified. Six have had holes placed in their apex and their internal structure removed (presumably with a hardened stick)—so hollowing out the whole shells. The remaining shells have had their apex removed and a hole perforated through the middle to create a small shell ring. As is the case with the beads at Riwi (1000 kilometres to the northeast), the beads show wear from being hung on a threaded necklace which, when strung, would have formed a decorative display about 18 centimetres long. This site, like Riwi and Carpenter's Gap, reveals an ancient tradition of design and creativity, and a sense of self-respect and aesthetics that is surprising for so long ago. The existence of these decorative objects places the people who made and wore them outside common perceptions of ancient nomadic survival and implies notions of choice, outlook and opportunity. The existence of these shell beads means, in effect, that the people who wore them had taste, social aspirations, social structure and broader empathic human relationships.[17]

Engraved in stone

What shell beads say about human behaviour so long ago is stated again with particular frankness in the artistic heritage in the Pilbara. The Pilbara is a pile of rocks that faces the sea and dovetails with the desert. The rocks are granite, rich in iron, and are over 3 million years old. They are so old that the rocks have rusted brown over time. They have also weathered round and fractured square to create enormous, artificial-looking rock piles on which people have abraded, bashed and hammered (pecked) the greatest art gallery in the world. Wherever one turns in the Pilbara there are engravings: over 3000 engravings on 200 boulders near Woodstock Station on the Yule River; more than 10,000 engravings on the Burrup Peninsula. There are individual locations with over 1000 engravings and countless other artworks throughout the greater region—perhaps over 1 million engravings all told; more art here than any other place on earth. The artistic technique was to cut through the rusted skin of the rocks and expose their inner flesh—soft yellows, brighter oranges—against which wondrous abstractions were carved in contrast to the rock's darker patina. The people of the Pilbara were engravers—the best, the most prolific and the most accomplished of their time.[18]

The earliest petroglyphs consist of lines and geometric patterns, various figures and terrestrial animals. They are engraved deep into the rocks and are so old that their abraded surfaces have themselves been eroded and have long since returned to the weathered stain of the rocks they were engraved on. No one has yet determined how old these original works are; suffice to say they are very old, probably at least 25,000 years old. Younger engravings sit among the older. They do not have the veneer of age and display marine animals[19] dating from the time when the sea level rose and stabilised 7000 years ago. There are tracks of all kinds, artefacts of predictable kinds (spears, boomerangs, shields), and figures of wondrous kinds, such as Murujuga Man (with antennae, huge genitals, strange projections from their heads) in less wondrous positions (fighting, running, dancing, hunting, having sex).

Among this vastness of fine art is one panel of particular interest. It is not an especially old panel, perhaps 3000–4000 years old,[20] but it is notable as it conveys something about the nature of human society in the more distant past. The panel is comparatively small and consists of a triptych formed by a repeated pattern of figures on both sides of tracks they appear to be following. The engraved panel is aligned vertically, giving the appearance of figures climbing. Each panel is focused on an engraved line—perhaps a track, a branch or an imagined pathway—and the figures are parallel, each facing the other across the engraved line. The figures are attached to the engraved line by their forearms, so that they appear to hang (rather like leaves from a branch), but they could be leap-frogging, dancing or swinging—or climbing or crawling. All are in-filled, varied and stylised so as to suggest children, men, women and strange human-like figures. The entire composition also hangs, aligned but otherwise disconnected from anything but imagined surroundings. Each figure has a small circular head detached from its body. The complete effect is an engaging exposition of wondrous possibilities: it conveys movement and meaning but is in all respects motionless and meaningless. But, to senior religious leaders from the western deserts of Australia, it immediately conveys ritual and dance in the context of the Wati Kutjara (the Two Men) and Tjukurrpa.

The 'climbing men' stand out in this otherwise diversified collection of art because of their peculiarity and singularity. They are also noteworthy because there is another panel like them in the Little Sandy Desert over 600 kilometres to the west. This painting is, as Aboriginal people would say, the 'same but different'. It contains two figures. One is in-filled and faces the viewer. It looks male and is placed halfway along an engraved line to which it is attached by its left hand and left foot. The position midway along the line suggests the figure is climbing. A second figure is represented in profile and appears to be walking or stepping, leaning slightly forward. The track here is more elaborate, consisting of two parallel lines, path-like, terminating in a circular 'head' with a banded neck and linear protuberances. The figure sits to the left, approaching one of 11 pecked dots adjacent to the path. There are also 11 similar dots to the right of the path.

The engravings are clearly part of the same tradition, even though they display regional stylistic differences. There is a covert relationship between subject, society and space, with the similarity of the engravings suggesting a common cultural tradition across a large socio-geographic area. The relationship between geography and style suggests the people in the Pilbara and the people in the Little Sandy Desert shared the same religious beliefs, saw the world in the same way, and expressed it accordingly. The people in these disparate locations may never have met, but the concordance of their artistic symbolism indicates they followed similar codes of social conduct and religious attendance. The 'climbing men' thus draw us towards a realisation of large-scale social relationships across vast territorial space some 4000 years ago. The similarity of the engravings suggests common traditions that necessarily imply broad-ranging social traditions: similar language, kinship, religion and territorial protocols. Traditional society in the western deserts of Australia is configured in this way today.[21] The art of the 'climbing men' suggests it was similar in the past. The analogous relationship between the Wati Kutjara, its ritual meaning and the 'climbing men' implies current traditions with ancient roots and great geographic meaning: the past lives on in the present.

The 'climbing men' are thus small figures with big implications. They sit beside, and exemplify, an even greater, older and more widespread artistic tradition known as the 'Panaramitee'.[22] Found throughout arid Australia—from the Pilbara to the margins of Cape York, and from there to the Flinders Ranges in South Australia—the Panaramitee is characterised by symbols most people would be familiar with and which are ubiquitous in contemporary Aboriginal art—tracks, lines and circles in various forms and combinations.[23] The Panaramitee tradition consists of thousands upon thousands of such symbols engraved in rocks throughout most of Australia. In central Australia there are sites with 2000–3000 engravings. At Sturts Meadow in northwestern New South Wales there are over 18,000 motifs on rocky outcrops. In northeastern South Australia there are over 12,000 engravings at 20 sites in the Olary area.[24] The geographic spread seems to have been the arid zone and its arid edges, with that environmental zone having been more extensive in the ancient past than it is now. The universality of artistic creation carries with it an implication of great social concord—of an established Australian population with shared traditions across all of the country by the late Pleistocene. What we see as a human sketch in the earliest phases of human settlement is now seen with textured and patterned infill: the art of all people in all places. This is the art of the ancients within which there is general and regionalised uniformity that suggests social coherence and communication on a scale that spans the continent. The art speaks of an ancient society of image-makers with imagined realities and diverse symbolism that was at once provincial yet set within a coherent social universe.[25]

The age of the Panaramitee artistic tradition is yet to be determined. Great antiquity is always implied—as nothing seems older than it—but enticingly, that antiquity remains elusive. Evidence of age is suspected through its representation relative to more recent imagery superimposed on it. Antiquity is also supposed by the old weathered nature of the engravings themselves: the dark patina and the mineralised coatings of 'desert varnish' that cover it. Its presence in northwestern Tasmania suggests its transportation before the closing of the land bridge (14,000 years ago), although there is no reason to suppose that this event defines the tradition. Its association with occupational locations of great antiquity (such as Puritjarra rock shelter in central Australia) provokes circumstantial arguments for a similar antiquity in the art, but at present the oldest antiquity rests at around 9000 years ago.[26]

Great antiquity is further implied by archaic design and composition, and its location in regions where extant tradition no longer recognises the design or the composition—it is an artistic tradition of people long forgotten and of culture before remembered time. I recall visiting an isolated range called Yiripanta in the remote eastern margin of the Great Sandy Desert with people who had been living there until 1985. Here there are a series of rust-coloured stone panels displaying ancient circular and linear engravings. When I asked the local people what the engravings meant and who made them, they shrugged their shoulders. They did not know who made the encryptions and could not interpret them. More recent engravings could be seen scratched into the older patina, cutting across the ancient petroglyphs beneath. These recent artistic attempts are rather frail, sketchy and tentative in comparison, as if the artist were mimicking, rather than maintaining, the older artistic tradition. The Panaramitee art at Yiripanta was more difficult and labour intensive to create than contemporary art in this part of the desert (which consists of sweeps, smears, washes and dots of charcoal, ochre and pigment), and is certainly more substantial than the more recent intaglios overlaying them. One might conclude, therefore, that greater amounts of time, effort, social organisation and resource allocation were dedicated to the production of the older art, compared to the more recent and ephemeral art seen in the region today. That supposition might be reflected upon in the context of the 18,000 engravings at Sturts Meadow in New South Wales. These are thought to have taken over a year to engrave.[27] A limited socio-economic correlate might be drawn from this in so far as the more substantial, older artistic tradition implies a more substantial human presence and thus a more productive subsistence environment than is seen in the region today. The physicality of the art conveys a sense of an enduring human presence during the period in which the art was produced.

But confirmatory evidence of that period is missing. There are some ancient engravings at a site called Early Man in Cape York that are covered by sediments older than 14,000 years. The engravings continue below this and are clearly much older. No one knows how much older. An ancient panel of engraved rock is reported from a site in Sandy Creek in Cape York, and engraved fragments of rock have also fallen from a cave into sediments at Ingalaadi in the Victoria River district. The sediments are 5000–7000 years old—but who knows when the engravings were actually carved into the cave walls.[28] Mineralogical examinations have suggested that engravings at various locations across southern Australia are 25,000–40,000 years old, but these estimates have proved to be complicated and contested.[29]

Regardless, archaeological intuition considers the Panaramitee to be ancient. And, in the same way that the artistic specificity and geographic disparity of the 'climbing men' points to regional social networks defined by common artistic and religious traditions, so the pan-continental parity of the Panaramitee reinforces that breadth of tradition as a substantive feature of late Pleistocene Australian society: one people firmly established in one country. The Panaramitee is art of homogeneity and regional variation that is indicative of ancient traditions, social commonality and emergent autonomy across the continent in the very distant past.

Archaic faces

The Panaramitee makes the legacy of a widespread culture obvious in Australia, and brings with it something that existed nowhere else in the world at that time—the portrayal of the human face. It is a fact

1. An artist's impression of Sydney Harbour 18,000 years ago at the end of the last ice age. The sea was 135 metres lower than now and the Australian land mass one-third bigger. The harbour was a series of canyons.

2. As the sea rose, the canyons were inundated, forming the coastlines we are familiar with today. Smoke from campfires appears along the shoreline: the rich harbour resources supported a large population.

3. Tracker Johnny Jupurrla Angus interprets 20,000-year-old footprints at Willandra Lakes, New South Wales. The tracks reveal families walking and men hunting, and tell us much about the people and their activities at this ancient cold time.

4. This 20,000-year-old footprint is one of the over 560 footprints forming a remarkable record of human activity in the Willandra Lakes at the peak of the last ice age.

5. Skull of Mungo Man, found at Willandra Lakes. The body, dated to 38,000–42,000 years old, was covered with ochre from 200 kilometres away, suggesting ancient funerary rites and reverence for the afterlife.

6. Yingana Creation Mother, Gunbalanya, Arnhem Land. This is one of a number of intense paintings that accompany religious accounts of the arrival of people in Australia and the colonisation of the country.

7. These 20,000 year old hand markings, at Koonalda Cave, South Australia, were made with the aid of firesticks, in complete darkness far underground. The stable conditions inside the cave have preserved them perfectly.

8. Scott Cane, inside Koonalda Cave, recreating something of the ambience of the activities that took place there 20,000 years ago.

9. Pitjantjatjara Elders Roy Underwood, Lennard Walker, Ned Grant and Fred Grant at Koonalda Cave after a ceremonial song (inma). They believe evil spirits now inhabit and emerge from the caves on the Nullarbor.

10. Arnhem Land in the Northern Territory had ideal living conditions for nomadic people—abundant water, fertile lands and sheltered escarpments.

11. An artist's impression of the 'marsupial lion' (*Thylacoleo carnifex*), reconstructed from fossilised skeletal material. This large, powerful predator hunted from its lair in trees and became extinct about 45,000 years ago.

12. Painting of a marsupial lion from Arnhem Land, capturing the striped fur, long limbs, powerful forequarters and head of the giant animal. This painting may be over 45,000 years old, one of the oldest paintings in existence.

13. A painting of *Genyornis*, a large flightless bird, from Arnhem Land, that may well be over 45,000 years old. Along with the painting of the marsupial lion (opposite), it is one of the oldest paintings in the world.

14. An artist's impression of *Genyornis*, reconstructed from skeletal evidence. The solid form of the animal is captured in the rare and remarkable painting above.

15. Dr June Ross looking at the Gwion figures in the Kimberley, Western Australia. The paintings are full of movement, the figures adorned with a rich array of tassels, headdresses, armlets, boomerangs and spears.

16. An extraordinary image of a small child reaching out for their father. This detail of the Gwion figures was painted perhaps 25,000 years ago.

that 90 per cent of all communication is non-verbal and that most of this is expressed through the face—described as the most entertaining surface on earth.[30] It is noteworthy, therefore, that there are almost no faces portrayed in prehistoric art anywhere in the world. The principal artists of antiquity did not paint themselves but painted animals, and where humans are depicted they are seen in part or as headless figures. Even where ancient portraits do have heads they do not have faces (although they may have hair or headdresses).[31] Today, in comparison, the face is the single most common representation in

Murujuga man engraved in granite: an ethereal person with scarified chest and sacred belt. The enlarged head and penis point to a well-developed sense of emotion and desire.

Western art. What does that say about human understanding and self-image in the remote past?

The best-known and earliest human representations in Europe are the Venus figurines, carved between 22,000 and 16,000 years ago. They are abstracted images of women with exaggerated proportions: large buttocks and huge breasts. Heads are rare and, where figurines do have them, faces are missing. The Venus figurines were followed by another phase of human representation, around 12,000 years ago, where human figures were painted in concerted action (such as hunting and fighting). Again, there is a notable absence of the human face; the paintings are not concerned with individuals or personality, but express a broader social consciousness in which people are represented similarly, regardless of gender or age.

The evolution of human representation has been interpreted accordingly, as mechanistic representations of demographic and social circumstance: the homogeneity of the earlier figurines pointing to open social networks, mobility and low population density (societies of similarity), while the regional variability and complexity of the later action figures points to closed social networks and higher, more sedentary, competitive self-defining populations (societies of difference).[32] Images of the human face emerge in the West late in human history, less than 5000 years ago: at first slightly distorted, and subsequently as cold, expressionless, stereotypic images of men—think of the lifeless faces encased in Egyptian sarcophagi or the cold marble eyes of early Greek statues.[33]

Not so in Australia. Here, within the Panaramitee tradition, are faces engraved in the very earliest phases of human history, at least 10,000–15,000 years before any other facial representations appear in the world. These are the first human faces. They appear in the arid reaches of Australia, across the desert, from the Burrup Peninsula to the Calvert Ranges in the Gibson Desert and the Cleland Hills in central Australia: across a landmass of some 666,000 square kilometres. The faces are engraved in stone. They have pecked eyes surrounded by concentric circles, with mouths, noses and ears set in heart-shaped heads. Their age remains undetermined, but associated weathering suggests they are between 10,000 and 25,000 years old. The earliest date provided for them is circumstantial, but indicates an antiquity of 29,700–37,700 years.[34]

The faces speak of individuality and empathy. They do what faces are meant to do: express emotion and convey, for the first time in human history, an awareness of self in the context of others.[35] The engravings are expressive and, at times, comical in their ability to convey feelings and moods: surprise, happiness, anger, horror, frustration, distress, stupidity, annoyance and disillusionment. The faces indicate the early occupants of Australia were thinking, feeling, expressive people, aware not only of their emotions but of the emotions of others—and of the effect of emotional expression on others. The people who engraved these faces at these disparate locations were clearly capable of expressing feelings and empathising with the feelings of others. The faces convey the first notions of personality anywhere in the world: of people as individuals within the society and environment they belong to. The engravings thus imply the emergence of subjectivity through the embodiment of self and the singular expression of human identity and personality in the context of society and its geography.

The representation and composition of these faces at distant and separate locations across the vastness of the desert imply, like the engravings of the 'climbing men', that the people who made them belonged to the same social system. That system was probably defined by mobility, communication and religious conformity within which the artistic representation of the faces suggests the development of regional social identity. The recognition of the human face implies distinctiveness within the greater social context and so necessitates a realisation of others in social relationship. Engraved faces thus allude to both an emergent sense of self and an emergent sense of regional difference (and perhaps competing political and territorial perspectives) in the larger social landscape.[36] The archaic faces thus paint a portrait of nomads with a common culture and an emerging regional identity.

Cold comfort

By the late Pleistocene almost every corner of Australia appears to have been occupied. In the very north, for example, people were living in the inter-mountain valleys of New Guinea more than 40,000 years ago. The mariners of first settlement mastered the mountains and subalpine ranges by 25,000 years ago, occupying everything up to 4000 metres above sea level. There is even archaeological evidence for them travelling through glacial mountain passes 4600 metres above sea level—through country that could hardly have been imagined by their ancestors. *Pandanus* nuts provided a seasonal bounty and secured life through their ability to be stored. The palms and their produce appear to have been managed through clearing and burning. The people 35,000 years ago were among the first in the world to deliberately and significantly modify their environment to improve subsistence opportunities and settlement outcomes. The evidence of these people's activities thus pushes the threshold of pre-agricultural activity back by tens of thousands of years. The people of the highlands were also hunters, preying on strange fauna that included possums, large rats, small echidnas, birds, and megafauna that are now extinct: the large echidna (*Zaglossus*), captured in ancient Arnhem Land art (and long since extinct on mainland Australia), and other extinct marsupials such as *Protemnodon* and *Diprotodon*.[37]

Settlement was also established at the very opposite end of greater Australia in similarly bitter climates at more or less the same time. Here people settled colder country at higher latitudes and lower altitudes. They were cave people living in the remote glacial valleys 200–400 metres above sea level. There are over 50 known Pleistocene sites in Tasmania—more evidence of ancient regional settlement here than anywhere else in Australia. Their primary business was hunting, and the cave dwellers hunted localised herds of wallaby as a seasonal staple. They sought protein, animal fat and thick fur. They hunted across the frostbitten plains from the protection of large limestone caves deep within Tasmania's glacial lands.

The massive quantity of bone in these caves is witness to the environmental tenacity and economic perseverance of these archaic hunters: there are hundreds of thousands of bone fragments mixed with tens of thousands of artefacts in the deep limestone caves across these rugged lands.[38] The density of material is astronomical and tells a remarkable story of human settlement and activity. It is a story of seasonal settlement and regional strategy, different caves utilised at different times as people tracked the availability of the animals they sought with expeditious caution. The hunters moved in and out of the mountains with care. They hunted beside glaciers, constantly at risk in the sub-Antarctic conditions. They were cautious, dexterous people, and the archaeological record shows them to be purposeful and efficient: phantom-like in the extraction of the resources they needed, a distant image of people in cold, forgotten landscapes, translucent as spectral silhouettes through veils of sleet on forgotten hill slopes.

Their archaeological legacy accumulated slowly, foray by foray, at rates of just 2 centimetres every 1000 years. So much stone and bone deposited so slowly over so much time shows that the dangerous lands must have been occupied carefully: tactically and seasonally—different caves at different times. The people hunted in the higher colder highlands in the summer and the warmer lower valleys in the winter. They were responsive to weather patterns and utilised the best and most accessible locations when the harsh conditions allowed. They were after wallabies, but they also hunted wombats, platypuses, kangaroos, quolls, marsupial rats and birds. Selected parts of the animals killed were returned to the shelter of the deep caves for communal consumption. Bones were cracked, split and broken to retrieve bone marrow. Some bones display cut marks where muscle was removed for cooking and eating.[39] The inhabitants of the mountains probably supplemented their meat diet with vegetables—wild yams (*Microseris*) and native bread (*Polyporus*). The remains of their fires have survived, around which the echoes of ancient families linger, warmed and satiated after a cold day's hunting. They collected emu eggs, and one might imagine women and children out on the cold grassy plains looking for them in late winter or early spring some 30,000 years ago.

The ice age hunters made stone tools from local quartzite and also travelled great distances at implied risk to obtain better raw materials. By 27,000 years ago, for example, volcanic glass appears in sites that are over 100 kilometres from its source.[40] This means people had to walk at least 200 kilometres return in the freezing conditions to obtain it. But perhaps it was traded: mountain furs for volcanic glass? The stone materials (and a fine-grained chalcedony from the Ragged Range near Lake Gordon) were carefully flaked and shaped into small scraping and cutting tools for working bone, skin and plant materials. They made (and left behind) tools from bone that appear to have been used as spear points, and for piercing and stitching skins.

The people of the mountains of southern and northern greater Australia demonstrate human adaptation to extreme environments in extreme climatic conditions. They also reveal the completeness of human settlement in this early phase in Australian history. But people had also settled the country in between. They were in the Great Dividing Range, the central highlands of Queensland, the Blue Mountains and the margins of the Australian Alps.[41] Their existence is shadowed by the appearance of charcoal in sediments at Lake George on the Southern Tablelands at least 60,000 years ago,[42] and by hard evidence in rock shelters from 23,000 years ago. Temperatures were 9 degrees Celsius colder, and the Snowy Mountains were glacial: a huge ice cap between 20 and 50 square kilometres covered the mountain tops—across mountains where there are no glaciers today. Periglacial conditions extended down into the valleys where people lived 1000 metres below.[43]

Scarce settlement

The settlement of these extreme environments is telling, for if people were living in the highest, coldest lands of greater Australia, then they were also likely to be living in the lower, warmer ones as well. We know they had settled parts of the deserts in the earliest phases of occupation and the profusion of their art suggests they had settled its entirety as well. That suggestion is verified by archaeological evidence for human settlement across the desert by 30,000 years ago.[44] The deserts had been drying steadily from the time of initial occupation but were still wetter and cooler than we find them today. Stronger westerly weather systems carried more rain further inland in the winter, and the cyclic nature of the winter cyclones and the summer monsoons meant that phases of wet and dry cycled across the desert over the millennia.[45] People had adapted to the desert's various moods, taking shelter in caves and protected overhangs as the need arose. We find their legacy in almost all desert habitats: in the centre of Australia, on the Nullarbor Plain, the Pilbara, the western coast and the southeastern margins of the desert: in remote barren parts of the Pilbara by 32,000 years ago, in the Little Sandy Desert 28,000 years ago, in the Simpson Desert 31,000 years ago.[46] The archaeological evidence is meagre, typically consisting of a few hearths, limited bone and small numbers of artefacts. At Djadjiling rock shelter, in the Pilbara, for example, occupation in the oldest layers (from 35,000 years ago) consists of just 664 artefacts. Settlement in the barren parts of the Hamersley Range 32,000 years ago reveals less than 300 artefacts. In the Little Sandy Desert human settlement at Serpents' Glen 28,000 years ago is revealed by just 32 pieces of flaked stone.[47]

West from Puritjarra (in central Australia) there is evidence for intermittent shelter in a large cave called Kulpi Mara (meaning 'cave of hands' [stencils]) in the Levi Ranges.[48] It was occupied from 35,000 to about 29,000 years ago. The cave overlooks the Palmer

River and was an attractive place to live when conditions demanded. Human presence is indicated by small numbers of well-made artefacts, indicating incidental visitation through time: the occupants left about 140 to 250 artefacts behind every 1000 years. This rate of discard at Kulpi Mara accords with other sites in the arid zone, such as Puritjarra, and paints a picture of settlement that is different to that seen in the more fertile environments.[49] Desert people were few and nomadic by comparison. They lived on the desert plains, seeking shelter in rock shelters as weather necessitated and particular activities required. They left little trace of their presence.

The late Pleistocene occupation of Allen's Cave on the Nullarbor Plain makes the point quite dramatically. After the first occupation 40,000 years ago, people visited the site occasionally—so occasionally that they left behind only three artefacts every 1000 years. More startlingly, no one lit another fire in the cave for 18,000 years: people did not warm themselves again at Allen's Cave until the height of the last glaciation 22,000 years ago. Clearly rock shelters only tell part of the story. Life in rock shelters was limited, and its archaeological signature is limited as a consequence. That part of the story is nonetheless told across the entire desert in the late Pleistocene.

Modern cave floors display signs of life as people live in and leave them—shavings from wooden dishes, dry tinder left for use the following wet season, piles of firewood stored to keep dry until the next visit, low walls of sand and silt pushed up to deter invading water during rains. There are grindstones, ochre and pigments, fragments of boomerangs, broken spears and spear-throwers, pieces of bone, seed-grinding implements and seed-grinding grooves in the bedrock, artefacts with spinifex resin adhering to them, hearths, flat rocks aligned as pillows and spinifex bedding. There are sacred caves that contain sacred boards resting on stone pedestals (to protect them from the damp and termite damage), and hand stencils and finger markings, and paintings of emu tracks, circles and snakes.[50] The present informs the past in this regard, and reveals people sheltering in desert caves to avoid heavy rain and extreme heat. Thus it is possible to imagine ancient caves as they might have also been left and to visualise the organic materials that have long since perished. And so the cumulative experience of great ages is seen through small windows, limited both by occupational content and occupational strategy. Rock shelters were, as the name intuitively suggests, places of temporary shelter. They were not the only places people lived; in fact they were places where people rarely lived.

The truth of this was brought home to me recently when working in a remote part of the northern Nullarbor Plain. Here there was a sinkhole, weathered through the hard crust of limestone into a large chamber below. The opening formed a chute that dropped, dangerously, into an open bell-shaped chamber.[51] The people utilising this shelter had placed a long branch of mulga at the base of the chute, allowing them to climb down into (and out of) the chamber. In the past, people wedged themselves against the walls of the limestone chute and edged themselves down to the roof of the open chamber. They then straddled the hardwood 'ladder' and climbed precariously into the chamber below. If they fell, or the branch broke, they died: there was no other way out. Such was the requirement of survival in the heat of summer—a desperate bivouac for the day, before a family would resume their travels in the cool of evening and through the subsequent night.

What they left behind was an anomalous fragment of the lives they led, the remains of a resting place from the heat of the day. As a consequence, material culture in rock shelters reveals information of a particular kind: a story that is contextualised by the circumstances that give rise to it. This is not a limitation to archaeological interpretation but a condition of it. In ice age Tasmania the caves formed permanent protective base camps, and in Arnhem Land shelters in the escarpments had seasonal and cyclic residential and religious significance, but across arid Australia they were short-term camp spots, hideaways from bad weather, that contain few artefacts. The residues are typically disturbed, as new residents prefer not to sleep on the refuse of others and tend to clean the cave floor, pushing the material outside before sleeping—a point reinforced through investigations of a site in the eastern Kimberley, where evidence of Pleistocene occupation survives in sands outside the shelter while the shelter itself only contains cultural material that is 5000–6000 years old.[52]

Ancient lakes

Desert people were plains people, living away from caves in the open air near waterholes, along rivers and around lakes. These locations are not the types of places where evidence for antiquity most easily survives. This is because outdoor locations are prone to destruction through erosion and reoccupation. Ancient cultural material is destroyed and deflated, washed away, wind-abraded and burnt. Favoured living areas are reoccupied, and any remaining human refuse is reused, mixed, confused, damaged and moved. But evidence does survive and there are sufficient amounts of it to see human occupation across the desert plains a long time ago: at Yantara in the Lake Eyre Basin, for example, 30,900 years ago, and near Hookina Creek in the Flinders Ranges 27,000 years ago.[53]

People were living across the lower Darling River 30,000 years ago[54] and, of course, occupied the Willandra Lakes from the earliest times.[55] The people living here utilised a number of large flaked stone implements and small bone ones. Use wear on the latter indicates scraping of skins and spearing animals—perhaps even sewing skins together. The bountiful resources of the Willandra Lakes complemented the food people obtained from the land. The people fished, their favourite catch apparently being golden perch—these make up 70 per cent of all the fish remains recorded near the Willandra Lakes. The fish people caught were generally the same size and suggest the use of gill nets and fish traps—indicating coordinated social activity and sophisticated technology. Fish remains at one location, for example, account for over 370 juvenile fish—enough to feed 60–70 people. If

Increased populations along waterways across southeastern Australia led to advances in aquaculture. Here a man is harvesting fish from extensive fish traps aligned across the Darling River.

the fish were netted the fishers would have required a net with about 7000–9000 metres of string. Such a net would have taken almost half a year to make.[56] Freshwater mussels are more easily collected, although their remains are found in surprisingly small numbers. Particular resources such as frogs, mussels and freshwater crayfish were selectively targeted: one ancient campsite contains the remains of over 500 freshwater crayfish consumed in one meal, 30,000 years ago.[57]

People hunted marsupials and birds away from the lake. Rat kangaroos, quolls, bettongs, wallabies, wombats, shingleback lizards and emu eggs seem to have been popular. The consumption of emu eggs and the exploitation of juvenile fish points to seasonality in the regional strategy—exploitation of the hinterland in spring (emu eggs) and the lakes in the summer (juvenile fish)—although it would be equally reasonable to assume that nomadic life was variable and resource driven, and that people travelled and hunted in a relaxed, integrated fashion across the region: fishing as water levels concentrated fish, gathering emu eggs as they were laid, collecting freshwater mussels as they desired, and hunting marsupials and reptiles as they found them.

Starch residues on stone tools indicate that people were harvesting local sweet potato. Tubers, smaller marsupials and reptiles were cooked in shallow earth ovens with the aid of heat retainers made from rocks or rounded fragments of clay and termite nests.[58] The baking of these clays captured the orientation of the earth's magnetic field at the time and reveals that the magnetic field underlying the Willandra Lakes 30,000–39,000 years ago was 120 degrees away from its current alignment. North was then southeast, the divergence drawing mysterious attention to the difference in life and environment in ancient times. The geomagnetic reversal was not catastrophic and it is possible that nobody even noticed it. It was caused by a regional realignment of molten rock under the earth's crust which returned to normal after a period of a few thousand years.[59]

There are over 100 burials known from the Willandra Lakes dating from the late Pleistocene. The remains constitute the largest body of ancient burials known anywhere in Australia. The original settlers are found buried and cremated in sand dunes around the lakes, dating from 15,000 to 40,000 years ago. The general appearance of the skeletal remains indicates living conditions were reasonably good. There are few signs of malnutrition and little evidence of disease. Those people who were unlucky enough to break bones healed with comparative ease. Generally, the people appear to have been strong and muscular but small with light frames, with heights varying from

151 to 178 centimetres (4'11" to 5'10"). One particular individual stood out from the crowd. He was buried about 25,000 years ago and was a giant compared to his compatriots. He had an unusually thick skull that may have been due to a genetic blood disorder, and a brain capacity that was almost 25 per cent larger than modern human skulls.[60]

Bushfires

Each and every environmental region within greater Australia seems to have been occupied by 30,000 years ago. By then, the archaeological evidence suggests there was an established population connected through a regional network of religious artistic tradition. The society of greater Australia had grown from a select group of pioneers who faced daunting environmental risk, in the possible circumstance of near environmental devastation, to settle a new continent that they could have hardly known existed. That elite group of settlers came, saw and settled, and in their affluent new world excelled and expanded. They were masterful colonisers. The emerging community was generally healthy and, save for unexpected encounters with over-sized predators, life was long. Domesticity established itself well and, we might envision, provided a platform for successful subsistence, socialisation and survival. The first people were, in many respects, special—a force of pioneers whose particular psychological and physical attributes set the scene for the future. They appear to have been tough, intelligent, creative, adaptable, sociable people. They and their descendants became part of a successful and elaborate society, born from the spirited gene pool that travelled with them, fertilised by the riches of the country they discovered and ultimately manifested in the coherent diversity of the traditions that developed to guide them. That society left its insignia across the continent—the art of original existentialism and the material culture of existence. They settled the savannahs and the rainforests, the highlands and the deserts, the coasts, the temperate forests and the glacial moorlands—within ten millennia of first settlement.[61]

Life might have been described, under the circumstances, as going rather well. But, as is often the case when everything looks rosy, things were about to change.

The flipside of successful colonisation is successful exploitation. Exploitation is fundamental to survival, and survival on a continental scale necessitates exploitation on an equally large scale. Human impacts thus shadow human settlement, and it might be expected that the successful colonisation of Australia led to notable environmental changes.

One of the earliest and most efficient land management tools used by the first colonisers was fire. Fire is evident in the environmental record paralleling human colonisation. There are, as a general indication, very few locations so far examined in and around greater Australia that show a clear or definite record of firing prior to 70,000 years ago. Then there is a steady increase in burning through until 60,000 years ago that remains high until the last glaciation about 30,000 years ago.[62]

Fire was a necessary and ancient tool. It was used, for example, to clear, settle and exploit forests in the northern highlands of Greater Australia (now Papua New Guinea) over 42,000 years ago.[63] The savannah of Arnhem Land was burnt from first settlement. In Arnhem Land sediments, washed from the escarpments devastated by fire, filled the valley floors.[64] In Cape York ancient sediments have been captured in old volcanic craters that reveal an almost total replacement of rainforest by sclerophyll vegetation from about 40,000 years ago. The change is accompanied by a substantial increase in charcoal. Oceanic cores to the east, just beyond the continental shelf and not far from the edge of greater Australia, reveal a decline in conifer pines (*Araucaria*) and an increase in fire-adapted melaleuca and eucalyptus. Again, charcoal peaks indicate high levels of firing activity.[65]

The pattern is reinforced by degrees in southern latitudes where proportional differences in pollen grains washed into Lake

George, near Canberra, indicate that fire was responsible for a notable shift from fire-sensitive she-oaks (*Casuarina*) to fire-tolerant gum trees (*Eucalyptus*) 60,000 years or more ago. That change is again accompanied by a large increase in the amount of charcoal washing into the lake.[66] High levels of charcoal are seen in pollen sequences in the Snowy Mountains, and fire also seems to have been a factor in vegetation management in glacial Tasmania. Charcoal increases in sediments from about 40,000 years ago and is shadowed by evidence for increased erosion. Both allude to increased burning. The increase in charcoal and erosion seems to indicate the use of fire to maintain open fire-adapted button grass (*Gymnoschoenus*) plains for access and hunting.[67]

The extent of burning across the continent was sufficiently wide for its signature to be captured in the Indian Ocean, some 800 kilometres from the present Australian coast (and about 600 kilometres from the ancient one). Here deep oceanic cores have revealed pollen and charcoal have blown with the southeast trades out across the ocean to settle on the sea floor. There is a substantial amount of sedge (*Cyperaceous*) pollen, and considerable quantities of grass and eucalyptus pollen—indicating the now submerged continental shelf was then covered with open forest and woodland, and swamps vegetated by rushes and sedges. The plains were flat, poorly drained and flooded by summer monsoonal rain. They were subject to burning 200,000 years ago and again at 95,000 and 80,000 years ago, with a sustained increase in frequency of burning from 60,000 years ago.[68] A similar biological trend is revealed off the North West Shelf. Here there is a sustained decline in eucalyptus pollen and an increase in chenopod (salt bush and blue bush) pollen. The decline coincides with a sharp increase in the abundance of charcoal, suggesting an associated change in the fire regime.

The ancient ecology revealed in these pollen cores suggests families camping, hunting and burning the plains as they travelled. Parallel to that scenario is a continent drying as a consequence of climatic change and becoming increasingly prone to natural fire—large lightning strikes creating fires that engulfed the ancient coast and spread charcoal widely across the adjacent seas. The ancient sedimentary records are silent on the balance of impacts—the impacts of people are always implied but the momentum of climatic change is ever present.

Such is the situation across the drier parts of the continent, where natural fire, human fire and climate interacted to effect discernible environmental change from about 60,000 years ago. In the Lake Eyre Basin vegetation seems to have changed from a tree–shrub–grassland mosaic to modern-day desert scrub between 60,000 and 45,000 years ago.[69] Human burning may have produced that change or it may have been a consequence of ongoing climatic drying—or a combination of the two. The northern summer monsoon was weakening around this time and less water was getting into the northern catchment of Lake Eyre. The weakening was part of a long-term climatic trend that was independent of humans but which may have been inadvertently aggravated by them. Extensive burning of the vegetation in the north of Australia may have reduced vegetation cover to the extent that it also reduced the transfer of moisture from the tropical rainforests and savannahs to the atmosphere, thereby weakening biospheric feedbacks and resulting in long-term desertification of large parts of the continent.[70]

A late Pleistocene adage might have it that where there is charcoal there is fire and that where there is fire there are people lighting it. That saying may not always hold true and there is reasoned opinion to the contrary: where there is fire there is climatic change,[71] people being less visible in the broader environmental equation. But the absolute dependence of people on their environment suggests they are likely to have had an impact on it—while the climate also changed around them. One might ask, in terms of this likelihood, could the early occupants of greater Australia have got by without burning? The answer is self-evident.

How could people, as an immediate consideration, confront the threat of giant monitors, terrestrial crocodiles, giant snakes and lion-like possums concealed in the bush without wanting to do something about it? A positive and obvious step in their risk-management strategies would have been to burn—clear the scrub these animals lived in; burn the bush to expose the ground so both animals and their tracks could be seen; burn them; drive them from their burrows and lairs; and remove their habitat.

It might be possible to envision ancient people burning the bush in the same way and for the same reasons that traditional Aboriginal people do today. Burning comes first. This is the first activity, in my experience, of tribal people in the northern deserts when setting up camps. I cannot recall the number of times we have camped in a secluded glade adjacent to a picturesque waterhole only to see it decimated by fire before camp is even established: the harmonious and photogenic colours of khaki, yellow and lime green against red sand reduced to grey ash and black charcoal on red within hours. Remote homeland communities are managed in the same way. The surrounding bush is either burnt or graded so people can see snake tracks near their camps. The environmental impacts are frightening, matched only by people's fear of snake bite, external fires and imagined attacks by human and spiritual forces. Their fear is, in part, justified—a child bitten by a snake in the remote desert means death. Parents are understandably keen to protect their children at the expense of the environment. Parents 50,000 years ago might have been equally concerned.

The reader might also reflect on how the first settlers may have kept fire if they could not make it. The only way to maintain it is to carry it and to keep it alive in the local environment. Anyone who has ever travelled with Aboriginal people in traditional contexts has experienced this: from Peron in Tasmania in the 1800s, to Rhys Jones in Arnhem Land in the 1960s, and myself in the desert in the 1980s and 1990s.[72] It is conventional for people to walk with a firestick informally lighting the spinifex as they go—sometimes intentionally and sometimes incidentally as coals and sparks fall from their firestick. Bushfires were a natural consequence of the need to keep fire.

One might also reflect on the combustible character of the Australian bush, and imagine what it might have been like living and managing that greater threat as a mobile family group. Huge wildfires represent substantial dangers for people who have no choice but to walk (or run) away from them. The image of a band of nomads confronted by a multitude of wildfires on a hot windy day is disconcerting to anyone who has experienced bushfires of this intensity. Our own recent history allows us some idea. Think of the horrific bushfire in southern Tasmania in 1967. The consequence was 110 fires that killed 62 people and 62,000 farm animals in about 12 hours, with the death toll of native animals not counted. The fires burnt some 2600 square kilometres of land, and destroyed 1200 homes, 1500 motor vehicles and 80 bridges. Sixteen years later 180 fires were driven by northerly gales across southeastern Australia. Seventy-five people were killed as well as 340,000 sheep, 18,000 cattle and untold native animals. Eight thousand people were evacuated, and over 6000 homes and buildings were destroyed. Another 16 years later 400 fires in Victoria killed 173 people and injured another 414.[73] Two thousand homes were destroyed, 7500 people were displaced and 450,000 hectares were burnt. How would the ancient nomads have managed such danger and devastation? They would have burnt the land first.

Fires on this scale are almost impossible to escape, and carry enormous risk to life and livelihood. My own memories of the Tasmanian bushfire of 1967 as a child are of hiding on the shore of the Derwent River under a totally black sky, hoping not to die. More recently, on the Eyre Peninsula, a wildfire burnt 145,000 hectares, and was so aggressive that people (including four children) were burnt alive trying to run and drive away from it. Over 47,000 animals were killed in an afternoon. Such is the scale of uncontrolled fire in the Australian landscape.

An analogous situation comes to mind that occurred in the Kimberley in 2011. Here a band of marathon runners were trapped by fire during an ultra-marathon. These runners, like the people of the past, were fit and strong, equipped for survival under extreme physical duress. They ran on an unexceptional spring day. Fires were seen in the vicinity, but none were recognised as a particular threat. How familiar that scenario must have been in the past. When the fires did become a threat they could not be outrun. People were trapped in terror. Some escaped by running through the flames, others were burnt, with two suffering third-degree burns to over 80 per cent of their bodies. Transpose that scenario to a time 40,000 years ago and imagine how people might have coped, understood and managed the risk to prevent such disaster from happening in their lives.

Natural fires are frequent in the Australian bush and, when ignited in unmanaged lands, create havoc beyond comprehension. The scale of destruction is simply massive, and the costs to the ancient Australians, in terms of people, resources and livelihoods, must have been near catastrophic. A recent fire in Yellabinna Regional Reserve in South Australia makes the point. It was ignited by a lightning strike in the summer of 2013 and burnt uncontrolled for three months, devastating 134,000 hectares of land. Yellabinna is remote and the fire went largely unnoticed. No human lives were lost, but a major habitat of the endangered sandhill dunnart (*Sminthopsis psammophila*), southern marsupial mole (*Notoryctes typhlops*) and malleefowl (*Leipoa ocellata*) was destroyed. The parallels with the past are obvious.

It is my experience across 30 years of desert life that traditional people are keenly aware of the risks of wildfire and of the advantages they gain by managing it. In the early 1980s I travelled with people who were returning to the desert for the first time in several decades. Desert vegetation had changed dramatically in that short time and landowners frequently lamented the state of the country they were returning to. They said it looked like 'jungle' and set about returning it to a livable productive state. They did so by burning. Sometimes burns could get out of hand, particularly if a long time had passed between last occupation and revisitation. On a recent occasion, for example, landowners burnt the bush in an area that had not been burnt for over 100 years. This resulted in a massive fire that burnt for over four months (when I last saw it). Recent Google imagery shows over 450 square kilometres of bush burnt in that fire and perhaps provides an insight into the sort of impact first peoples might have had on the Australian bush in their early attempts to clear and maintain it. It is easy to see how charcoal signatures might have found their way into oceanic sediments 40,000–60,000 years ago.

But normally the impacts of traditional burning are contained through timing (burning in the cooler months), proximity (burning adjacent lands, typically within a day's walk from a waterhole) and repetition (normally a five-year cycle). Much has been written about traditional burning and, in my experience, the advantages are as obvious today as they were likely to have been to the first settlers. Matchstick farming today tells us much about firestick farming in the past: it made the bush safe, it made it easier to access, it provided a means of communication, it improved hunting and gathering, and it encouraged productive regeneration.[74]

Burning clears the ground, flushes animals out of hiding, exposes animal tracks, reveals goanna burrows and regenerates vegetation. That regeneration attracts marsupials and effectively localises them for the period of regeneration. The animals feeding on the soft green shoots of regeneration in freshly burnt country can be hunted more easily, some in the past being maimed so they could be killed and eaten later on. Fire also kills and injures insects, which in turn attracts bird life: bustards (*Ardeotis australis*) particularly gather in large numbers after burns and are hunted easily. Burning also improves goanna hunting as burrows are easily spotted and the firing 'tricks' them out of hibernation so they can be tracked and caught. They mistake the heated sand for warming spring weather.

Fire also increases the availability of fruits and tubers, with country being burnt in spring to improve the harvest the following season. I have seen vast paddock-like fields of grass seeds maintained (at the expense of spinifex) through burning. Some wild fruits, such as the bush tomato, respond spectacularly to fire, with as much as a tenfold increase in fruit production after firing. Sweet potato tubers respond similarly, as the burnt bushes send out additional runners after burning that produce abundant fresh shallow tubers. Biological benefits of this kind continue for some years. Acacia seed production, for example, peaks about five years after burning and establishes a typical timeframe for the harvesting cycle: the initial burn creates access, exposes animal tracks, assists goanna hunting, attracts birds and kangaroos; grass seeds, fruits and tuber production increase over the following years as acacia seed production comes on line, after which the bush is thick enough to burn, and the cycle of production and harvest starts all over again.[75]

The cyclic firing of the bush varies in different regions and across different ecological regimes. The variation creates different produce in different stages of production. Some parts of the desert are rarely burnt: mulga woodlands, for example, are not generally burnt, as the woodland fires are hot and decimating. Mulga is a valuable tree for food and wood implements. It responds badly to fire, grows slowly and loses value through burning. In some areas many trees are sacred and cannot be burnt for fear of desecration. But in everyday situations the spinifex plains were (and are) burnt. The regularity creates corridors of differentiated bush that contains successive burning and produces a mosaic of country in variable stages of regrowth and production: grass seeds in one area, tubers in another, hunting somewhere else. The small paddock-like mosaics eliminate the risk of large, hot wildfires—in stark contrast to the massive firestorms recorded historically over country that has not been regularly burnt.

Thus there is every reason to assume, and sufficient evidence to indicate, that the people of the late Pleistocene were managing their country through burning: its advantages were obvious and its application straightforward. Fire was the easiest and most effective management tool available. The ancient people, we might anticipate, were mindful of their ability to manipulate the environment and were aware of the most effective tool available to control its productivity. But fire had an effect on country as well, and those same people were probably less mindful of the incremental and eternal changes they were making to the country they inhabited. And they were probably less likely to have realised that the world they lived in was changing, for reasons beyond their control, in a way they could hardly have imagined. For as they moved across the country with fire in their hands the climate moved with ice in its teeth. The world was cooling and drying towards the greatest drought in the coldest and longest ice age ever known to humankind. The environmental pendulum was swinging out of the first settlers' favour, and as it moved with omnipotent momentum a convergence of incremental human impacts, climate directives and environmental changes took their toll.

Disappearing giants

One of the first and greatest casualties were the giant animals, or megafauna, living in greater Australia at the time. Mammalian extinctions had occurred across Australia before the arrival of humans, but after their arrival at least six genera of an original 22–24 genera died out. This final loss included 50 species of animals, encompassing 90 per cent of Australia's large-bodied marsupials and 40 species of its kangaroos.[76] Those that became extinct after humans arrived included the biggest and most spectacular of the giants: *Diprotodon*, the largest marsupial to have ever lived; *Procoptodon*, the biggest hopping animal to have ever jumped on the earth; *Phascolonus*, the giant wombat; *Thylacoleo*, the predatory marsupial lion; *Protemnodon* and *Simosthenurus*, the large, heavily built snub-nose kangaroos; *Megalania*, the giant carnivorous lizard; and *Genyornis*, the large flightless bird.[77] These animals disappeared slowly, perhaps so slowly that the nomads scarcely noticed them going. The final curtain seems to have been pulled down about 45,000 years ago, in a window of extinction between 51,000 and 40,000 years ago.[78] There is a coherent pattern of extinction across the continent, despite the fragmented, regionalised and contested evidence for it.[79] There is no evidence for associations between humans and megafauna in the core deserts of Australia, and the great animals had probably died out there long before human occupation, perhaps as early as 130,000 to 115,000 years ago.[80] In Tasmania *Procoptodon* and the giant kangaroo *Macropus giganteus titan* survived until the arrival of humans, to become extinct between 45,000 and 41,000 years ago.[81]

There is evidence for more recent survival of other megafauna but the antiquity of this evidence is under revision.[82] The most significant among the younger megafaunal sites is a suite of remains at Cuddie Springs near the junction of the Darling and Macquarie rivers in New South Wales. This swamp was once an old lake in the semi-arid corner of the Murray–Darling Basin. The remains here are of animals originally thought to have survived until 30,000 years ago, but examination of dental enamel in the fossils suggest they are more likely to have become extinct 15,000–20,000 years earlier.[83] Similarly, there are tens of thousands of megafaunal remains—mostly of the large kangaroo *Macropus giganteus titan*—at an extensive fossil site at Lancefield Swamp, in Victoria, that were originally thought to be 26,000 years old, but more recent assessments suggest them to be 40,000–60,000 years old.[84] There is another site in northern Queensland that promises a younger timeframe for survival, but the research is still young and no firm conclusions can be drawn about its final antiquity.[85]

Such temporal particularities and peculiarities are, in many respects, immaterial to the greater human experience of ancestral association: the evidence is sufficient for us to know that the nomads of Australia lived alongside these great animals for many, many thousands of years. We thus appreciate that the ancients must have seen the giant marsupials browsing and grazing across the plains and we can imagine they heard them as they passed by in the still of night. The people and the animals were in the land together. Small children must have gazed (with some incredulity) at the sight of the 3-metre-high *Procoptodon goliah*, and been at least a little intimidated by herds of *Diprotodon*: bulls, pregnant females and calves. The reflection causes a degree of ancestral envy: environmental wonders recalled in absentia across great ages. What we see in our mind's eye is what the original people saw for real. They saw them, lived with them, heard them, smelt them, tasted them and painted them. They hunted them and were probably hunted by them. But why did the animals disappear?

The archaeology is frustratingly silent on the subject of human predation, but who really doubts that these large animals were a likely source of food? A slow-moving, defenceless, 1000-kilogram *Diprotodon* would be an easy target, hard to pass up. Even a medium-sized animal would have provided enough food for around 30 people.[86] But how likely is it that the remains of a *Diprotodon* meal consumed on the open plains 45,000–50,000 years ago would survive to become contemporary archaeological evidence of the fact? The destructive forces of nature count against survival. The greater part of the Australian archaeological record is, in this regard, almost bare bones. Even the most recent sites contain limited amounts of bone and, in the arid and semi-arid parts of Australia there are hundreds of thousands of sites that contain no bone at all. In a long-term investigation at Olympic Dam, between Lake Eyre and Lake Frome, over 16,000 sites are reported with over 20 million artefacts—without a single bone being mentioned.[87] If a literal interpretation were made of human behaviour at these sites archaeologists would be forced to conclude desert people were vegetarians. Yet we know and accept they were not, as a consequence of limited behavioural windows provided by stratified sites in rock shelters, ethnography and intuition. There is a lesson here for the interpretation of ancient archaeological remains: the absence of evidence for ancestral megafaunal kill sites is not necessarily evidence for the absence of ancient megafaunal meals. Sometimes too much is expected of the ancient archaeological record. But what we have is suggestive of human predation.

In the northern highlands of greater Australia, for example, there is evidence people hunted the large monotreme *Zaglossus*—a marsupial now extinct on mainland Australia but seen in ancient Arnhem Land art. There is also an association of artefacts and megafauna—the thickset kangaroos, *Thylogale* and *Protemnodon*, and a *Diprotodon*-like marsupial, *Maokopia*—in several caves in the subalpine grasslands 1700 and 3000 metres above sea level. In the Nombe rock shelter, located in the rainforests of the New Guinea highlands, there are remains of extinct kangaroos, including *Protemnodon*, in the older occupational deposits.[88] At the other end of the continent, in the far southwest of greater Australia, there are large marsupial bones associated with artefacts at Mammoth Cave, not far from Devil's Lair. Some of the bones appear to have been deliberately broken, cut and burnt.[89] Giant marsupial bones are also found in Devil's Lair (but may have been carried to the site as ancient souvenirs rather than as part of a meal).[90]

In the semi-arid lands to the east, stone artefacts and giant bones have been recorded at lakes Menindee and Tandou on the Darling River in New South Wales.[91] A burnt long bone and a fireplace are also associated with megafaunal remains at Lake Menindee—although the association begs further investigation[92]—and there is a hearth at Dempsey's Lagoon on the western margin of the Flinders Ranges that seems to be associated with the eggs of the flightless bird *Genyornis*.[93] Cooked and burnt eggshells are relatively common around Lake Eyre, and there are a number of eggshell fragments that have been pierced at one end, perhaps to prevent them bursting while baking in the coals.[94]

There are three teeth of an extinct kangaroo (*Sthenurus*) associated with cultural materials in the oldest levels of a cave on the southern coast of greater Australia (Seton site on Kangaroo Island).[95] At Spring Creek in Victoria there is a *Diprotodon* tooth with 28 parallel grooves engraved on it. The engravings were made soon after the death of the animal.[96] At Lime Springs, near Gunnedah in northwestern New South Wales, there is an accumulation of *Diprotodon*, *Procoptodon*, *Protemnodon*, *Sthenurus* and *Macropus* bones with stone artefacts, and a high proportion of burnt bone.[97] There are stone artefacts mixed with bones, and bones with cut marks, at Cuddie Springs.[98] And, of course, they were painted and implicitly hunted in Arnhem Land and the Kimberley (as described in Chapter 2).

The accumulation of evidence points incrementally and invariably to the coexistence and interaction of people with megafauna. The evidence indicates that people collected and transported megafaunal bones, cut and engraved bones, painted them (perhaps from dead specimens), left stone tools at sites that they either shared with them or took their remains to. Burnt megafaunal bones have been found, and burnt *Genyornis* eggs appear to have been eaten. But the evidence can be interpreted any number of ways. Investigations into the fossil bed at Lancefield in Victoria make the general point.[99]

A hunter at Uluru. Note the open burnt terrain surrounding the rock. The hunter holds a perentie goanna weighing about 13.5 kilograms.

A catastrophic death

Lancefield Swamp is small. It is located on a creek in a depression on a grassy plain with a spring at its head. Water from the spring has eroded a natural amphitheatre about 80 metres across around the creek in which the swamp has formed. The swamp contains a layer of megafaunal bones that is just 20 centimetres thick. The bones are spread over about 2000 square metres (or about the area of three or four suburban house blocks). It is not a large area, nor a thick deposit, but it contains the remains of a staggering 10,000 animals. Ninety per cent of the remains are the giant 3-metre-high kangaroo, *Macropus giganteus titan.* The rest are other *Protemnodon* and *Sthenurus* kangaroos, *Diprotodon* and *Genyornis.* The population of *Macropus* is largely adult, reminiscent of a modern population of kangaroos after several years of drought.

This deposit appears to be an accumulation of dismembered carcasses and broken bones. The skeletons were disarticulated (limbs removed without cutting through bone) and many bones were broken before final deposition. A small proportion show cut or chop marks.[100] There are no complete skulls in the entire deposit. The bones appear not to have been moved significantly after final deposition. Two artefacts have been found associated with the bones. One is a large quartzite blade, 21 centimetres long and at the extreme end of similar blades found throughout Australia.[101] It is firmly embedded in the bone bed. The other is a 3-centimetre flake found in adjacent channel fill. Both are contemporaneous and both are made of the same material—a quartzite not found in the local area.

Archaeological interpretations of the site are conservative—with the array of related evidence interpreted ambiguously or implicitly as indicating a large number of animals trapped in the swamp and consumed by marsupial lions. Yet the question of human impact remains decidedly open—despite caution and qualification, the evidence has a way of speaking for itself. Lancefield presents, in this regard, evidence for a remarkable number of animals trapped, somewhat inexplicably, in a small, shallow swamp. The bodies of the animals were dismembered, bones were broken and skulls were smashed or removed. Someone left an unusually large stone knife among the bones. The knife is as long as the bone deposit is thick. How would you interpret it?

Perhaps, inconceivably, all 10,000 animals were unlucky, and became stuck through time in the little swamp, in the same way that stray cattle accidentally get bogged in drying dams on pastoral stations. And perhaps they were trapped, attacked and consumed by possum lions (*Thylacoleo*). But perhaps they were driven (incrementally, en masse and individually over a period of time) into the swamp, and scavenged at the swamp by people who then disarticulated the kills, and broke the bones and skulls—in much the same way the periglacial Tasmanians disarticulated Bennett's wallabies around the same time (and traditional desert people dismember and consume kangaroos today). Perhaps the unfortunate animals were both trapped by nature and driven by humans, to be predated by both people and marsupial lions, although the remarkable absence of skulls, the dismembered skeletons and the large quartzite cutting tool points heavily to the hands of people.

Yawa and his camel

The hand of the hunter need not be heavy to effect a megafaunal kill. In 1989 I was travelling to a large, important rock hole near the Carnegie Range in the Great Sandy Desert. As I walked up the dry lateritic creek bed to the rock hole, I passed the remains of a small shelter constructed against the trunk of an isolated acacia tree. The shelter belonged to a man called Yawa and was used by him as protection from the heat of the sun in the preceding 'hot time'.

Yawa and his brother Tirinja had a violent and murderous relationship with remnant populations living in the area in the 1950s.

He was known as a violent man and, in proof of the point, razed a homeland camp we had built in the area in the early 1990s. Grass had accumulated in the camp over the wet season and, before the local families returned in the dry season, Yawa burnt the place to the ground. He was an unforgiving, territorial individual with an eye for seclusion.

Yawa had originally travelled into Christmas Creek near the Kimberley as an adult in the 1960s, but disappeared not long after his brother died shortly after coming in. At the time, Yawa had been disciplined and hit by missionaries for not working hard enough. He waited till they had gone, then set down his axe, picked up his spears and spear-thrower, and left the station. Alone and on foot he headed south, back into the desert, and was never seen again.

It is said he left no trace, but in 1982 his tracks were seen.[102] People looked for him and found evidence of recent habitation: charcoal, half-burnt sticks, flakes of stone in a small cave. This, they said, was his wet season camp. The next day they found more tracks, and later that morning came upon a tree from which a large piece of bark had been removed. The men went to look and found he had cut the bark to carry a large number of eggs he had collected from an emu's nest. The group did not contact Yawa and the party returned home. They felt Yawa could not have failed to know they were around: he was on foot, never far away, and he would have seen their campfires, heard their vehicles and seen their tracks. Some of the footprints would have been familiar to him, as his were to the people looking for him. He could have shown himself at any time, but he chose to stay away—not quite alone, for wherever his footprints went they were accompanied by the tracks of a dog.[103]

The camp I saw in 1989 was within a few hundred metres of the rock hole I was there to visit. Not far away were the remains of a dead camel. In those days camels were rare in the desert and the sight was worthy of consideration. The camel seemed to have died looking for water during the previous 'hot time'—the intensely hot months leading up to wet season rains. This part of the desert is the hottest part of Australia and the heat at that time of year is virtually intolerable. Dingoes had disturbed the camel bones, but the people noticed something about them I failed to see: the bones of the left leg were missing. Their interpretation was that the camel had come to the rock hole for water and, being weakened, thirsty and unreplenished, it had been speared by Yawa, who then removed its leg for consumption. There is an obvious megafauna moral to this story.

The wild camels' occupation of the desert at that time was, in effect, a return of the megafauna—they are the first giant browsing and grazing animals to have walked and fed in the Australian deserts for over 40,000 years. They are a similar size to the ancient megafauna (camels weigh about 600 kilograms and stand about 2 metres tall at the hump), but are perhaps better adapted to desert life.[104] They are nonetheless reliant on water and, like the giant marsupials, require more of it in critical periods than might be supposed. This reliance is considerable among females with feeding calves, as they need to obtain at least 40–60 litres of water per day to survive and produce milk for their young. This reliance determines herd structure and location, as the young are dependent on their mothers, and females lead camel herds (except during mating season). Lactation requirements and herding instincts mean that camels become tethered to water bodies (and the more succulent vegetation surrounding them) when they have feeding young. This tethering becomes so marked in the summer months that huge herds now gather around standing water, wherever that may be found in the desert. The size of the herds are notable—as recent culling activities indicate. In April 2013 over 10,000 camels were culled (from a helicopter) around one lake system in the Gibson Desert. The previous month 1000 were culled around another lake in the Great Victoria Desert: 800 the first day and 200 the next.

There is a parallel here with the past. In place of massive herds of camels we might imagine massive congregations of megafauna. And, just as Yawa took down one large camel in the historic period, many of his forebears may have hunted large marsupials in the past. And while the disarticulated remains of Yawa's camel provide no direct evidence of his involvement in its death (there were no burnt bones, cut marks or associations of stone tools to prove he had killed or eaten part of it), nor might the disarticulated remains of megafauna in swamps provide direct evidence for human involvement in their demise. Yawa's principle is that neither novelty nor mammalian gigantism is insurance against human attack and consumption. In the same way that Yawa recognised and exploited a large and novel food source near a waterhole in the desert 24 years ago, so we might anticipate his ancestors would have similarly exploited large and novel food sources near waterholes in the late Pleistocene.

Climatic change

If one accepts the likelihood that people hunted giant animals in the past, then one is obliged to consider the impacts hunting may have had on the ancient megafaunal populations. It is generally believed that the ancient animal population was, by and large, a slow moving and slow breeding one, and that sustained hunting could have had a considerable impact on it. Herding and trapping of the kind implied at Lancefield suggests significant impacts, erring towards overkill. But even underkill, in the form of individual hunting, may have taken an unexpected toll. Estimations are, for example, that a group of ten people would only have to kill one or two juvenile *Diprotodons* a year to drive the species to extinction within a few hundred years. Put another way, this means that one person only had to kill one juvenile *Diprotodon* every ten years to effect speedy extinction.[105] Similarly, it has been recognised that low levels of hunting and predation of *Genyornis* eggs may have been sufficient to threaten the long-term viability of the great bird during times of environmental stress.[106]

But the implied immediacy of the predatory consequences stands in contrast to the bio-ancestral reality—human impacts were not so instantaneous. Humans arrived in Australia over 60,000 years ago and the great animals did not become extinct until

45,000 years ago, perhaps even later. People and giant animals thus lived and fed together for at least 15,000 years (and perhaps longer) before the giants became extinct. This is an extraordinarily long time in human terms—even if it is short in broader evolutionary ones. It thus seems reasonable to accept that if people hunted the great marsupials they did so reasonably, in a timeframe that was so slow in the context of colonisation as to be virtually indiscernible in generational memory—until it was too late. The duration of coexistence amounts to 25 per cent of the total colonising experience; long enough for megafaunal history to have become embedded in elemental tradition, defined in art, integral to ancient cosmology, and to have remained as an expression of contemporary mythological history.[107]

One need not take a particular view on the matter, but it is reasonable to ask, nonetheless, why, if people had not decimated the population soon after their arrival, did the giant marsupials die out at all? What was it that beat them 15,000 years or more after human settlement? Evolutionary history is replete with extinction stories—and humans had nothing to do with most of them. Australian megafauna had been in existence for millions and millions of years, and many had become extinct well before humans set foot on the continent. Extinction was a factor of Australian bush life for a long time before humans arrived—80 per cent of the 20 or more genera of mega-animals in Australia became extinct over 80,000 years ago. Was the arrival of humans little more than a mosquito bite on the skin of greater extinction? The possibility exists, and would see humans subsumed within the greater momentum of climatic change, of the global cooling and drying then underway.

The Pleistocene encompassed a long period of increasing desertification. It was an era of climatic extremes, of global cooling and global warming: heatwaves and ice ages, and fluctuating environmental conditions in the context of ever increasing desiccation. If climatic and related environmental change did not play a predominant part in the extinction of the megafauna, then it must surely have put them under cycles of extreme stress. That stress was sufficient to wipe out the great majority 80,000 years ago and may well have finished the job 45,000 years ago. The actual mechanisms of extinction—the final climatic trigger—are yet to be detailed, but a link between long-term desiccation and eventual extinction is broadly accepted.[108] It is unfortunate for the equanimity of the association that the final extinctions occurred during a wet phase in the greater climatic dehydration. The estimated era of extinction coincided with a drier and cooler climate in which reduced evaporation led to generally wetter surface conditions. The Kimberley and northern deserts were wetter. The North West Shelf was wetter and more humid than today. Groundwater replenishment and moderate rainfall characterised central Australia. There was a period of pluvial (rain) activity in the western Simpson Desert. High lake levels persisted, with minor short-lived episodes of aridity until about 40,000 years ago.[109] Even Lake Eyre experienced a notable wet phase between 50,000 and 47,000 years ago, and Lake Frome was full around 30,000 years ago.[110]

Climatic desertification might have led to many Pleistocene extinctions, but the final curtain fell during a wet phase, suggesting other factors were involved. Climate might therefore be seen as a factor contributing to, rather than a primary driver of, extinction, and it is probably reasonable to consider that some species of giant marsupials, birds and reptiles might still roam the land had not humans arrived on the scene. Humans did, however, arrive on the scene, and with their hunger and their burning probably antagonised an already difficult situation: people as protagonists, humans and their fires as aggravating agents in the long history of extinguished life. Things may not have been going well for the last genera of megafauna, and the arrival of humans with firesticks can hardly have helped. So the megafauna declined and, in time, became extinct. There was, in effect, a convergence of certainty, in which the consequences of increasing aridity (and linked environmental change) and human predation and burning (and linked environmental change) led to the extinction of the megafauna. Whatever the cause, or the weighting of causes, the outcome was the same: at the commencement of the last ice age there was only one species of megafauna still standing—*Homo sapiens.*

Ice age

The globe cooled and dried dramatically from about 30,000 years ago.[111] Ice caps enlarged and the frozen poles grew. The cold created landscapes of ice and the growing ice consumed the sea. The sea levels fell, lower than they had ever been, to expose more continental shelf than ever before. The Australian landmass expanded to its largest extent—a third larger than we see it today: to some 10 million square kilometres then compared with 7.7 million square kilometres now. At first the sea levels fell rapidly, probably dropping by as much as 50 metres in just 1000 years: 5 metres every hundred years. The millennium was, in effect, snap frozen; the oceans contracted by cold, the bush withered by drought. The cooling and drying slowed over the next 5000 years, and then began warming and cooling in pulses that caused the seas to rise and fall in small magnitudes over 1000-year cycles. The aridity and glacial cold finally peaked between 25,000 and 18,000 years ago, and the sea stopped falling—135 metres below where it stands today. It was then possible to walk where oceans now stand: from Cape York to New Guinea and from Cape Otway to Tasmania.[112] Sydney Harbour was a beautiful valley and Port Phillip Bay was a broad, flat plain. It was an energetic walk from Adelaide to Kangaroo Island and a jog from Perth to Rottnest Island—but it would have been wise to wear furs. The sea had gone so far that it could not have been seen from modern homes with coastal views. Open plains and valleys replaced oceanic and estuarine panoramas: bleak, cold and dry—colder and drier than any other time in human history.

Opposite: Woman wearing a traditional possum skin cloak with an extended hood for carrying a child, supported by a skin belt around her chest. These cloaks were worn all over south and east Australia.

The last great ice age placed its hand over Australia for over 10,000 years. It gripped the continent both completely and awkwardly. Its hold was punctuated with abrupt periods of increased aridity, offset by intervening periods of relative humidity. Its grasp was particularly strong at the start and even stronger near the very end: first at 31,000 and then at 22,000 years ago. The intervening time was ameliorated, slightly humid, the chill of glacial westerlies sometimes softened by southeasterlies warmed by the sea.[113] Climatic extremes and instability created geographic variability that both tested humanity and opportuned its survival—and, when it was over, became testament to human ingenuity, its spirit of survival and its ability to endure and adapt.

The general patterns of glacial cooling saw the northern coastal plain enlarged by at least 200 kilometres, stretching northwards towards Timor and encompassing the Aru Islands west from Papua New Guinea. It was a 400-kilometre walk from the Admiralty Gulf in the Kimberley to Ashmore Reef near Timor, across broad basins, open sand plains, high ridges, vast plateaus and deep valleys.[114] Seventy per cent of the expanded landmass of greater Australia belonged to northern Australia.[115] Falling seas consolidated the land bridge between Cape York and New Guinea, and created an enormous coastal plain extending out to the limestone ridges and canyons underpinning the Great Barrier Reef today. As water levels began to fall the sea lost near-shore productivity, changing, in places, from open marine to shallow brackish water. The huge land bridge between Australia and New Guinea blocked the east–west flow of ocean currents and weakened the northern monsoon. Cyclones decreased across the north as a consequence. As the monsoon weakened, the southeasterly trades blew stronger, all year round.[116] Rivers dried without seasonal rains and lakes dried in sympathy. Vegetation became sparse, the ground became bare and dust storms became greater than before. Sand and dust blew from the ancient continental shelf as far inland as the Kimberley and Cape York.[117]

The Kimberley became increasingly arid, windier and colder, although gorges and sheltered valleys retained levels of moisture that supported sedges, perennial grasses, fruit-bearing trees and red river gums.[118] Beyond and across the North West Shelf summer rains decreased, and winter rain increased sufficiently to support drier vegetation of *Callitris* pines, salt bush, daisies and grasses. Levels of atmospheric dust rose and rainfall fell (by about 30 per cent, from an average of 275 millimetres per year to around 200 millimetres).[119]

Glaciation cooled Arnhem Land, mixing the great savannahs with a mosaic of grasses and sedges. Coastal mangroves declined.[120] The falling seas created perfect conditions in the Gulf of Carpentaria: the climate remained mild and Lake Carpentaria formed as the sea fell. The embayment turned into a freshwater lake and the lake changed, as sea levels ebbed and flowed, from 29,000 square kilometres to 70,000 square kilometres—eventually reaching 190,000 square kilometres in area.[121] The largest freshwater lake in the world today, Lake Superior in Canada, is 82,000 square kilometres—against which the warm temperate vastness of Lake Carpentaria might be fully appreciated. The lake increased in productivity as glaciation elsewhere became more extreme. It was a giant freshwater lake surrounded by swampy floodplains, grasslands, vine thickets, palms and water lilies—a foraging environment of fortuitous proportions in a desiccating country: there were freshwater mussels, crustaceans, fish, turtles—and crocodiles. A vast eroded escarpment of gorges and canyons rimmed the gulf country. The escarpment rose some 120 metres above the surrounding plain and extended for at least 350 kilometres, offering ideal habitation for homeless hunter-gatherers.[122]

The mountainous country in the north became excessively cold until the highlands of New Guinea were covered by an ice cap 2200 square kilometres in area. Alpine grasslands extended around the highlands for another 50,000 square kilometres.[123] Conditions were better at lower altitudes, where savannah, eucalyptus woodlands, grasses and sedges grew. Cape York received less than a third of today's rainfall. Southern Queensland and northern New South Wales supported more open she-oak vegetation, although pockets of rainforest survived.[124] The Capricorn Coast was probably sufficiently warm to experience subtropical conditions and cyclonic events. A pool of warmer water from the Pacific Ocean sat against the coast, trapped in the arm of the greater land bridge between Queensland and New Guinea. The blockage created a semi-permanent 'La Niña' that triggered instability and storms as it interacted with colder glacial air and sub-Antarctic waters from the south.[125]

Further south, the eastern coast was cold and vegetated in a manner that brings images of Patagonia to mind. The Southern Alps were covered in snow and ice, and experienced particular glacial advances at 30,000, 19,000 and 16,000 years ago. Maximum summer temperatures were 9 degrees Celsius colder than today and an ice cap covered some 50 square kilometres of the mountains. Glacial melt waters flooded the Goulburn, Murray and Murrumbidgee rivers, and increased river discharge by 5–10 times that seen today. The pan-continental glacial impacts were schizophrenic in this regard, for while the northern rivers dried with the disappearance of the summer monsoons, the southern rivers swelled with the appearance of glacial melt waters. Lake George on the Southern Tablelands filled to its maximum extent, as did other lakes in the eastern catchment of the Murray–Darling Basin.[126] Here, lakes remained full, assisted by glacial melt waters and low evaporation of surface catchments. But lakes to the west dried as stream discharges reduced and watertables fell. Yet the pattern of aridity was complicated and saw periods of devegetation and dune building interspersed with periods of flooding and fertility. In the Willandra Lakes, for example, lake levels were high at 27,000 years ago, low across 24,000 years ago, and high again between 23,000 and 20,000 years ago.[127]

The general environment of southeastern Australia was an oxymoron of wet aridity: of dry plains and wet rivers, a land of droughts and floods writ large. Forests declined across the plains and were replaced by fields of grasses and daisies. Reductions in vegetation, sparse ground and higher winds produced levels of atmospheric dust that were three times the levels of today. Most of Victoria and South Australia was virtually treeless. There is evidence of high levels of burning in some areas but not others. Elsewhere in New South Wales, for example, there is little evidence of burning, perhaps because there was little bush to burn.[128]

The further south the nomads lived the colder and crueller the climate became. It may well have been possible to walk from Victoria to Tasmania but it would have been a testing journey. The Bassian Ridge was a dry, cold grassland, frosted in the winter, coloured with daisies in the summer. A giant lake filled the Bassian depression. It covered about 400 square kilometres but was only 15 metres deep. It must have been chilled to the base and may have iced in winter. It was cold, brackish and infertile. Yet the coastline was comparatively fertile. Increased deposition of dust and increased nutrients from sub-Antarctic upwellings enhanced offshore productivity. Central Tasmania was fearfully cold, with over 400 glacial head lakes within and two giant ice caps covering possibly 5000 square kilometres.[129] Temperatures were between 6 and 10 degrees Celsius colder than today, but sub-Antarctic winds were little, if any, stronger: wind chill was minimal. The vegetation was characterised by alpine and sub-alpine herb- and shrublands, and button grass filled the valleys, which were burnt regularly by the people living there.[130]

The coast of greater Australia extended south and west, encompassing Kangaroo Peninsula (now Island) and a vast limestone plain stretched 200 kilometres seaward beneath an escarpment that now forms the Nullarbor Cliffs. Southern storms chilled the days and clear continental skies froze the nights. The thin coastal woodland plain that hugs the coast today was gone, treeless—reduced to chenopod scrublands similar to the treeless plain of the inland Nullarbor Plain today.[131]

Droughts were both common and prolonged in the central and southern parts of the expanded country. Vegetation cover declined, sand sheets mobilised and sand storms increased. The centralising weather patterns that characterise the region now moved north and enlarged so that vast high pressure systems hovered above the land; clear and cold over a continent that became larger and larger. As the distance to the sea increased, diurnal extremes in temperatures magnified in a

Mongolian effect of continental cold and aridity. The great distances weakened ameliorating opportunities and enhanced elements of aridity the further people walked from the sea: weaker sea breezes, drier winters, reduced atmospheric moisture and weaker summer monsoons.[132]

The desert expanded in every direction to encompass virtually the entire area we recognise as Australia today, a desert of almost 7 million square kilometres. The land gained from the sea never compensated for the land lost to the desert. Australia had become less fertile than ever before even though it was now a third bigger than it had ever been. Deserts spread north towards Lake Carpentaria, and east across the Murray–Darling Basin as far as western Victoria. Desert dunes rolled across the land and expanded to such a degree that they now lie submerged under the sea in the estuary of the Fitzroy River in the Kimberley (Kings Sound). Vast quantities of dust and salt blew east as far as the slopes of the Great Dividing Range. Many of the Pleistocene lakes and river systems vanished in semi-arid Australia. Deserts, woodlands, and communities of spinifex and saltbush expanded north and east. In the desert itself woodland communities disappeared, eucalypts began to die and even spinifex grasslands failed. The *Callitris* forests around Lake Eyre disappeared. As summer rains slowed, rivers feeding into the desert lakes stopped. Dry lakes were scoured by wind and dust storms intensified—the continental rain gauge was empty.[133]

The overwhelming image of glacial aridity sees greater Australia under relentless glacial attack and a human population under continual and extreme ecological stress. It is a scenario of variability and unpredictability characterised by widespread environmental strain compounded by unimaginable, unmanageable and irresolvable environmental complications. The conditions find no counterpart anywhere on the continent today: climatic behaviour was delinquent in its annihilation of watertables, lakes and rivers, and in its desiccation of biological resources.

But in the same way that the last glaciation caused massive changes to the massive country it affected, it affected it erratically at different times and in different places. So while there is a general and obvious indication of glacial desertification across Australia's heartland, not every part of it dried or de-vegetated. In the northwest, for example, aridity took a gentler toll. In the Gascoyne area, near the Pilbara, the vegetation changed from eucalypt and spinifex to native conifers and saltbush—the latter being comparatively vigorous and providing reasonable ground cover. There is no evidence for excessive erosion or atmospheric dust here.[134] Similarly, it is apparent that river systems in the Kimberley continued to flow at levels that supported red gums along them and there was no significant change in local grassland communities.[135] Eucalyptus and acacia woodlands also persisted in the mountains of central Australia, indicating the region, while more open, did not reduce to a treeless steppe.[136]

Despite the general aridity of the Lake Eyre Basin, some rivers continued to flow. Seasonal flows continued, for example, along Cooper Creek. These appear to have been sporadic but powerful, giving rise to intense episodes of riverine activity at the very peak of glacial cold and aridity. These were associated with high short-lived lake levels in Lake Frome and Lake Eyre. The Finke River was also active and substantial flooding occurred in the Lake Lewis basin—in the very centre of greater Australia.[137] Discharge was, at times, higher than seen in the area today, resulting perhaps from cyclones and cyclonic clusters drifting into the desert from turbulent atmospheric convergence between warmer Pacific and cold sub-Antarctic atmospheres along the eastern coast.[138]

South of Lake Eyre, in the Flinders Ranges, wetlands survived between 33,000 and 17,000 years ago. The depositional history indicates more humid conditions between 35,000 and 25,000 years ago, and increasing cold, wind and dust between 25,000 and 21,000 years ago.[139] Regional ecological impacts also varied across the arid margins of eastern Australia, with fluctuating lake levels in the Willandra Lakes and high lake levels in the eastern Murray–Darling Basin.

Regional environmental diversity thus appears cloaked within a cape of desiccation, and suggests a complicated mosaic of differing environments and environmental impacts across the country—within which humans survived and adapted. The greater picture of desiccation is marked with variability in detail, and points to complicated environmental outcomes influenced by differing gradients of effective moisture across the country: an endless and ever-changing relationship of precipitation and evaporation, runoff, humidity, temperature, vegetation and atmospheric carbon dioxide—not to mention variable unquantified environmental impacts caused by people through fire.[140] The broader reality was a complication of inter-relationships between climate, hydrology, vegetation, atmospherics and humans.[141] It is in that environmental complexity of extreme hardship and unpredictable diversity that people found a place to live and survive. Their survival is an extraordinary testament to human resilience and adaptability.

And people see that sun

There is no doubt about the toughness of nomadic Australians—the survival of Tjantjanu, Lantil and Yawa in the desert and the Kimberley, and the waterless walk of Napin and Nunyarangu across the treeless Nullarbor Plain make the point well enough.[142] The desert is replete with such accounts, and each provides insight into the resilience of humans in hard lands and alerts us to the human capacity for survival. That reality was brought home to me in 1986 when returning to a remote part of the desert with a family of bush people who had lived there until the previous year. My youthful enthusiasm for, and romantic notions about, their nomadic life created a strong desire to experience it, and, after careful consideration, I asked the older bushman we were travelling with, Wallimpirri, if he would consider returning to the desert and living in it for one year, with me. The bushman looked at me steadily and replied in Pintupi, 'You'll die.' There was no bravado here, simply a statement of fact. The frank intent of the short response was as obvious as it was humiliating—despite my years of camping in the bush and my affinity with their life, I was being told I had *no* idea how hard nomadic life in the desert was.

As if to prove that very point, some years later I was travelling with the same family in vehicles along a little-known and rather ill-formed track between Kintore and Nyirripi—near the great Pleistocene mine of Karrku—in the Tanami Desert. The family asked me to stop in the shade of a slender corkwood tree and told me a horrifying story. Two of Wallimpirri's sisters had made the same journey in the dry heat of early summer several years previously. They knew the country well, and if anyone in Australia could be trusted to traverse it safely at that time of year it was they. But their vehicle had broken down 80–100 kilometres from Nyirripi, and the group was stuck in a life-threatening situation on an unused track in a large, open, waterless plain. The circumstance was serious, as Wallimpirri's sister, Yarti, was heavily pregnant. The men in the group set out on foot to get help. Yarti and her bush sister, Takurri, stayed behind.

They 'saw the sun' on that baking plain, and sheltered under the very slight shade of a single hakea tree. The men walked, without food or water, all the way to Nyirripi. They survived, borrowed a vehicle, and began the return journey to save the two women. While they were gone Yarti gave birth. She had no medical assistance, no food or water, just the traditions of her desert life, the care of her sister and her natural strength to get her and the child through. The sisters waited—Yarti weak, the child vulnerable—without water or food, for help to come.

Unknown to them the rescue car had broken down. Now, in dire straits, some of the rescue party returned on foot to Nyirripi to raise the alarm. Two of the rescue party set off to tell the women that things had gone wrong. They died attempting to do so.

So the women waited, Yarti recovering from childbirth, trying to keep the child alive. They realised that something was wrong when days passed and no one had come. Then they heard the sound of a helicopter. It was looking for them. They waved and shouted, but

Unlike men, women's hair was worn loose. It was also typically short, having been repeatedly cut for hair to weave into twine, usually for threading beads and other decorative purposes (Mann Ranges, northern South Australia).

had no means of lighting a fire and attracting attention. The search party did not see them and the helicopter flew away.

So the two sisters began to walk as nomads had always walked—resiliently. They were hungry and thirsty. Yarti was weakened from childbirth. They were alone in the hottest and driest place in Australia.

They carried the child, walking at night and resting in the day. There was no food and the sisters chose not to hunt. They had to conserve their energy for their desperate plight. They made it to Nyirripi.

The birthplace remains—a slight hollow in the spinifex under the speckled shade of a small tree in an endless desolate plain. The imperceptible fragility of the birth site in the unforgiving invincibility of its arid surrounds gives cause to reflect and to feel both humbled and inspired. Their story is a tribute to the psychological and physical stamina of desert people (and perhaps all people), in whose ability to survive we see the nomads of the glacial past.

A precarious existence

Climatic reconstructions of glacial conditions imply, and are in many respects set in the context of, imagined human responses to them. But human responses to change, and human capacity for adaption, cannot be properly imagined or easily assessed. That assessment is, by definition, based on our own experiences and, as my conversation with Wallimpirri demonstrated, may have little or no relationship to the reality being imagined. The human dimension of the nomadic life (it might be inferred) is not properly understood—and certainly not properly felt—from the generalised vantage point of ethnography and archaeology. How, therefore, is it possible to imagine nomadic life in the glacial period 20,000–30,000 years ago?

There is, however, an inverse message in the advice from Wallimpirri and the experience of his sisters that is worth drawing attention to: the most difficult and dangerous thing about surviving in the desert today is the extreme, desiccating and deadly heat. In the desert of these nomads evaporation outstrips precipitation by a factor of five so that the 'hot time', at the end of the dry and before the wet season rains fall, is an extremely difficult and dangerous time of year: the cruel link that almost breaks the chain of permanent desert settlement.[143]

And so, it might be speculated, a cooler glacial environment in the past may have been more conducive to regional occupation than our notions of glacial aridity incline us to think. A fall of between 6 and 9 degrees Celsius in annual temperature would be a welcome reduction in the desert today, as long as there was enough firewood to burn and enough water to drink. Perhaps it was so in the past. Decreased precipitation in the glacial past may have been problematic for, but not fatal to, occupation of the deserts. Precipitation levels vary significantly across the arid zone but do not prevent permanent settlement in those drier deserts today. For example, the country of Wallimpirri and Yarti receives a quarter of the rain the same desert receives a few hundred kilometres to the north. Yet they lived in the driest part of the Great Sandy Desert until 1986, while more fertile areas were vacated. The viability of their country was maintained not so much by proportions of precipitation as by the proximity of the watertable and the abundance of underground soaks available to them.[144] Their example is not isolated, and many parts of the Australian arid zone were permanently occupied despite having very low rainfall. The western side of the Simpson Desert, for example, receives half the rain (125 millilitres) of the Great Sandy and Gibson deserts, but was permanently occupied nonetheless. The reason is that the western Simpson is blessed with large, long river catchments (such as the Finke and Alberga rivers) that allowed an extremely mobile resident population to sustain permanent, and typically consolidated, settlement in the greater area.[145]

It is also apparent that when monsoonal rains come to the northern deserts they flood the landscape, creating massive runoff and overflowing rock holes. Monsoonal rains effectively overfill local rock holes—there is too much rain for the size of the permanent reservoirs—and the floodwaters spill out onto the plains, evaporating in the desert sun and disappearing through porous desert sands. It is thus possible that rainfall totals could be reduced by 30 per cent without altering the amount of permanent water available to occupants, particularly if that fall in precipitation was matched by a fall in evaporation. Thus lower temperatures and lower rates of evaporation in the glacial period may have balanced decreases in rainfall and effected a milder living environment than we know today, in much the same way that the Flinders Ranges and the eastern Murray–Darling Basin retained water at the height of the last glacial period.

Differences in desert climates resulted in variations in desert adaptations. Not all deserts are the same and not all parts of the desert react in the same way to differing climatic conditions. Desert occupation was conditioned accordingly and people employed alternative occupational strategies so they could live in these varying environments. The generalised notion of a wandering desert nomad is essentially flawed. In the northern deserts, for example, summer cyclones fill available water catchments and underpin human occupation. These are vast sand deserts with sparsely vegetated sand plains and dunes. These plains are interspersed with ridges, mesas and escarpments that contain gorges, creeks and rock holes. Such features provide the primary supply of drinkable water and are thus the nucleus around which traditional human settlement revolved.

There are some areas, such as Wallimpirri's country east from greater Lake Mackay (Wilkinkarra), that contain a disproportionate number of soaks, but there are very few springs—only two that I am aware of across some 40,000 square kilometres—in the region of the Great Sandy Desert that I have worked in. The seasonal nature of the regional water supply meant that traditional life here was both highly nomadic and highly concentrated at different times of the year. People spread out across country in small family groups after wet season rains. They moved sequentially from the least reliable water sources to the most reliable as the year progressed and the surface water dried. Families amalgamated as the number of rock holes containing water decreased. By the end of the dry season few rock holes were left, and those that were left attracted large concentrations of people. These rock holes were known as 'living waters', as it was these that allowed people to survive.[146]

This pattern of dispersal and contraction contrasts with the adaptive strategies of people living in the southern deserts. The Great Victoria Desert is a sandy desert with multiple poorly aligned sand dunes vegetated by mallee, mulga and spinifex. It is exceedingly waterless, with an annual rainfall of about 250 millimetres a year, has few ridges in which surface water can be trapped and no river systems. Traditional settlement here concentrated on a number of large soaks. Some of these, such as Ooldea and Mirramirratjara, are huge compared to elsewhere in the desert. Ooldea, for example, was once used as a water resource for steam trains on the Indian Pacific Railway. Over 200,000 litres of water were extracted each day (before the soak was punctured by drilling for more water and the soak drained away).[147] These (and similar) soaks appear to have supported relatively large numbers of people for extended periods in a consolidated pattern of settlement: the people of the Great Victoria Desert were essentially sedentary, sustained by giant soaks—with movement between them difficult and typically reliant on heavy regional rains or the extraction of water from particular plant roots.[148]

Religious maps

The varying adaptive strategies of the present provide clues as to the adaptive strategies of the past, and might see social convergence, dispersal and consolidation across the desert at different times through the glacial period.[149] How this was achieved might be glimpsed in the religious tradition of the Tjukurrpa. The Tjukurrpa conveys many meanings and has many social and political functions.[150] One of those is to provide an oral map, learnt through recital and song, of every waterhole in the country over which the tradition is manifest. The application and importance of this map is difficult to overstate and, without implying nuances of romance and affectation, I have had many experiences of its profundity. I recall, for example, sitting in a hotel in Fremantle with people from the Great

Victoria Desert who had never been to the city and listening to them sing the sacred songs of Rottnest Island. This is not an uncommon occurrence. Every senior man I lived with in the Great Sandy Desert knew the location of every waterhole, through the narratives of the Tjukurrpa (the most important of which are called Tingarri here) in every place we visited over areas of at least 40,000 square kilometres. I recall crossing the Nullarbor Plain with senior men who had never seen the sea, yet who took me to gorges and other locations on the Nullarbor coast they knew through song. The mythological memory was so complete that in one location they could identify and name individual boulders.[151]

A more startling example occurred after I had invited people from the desert to my home on the Lower Eyre Peninsula, over 1500 kilometres from their desert homes. They had never been to the area before but named locations wherever I took them—and took me to locations that had particular meanings I did not know existed. They knew the country through oral narratives: the songs and stories of the Tjukurrpa. One of the most important locations was called Yula (pronounced *Yulanya*, with *nya* placed after all words ending in a vowel). The narrative comes from the Pilbara, travels over 3000 kilometres through the desert to the Lower Eyre Peninsula before heading north, crossing the continent and terminating on Groote Eylandt in the Gulf of Carpentaria. The account given to me in the land of my home was astounding—the detail of religious geography difficult to accept from people so far away. The account could have been one of inferred application—the application of a likely account that accorded with the landscape—except that the religious place names they used were replete across the countryside (corrupted as Yulina, Yellana, Yellanda, Yuli, and so on). History verifies the authenticity of the ritual account.

The Tjukurrpa, as geographic narrative and atlas, penetrates the mysteries of ancient desert survival in arid glacial times. It alone counts the names, codes and descriptions of all the waterholes—all the places where survival was possible—across the entire arid zone (and the greater Australian continent). The Tjukurrpa thus provides the ultimate survival guide in the context of environmental extremes and extreme glacial aridity. It is, in this sense, the last word on the matter. This is not to say that the Tjukurrpa was a religious tradition that survived from the late Pleistocene or emerged in the last glacial period (although it may well have done so), but it is to say that a person armed with its content stood a vastly better chance of survival than a person without it. The religious cartography is complete. Even I know 21 narratives that cross the greater part of arid Australia, and I am aware of 170 others that identify, associate and define waterholes and territorial associations in a manner that makes desert access reasonably easy.[152] It is this tangle of narration that models desert survival (ahead of any climatic or archaeological speculation) and allows us to envisage the complete and complicated cultural heredity that gave past desert nomads the best chance for survival.

There is, therefore, a cultural template for past survival. This does not imply easy occupation or unbroken settlement of the huge area of Australia that was struck by glacial aridity. Quite the reverse is likely—many parts of the desert probably became uninhabitable at different times during the glacial chill. And there are, as one might expect, mythological insights here.

The first account is paraphrased at the start of this chapter. It is a restricted narrative that is described as 'the first' Tjukurrpa in the part of the desert to which it belongs. The story has a strong ritual meaning but, if removed from that elaboration and reinterpreted structurally, in a secular context, it describes people leaving and reoccupying the desert at some distant time. The occupation, abandonment and reoccupation conveyed in the narrative sounds like a scenario before, during and after the last glacial maximum: but it may not be.

A second account has two parts, and is described as the 'second' Tjukurrpa of the people who inhabit the country it belongs to. The first part of this Tjukurrpa relates to the loss of water. Its second part relates to the rising seas encountered in the Holocene (and can wait until the next chapter). The first part carries a strong message of landscape protection and water conservation. The story commences in the ranges of central Australia and travels to the southern ocean. It revolves around a troublesome old man who hoards and wastes water, destroying the country as he does so. A central part of the story sees the old man uproot desert mallee trees that contain water in their roots, and this causes all the water in the desert to be lost, drained away into the ground, from where it seeps out to the distant sea only to return as a great flood (part two of the story).[153]

Another account heads south through the desert and ends abruptly and ambiguously at the very edge of the Nullarbor Cliffs. The story seems to have no conclusion. Perhaps it once continued out onto the plain. The story relates to two men—not the Two Men (Wati Kutjara) of the greater desert, but another two men who find they are struggling to preserve water. The story is about water shortage and the loss of underground water. It sees the ground 'punctured' by one of the men with a giant spear, and the underground water draining away as a consequence. Another curious element in the story relates to the transportation of water in a large skin bag. The bag is ultimately torn by one of the men and the water is lost, to great catastrophe. The curious thing about this part of the story is that there are no skin water bags in the desert today. Such items are not part of today's material culture; they do not exist. Clearly, however, the concept does exist and perhaps the bags themselves existed in the past. Were skin bags a feature of water storage and desert survival a long time ago? Is that how people moved great distances across the desert in the glacial past? Was the importance and manufacture of skin bags one of the reasons bone points seem so abundant in sites across the country in the late Pleistocene?

The parallels of these Tjukurrpa with the character of glacial aridity in the last ice age are reasonably obvious: land was abandoned and reoccupied, vegetation was destroyed, water was lost, underground water disappeared and the sea departed. The rituals of desertification in the desert are so profound that it strikes an environmental chord.

Clearly the people never forgot it. The structural similarities in the Tjukurrpa to the fundamentals of the ice age experience are worthy of wonder. It is risky, however, to draw too many parallels with the past—but that does not mean there are no parallels at all.

Desert chill

No country is ever abandoned in the desert—even the largest, most infertile and unlivable parts of it are incorporated in the human experience through story (Tjukurrpa). Some of the most unlivable and most 'abandoned' are, in fact, the most important in the metaphysical (and implicitly physical) experience of people's connection to country. But this is not to say that people did not vacate country at difficult times or that they did not die in it when poor judgements were made and conditions became too harsh. There are many stories to this effect in living memory. There must have been many more in the past—and perhaps even more across the last glacial period.

But, as a general characteristic of the time, there is no particular evidence for mass abandonment of the arid zone during the great glacial age. There are now, as mentioned, 50 sites dated to the late Pleistocene and 24 of them demonstrate occupation through the glacial era from 30,000 to 18,000 years ago. The sites are located across the arid continent: four in the northern desert margins, five in the arid west, eight across the inland side of the Pilbara, one in the western side of the desert, one in central Australia, two in the Lake Eyre Basin, one in the Flinders Ranges and two on the Nullarbor Plain.[154] The rest do not show evidence of occupation during the glacial time, and some sites with evidence of occupation reveal a decrease in site usage over the extreme glacial millennia—but that, perhaps, is to be expected. Given that caves and rock shelters were typically occupied for shelter from heat and rain it is not surprising that there is less evidence for people seeking shelter at times when it was less hot and there was less rain.

But in cases where the archaeological debris indicates a decrease in occupational intensity it might be inferred that this corresponds to a decrease in population across the desert generally. It is difficult to know. There is, nonetheless, reasonable evidence of social and economic adjustment in response to increasingly difficult environmental conditions across this period of time. At Puritjarra rock shelter, for example, in the centre of greater Australia, evidence reveals that social adjustments were made as people adapted to the difficult conditions through the glacial maximum.[155] Survival in the range country was underpinned by a number of semi-permanent springs. The permanent water was the intravenous drip of the age and allowed people to continue living in a desert they may otherwise have had to vacate. But while life continued in the central Australian ranges, it also changed. The archaeological material at Puritjarra between 35,000 and 24,000 years ago suggests a high degree of mobility, with people moving widely across the plains and making intermittent visits to the ranges. The mobile population obtained ochre from the famous Karrku mine, 125 kilometres away, on the sand plains to the northwest. But after 24,000 years ago visits to the cave became more frequent and extended, as if populations had consolidated around nearby water supplies. Social relations and mobility seem to have contracted as the glacial ages encompassed them. People began utilising local silicified sandstones for stone tools, rather than better quality chalcedony from further afield. The change in raw materials implies a community in lockdown, in the context of which more localised social relationships developed. That centralistion led to a reconfiguration of broader regional allegiances. By 15,000 years ago the range people were no longer obtaining ochre from Karrku; it was replaced with materials sourced within easier reach, in the ranges only 50 kilometres to the southeast. Customary behaviour remained—stone tools were still made and the ochre was still applied—but the social mechanisms of procurement were different. It seems the people of the desert ranges no longer travelled huge distances to obtain precious materials. Or perhaps the desert became depopulated, fragmenting regional alliances and breaking down trade mechanisms. Having seen the unforgiving plains around Karrku and heard the story of Yarti's remarkable survival in nearby country, it is not hard to see why things might have changed. The material adjustments suggest accompanying social adjustments across the glacial period: life became circumscribed, risks were not taken, and social engagement was confined. The people survived in the difficult conditions by doing the same with less; life was not what it used to be.

The period of glacial aridity may well have been an era of climatic extremes across the huge desert, and if so they seem to be mirrored with equivalent social and demographic extremes. Human behaviour at Koonalda Cave, on the Nullarbor Plain, for example, contrasts with the sensible and believable adaptive strategies seen at Puritjarra. At the time, Koonalda was 200 kilometres from the sea: a giant dark hole deep beneath a treeless barren plain. Yet people travelled great and inhospitable distances to reach it, to obtain precious resources and perform remarkable rituals. Their behaviour is seemingly counterintuitive in the context of the extreme climatic conditions: behaviour enriched by the impossibility of the environment in which it was conducted.

At this great cave we find that people travelled from places unknown across vast, desolate plains, and climbed into its massive doline to obtain a high-quality flint and nodules of ochre in the cave walls deep underground. The Pleistocene people penetrated the dark recesses of the cave, climbing and walking in precipitous caverns almost 250 metres beneath the surface of the earth, leaving behind incisions and hand markings on the soft chalk-like walls of the cave. It was an ancient land of inverted proportion where, to the people who lived on the flattest country on earth, the greatest topographic relief they knew existed underground. The people moved through cathedral-like chambers and narrow animal-sized tunnels in pursuit of their artistic and ritual objectives. They moved and worked in darkness disturbed only by the flickering light provided by firesticks, and left behind distinctive hand markings and vertical lines engraved with sticks and stones. Ice age people are seen here with particular vibrancy—fingers drawn across the fabric of the inner earth, the imprints of real hands belonging to real people who lived 20,000 years ago.

The cave was perhaps warmer than the air outside, and Koonalda was so deep that it penetrated the watertable—perhaps providing a vital source of water in that difficult time.[156] But Koonalda is not a singular site; there is another with identical markings 230 kilometres to the west in which the parallel artistry alludes to a parallel tradition, and the existence of territorial relationships articulated through shared ritual in the most difficult of lands and times. The artistic geography suggests the people of the Nullarbor were not random visitors struggling to survive at the peak of the last ice age—although the harshness of the country suggests they should have been. The commonality of their disparate artistic traditions points to shared beliefs and territorial purpose. There was, it appears, more to life in the glacial age than mere survival.

Footprints

The hands of the past are matched by its feet in another part of the arid interior in this cold and dry time. At the Willandra Lakes there are, almost impossibly, over 560 human footprints left by people walking on the muddy lake floor 19,000–23,000 years ago.[157] Twenty-three people made the tracks: 12 men, four women and seven children.

The footprints bring to life these cold, remote times and show us real people living normal lives in extreme places at extreme times. Six men in the group were running in a flanking movement. The distance between individual tracks indicates they were travelling at about 20 kilometres an hour—around half the speed of an Olympic runner—and suggests a purposeful sprint rather than an accelerated run across the lake. The men seem to be hunting in company. Surprisingly, one of the men ran on one leg with the aid of a crutch.

The men stood for a time, with the ends of their spears placed on the ground. They had at least nine spears. Nearby is a scuffmark where a spear ricocheted off the ground. (Traditionally, spears were bounced off the ground in the hope of breaking a kangaroo's leg rather than thrown as a clean shot through the chest, as might be imagined.) Not far away are the tracks of an adult walking with four children. What were they talking about?

The tracks reveal the people who made them were reasonably tall. The average height of the men was 168 centimetres (5'6"), and the average height of the women 156 centimetres (5'1"): considerably taller than their ancestors from previous millennia buried in the lunettes around them. The tallest person was a man, at 191 centimetres (6'2"). The people were thus taller than Indonesians and about the same size as Africans today. They were a little smaller than contemporary Australians,[158] but not by much, suggesting they were well fed, healthy and strong.

The tracks and trails imply companionship—an extended family who may have owned the country they were living and hunting in. There is an impression of a close, cooperative community: a parent or grandparent with children, a man with a crutch running with his compatriots. Ethnographic examples give colour to the one-legged man's life, and through his life the experience and outlook of his community. Donald Thompson met a man similarly handicapped, in the Tanami Desert in the late 1950s. He ran in a similar way, with a crutch made of a slender wooden pole.[159] I knew 'One Leg' quite well, and the man who cared for him after the injury even better. His leg was broken below the shin during a spear fight. The damaged part of the leg was then removed, and the bone properly broken with a boomerang and 'chucked away': a rough amputation in a time without anaesthetic. The wound became badly infected, perhaps gangrenous, and his friend Patatu nursed him. The injury was rubbed with natural antiseptic made from available bushes (*Cassia lanceolata* or *Acacia ancistrocarpa*) and, in combination with the antibodies of a desert hunter-gatherer and stoicism of steel, this allowed One Leg to survive. Such is the resilience of the desert hunter, and such is the compassion of his family and friends. Such may have been the nature of life in the Pleistocene where only the tough and the kind survived. Perhaps the one-legged man who lived in the ice age also damaged his leg in a fight. Perhaps a friend also nursed him back to health.

Food for thought

And so life went on across the glacial millennia. The tracks in the Willandra Lakes mean, if nothing else, that the lakes had not been abandoned. There were in fact times during the glacial maximum when parts of the Willandra Lakes were sufficiently full for people to be fishing and collecting shellfish within them,[160] and there is similar evidence in the form of middens and campsites elsewhere across the Murray–Darling Basin between 33,000 and 19,000 years ago.

It may also have been that people started processing cereals about this time. If so, they were about 10,000 years ahead of anybody else on earth.[161] While there is convincing archaeological evidence for the development of seed grinding within the last 3000–4000 years,[162] the ancient evidence is debated and worth reflection. The evidence includes what appear to be remnant pieces of larger seed-grinding implements on the lake lunettes in the Willandra.[163] The pieces look like 'grindstone' fragments in the last stages of reduction, rather than seed-grinding implements as such. Seed-grinding implements have a functional history so that once they wear out or break they are used for other purposes such as crushing reptile vertebrae, smashing marsupial long bones for the extraction of marrow, as heat retainers to cook anything from termites to kangaroos (where they are placed in the visceral cavity), sharpening and smoothing wooden tools (notably spears), and in the preparation of ochre for non-sacred purposes. Seed-grinding implements may thus remain in the archaeological record as amorphous pieces with other functions subsequent to their original purpose.[164]

In my experience, seed-grinding implements are highly valued and not discarded lightly. They are handed down from mother to daughter and reused until they are worn out. They thus tend to be degraded, fragmented and spread out across the country (rather than found whole at sites within it), or they move up through archaeological deposits (rather than being trapped within them). Seed-grinding implements are also rather large and difficult to bury in slow accumulations of ancient debris. In a site in the arid zone, where rates of deposition are high, a typical seed-grinding implement (5–7 centimetres thick) would take 500–1000 years to bury. It's reasonable to assume such an implement would be picked up and used, removed, reused, broken, reduced and dispersed elsewhere in that time: only the most recent are likely to survive human usage over time.

Seed-grinding implements are tools with ancestry and spiritual affinity, and are handed down through the generations accordingly. Everyone knows who owns them and, at any site I have been to, people know who left them there. Grindstones were typically left at sites because they were heavy and hard to carry from place to place. They were left at popular camping locations and at sites near primary seed-collecting areas.[165]

The following example conveys something of the importance of seed-grinding tools in the cultural context of past nomadism. On one occasion we had been travelling for three days in an attempt to locate an important soak on the far southwestern plains of the Great Victoria Desert. We finally located the soak and found, among other things, an excellent seed-grinding dish on its bank. The dish belonged to an old lady who had recently died. The soak belonged to her as well. Both were an integral part of the place and the place was an integral part of this important woman's religious identity. One of the senior men decided to take the seed-grinding dish home. People were very upset about it, explaining that the old lady had always wanted to go back to the soak and get that dish. It should be left where it was. That night the man had a frightening dream. He dreamt that evil spirits had reared out of the soak and screamed down

This woman is grinding Wangkanyu seeds to make unleavened bread. Seed processing may be as old as 30,000 years in Australia and was highly advanced by 4000 years ago. The seeds are ground with water, collected in a wooden bowl and baked in hot coals. The same species (*Eragrostis*) is widely cultivated across Africa, initially in Ethiopia about 4000 years ago.

at him. They lunged a huge spear at him, but he rolled away and the spear missed. They then picked him up and threw him against the ground. He landed hard, on his back.

A few days later he developed an extremely sore shoulder and was in such pain that he could barely move. The community nurse said he should be evacuated, but the old man would not leave. He became so sick he had to be administered intravenous antibiotics. He survived, but was lucky to do so. The clinical diagnosis was that he

This wild damper was made from chenopod seeds by cleansing with ash and soaking, then grinding and baking. Preparation time was 95 minutes; the loaf weighed 280 grams and provided 1885 kilojoules of energy. It is one of the only quantified records of seed processing in hunter-gatherer societies in the world. Chenopod seeds have been found at Carpenter's Gap in the Kimberley that are between 18,000 and 26,000 years old.

had a haematoma caused by a major impact on his shoulderblade. The impact had caused internal bleeding that had then become infected. The community attributed the injury to his dream and his subsequent sickness to him having removed the old lady's seed-grinding dish from the soak. We had been with the old man all the time and knew he had not suffered any fall or physical impact that could explain the injury. The psychology of spiritual association with the old lady and her seed-grinding dish seems to have been the cause.

The example indicates that grindstones were not left idly unattended to become part of miscellaneous archaeological deposits and that the discovery of any grindstone of great antiquity would be a rare thing. Some are located on the Willandra Lakes and some are found in deposits that might be 30,000 years old, at Cuddie Springs, in the northern Murray–Darling Basin. Chenopod seeds have also been discovered in Carpenter's Gap between 26,000 and 18,000 years ago that suggest their consumption.[166] This was a time of great desiccation. Australia was drying and the woodlands of the Willandra and Murray–Darling Basin were contracting and grasslands were expanding. The time would come when the basin was virtually treeless, and grasses would abound and provide abundant new resources. It would seem likely that women living there at the time would recognise the foraging opportunity and seek to maximise the ubiquitous new source of carbohydrates.

But seeds can be eaten without grinding them. I have eaten unground seeds and have seen many eaten, stripped directly from the grass. A handful of seeds stripped in this way need only be rubbed between the palms of two hands and the husks blown away, for consumption. Other seeds, such as the succulent, *Portulaca*, are contained in a little capsule that can be de-capped with ease. Ants also collect many of the more edible wild seeds and conveniently leave them in neat piles. The ants eat a nodule attached to the seed and leave the rest in piles around their nests, ready for collection by people.[167] It is hard to believe that ancient people living in difficult times would not have recognised the food source accordingly. And it would be an odd thing if seeds from grasses and succulents did not become part of the glacial diet given the difficulty of the times and the fact that the greater part of the Australian landscape was, at that time, covered with them.

A spectacular sea view

Glacial aridity clearly put pressure on human populations, and we see evidence of them moving and regrouping in more fertile locations beyond the deserts. The plains and escarpments south of Lake Carpentaria were perhaps the best place to be. Here the limestone gorges contained deep pools of water and permanent lagoons that supported fish, molluscs, turtles, crocodiles and freshwater rats. The plains nourished wallabies, kangaroos and wallaroos, and were a very different foraging environment to the neighbouring deserts. The area was a comparative oasis and drew increased populations across the glacial maximum. At Colless Creek, for example, there is evidence of human occupation from 30,000 years ago that intensifies between 21,000 and 17,000 years ago. Given the fertility of the area, the reasons are obvious.[168]

Similar environments in escarpments elsewhere were also occupied through this time, with settlement through Arnhem Land dated to around 23,000–18,000 years ago. The great cave of Nauwalabila shows continual occupation from the very beginning, and it is implied at Nawarla Gabarnmang to the southwest.[169] Sites of ice age antiquity are spread across Cape York and down the east coast, in the Great Dividing Range, the Blue Mountains and the Southern Highlands.[170]

Settlement continued in the glacial valleys of Tasmania but was pushed to the limit. There are 40 sites across the frozen mountains of central Tasmania that show people hunting and living in that environment between 30,000 and 14,000 years ago. But settlement appears to have been interrupted by the extreme conditions at the very worst of the glacial era: the cold became too great for even these hardy folk. Occupation in the ice age caves concentrates in two peaks, one between 25,000 and 22,000 years ago, and another between 18,000 and 14,000 years ago.[171] There is little evidence of people hunting in the sub-Antarctic valleys for almost 5000 years across the worst of the glacial period.

As the desert dried and the mountains froze and the sea fell, it is easy to imagine people migrating to more manageable lands. The coast beckoned as people were drawn to new lands in milder climates. We might see in that past something we see in the present: a population looking out, their backs to the land, living by the sea. But the sea dropped so much and the coastline moved so far away it is virtually impossible to catch a glimpse of their lives and the conditions they experienced in that distant time. For where they lived then is now well under water. Past reconstruction of ancient coastal colonisers is thus a thing of great imagination, although some sites give us small clues.

Mandu Mandu rock shelter on the northwest coast is a perfect example. The ancient coastline here is steep, the site never far from the sea. But the evidence for coastal life is small. There are just 123 artefacts in the oldest part of the site, indicating less than 30 artefacts were made and left behind every thousand years. And there is just 30 grams of shell over a 10,000-year period leading into the glacial maximum: a piece of nautilus shell (perhaps an ornament), a fragment of baler shell (*Melo*), some pieces of *Turbo*, mud whelk (*Terebralia*) and chiton (*Acanthopleura*). The clues are small but nevertheless indicate varied resource use congruent with the times: the chiton and turbo indicate people foraged on rocky ocean shores, and the mud whelk sees them up to their ankles in mud among the mangroves. There is a tiny amount of fish bone—the possible jaw and teeth of a rock cod (*Epinephelus*)—suggesting they perhaps fished in oceanic rock pools. People were camped in the cave looking across the coast but the evidence for their use of it is tantalisingly small. Then the site was vacated as glacial conditions intensified.[172]

The occupation here is reminiscent of desert people living by the sea—their homes and economy were centred on the arid lands, but they had access to and used the resources of the sea. Such is the situation nearby, on the Peron Peninsula in Shark Bay. About 35,000 years ago people camped on a sandy ridge (the Silver Dollar site) about 50 kilometres from the coast. They visited the area until about 22,000 years ago, hunting wallabies and collecting emu eggs. But they also visited the coast, or were visited by people from the coast, as there is a fragment of baler shell in the lower levels of the site. Perhaps it is a fragment of a larger shell used to carry water. The people living here also left the area once the sea level dropped.[173] The same pattern is seen further north. At the time people were living near the Pleistocene coast of Mandu Mandu shelter they were also living near the coast in the Kimberley. The coastline here shelves steeply before flattening across a broad coastal plain, and people once lived around the steep mesa-like plateaus that now form the Buccaneer Archipelago. People lived here 28,000 years ago. They hunted animals that, with the exception of the remains of red kangaroos (*Macropus*), Tasmanian devils (*Sarcophilus harrisii*) and Tasmanian Tigers (*Thylacine*), were similar to those of traditional diets in the Kimberley today: these were desert people on the seashore. And like the occupants of Mandu Mandu shelter and the Silver Dollar site, they also left the site as the extremes of glacial aridity encroached and the sea moved further away 19,000 years ago.[174]

In this flat and expansive land the sea retreated over 200 kilometres. We might imagine people followed it and, remarkably, there are traces of them having done so at Noala Cave, 120 kilometres out to sea, on the Montebello Islands. These islands were then hills 8 kilometres from the coast of the great continental plain across northwestern Australia. People lived in the cave and hunted along its nearby shores 31,000 years ago. They ate kangaroos, bettongs, bandicoots and goannas, collected clams and caught fish.[175]

But for all this remarkable evidence for life on the margins of the glacial shores, evidence for life on those shores remains frustratingly, perhaps impossibly, out of reach. The archaeological record remains a hand's width away from the place we want it to be. The

17. An artist's impression of Murujuga in Western Australia, before the seas began to rise around 18,000 years ago. When sea levels were low, this area of the Pilbara was a rugged, rocky hill surrounded by plains.

18. Murujuga today. As the sea levels rose, the plains were flooded. The engravings found there feature marine animals, turtles, dugong and fish, superimposed on older engravings of terrestrial animals.

19. Dr Ken Mulvaney and Ivan Dale look at a particularly radiant engraving of two archaic faces linked with geometric designs at Murujuga.

20. This is just one of the at least 70 engraved faces found across the Pilbara region. They are the earliest representations of the human face in the world, perhaps dating back 25,000 years.

21. An example of one of the more recent engravings found at Murujuga. The engraving shows the life cycle of a turtle, through the seasons. There is a mating pair, hatchlings and a turtle speared for food.

22. An engraving of a Tasmanian Tiger (*Thylacine*) found on the rocks at Murujuga. The Tasmanian Tiger survived until modern times in Tasmania, but became extinct on mainland Australia 3300 years ago.

23. A map, carved into rock, pointing to Binpi in the Western Desert. The locations of waterholes and resources were recorded and retold in the arid parts of Australia through oral history and religious narratives (Tjukurrpa).

24. Close up of the engraved map. Oral accounts were painted and engraved on stone. These engravings appear to be the oldest maps in the world.

25. Climbing Man engraving from the Western Desert (Little Sandy Desert). This remarkable engraving is located over 800 kilometres distant from the similar image below.

26. Climbing Men engraving from Murujuga in the Pilbara. These engravings indicate that a network of social and religious tradition was established across huge parts of Australia a very long time ago.

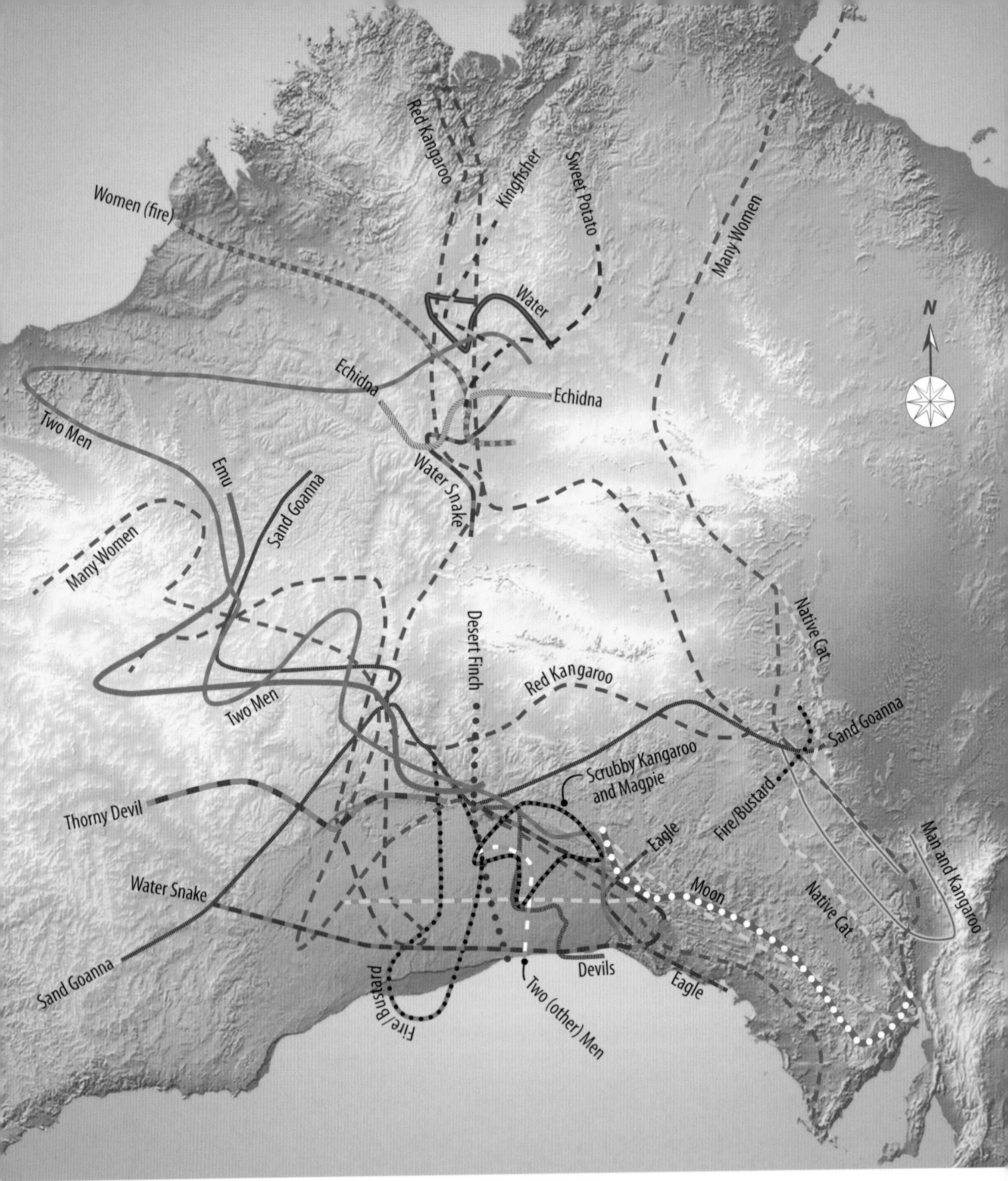

27. The enormity and complexity of the religious geography across arid Australia is indicated by this representation of the desert dreaming, or Tjukurrpa, tracks. There are many hundreds more tracks and stories than are represented here and each provided a pathway across the desert, between countries, linking waterholes with reliable living areas and places of religious importance. These highways of subsistence, ceremony and society conditioned life in one of the hardest landscapes on earth. Armed with this oral tradition, a desert nomad could survive anywhere, at almost any time over the last 45,000 years of settlement in the desert.

28. Martu Elder Timmy Patterson interprets a Western Desert map. This representation of the Tjukurrpa is more recent, but is a continuation of the same artistic geographic tradition seen in plates 23 and 24.

29. Engravings are also numerous in the sandstone escarpments of eastern Australia. There are over 3000 such sites in the Sydney basin alone—more ancient art than in any other urban environment in the world.

30. Spinifex children from the Great Victoria Desert are photographed on first meeting white people in the mid-1950s. Their camp is behind, spears on the ground. They seem embarrassed, even though they have never seen a camera before.

31. The children of Tjantjanu and Lantil with Lantil's brother in 1992. These are the great nomads of the Great Sandy Desert and share adjacent countries few white people have seen, west of Lake Mackay.

same frustration, mixed with the same tantalising desire to find out more, echoes through the Pleistocene archaeology off the eastern coast of greater Australia.

At Wallen Wallen Creek, for example, on present-day North Stradbroke Island, people were camped on a high dune field, overlooking a coastal plain that extended east for 12–20 kilometres from their camp. They were not eating shellfish, but they seem to have been using the coastal plain. We know they walked across the plains as they made stone tools from a high-quality chert that disappears from the record after the sea begins to rise—it was probably obtained from the old drowned coastal plain.[176]

Similarly, there is evidence of people overlooking the coast further south, on the south coast of New South Wales. This campsite sits in a cave overlooking an estuarine embayment called Burrill Lake. Then people lived in the cave overlooking a relatively small valley in an inclined coastal hill; the sea was only 13–16 kilometres away.[177] People lived there occasionally 21,000 years ago and developed a remarkable technical innovation. The occupants began using heat to alter the crystalline structure of rocks they wished to flake into stone tools.[178] They used fire in a controlled manner to decrease the tensile strength of the stone and improve its flaking qualities. This is a remarkable application of fire and reveals a keen awareness of the physical properties of stone. That level of innovation and application is consistent with the general remarkability of human settlement across greater Australia in the late Pleistocene.

Wallen Wallen Creek and Burrill Lake help us appreciate settlement on the ancient coastal plain in the ice age—we can imagine people living there and looking out across the coast: small groups living in forgotten landscapes, the mementos of their lives now buried deep under water. There is, it seems to me, sadness in that coastal panorama for wherever one looks there was once land, and where that land once stood, people experienced life on it. Who were they? How did they live? What were they like? The questions are tantalising, and our inability to answer them somehow enhances the romance of their enigma. While we might never know what life was like for these people in the lands now submerged, we nonetheless have glimpses of them and a sense of their lives.

There is evidence of people sheltered in a large cave overlooking the western side of the Bassian Ridge. They lived on a low peninsula (now Hunter Island) for about 2000 years at the height of glaciation, 23,000 years ago.[179] The region was a cold steppe and people made repeated visits to the cave. They used poorly shaped pieces of quartz and smashed marsupial bones to extract marrow like their glacial relatives in the mountains further south. They also made and polished bone tools from the long bones of kangaroos—again, like their mountain compatriots. The tools may have been used as awls, spear points or netting needles, to make clothes or nets and baskets for catching fish—cold work even by Tasmanian standards. There was also, curiously, a bone from the foot of a swan. Its ends were broken, it was deeply incised and it was slightly polished in the manner of a pendant. The artefact creates an ethereal image of the environment and the people whose lives associated with it—one of ancient lakes and gliding swans, open grasslands and daisy fields juxtaposed with people hunched among marshes and reeds on periglacial lakes, stooped low on frozen shores and, at day's end, warming themselves around fires in home caves while sleet is driven by the sub-Antarctic wind outside. Glacial life cannot have been pleasant in the cold latitudes, but it was not destitute.

People also lived in the very heart of the bleak Bassian Plain—on hills that now form the Furneaux Islands.[180] There are caves here that display a fascinating array of cultural material over 21,000 years old. There are hearths, artefacts made of fossilised shell, quartz flakes, small amounts of ochre, ornaments made from scallop shell, and food remains including emu eggs and grey kangaroos (now extinct in the Bass Strait region). The material culture reveals people whose lives were comparatively rich given the difficulty of the times. Their subsistence base was diverse and their sense of self and community is recognised through ornamentation and ochre. A glimpse into their

A proud father, and embarrassed children, at home. Life in a windbreak is surprisingly snug and sociable, protected from the wind next to a soft glowing fire. The father's spears and spear-thrower are at hand in the windbreak.

lives is not one of impoverished hardship, despite the rigours of the world they lived in.

And, perhaps fittingly, there is a rare opportunity in this coastal land to obtain a sense of the people themselves. There is an ancient burial in a sea cave on King Island. The cave now has a spectacular view of the sea but at the time it looked over a cold, treeless plain. King Island was then a large hill and the cave was perched in a cliff on the side of a raised plateau. The burial is 18,000 years old.[181] It is not clear how the person died, but after death the body was laid on its right side and left exposed for some time. The bones then appear to have been gathered together into a pile. Small pieces of ochre are attached to the skull and the thighs, suggesting the person either had ochre on them or the ochre was brought in later and placed with the body. Once the burial mound was constructed the cave was vacated. There is no other evidence of human presence, no artefacts or food debris of any kind.

The person was a male between 25 and 35 years old with a large muscular face. He is the most southern representative of the nomads at the end of the Pleistocene. His burial implies ritual attendance. The ochre suggests personal adornment and considered mortuary rites. The lack of accompanying or subsequent cultural material suggests the cave was a mausoleum, a place for the dead. There is a sense of place and purpose in the lives of these people of the past.

The burial captures the life of an ice age man at the peak of the ice age in greater Australia. He might be seen to represent the social and geographic achievements of all the nomads who lived throughout the era and whose lives are etched with such remarkable diversity across the land. We see in his death much that we see repeatedly across the ages and across the continent: a viable people in varied environments linked through shared traditions and common ideology, who survived in extreme environments through testing times. There is artistic achievement and social development through deep history enriched with notable creativity, technical innovation and diversified subsistence. These were people who changed the environment they lived in and left their mark accordingly. They were great and successful colonisers who adapted to the deserts, mountains, plains and coasts with erudite diversification. The nomads of Australia had settled extreme environments and adapted to extreme conditions. And, as they mastered the difficulties that confronted them, the world they knew changed dramatically once again.

4
The Great Flood

FROM 18,000 YEARS AGO

'The People of the Sun and the People of the Shadow moved south from the deserts. They carried huge numbers of spears. The Sun People faced the encroaching water from the cliff tops. The Shadow People blocked the valleys and gorges. They built massive ramparts with their spears. Together they blocked the rising sea.'

— Traditional account of the Spinifex People, documented in 2002

Water

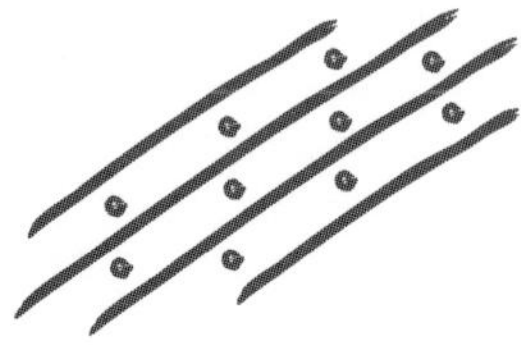

She looked at her grandfather's body and could not stop crying. She held her lips, pressing them against her teeth, hoping the grief would push away. But sobs erupted through her chest. She couldn't understand. She knew he was old but he seemed so strong. His voice made her feel safe. He was always there. She sat in his lap near the fire. He talked to her and told her funny stories. She slept warm in the cradle of his body. He had died like that, silently in the night, his arm around her. She hadn't realised he was dead; his body was still warm.

Now she looked at him. He was wrapped in his skin cloak and wore a headband woven from human hair and coated in ochre, dark red against his grey hair. The men placed a small bag next to his body. She wondered what was inside and caught a glimpse of a white feather through a small opening. The men knelt next to the grave and pushed sand softly over his body. They bled where they had sliced their thighs, intensifying their anguish. They covered the low mound with branches and stood up, grief accentuated by despair. Now the old man was gone, what could they do?

It was all he had talked about for years. They were sure it had killed

Previous pages: Men watch as strangers arrive at Pukatja soak in 1933. A well was sunk in the soak and Ernabella Station was established that year (Musgrave Ranges, northern South Australia).

him. He had tried everything but nothing had worked. Then he stopped trying. What could they do? The sea kept rising. The old man said it had covered the place where his grandfather was born and was now close to his own birthplace. They had placed his body on a high sand dune hoping it would be safe there, but nobody was sure.

Her grandfather had told her about the sea. He always talked about it. He talked about it so much that sometimes she stopped listening. He had told her there was nothing more he could do. He said it was his fault that the sea would not stop. She would lean on him then, feel for his hand and squeeze it gently. He always smiled but the worry stayed on his face. She felt worried now, now that he was gone. She missed him and felt scared.

All the people had been saying that the desert people were coming and that they would stop the sea. She had heard about the desert people. She looked out at the ocean. And she thought of the desert people. She didn't know which frightened her most. She sobbed deeply. She needed her grandfather to hold onto.

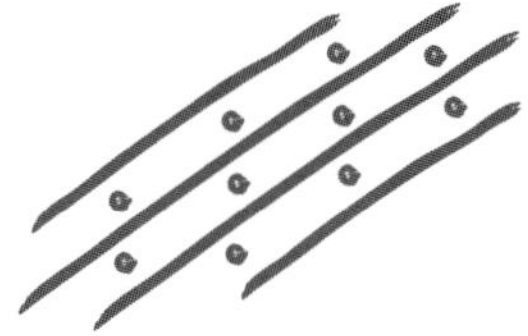

The waters rose and increased greatly on the earth

There is perhaps only one thing worse than a land in absolute drought and that is a land in absolute flood. For no sooner had greater Australia expanded to its coldest, driest and largest extent than it began to contract to its warmest, wettest and smallest. As the glacial era started to unwind, the climatic and environmental conditions of the previous 15,000 years reversed and inverted. The seas rose and the climate warmed. Tropical influences began to dominate, monsoons intensified and warm trade winds stimulated ocean currents bringing warmer temperatures and more rain. Ice disappeared rapidly. Deglaciation commenced about 18,000 years ago and was virtually complete 15,000 years ago; shrublands replaced tundra by 13,000 years ago, and forests replaced shrublands by 10,000 years ago.[1] Monsoons had returned by 14,000 years ago and peaked 8000–6000 years ago, with high rainfall and summer temperatures promoting the growth of sclerophyll and rainforest across the northern, eastern and southern parts of the country. Tropical grasslands and rich woodlands returned to the Kimberley, and boab trees were growing there 11,000 years ago. Across Arnhem Land coastal rivers became estuaries and mangroves choked their shores, reaching their maximum extent 6000 years ago.[2]

The northern rivers started to flow again and the southern rivers started to slow as glacial meltwaters ran out. Southwesterly winds increased from about 14,000 years ago and declined between 11,000 and 7500 years ago, bringing wet, warmer conditions across most of southeastern Australia. Lake levels increased. Eucalypts and casuarina replaced herb, shrub and grass fields across temperate Australia. Open woodland returned to the Murray–Darling Basin. Rainforest grew over western Tasmania and levels of burning increased everywhere.[3]

Conditions fluctuated in the desert, with temperatures climbing a few degrees above today's temperature about 9000 years ago. The climate stabilised by 8000 years ago, and was at its optimum over the next 3000 years: woodland and grassland communities were re-established and the watertable was replenished. Trees grew along the coast of the Nullarbor Plain. Inland lakes started to fill again with increased monsoonal flows, more winter rains and a higher watertable. Lake Eyre was a shallow lake around 12,000 years ago, and Lake Gregory (Paraku) was semi-permanent from 14,000 to about 6000 years ago. The great deserts of the glacial era reduced by half their size across this time.

Just as everything was warming perfectly, the climate dried again and the weather became unstable. The change in the later part of the Holocene was distinct and saw decreasing summer rain, increasing winter rain and decreasing temperature after 5000 years ago. This was a time of climatic variability and enhanced droughts and floods—Australia became dry more often.

In southeastern Australia lake levels rose and fell. Six thousand to 5000 years ago, southeastern Australia was substantially drier and lake levels were lower than today. Then the climate warmed and became wetter again before drying more severely between 3500 and 1000 years ago, and returning to wetter, warmer conditions in the more recent past. There was a general increase in burning across southeastern Australia, although a decline in fires across southern Tasmania after 6000 years ago.[4]

The desert also became drier as monsoons weakened and rainfall became more variable. The estuaries across the north filled with sediment and became the vast floodplains we see today. Most desert lakes became ephemeral, dunes mobilised and vegetation cover changed from woodlands and tall shrub to more open scrub. Grasslands recovered over the next two millennia, and by 1500 years ago the vegetation we recognise today became established: a desert of increasing seasonality and climatic variability.

The most immediate effect of climatic change across the Holocene was sea level rise. The ocean rose for 13,000 years. It was a flood of incremental magnitude and great variability but, in the longer scheme of things, the seas rose at an average rate of 1 centimetre every year. It was a relentless flood equating to over half a metre in a lifetime, with a lateral consequence of many kilometres over flat coastal plains across each generation. But the sea level did not rise neatly, in measured increments of equal proportion. It moved both imperceptibly slowly and disconcertingly fast. At times, great swathes of the coast disappeared in front of people's eyes. At other times it moved so slowly the ancients might have been forgiven for thinking the great flood had stopped.

At first the sea rose quite slowly, then more quickly and spasmodically. It rose at a general rate of 1 metre every 100 years from 19,000 to 14,600 years ago. But then it rose very fast and increased by 5 metres every 100 years for 300 years, reaching 80 metres below current levels in that time. The sea then slowed until 13,000 years ago, by which time it had reached 60–64 metres below current levels. The sea rose another 20 metres by 10,000 years ago and continued to rise, reaching a metre or so above today's levels 7000 years ago. It then oscillated significantly with great variation around the country, reaching levels we see today by about 6500 years ago, rising again by a metre or so around 3600 years ago, and then falling to the present levels by 1500 years ago.[5]

As a consequence of this eternal flood, 25 per cent of greater Australia was drowned, almost 2.5 million square kilometres of land lost over a 13,000-year period. The average loss was over 190 square kilometres of land each year. At least 1.6 million square kilometres were drowned across the northern coastline of Australia. The land bridge underlying Torres Strait was breached between 8500 and 6500 years ago, and New Guinea became a distant and somewhat foreign island. The Bassian Plain was inundated, isolating Tasmania from 10,000 years ago. The seas had invaded Lake Carpentaria by 12,000 years ago, and over the next 2000 years turned the lake into a salty embayment. The vast coastline fronting the Pilbara was gone by 9000 years ago and the sea rushed across the Nullarbor Plain to reach the base of an escarpment we see as the Nullarbor Cliffs today by 11,500 years ago. Kangaroo Island was disconnected 9500 years ago, and the islands dotted along the western coast of Australia were formed between 12,000 and 7000 years ago.[6]

Castaway

What happened to the people who once lived on the millions of square kilometres that were drowned? What was their experience as landscapes they knew were lost under water? What happened to the social structure of communities whose ritual politic was embedded in land sequentially drowned? What were the social and political consequences for those responsible for that land, when their power to stop the flood was revealed impotent? And how did communities respond to geo-political tensions as their country was lost and they encroached on the lands of others? And what about the people whose country centred on the coastal hills and ridges, the broad plateaus and mountains that would in time become islands? How could they tell, as the sea rose, whether it would continue to rise: whether a mountain range would become a peninsula or, in time, an island—and whether that island itself would also go under water?

The rate of sea level rise was not so fast for these decisions to have been made immediately, but there was a time when decisions had to be made nonetheless. At some point a peninsula became an island,

and the island moved further and further from land. At some point people had to decide whether to stay or go—to leave their country or to stay, forever isolated from greater country and their broader community: isolated on home country now insular, with the ever-present possibility that the sea would continue to rise and consume it too.

The geographic impacts of the sea were comparatively minor on the more precipitous parts of the country—east of Wallen Wallen Creek and Burrill Lake, and west from Mandu Mandu shelter. Here the social and territorial changes required to cope with the rising seas were minor—the people had effectively always lived on the coast and the lateral impacts of sea level rise were small in the context of the vertical shores they encroached. But within that vertical displacement was an insidious threat—coastal people ran the risk of becoming island people, isolated from the mainland, without realising it.

In the Whitsunday Islands, for example, that very process of entrapment took place over 2000 years. People had moved to higher ground on Hook Island 10,000 years ago. They were camped in a small cave in Nara Inlet and the rising sea was just a few metres from their door. The island was then connected to the coast by a long, narrow peninsula, but this was cut 1000 years later, and over the next 2500 years the peninsula converted to a chain of islands. At first people travelled between the islands—they took water craft 2 kilometres to newly formed South Molle Island to obtain stone for tools. Perhaps they also travelled to the mainland coast. But then the distances eventually became too great, with the mainland over 30 kilometres away, and the people were left to cope on their own. They did so by becoming specialised marine foragers. They developed their own artistic traditions and a distinct social and linguistic identity. They invented new tools to suit their particular subsistence needs: fishhooks from shellfish and turtle shell, spear points from bone and wood, as well as nets and shell-scraping tools. They hunted everything from turtles to small pilot whales, as well as fish, crabs and shellfish.[7]

Further south, people also stayed on the mountain tops that were to form the Keppel Islands. Settlement contracted back to the newly forming islands 5000 years ago. These islands are 13 kilometres from the mainland coast and the people could connect over shorter distances by a dogleg through Pelican Island. Visits to the mainland were possible but distances were large and trips few—the remnant population was effectively isolated. Their language changed, rituals developed, the people became considerably smaller and inbred. Their material culture changed to suit their particular subsistence requirements. Implements that had little application disappeared from their tool kit: boomerangs disappeared and ground-edged axes were no longer made. The people had no shields (perhaps there was little conflict), and they stopped flaking stone for tools; natural rocks sufficed and they used shells when needed. They invented other tools instead: fishhooks made from turtle and coconut shell, stone drills for making fishhooks, sticks for digging yams, and harpoons with detachable heads for hunting turtles and sea mammals. They accessed the sea and other islands on communal logs paddled by hand.[8]

The rising sea was not devastating to the people on the northern Queensland coast—but it had an impact. Their experience creates a sense of the times: a forlorn sense of adaptive pressure, necessary specialisation and society lost, partnerships denied and territorial opportunity relinquished. One can visualise these small populations alone, but it's hard to imagine how they felt—within sight of the smokes and fires of their countrymen on adjacent shores, but just out of reach.

On the flatter coasts the lateral encroachment of the sea was more apparent, and people vacated the hilltops, ridges and peninsulas as the seas started to surround them. On the western coast, Noala Cave and the Montebello Islands were vacated between around 9000 and 8000 years ago. People also seem to have escaped the nearby Barrow Islands, and left the Recherche Archipelago and Rottnest further south before the seas cut them from the mainland.[9] But the people occupying the larger uplands, promontories and peninsulas were confronted by a more difficult situation. These larger areas may have seemed big enough for people to stay and survive. They might also have contained regional territories within which people preferred to stay. How could the occupants be aware of the long-term consequence of their attachment?

People lingered on the Bassian Plain, for example, as the seas closed in around them. There is a hearth in Cave Bay Cave on Hunter Island that is 15,400 years old and sees people still living there as the sea rose around them. Occupation then intensified as more people were compressed into the contracting country: the plains people were now living on an ever-decreasing peninsula. The peninsula became an island 6500 years ago. The last camp is 6600 years old: then cultural materials disappear—the people got out just in time.[10]

The people on Flinders Island to the east were not so lucky. They were forced back as the uplands were surrounded by water and became a large island (1300 square kilometres in area). The people of the plain seem to have known the sea was rising as the hills, forming smaller islands, were abandoned in time: human occupation on Badger Island and Prime Seal Island ceased abruptly 9000 years ago, after having been occupied since the glacial maximum 21,000 years ago. The retreat to Flinders Island was a miscalculation, but it must not have seemed so at the time. How could the people have known that the climate would change again and the island would not be big enough to sustain them? Nobody knows how many people stayed as the island formed, but they managed to live there for another 2000 years after the seas stabilised. One can only imagine what happened over those two millennia. The population may have declined slowly, until there were too few people to survive genetically. They are unlikely to have run out of food as they did not exploit all the resources available to them: the people were coastal foragers and did not exploit near-shore resources such as abalone and crayfish. They may have died of thirst, as the Holocene climate became more variable and drought became more common and extreme.[11] Climatic conditions declined drastically in the late Holocene and the people had no escape. Even with watercraft the seas are notoriously treacherous: the tidal current between Flinders Island and Tasmania is one of the strongest in the world, running at 10 kilometres an hour.[12] There was no way off and, as the climate dried, the people died.

The same thing happened on Kangaroo Island. Here people also contracted to the higher ground as the sea encroached. Kangaroo Island was at first a substantial promontory adjacent to the coast, becoming the island we see today about 6400 years ago. It is a large island—four times the size of Flinders Island—but was still not big enough. People had been living on the promontory and the surrounding plain since 16,000 years ago and seem to have withdrawn to it about 11,000 years ago as the sea encroached. There is evidence at the Seton site for more intense occupation at this time: more stone, more bone and charcoal, including two bone points that seem to have been used for working skins. But after this period evidence for occupation decreases: sparse scatters of stones and shell tell of a small, isolated population staying on the island. The last sites are 4300 years old, but people may have lived on, as the island was regularly burnt until 2500 years ago—perhaps the cessation of burning at that time marks the last signs of human life on the island.[13]

Flooding memories

The seas continued to rise on the adjacent coasts as the people on Flinders and Kangaroo islands were left behind. When the sea rose quickly, vast strips of coastline were lost. The sea moved inland at a rate of up to a metre a week on the Nullarbor Plain and covered so much lateral territory that an old man might have seen 2–3 kilometres of his country inundated in his lifetime; a favoured wombat hunting area under water in the space of one hunting season. Territories were lost, subsistence regimes altered, spiritual locations and religious pathways drowned at sea. Across the northern coasts of Australia rapid sea level rise may have consumed up to 5 kilometres of land in a year.[14]

Rising sea levels were a global phenomenon of such proportion and human impact that they appear to have been captured in cultural memory: there are over 500 myths about great floods across the planet.[15] The biblical flood may be one of them, the Australian narratives may be others. These narratives are of particular note as they invariably account for sea level rise in the context of the land that existed before it—they are myths of palaeo-environmental context, less about the formation of the sea as it is seen and might be understood in the present and more about the coast as it changed through antiquity. Together they form a remarkable body of religious lore that must be at least 6500, if not 10,000, years old. These narratives are thus among the oldest known parables in the world.

The Australian accounts are typically associated with the flattest country—where the impacts of post-glacial sea level rise were greatest and most visible: the Gulf of Carpentaria, coastal Arnhem Land, the Bassian Plain, the Nullarbor Plain and Rottnest Island.[16] On the northern coast, for example, mythology describes how the Gulf of Carpentaria was formed when a raft was dragged across the land and created a channel that filled with sea water. On Groote Eylandt there are two mythological accounts that relate to desert Tjukurrpa and reveal connections to the desert when the Gulf of Carpentaria was land. It is also told that Elcho Island, off the coast of Arnhem Land, was severed from the mainland when a stick was pushed into the ground and the sea rushed in. Joseph Bonaparte Gulf was flooded when endless rains came and the sea rose, threatening to extinguish fire then maintained by mythological beings.

On the southern coast of Australia the Bassian Plain was drowned after children found a sacred object. The land gave way, the seas moved in and many people died. Port Phillip Bay is described in mythology as a flat, fertile plain, inundated when a large storm blew up and the sea flooded in. Backstairs Passage, between Fleurieu Peninsula and Kangaroo Island, was formed when an ancient mythical being ordered the waters to rise and drown his fleeing wives. Stories of a great flood account for Spencer Gulf in South Australia, and a great fire swept across the ancient coastal plains of the Swan River and cracked the earth, letting the sea flood in and separating Rottnest Island from the mainland.[17]

All desert Tjukurrpa on the Nullarbor Plain relate to the emergence of the sea. The myth of the Wati Kutjara ends abruptly where the Two Men went into the water, via a soak at the Head of Bight.

A man sitting under the shade of a shelter made from dry mulga trunks, surrounded by mulga trees. Mulga was rarely burnt as it provides excellent wood for tools and was an ideal habitat for kangaroos. The shelters were also used during wet weather (Tomkinson Ranges, northwestern South Australia).

They are immortalised as two pillars out to sea (one having fallen over recently). In another story, fire is almost extinguished by the rising sea—in an analogous manner to the account from the Joseph Bonaparte Gulf—while the aunty of those who saved it sat cross-legged on the plains pushing up a barrier in an attempt to stop the sea rising any further. In another story, large numbers of mythological birds, embodying the People of the Sun and the Shadow, crossed the desert to build a rampart of spears. The first part of this story relates to the desiccation across the desert (described in Chapter 3), and the second part concludes with attempts to contain the great flood that followed it. The plight to stop the rising seas is replete with consequence and desperation—of land being lost, of people and animals dying, and country submerged; a story of distress lest the attempt fail. The story has other sequential components that describe the re-watering of the desert: the filling of rock holes and the re-emergence of the underground waters that support human life today. It is a story of prevention and rectification, completing the Tjukurrpa already described about the desiccation of the desert that took place beforehand. The mythology is consistent with what we know of climate change in the Holocene.[18]

War and conflict

The impact of Holocene sea level rise on the Nullarbor Plain is as dramatic as anywhere in Australia and, perhaps because of this, it is possible to see an archaeological signature of its social and economic consequences. The first sign we have of an encroaching sea is the appearance of a fragment of abalone (*Haliotis*) in Allen's Cave 14,700 years ago. The sea had then risen to be 65 kilometres from the site. The shell fragment shows wear reminiscent of having been hung as a pendant—and suggests coastal people were on the move (or that local trade with them was activated for the first time). Two fragments of cockle (*Katelysia*) then appear in the site 3000 years later, equivalent to about 11,000 years ago when the sea had reached the base of the present Nullarbor Cliffs, 8 kilometres to the south of Allen's Cave. The cockle fragments sit just below a massive hearth dated between 9500 and 10,000 years ago. This hearth is the largest feature and is associated with the greatest concentration and diversity of artefacts in the occupational history at the site. Discard rates are three times higher than average, and the range of raw material diversifies from local limestone to include flint, tektites and silcrete. The flint was acquired from the eroding cliff face not far away, but the tektites and the silcrete must have come from the sandy deserts over 300 kilometres to the north.[19]

The appearance of shells and exotic stone means that people were on the move. The artefacts suggest coastal people were in contact with desert people—if not through physical movement then through trade. The increase in occupational intensity suggests more people sheltered at the site as the sea lapped against the cliffs nearby. This occupational peak alludes, in the context of the spartan cultural profile preceding it, to a time of cultural change—mobility, demographic readjustment and social adaptation—in response to extreme geographic change. The concentrated occupational event suggests a demographic ripple, a human bow wave, in the face of the encroaching seas.[20]

Other examples of occupation intensity and social reconfiguration are seen elsewhere across the southern coast, in similar locations and geographic settings. Seashells and coastal flint are found at the Seton site on Kangaroo Island, for example, between 16,000 and 11,000 years ago—when the sea was 50 kilometres away from the cave. At 11,000 years ago there was an intense phase of occupation when the sea was 16 kilometres from the site. It suggests people compressing back to the large promontory that would soon form an island. To the west there is a peak in occupation at Cheetup Cave, near Cape Le Grand, between 13,000 and 8000 years ago. In the southwest of Western Australia, fragments of marine shell appear in Tunnel Cave at a time when the cave was still 35 kilometres from the sea. Mussel shells appear in Devil's Lair 12,000 years ago, and there is a rich phase of occupation between 13,000 and 12,000 years ago—thought to signify increased population levels resulting from sea level rise.[21]

The archaeological signature is as strong here as the perceived consequences of sea level rise on the resident population are likely to have been. But there is also a signal of occupational intensity across the entire continent at this time. There is a small increase in the number of new sites and newly occupied sites across the continent between 12,000 and 10,000 years ago. The change is just a blip on the ancestral radar, but it is there nonetheless. It becomes a step in south-eastern New South Wales between 11,000 and 9000 years ago, and in the Queensland Central Highlands 13,000–9000 years ago. That step becomes a prominent and abnormal peak in the Magnificent Gallery in southeast Cape York between 12,000 and 9000 years ago. Here there is a major increase in ochre residues accompanied by a lesser peak in stone artefacts. The peak in ochre is notable and indicates an unparalleled increase in the use of the pigment at the site.[22] One might ask why.

Ochre is used in a number of social contexts. The most obvious is rock painting, and the massive increase in ochre at the Magnificent Gallery suggests a proportional burst of artistic activity. But ochre also has other functions. It is also used to decorate wooden implements and people—notably men in social and ceremonial contexts—and it is used medicinally when mixed with goanna fat or saliva as an antiseptic.[23] The variety of functions point to multiple reasons for the abnormal increase in ochre at the Magnificent Gallery: more artistic activity, more decoration of more wooden implements, more social visitation, more ceremonial activity and more injury in need of attention. Some interpretations are more likely than others, but nevertheless the peak in ochre (and the shadowed increase in stone tools) conveys a moment in time when people were engaged in greater social, ceremonial and creative activity. This moment was in fact a period of a few thousand years which coincided with the arrival of the sea at the door of contemporary geographic Australia. If there was a pressing need for social insignia (in so far as the decoration attached itself to people) and geographic tattoo (in so far as the decoration attached itself to land) this was the time. The ochre thus speaks of social and geographic identification at a time when land was in increasingly short supply. It may reflect emergent social and geographic demarcation in response to heightened social anxiety and territorial pressure.

There is more than a hint of this anxiety and pressure in the art of Arnhem Land. Here, for the first time in history, there are images of the ancient nomads in combat. These images are probably about 10,000 years old and are thus the earliest images of human combat anywhere in the world. The paintings portray men in various acts of aggression: running, dodging, waving weapons, throwing boomerangs and volleys of spears. The figures are highly decorated and their weaponry is detailed. There are paintings of people with spears, and paintings of people with spears through their bodies. Some images show people bending to help others who have been speared. Hand-to-hand combat is displayed, violent fighting, boomerangs impacting limbs and directed towards heads. There are images of prostrate bodies with spears plunged into them as well as individuals fighting and groups of people at war. In Deaf Adder Gorge 19 figures stand in a group. Nearby, six others bend with barbed spears grouped in sets of three above their heads. A man lies dead on his stomach. One reaches down to a wounded friend, their arms outstretched. Another bends, holding the arms of a countryman as he too receives a spear in his leg—such is the consequence of compassion. It is a scene of death and defeat against which 12 warriors walk away, their backs to the battle scene, in victory.[24]

The frequency of warrior art increases through time so that by 6000 years ago the battle scenes become larger and more complicated: groups of over 60 people in combat with arsenals of barbed, pronged and stone-tipped spears, spear-throwers, hafted stone axes, boomerangs and hooked clubs. There are figures painted with mouths open in pain and anguish. One painting sees a pregnant women carrying

Extracting a spear-thrower from a mulga trunk was a slow process. The weight of the stone and the strength and skill of the craftsman counterbalance the limitations of the tool.

The craftsman holds a spear-thrower with a hafted adzing blade in his left hand and the tip of a composite hunting spear in his right. The tip and the barb of the spear are attached by kangaroo sinews, an ideal strapping as it is pliable when wet and shrinks tight.

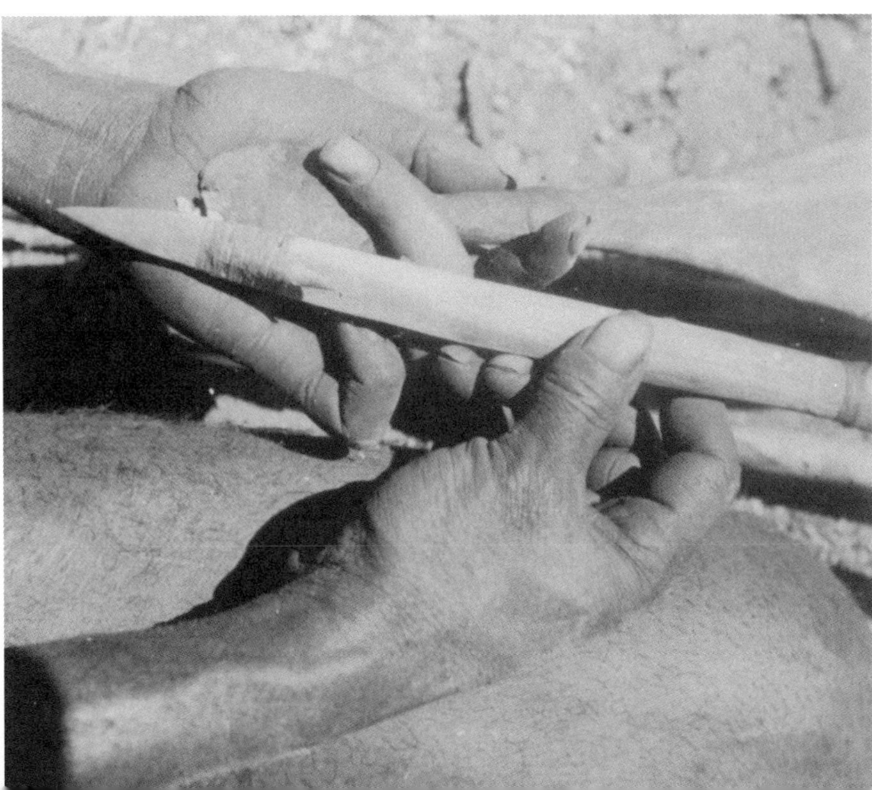

a dilly bag lanced by 18 spears. The violence is apparent, the reasons for it implicit.

The social dynamic had changed from the remote past: the climate had warmed and the seas had expanded. There was less space for the people to live in. Competition for resources had increased in proportion to the need to defend them: Pleistocene systems of social inclusion became Holocene systems of exclusion. Combat was a predictable outcome of the great climatic shift, and saw the development of more particular mechanisms for demarcating communal space and defining individual rights to land.

Technological innovation

People also responded to the increased demands on country and resources by developing a more efficient tool kit. The boomerang, barbed spears and spear-thrower seen in the warrior art of Arnhem Land are perhaps the most obvious examples of those new developments, but people also used a range of smaller, more effective stone tools. The artistic vision of technological innovation in the north is given material form in the south where 25 ancient wooden artefacts were discovered at Wyrie Swamp, near Millicent, South Australia. The artefacts include digging sticks, pointed stakes, short spears, two barbed spears and nine boomerangs. They are over 10,000 years old—which makes the barbed spears and the boomerangs the oldest in the world. The boomerangs are returning boomerangs—a remarkable invention for the time that required each end of an elbow-shaped boomerang to be shaped to a different aerodynamic plane. The boomerangs were developed as artefacts of decoy: thrown into the air to unsettle birds so they could be trapped in nets raised on poles. The boomerangs speak of sophisticated technological and strategic thinking—a communal solution to individual need.[25]

Elsewhere, boomerangs are used as throwing sticks,[26] designed to kill or knock out an intended target. I recall quite recently on a

The oldest returning boomerang in the world, dated to over 10,000 years, from Wyrie Swamp, South Australia.

bush trip in the Great Victoria Desert seeing a goanna in a branch of a tree. I radioed the car behind me, and before I had even got out to observe, the driver of the rear vehicle had snapped a dry branch, thrown it and knocked the goanna from the tree, where it lay stunned on the ground. The accuracy and speed of the kill was worthy of Test cricket, and gives some idea of how deadly boomerangs were in the hands of the hunter. Throwing-boomerangs were designed with aerodynamic twist to fly straight and fast. They were cut from branches that were already curved, and then carved, heated and twisted with visible mastery. Throwing-boomerangs were asymmetrical in plan, the longer end used for leverage, and the shorter end weighted and shaped to cartwheel the blade, enlarge the parameter of attack and enhance the chance of a successful kill. They are made from extremely hard wood and so form a deadly blade-like club.

I once saw a man hit on the head with one, resulting in severe brain damage, and can appreciate how effective they must have been as a weapon 10,000 years ago.

Other technological improvements included the development of composite tools: tools with spare parts and tools that could be mended rather than replaced. Spears are a good example, and were developed with detachable heads and ends so the parts most subject to damage could be replaced with ease. Multipurpose tools were also invented. The spear-thrower is the best example. It was, in a sense, the original Swiss Army Knife: one implement, many functions. Its primary purpose was to launch a spear further, more easily, without loss of accuracy. The design was ingenious: the spear-thrower was arched and curved so as to enhance longitudinal strength while lowering its weight. The lateral curve improved rigidity and created a container. Its handle was bulbous for grip and allowed the attachment of a stone blade (for cutting) or a discoidal flake (for adzing). The fine outer lip of its lateral margin was hard and sharp, and could be rubbed across a dry branch to make fire: a spear-thrower was a weapon, a woodworking tool, a container and a fire lighter.

The discoidal adzing flake and the stone blade were part of significant technological improvements to the traditional stone tool kit in the Holocene. Improvements in stone tool production, craftsmanship and design allowed the production of lighter, more efficient tools: blades for cutting, adzes for woodwork, scrapers for scraping, engravers for carving—for all aspects of food processing, woodworking and home maintenance. The benefits were both direct and indirect. Engraving tools, for example, had artistic ritual intent and functional benefits—they were used to engrave sacred religious narratives on wooden tablets and to flute boomerangs to reduce drag in flight.[27]

One of the signature tools of the recent era was a small blade that, when flaked, was chipped blunt on one side, forming a 'backed' edge on a sharp blade, not unlike the blade of a small pocketknife. These artefacts first appear in the archaeological record 15,000 years ago.[28] They increase in quantity and frequency through time, with more appearing 9000 years ago, and peak astronomically about 4000 years ago, when at some sites their production increased 200-fold, with literally thousands and thousands of them in primary areas of production across the southern part of the country.[29] Their abundance, diagnostic symmetry and aesthetic appeal allude to a range of interesting and arresting functions. They were effective cutting and scraping tools, and were clearly used for these purposes. But they were also hafted and aligned as serrations on saw-toothed knives and as blades on the tips of spears. Examination of microscopic residues on the tools reveals bone, red blood cells, collagen fibre, muscle fibre, fat and feathers as well as resin, plant fibre and cellulose.[30]

The tools had many functions, but an important one seems to have been killing: if not animals then people—death through impact, laceration, blood loss and infection. A rather unpleasant contextual example comes from a body at Narrabeen on the northern beaches of Sydney. The burial is of a man of about 35 years of age who was killed 3700 years ago—at the height of backed-blade production and near the peak in glacial sea level rise. Fourteen artefacts were found with the body, 12 of which were backed blades. The blades show damage from impact as either spear barbs or knives. One is wedged into the man's spine, and another seems to have been used as an awl for puncturing and working skin; its position with the body suggests it was being carried in the hair of the man when he was killed. The man was speared in the back. The spear entered his body just above the left hip, where it passed through his small and large intestines, and possibly his kidney, before lodging in his spine. He was also speared from the front, and then killed on the ground by being clubbed on the head (perhaps with a stone axe) and speared in the skull. His body was left unburied on the sand dune.

The manner of the unfortunate man's death points both to the use of backed blades in conflict, and to the extreme social and environmental circumstances at the time. The death occurred at, and is seen to be associated with, a time of social change and increasing cultural proscription, when sea levels were at their highest and increased territoriality and social conflict were at their greatest. The death also coincides with an increased production of rock art in the area and, in the same way that art in the Magnificent Gallery in Queensland may indicate ancient social and territorial adjustment, the diversity of engravings here seems to demonstrate territorial division—in a time of highest sea level, diminished territory, climatic variability and contingent population pressure. Human conflict was a national characteristic at the time, with evidence of violent disputation across populated areas such as the Murray River bordering on organised warfare.[31]

The killing at Narrabeen may of course have been a judicial killing, an isolated event in an otherwise peaceful world. This was a common enough activity in the past, and might place the death less as an indication of territorial conflict and barbaric murder than the execution of unflinching social justice. A comparative example comes from the desert. I did not know the central figure in this saga, but I knew his children well and was taken to the location of his killing. He was renowned for his strength and size, and for having 'too many' wives. One wife ran away with her lover. The big man pursued them, tracking them for over 100 kilometres before killing the lover. The big man was then punished in kind. Senior men travelled from each of the neighbouring districts to attend his killing, possibly to ensure his successful execution. Each witness participated in the killing, conducted with large stone knives. The big man was stabbed to death, 'nobody stopping' until he was dead.[32] The killing appears to have been rather brutal; the big man was, by all accounts, chopped to pieces. With the killing complete, the unfortunate matter was over.

Domesticated dogs

Regardless of the context of and reason for the death of the Narrabeen man, the associated technology and timing of his death point to a general conclusion: the mid Holocene seems to have been a particularly turbulent time. People were seeking efficiencies and security in a time of social and territorial adjustment that was congruent with the rising seas. People were on the move and their technology and social systems were evolving. People began to demarcate space more rigidly and exploit most resources more effectively. They developed mechanisms for storage, domesticated food and improved its production. People everywhere became more sedentary, more aware of their territorial limits and necessary rights—and developed ways of protecting both. The whole world was suffering in the same way: less land, more isolation and greater geographic fragmentation. Britain became an island, the Americas were severed from the Euro-Russian continent. The coastal catastrophe of the Australian shores was magnified to the north. While Australia lost about one-third of its landmass, Indonesia lost two-thirds: the huge glacial landmass of ancient Indonesia reduced from 6 million to less than 2 million square kilometres across 13,000 islands. One might imagine a degree of displacement, and the movement of some of the displaced to Australia.[33]

There is evidence for at least two such migrations in the Holocene. The first occurred 7000 years ago, when people arrived from Indonesia with an individual carrying a neurodegenerative disease called Machado-Joseph disease. People in communities in eastern Arnhem Land have that disease today. It is a terrible affliction that results in loss of muscle control and coordination. The localised nature of the disease on Groote Eylandt in the Gulf of Carpentaria and Yirrkala on the Gove Peninsula indicate this is where the original migration took place, and where the immigrants subsequently stayed.[34]

The second migration occurred about 5000 years ago. We know people came to Australia then because they brought their pet—the Asian dog, or dingo. The dogs caught on as a domestic pet in Australia and soon became family friends and hunting companions all over the continent. They appear to have been eaten as well: a kind of all-purpose pet. Dingo remains are found everywhere across Australia by 3000 years ago. Genetic indications are that they were

originally domesticated dogs from southeastern Asia and came from a small number of dogs brought here in a single migratory event. Their arrival was followed by the mainland extinction of the thylacine 3300 years ago.[35] The two are probably linked: both directly in so far as the dingo hunted in packs and may have outcompeted the tiger, and indirectly as an added burden in a world already under strain from climate change, more effective human predation and the likely conjunction of people and dingoes as a hunting team.

Beside the seaside

One of the positives of the rising seas was the creation of an intricate and productive shoreline around significant parts of Australia's new coast. That coastline is so convoluted it has never been properly measured: different scales of linear detail produce different estimates of distance. A generalised outline of Australia reveals about 15,000 kilometres of coast, but if measured millimetre by millimetre the coastline is over 130,000 kilometres in length. At mid tide (with mangrove swamps included but coastal reefs, tiny islands and small estuaries excluded) it is about 50,000 kilometres. If measured at 100-metre intervals the coast is 70,000 kilometres, but if plotted at 500-metre intervals it is just over 35,000 kilometres. It is nonetheless one of the longest coastlines in the world and is described in most atlases as 36,000 kilometres in length. But a large part of our coastline contains many islands and these add another 24,000 kilometres—40 per cent of the actual coastline of Australia—making the real total coastline closer to 60,000 kilometres long.

The difference in detail was probably significant to the hunter-gatherers, who lived off every metre of it. They occupied a new coastal environment, but one that varied significantly in terms of its

Opposite: A husband and wife carry all they need for desert survival: the man a spear and spear-thrower, the woman a wooden dish and digging stick. They are accompanied by their dog, part dingo (colouring and fur) and part kangaroo dog (length, curved back and long legs).

productive capacity and foraging opportunity: 50 per cent became sandy beaches or barrier beaches; 30 per cent became tidal flats and mangroves; 10 per cent stood as largely inaccessible cliffs with minor beaches; and the rest turned into estuaries. This was the environmental diversity that eventually presented itself to the coast-foragers in the mid to late Holocene. It was not a fertile coast by global standards, as nutrient levels are comparatively low, but it was productive enough: 3600 species of fish, 2000 species of crustaceans and tens of thousands of species of molluscs.[36]

That diversity saw coastal economies develop differently at different times in different places. The people of the temperate, humid east and south coasts became, or perhaps remained, specialised coastal fishers. They lived on a steep coastal shoreline and were never far from the sea: evidence for their fishing economies exists from over 9000 years ago and presumably goes back to the earliest of times. There are almost 20,000 sites recorded along the 4600 kilometres of the New South Wales, Victorian and Tasmanian coasts. They are the most frequent, densest and largest coastal sites in the country. Site densities might often be as high as 50 sites per kilometre, and an average of one to six sites per kilometre is quite normal. The largest middens contain over 30,000 cubic metres of cultural deposit, with between 30,000 and 40,000 shells per cubic metre. These are huge sites, testimony to the intensity of coastal settlement in this part of the country.[37]

On the north coast of New South Wales, for example, some sites are so large observers first thought they had been deposited by tidal waves. One of those, the North Creek midden, is over 33,000 cubic metres in volume with 45,000 shells per cubic metre: a tidal wave of human consumption. The Wombah midden on the Clarence River is equally large, and both indicate a particularly specialised foraging economy. The Wombah midden, for example, contains 97 per cent shellfish—mostly oysters, with small amounts of quoll, bandicoot, possum, wallaby and dingo. There is enough food at this site to feed 30 people for four weeks every year over the 3200 years of the site's occupation. The surrounding country was then scrub and grasslands maintained by fire—considerably different from the impenetrable cedar forest growing in the district when settlers arrived in the 1900s.[38]

The Clybucca midden complex, near Stuarts Point, is even bigger—over 200,000 cubic metres in size. It is also a shell-fishing camp and is mainly composed of cockles. The camping area was originally established 5000 years ago beside a newly formed estuary, but the estuary began to enclose following sedimentation from devegetation caused by burning. The estuary became a mangrove swamp 3700 years ago and the economy switched to mud oysters (with a tiny contribution of fish and marsupials). The swamps then silted up completely 2500 years ago and the people moved on.[39]

Further south, there is evidence of greater diversification in the marine economies of the Holocene as time went on. At Birubi Point near Newcastle, for example, people collected masses of pipi, limpet and periwinkle shells as well as mussels, turbo and sea urchins 500 years ago. Fishhooks had been invented a few hundred years previously and the fishers caught an impressive array of fish: 23 species including bream, drummer, flathead, mullet, shark, snapper, salmon, trevally and whiting. A few land animals were eaten there as well—a small amount of bandicoot, some kangaroo, a dingo, half a dozen lizards and a dozen mutton-birds.[40]

At Currarong in Jervis Bay people collected oysters near their camp, and hunted and gathered every other imaginable resource over a period of 4000 years: bat, rat, dingo, whale, wallaby, shellfish, crow, cormorant, gull, shearwater, abalone, turbo, crab, to name a few of the 56 species represented. They also employed a diverse tool kit, including small stone tools, fishhooks, fishhook files and bone points.[41]

The vision of dense populations on these temperate humid coasts contrasts with the more sparsely populated temperate arid coasts of southern and western Australia. Here there are about 9000 recorded sites (excluding the Pilbara) along 18,000 kilometres of coastline—an average density of just half to one site per kilometre of coastline. There are huge stretches of coast where little site recording has taken place, and there are huge stretches of coast with few sites on them. Shell middens are almost non-existent. There are, for example, just 60 sites containing shell out of 1200 sites recorded along 1300 kilometres of coastline around southwestern Australia. There was no specialised fishing technology (such as fishhooks), and there were no watercraft between Kangaroo Island in the south and Shark Bay in the northwest of Australia.[42]

The largest sites on the arid South Australian coast (approximating the smallest shell middens on the east coast) are 6700 years old. They convey a sense of coastal people compressing on the hinterland as sea levels peaked around them, with the subsequent economic tradition being terrestrial with selective input from the sea. These coastal people were not specialised coastal foragers like those on the east coast. Perhaps the reason was environmental—relating to limited fresh water, low population density, low coastal productivity and material survival. Perhaps it was also cultural. The remains of the past give an impression of people with desert traditions living by the sea: they hunted land animals and occasionally collected large shellfish and killed sea mammals.

A chance encounter with a recent coastal campsite on the far west coast of South Australia provides a fair insight into the nature of coastal subsistence on the arid coast in the past. This site, on Long Beach to the west of Ceduna, was exposed by an unusually large southwesterly storm. The people once camping there had eaten one tammar wallaby, four brush-tailed bettongs, one burrowing bettong, one western barred bandicoot, two dunnarts, one emu, one dingo, some hopping mice and stick-nest rats, as well as some skinks and goannas. They had also caught a few wrasse, one crab and one penguin. Beach subsistence at Long Beach sites sits in complete contrast to coastal economies on the east coast.[43]

Interest in marine foods is similar on the southern dry coasts today, where most Indigenous people have a shovel for wombat hunting rather than a rod for fishing. Curiously, the contemporary Australian population shares this dietary characteristic. Australians see themselves as beach-loving people and 85 per cent of us live on the coast, looking out to sea. Fishing is our third most popular sport, yet, ironically, only 14,000 people fish full time and seafood is an incidental part of our dietary intake: the average consumption of seafood is only about 8 kilograms per person per year.[44] In that sense, Australians are landlubbers who live by the sea, as were the old inhabitants of the arid coasts.

The arid coast of northwestern Australia reveals similar patterns of coastal subsistence. Coastal occupation is seen again here about 12,000 years ago when sea levels rose and people returned to old coastal haunts not occupied since the Pleistocene. People returned to the Jansz site, for example, 12,000 years ago. They ate mud whelks (*Terebralia*) from the establishing mangroves. Coastal occupation and limited marine subsistence continued through the Holocene, but people did not camp in Mandu Mandu shelter again until 2500 years ago. They were back at the Silver Dollar site in Shark Bay by 7500 years ago, with similar subsistence habits to those of 12,000 years before. They hunted bettongs and wallabies, collected emu eggs and shellfish, and caught some fish (whiting and snapper) in rock pools and coastal stonefish traps.

The Buccaneer Archipelago had returned from the coastal plain and people moved back to Koolan Island from about 10,000 years ago. People were also living near the sea on the mainland coast at Widgingarri rock shelter 8700 years ago. Their economy was a mixture of both terrestrial and marine resources. As the sea rose and settled around 6000 years ago, visits to the islands became intermittent. People occupied one island, however, called High Cliffy Island, as early as 7000 years ago, and appear to have lived there permanently from about 3500 to 1000 years ago. The island was then vacated and reoccupied about 650 years ago. It has a complicated history and a complex cultural heritage. The island is only 20 square kilometres in area but contains rock shelters, open sites, butchering sites, quarries and hundreds of stone structures. Some are aligned as pathways, cairns and standing stones. Some structures appear to be the remains of villages. The occupational intensity is notable, the diet largely marine: fish, shellfish, dugong, turtle and sea birds.[45]

People were also living along the Pilbara coast. There are many sites here, sometimes as many as 50 sites for every kilometre of coast. The new cultural regime is displayed visually with the appearance of marine species such as turtles, dugong and fish engraved over older engravings of terrestrial animals made when the rocks were a long way inland. As the sea level rose, mangroves colonised the coast and people began exploiting the resources they contained. The sites are small—in the order of 100 shells per square metre. The mangroves declined as a food resource as sedimentation increased about 6000 years ago, and people turned to the sandy beaches. One site in the Skew Valley on the Burrup Peninsula reveals the change: exploitation of mangrove species (*Terebralia*) around 6000 years ago and cockles (*Anadara*) from around 4000 years ago. Other foods included crabs, catfish, barramundi, wrasse and wallabies. Shellfish collection appears to have been a minor link in the wider chain of coastal settlement and resource exploitation.[46]

Coastal sedimentation was a major feature of the ancient coast and the ancient culture across northern Australia. The impacts of sedimentation were dramatic—more dramatic perhaps than the changes in sea levels that initiated them. In Roebuck Bay, near Broome, for example, there is a large coastal site that is now 20 kilometres inland. It contains at least 200,000 cockles and mud whelks spread over about 10,000 square metres. The site is 3000 years old and was once close to the sea. It became removed from it as sediments washed from the land and filled the bay.[47]

The coasts on the northern half of Australia reveal a consistent pattern of coastal adaptation resulting from this kind of sedimentation. From northern New South Wales to the Pilbara there is a millennial pattern of adaptation and change: successful settlement on newly formed coastlines followed by erosion and sedimentation resulting in abandonment and resettlement. People were in a constant state of economic and territorial unrest as the Holocene wound its variable way. It was a period of economic variability and difficulty, disruption and strategic readjustment in a constant cycle of reinvention.

The experience is writ large on the tropical coasts of Arnhem Land and Cape York. Here the rising seas created large gulfs from existing valleys, such as the Van Diemen Gulf facing the South Alligator River. Mangroves then grew on the muddy estuarine shores. They extended massively—in the case of the South Alligator River, mangroves covered around 80,000 hectares. People exploited the estuaries about 8000 years ago before they were choked by sedimentation, became more saline and were vegetated with sedges and grasses (6000–4000 years ago). Marshes and swamps began to form, from which the floodplains we see today developed over the last 1500 years. New economic strategies were required. Marine subsistence continued on the ocean shores many kilometres away, where people exploited huge quantities of cockles (*Anadara*), and left massive mounds and long, thick shell middens along the sandy beaches from about 3000 years ago.[48]

Painting new country

The history and character of the estuarine period in Arnhem Land is captured in its imagery. Images of combat disappear. Boomerangs are no longer in use (presumably ineffectual in the swampy, forested floodplains), and new forms of spears and spear-throwers emerge.[49] Extraordinary figures of men shaped and attached in beeswax replace warriors on rock walls. These figures are sculpted as much as painted, and contain creative material additions of stones, feathers, flowers, seeds, sticks and grass: hippies replace warriors. The oldest beeswax figure is 4000 years old. The terrestrial animals of the great past have gone, to be replaced with barramundi, mullet, catfish and saltwater crocodiles. This is the X-ray art for which Arnhem Land is so famous. It is descriptive and decorative art that seeks to portray both animal form and animal anatomy. The paintings depict muscle fibre, bone structure, fat, nerves and organs: heart, lungs, liver, kidneys, and so on. This is art of elaboration, vastly complicated and abundant—typically featuring white pigment, purple haematite and red ochre with polychromatic additions. Humans also appear—perhaps the first anatomical drawings of people ever made. The drawings of human anatomy are less detailed (presumably because the insides of people were less frequently seen), with depictions limited to exposed, notable and inferable anatomical features such as the aesophagus, ribs, backbone, long bones, joints, testicles, scrotum, labia and vulva, and nipples (and milk ducts, interestingly).[50]

As the estuaries began to close, the merging plains caught more sediment and large wetlands slowly grew across northern Australia. The ecological change is mirrored in the artistic accounts of the country. Freshwater birds and water lilies appear in the galleries, as do people hunting from paperbark rafts with specialised spears and iconic goose-wing fans. Didgeridoos appear for the first time. The art becomes distinctive and artistic distinction is accompanied by linguistic variation and differing mythological representations of country. There is a sense of regionalism in the social and cultural geography. Differences in style and story seem to reflect differences in claims on and rights to country: named clans in known country inherited and managed through descent, diagnosed through art and religion.[51]

The depiction of country and the expression of belief about country is also apparent in the artistic style elsewhere in northern Australia. Motifs of regional identity, for example, are recognisable through northwest and central Queensland, where connection between life, fertility, death and country is captured and expressed through art. The association is sensed through graphic emphasis and physical association between country, artistic representation, human burials and burial goods. The conjunction between image and material and between spirit and place is explained and asserted through motif. Artistic insignia becomes emphatic and emotive demonstration between people, their country and their ancestral spirituality. Similar correlations are seen through the highlands in northern Queensland (after about 3000 years ago) and in Cape York: art as social identity and regional association.[52]

Differing art appears to have indicated differing territorial relationships in the range country of the Hawkesbury River around Sydney (as mentioned already in relation to the death of the man at Narrabeen). In this region engravings are the dominant visual representation. Common motifs include emus, fish, macropods and men. There are also other less common depictions of women, mythological beings, snakes and various tools (such as shields and axes). The way these less common subjects are drawn varies across the region and, in conjunction with the more common motifs, implies regional cultural diversity within a broader social universe. Combined, the works convey a stylistic patterning synonymous with regional social cohesion and

Gadigal elder Allen Madden and Jo McDonald examine an engraving near Sydney of a family that portrays a man with his stone axe and a woman with her dilly bag. Slight differences in rock art design point to slight differences in territory.

linguistic identity (associated with the common motifs), and internal cultural variability, territoriality and social identity (associated with the style and distribution of the less common motifs).[53]

Agriculture and aquaculture

In southeastern Australia and the lower Murray–Darling Basin similar shadows of territoriality can be seen through the distribution of material goods during the last 3000–4000 years. Here it is possible to trace the movement of precious ground-edged axes from their source quarries across country to their final destinations. Some axes were traded up to 300 kilometres from their source, through recognisable redistribution centres. The distribution of the axes mirrors linguistic areas, accords with known traditional territorial relations, and reflects social affinities (where the axes were traded) and hostilities (where they were not). Redistribution centres are known ceremonial locations.[54]

The pattern here represents degrees of socio-geographic definition—of groups aligned and unaligned, and populations in conflict and accord. The strength of demarcation suggests high population density and alludes to a concurrent need to define, manage and protect territory. This was also the case across the Murray–Darling Basin, where the population seems to have been particularly high. Hunting and gathering techniques became more specialised along the rivers as population levels increased. Freshwater mussel middens line the river banks for kilometres and stand in demographic contrast to the small, occasional middens seen around the Willandra Lakes in the Pleistocene.[55] Technology also became more sophisticated. People made fish nets up to 90 metres long, built extensive stone-walled fish traps, weirs and wickerwork traps. Animals were driven into communal hunting nets as well as speared individually.

The great importance of seeds becomes apparent about 3500 years ago. Seed production was managed through fire. Storage facilities were developed that included underground pits, grass containers (pottery-like with their coatings of mud) and bags of wallaby or kangaroo skin. There is a record, in arid Australia, of over 1000 kilograms of seeds being stored in 175 wooden dishes, each almost 2 metres long and 30 centimetres deep. The production of food from seeds was hard work and required hours of collection, winnowing and processing. Its emphasis in this era suggests a need for reliable food production in a time of larger, more sedentary, populations. The material inventory and system of food production in the later Holocene suggests social cooperation, strategic effort and maximised returns in an economy underpinned by planning and efficiency.[56]

In the southwest of Victoria, for example, there are over 70 large earth mounds set on high ground overlooking fertile land. The mounds are set over an area of 120 square kilometres, with the largest mound cluster covering about 4 hectares. This cluster was associated ethnohistorically with a village of 2500 people. The mounds were habitually maintained and resurfaced as hut foundations, campsites and cooking areas. The huts were made from a framework of boughs bent to form a dome. The oldest mounds were in use over 2500 years ago.[57]

There are also other mounds along the Murrumbidgee, Wakool, Murray and Macquarie rivers. On the Macquarie there are 63 mounds spread along the riverside, with a density of about three mounds per hectare. These also date to 2500 years ago and contain stone artefacts and food remains—marsupial bones, emu eggs, freshwater crayfish, frogs, fish and shellfish. Some have hearths, burials and hut foundations. The distribution of mounds within the Murray–Darling Basin conforms to the distribution of the yam daisy (*Microseris*), and suggests the mounds might also have been used as, or were associated with, gardens.[58]

The emerging sense of cooperative agriculture and communal food collection is reinforced by the development of large-scale drainage systems near Toolondo in western Victoria. The drainage system extended for over 3 square kilometres. The people who constructed it used natural elevations to create a hydraulic system that moved water at swift speeds between swamps so as to flush eels and fish into the drains where they were caught in funnel-shaped wicker traps. The drainage system had the added advantage of draining water from the plains during flood and maintaining water in the swamps during drought. It was a system designed to control water and harvest fish: perhaps the first aquaculture on earth. The system would have taken ten men about six months to construct (although the system probably evolved and grew over a period of time) and required ongoing maintenance: it was a feature of significant community effort, management and benefit.[59]

There is further evidence of ancient hydraulic engineering amongst the Gunditjmara, near Lake Condah in southwest Victoria. A complex series of channels and stone fish-traps were created over the last 9000 years (see Plate 45). The purpose of the channels and the traps was to drain and capture water, fish and eels as water levels changed around the lake. The older traps were low and small and worked during floods, but the operators saw the need to improve the traps and increase their size to maximise resources during normal lake levels. By 2000 years ago the engineers were overseeing the excavation of local basalt and the construction of stone walls 6 metres high. This improved water management and resulted in aquaculture throughout the year: these were the first fish farmers in the world.[60]

Another important land-management tool through the Holocene was fire. The intentional use of fire aided communication, improved access, maximised hunting and gathering, and maintained and extended productive human habitat. It was used so extensively that it represents a form of natural cultivation in so far as it aided crops for harvest and managed large herbivores for slaughter. Fire improved fruit and seed production, maintained fields of edible grass seeds, enhanced cycad production, and improved the growth and dispersal of the yam daisy and other tubers. The open plains and fields of grass seen at the time of European settlement throughout southern Australia were a product of Holocene practices. The colours

A semi-permanent village on the Mulgrave River near Cairns provides an insight into the nature of settlement in the fertile populated lands of eastern and southern Australia around 2500 years ago. The large stones in front of the house (second from left) were used to grind cycad nuts, which were then placed in string bags and leached clean in the adjacent river before cooking and eating.

of green and gold that so perfectly reflect our national identity and give meaning to our sporting complexion are a product of ancient land-management practices: they are the colours of fire.[61]

The later Holocene emerges as a time of settlement in the true sense of the word: it appears to have been a time of regulated security, of establishment and routine, and life conditioned by what would reasonably be described as hard work, social alliance and networks bound by family and tradition. There is a sophistication here that warrants reflection in the context of Australian perceptions and misconceptions of nomadic history. Labour-intensive engineering, intensified subsistence strategies, villages and well-defined socio-political relationships all point to significant population levels and regionalised land-management regimes across southeastern Australia in the more recent Holocene. Population densities appear to have been high: at least 250,000 people lived in the Murray–Darling Basin alone and perhaps 1–1.5 million people were spread across the whole continent.

There are certainly indications of a high population across the Murray–Darling Basin during the mid to late Holocene. People became smaller—about 20 per cent smaller than their Pleistocene ancestors—and suffered health-related problems associated with high population: dietary stress, anaemia, osteoarthritis, trauma (through violence and including surgery such as trepanning), tumours, parasites and diseases associated with weaning practices. Burial customs also appear to have become more formalised, and there was a preference for particular burial locations and regulated mortuary practices. Along the Murray River, for example, the dead were laid on their backs with their heads and arms aligned in a westerly direction. Women appear to have been cremated, and women and children were buried apart from men. The burial patterns imply tradition, the locations imply recognised territorial rights, and both imply a strong sense of social identity, localised settlement and descent-based rights to land.[62]

Many burial locations were used for a long time. People had been burying their dead, for example, at Roonka Flat on the Murray River from 7000 years ago, although 90 per cent of the 250 burials found there belong to the last 2000 years. They provide a remarkable insight into customary life at the time. There is, for example, a vertical burial of a young man. He has a child of about seven at his side. The man was buried with a skin cloak held fast on the shoulder with a bone pin. Other bone pins held the cloak together down the front.

Animal paws hung as tassels from the cloak and it was decorated with feathers down its left side. The man wore a headband patterned with 150 wallaby teeth: 75 pairs—indicating not just decoration, but evidence of serious hunting. The child was covered with ochre and wore a headband made of animal teeth strung on a single string. Another necklace of snake vertebrae strung in opposing decorative groups was placed on the child's stomach. The child also wore a pendant made from the skull of a brolga. The emotive magnificence of this burial is repeated across the area. At Lake Nitchie in western New South Wales a tall man was buried within a small pit. He suffered from a dental abscess. He was covered with ochre and was buried beside a small fire—perhaps part of the burial ritual. Small pieces of pearl shell and some tektites were buried with him, and he wore a necklace made of 178 Tasmanian devil teeth (from over 100 animals). He was buried almost 7000 years ago.[63]

Mining and industry

Further west, and across the major part of Australia, Holocene heat gave rise to an arid land inhabited by a dispersed population. These were the people of popular stereotype—see 'tails' on an Australian $2 coin and you see the face of the desert. Population densities varied with the seasons, the availability of water and the fertility of the land, with the desert supporting about one person every 50–160 square kilometres (depending on how hospitable the country was they lived in). Their diet was mixed according to the seasons and the country they occupied. As a generalisation, people consumed more vegetable foods in the autumn and winter, and more reptiles and marsupials in the spring and summer. People ate more vegetables and small animals in the northern deserts, and less vegetables and more large animals in the southern deserts. Desert people preferred the fertile landscapes between the ranges and the sand plains as these contained the most water,

Wooden dishes are designed to carry babies as well as food and water. This dish is a bit small, but otherwise provides the perfect mobile transport for a young child. The baby is clearly well fed (Haast's Bluff, central Australia).

the broadest foraging opportunities, and had the best supplies of wood for tools and fire—but not all desert people had access to them. Desert people generally worked communally, as families of subsistence. No one was averse to hunting a lizard or picking a bush tomato, but only men hunted large marsupials—particularly the red kangaroo.[64]

Occupation in rock shelters increased during the later Holocene, in part due to the greater frequency of rain and the more intense summer heat. At Allen's Cave, for example, people found shelter and lit warming cooking fires quite frequently between 10,000 and 4000 years ago. Curiously, they visited the cave less frequently after that time. The same decline in shelter occupation is seen across the Nullarbor Plain and may be a consequence of the drier, more variable conditions in the more recent Holocene. The Nullarbor people hunted widely, consuming possum, wallaby, bandicoot, bettong, stick-nest rat, numbat, bilby and kangaroo. Desert menus appear to have been similar across the country—small marsupials and reptiles as a staple, supplemented with bonus kills of larger game (vegetable foods are not preserved in those old stratigraphic cameos but probably made up a large variable proportion of the food consumed throughout the year).

In Allen's Cave only 2.2 per cent of the bone in the site comes from human hands. Evidence of human occupational intensity is thus low by eastern Australian standards, but is characteristic of the desert generally. Occupational intensity at Puritjarra, in central Australia, in the late Holocene reveals an idealised pattern of one visit by a small family for three to six weeks a year. The visitation rate is higher than in the Pleistocene, but hardly represents a population explosion.[65]

People lived on the plains in an open accessible society, where people were dependent on each other and each other's resources for survival. The all-embracing nature of desert communication and shared need is signified by the elaboration of its extensive trade networks. The narcotic plant pituri, for example, was traded over distances of 900 kilometres across an area of 500,000 square kilometres in arid Australia. The plant was picked and dried, mulled and packed in special net bags. The drug trade was substantial. Pituri was said to have been a hallucinogen, but in my experience the effects were more of relaxation and disorientation. The mull was mixed with ash for enhanced effect and rubbed around the gums or under the tongue[66]—rather how people apply cocaine in the event that their sinuses are damaged from overuse. (Drug users across the ages know the best ways to maximise the effects.)

Other valued items, such as pearl shell and baler shell, were traded, transaction by transaction, over 1600 kilometres from northern Australia to the south of the continent. One of the greatest and most obvious trade routes was down the huge catchments of the Georgina and Diamantina rivers from the Gulf of Carpentaria into Lake Eyre and the Flinders Ranges. The trade routes were as large as the desert itself. The further the material went the more valuable it became. Other items were traded in exchange. Boomerangs are a perfect example. Their manufacture had ceased in the north during the later Holocene and they were now obtained from the desert through trade—to be used as musical instruments, as clapping sticks, rather than implements of hunting and conflict as seen in the old warrior art.[67]

There was also an enormous trade in seed-grinding implements. There is a quarry at Anna Creek near Lake Eyre, for example, where over 200,000 grindstones were mined, manufactured and traded. Grindstones from Wadla Wadlyu quarry on the eastern margin of the Flinders Ranges were traded as far north as Boulia, 1000 kilometres away. There are over 370 quarry pits here, resulting in the production of between 500,000 and 1.5 million millstones: an activity of industrial proportions. The volumes of extraction and manufacture are as massive as they are extensive. In the Ashburton Range in central Australia there is another quarry that supplied grinding slabs over an area of 135,000 square kilometres (twice the size of Tasmania), from the Tanami Desert to the Barkly Tableland in the Northern Territory.[68]

Another valued desert commodity was ochre. People travelled all the way from western Queensland to obtain iridescent ochre from the Flinders Ranges. On the other side of the desert, people traded and travelled distances of 400–600 kilometres to obtain ochre from Wilgie Mia in the Weld Ranges near Meekatharra. This is an ancient open-cut mine of at least 1000 years in age. It has a quarry face measuring 30 metres by 20 metres from which ochre was mined from scaffolding. The mining face opened into a mineshaft that was 60 metres long. At least 24,000 tonnes of stone were quarried in the extraction of about 6000 tonnes of high-grade ochre. The Karrku mine, which has been in use since humans first came to the desert, is small in comparison. Here people mined about 500 tonnes of ochre by the light of firesticks from a seam tunnelled 35 metres underground. It is a mine of great antiquity from which ochre is still mined, used and traded today.[69]

The extensive trade routes across the Australian arid zone were possible because of the open social networks and inclusive territoriality of the people who lived there. Theirs was a society of inclusion, kinship, flexible territoriality, and shared religious tradition and language; a society of broad homogeneity and subtle distinctions: one people with many personalities; one language with many dialects; one religion with many sects. Religious traditions defined social behaviour and determined geographic association (along with mutable customs of birth and descent). Geographic principles were embedded in the shared mythologies of the Tjukurrpa, and its regional sects of Tingarri, Watjirra, Wapar and Wilyarru. This religious tradition connected and coordinated all people and all country. It was a tradition of subtle and significant definition configured through religious law enacted through codified patterns of human behaviour. The Tjukurrpa established a political community defined by belief in the religious narratives of the land that constituted it. The Tjukurrpa is, in this sense, a religious political tradition centred in country and enacted through political relationships in society. It is composed of metaphysical associations in the physical environment transformed through religious tradition into status and power in the social environment. The tradition is thus metaphysical in understanding, physical in definition and political in effect. Communal belief in the tradition gives rise to political processes at the broadest level, and so defines that society in the broadest geographic terms. The people living on the land touched by the Tjukurrpa are bound by its laws and are thus members of the same vast political community. In other words, the socio-political and the socio-geographical parts of the Tjukurrpa are co-dependent in the delineation of society, its politics and its territory.[70]

The inclusive character of the political and social tradition is one of real and customary family ties, of people bound together by biology and codes of social relation. The oldest system predated the modern by at least 1500 years and saw society divided into two groups, independent of but based on actual biological relationships and terminology. The system operated primarily in the sphere of ritual, death and marriage, but also configured allegiances in times of trouble—it dictated whose 'side' you were on in times of need, religion, grief and romance. The system developed over the years, so the two-part system became four, and the four-part system became eight. The brilliance of the tradition is that it converted every member of society into a family member. This was done by a series of named identities within which anyone belonging to one named identity knew immediately how to relate to every other person also named in the system (even if they had never met them). The system normalised and equalised human behaviour in a social environment where everyone was, by definition, family. The system meant that wherever a person might go or whatever need they might have, someone was obliged to help—there were always fathers, brothers, sisters, mothers, grandparents and in-laws in their social world. Codes of behaviour were assigned as if everyone was a blood relation. To appreciate the impact of that system in society it helps to imagine a situation at work where everyone is closely related: the boss is your grandmother, your assistant is a brother, your colleagues are your wives and husbands, the admin staff are your parents, and the middle managers are your children. Hierarchies, authority and opportunities either disappear or are realigned, and obligations, sympathies, allegiances and dependencies take their place. Such was the eternal nature of actual and constructed family across the entirety of the desert in the recent past (and as it is constructed today).

This system regulated marriage, and defined subsistence obligations and ritual relationships. The eight-part system emerged about 1500 years ago and entered the desert from the north. It then spread southward but did not reach the southern desert before white settlement. It was with the Warlpiri in the Tanami Desert in the 1890s, and with the Aranda and Pintupi in the central deserts by the 1930s. The ancient two-part system still remains with the Pitjantjatjara, Yankunytjatjara and Antakirinja in the southern deserts.[71]

It is, in light of the intensity of tradition so far described, something of a cliché to observe that the traditions of Holocene people were rich and diverse. Complicated and complex are also words that get overused in such socio-historic accounts, but they are, nonetheless, apt descriptions of Australian society as it then was. Needless to say, the cultures of the Australian Holocene were as emphatic and enigmatic as it is possible to imagine. It was a time configured from and constructed beyond nomadism. The Holocene saw a cultural movement from turbulence to tranquility. It was a time of great variability that was overcome through resilience and ingenuity. It saw adjustment and adaptation to extraordinary change: loss of land, variable and unpredictable climate, and greatly altered and altering ecosystems. People adapted through contrasting social and territorial systems of exclusion and inclusion, demarcation, trade and religious conviction. They created communities of great diversity, from the most extreme forms of nomadism to the most consolidated forms of settlement: a human spectrum of nomadism, opportunism, sedentism, agriculture and industry. The response of people to the new geography might be described as one of distinction: of conflict and community, and communication and competition across lands that were as variable as the traditions that developed upon them.

The people of the humid tropical lands, riverine plains, deserts and coastal environments had different strategies of subsistence, socialisation and survival. Territorial tension gave way to territorial organisation, and social conflict resolved itself through systems of social order. Religion and ritual pervaded life and gave meaning to the land. Religion created the political nexus between land and society, and the elaboration of kinship created societies of incremental difference and, implicitly, incremental similarity. The Pleistocene characterisation of similarity, expressed rhetorically as one people in one country, could be reframed in the Holocene as many people in many countries. There was productive social order in, and as a consequence of, the evocative immensity of country, culture, society and environment that had been played out upon it.

Such is the envisaged social history of over 1 million people after 10,000 years of volatile life in mainland Australia. What might have been the story in Tasmania, where the landmass and the population was 99 per cent smaller, and the community was alone?

The Tasmanian paradox

The Tasmanian landmass was just 69,000 square kilometres after the seas had stopped rising, such a small island that it would take a desert nomad less than three days to walk across it. The population was perhaps between 5000 and 10,000 strong, no larger than that of a small town and suggests everybody must have either known everybody else or known somebody who did. What happened to that small group of people on that little island across Holocene time? What happened to the world's most ancient and most isolated people on earth over that long era?

The first consequence of the glacial melt was, in many ways, unexpected: the ice caps disappeared, the glacial valleys thawed and the 20,000-year tradition of wallaby hunting collapsed. The climate became wetter and warmer from about 14,000 years ago, and the ice sheets had fully retreated by 13,000 years ago. As the climate warmed, rainforests and wet sclerophyll forests reclaimed the moorlands. There was, as a consequence, an almost complete cessation of occupation in the cold cave country of the mountainous valleys. By 12,000 years ago all but one ancient cave site had been abandoned. The exception, Nunamira Cave, was abandoned 10,000 years ago. The caves were not reoccupied until last century, when people refound the ancient heritage within them.[72] Occupation continued in the Holocene in some caves just outside the southwest—including the oldest of them all, Parmerpar Meethaner—but at much lower intensity. That great cave would remain in use until 200 years ago, when the colonial wars between the nomads and the British settlers commenced.

The apparent abandonment of the new forest lands seems an unlikely occurrence: one intuitively imagines the forests would have been easier to live in than the glacial steppes, and as the climate warmed life could only improve. But this appears not to have been the case—the people left the rugged country as the forests encroached. The reason seems to be that the rainforests did not support sufficient marsupial fauna to maintain settlement: Tasmanian rainforests contain fewer animals than ice age moorlands. Environmental documentation and historic records of trapping and hunting imply something of the ancient reality. In 1972, for example, naturalists conducted the equivalent of 2400 trapping nights in these rainforests and managed to trap five Bennett's wallabies. By comparison, in the drier forests to the east, trappers killed 1,586,308 brushtail possums and 1,802,600 Bennett's wallabies between 1923 and 1970. Over 2 million Bennett's wallabies were shot between 1981 and 1986. It is not difficult to figure out where the ice age hunters might have gone when the rainforests came to the west.[73]

Still, the demise of the ice age tradition is as spectacular as it is confounding. The biological rationale is convincing, but the broader notions of abandoned landscapes are difficult to understand. The Tasmanian rainforests are outwardly impregnable and low on marsupial content, but they contain a range of vegetable foods that were important staples in the past: various fruits, edible ferns, grasses, bulrushes, seeds, parasites, fungi and berries—as well as the intoxicating sap of the cider gum (*E. gunnii*), which was fermented and then drunk.[74] From this perspective, rainforest subsistence would have to have been worthwhile, and people perhaps exploited it even if they left little trace of doing so. My own experiences in the southwest recall the forests as more accessible than historic accounts suggest. And my experiences with hunting and gathering communities in the jungles of Siberut and Sipora (Mentawai Islands) and the Amazonian headwaters in eastern Ecuador reveal rainforests to be rather more productive environments than they outwardly appear. Hunters move through impenetrable jungle with the ease of dancers. Children forage all the time, and there seems to be an abundant, replenishing supply of tubers, leaves, saps, fruits and raw material for implements, weapons, string and clothing. The comparative vision is one of forested sustainability, but the archaeological cupboard is bare in Tasmania. There are not even signs of open campsites in the remote southwest and it was declared 'unoccupied' in ethno-historic accounts.[75]

If the rainforests were unoccupied then the people may have gone east to more open, productive and rewarding hunting environments. There is a trace of them at Warragarra rock shelter in the adjacent highlands 11,000 years ago, but it is fleeting. They are also caught at Rushy Lagoon in the coastal hinterland of the northeast, 8700 years ago, but again the visit is short. There are physical signs of them in deep caves in southern Tasmania—hand stencils in Ballawinnie Cave and Wargata Mina Cave that are 10,000 years old—and people were still in the forest nearby. The hand stencils are eerie—human hands bringing a shadowy awareness of people in this distant time and place. They are an articulation of existence in outline; great time, great isolation, great change stencilled in blood and ochre; human blood in deep ritual in the dark remoteness at the transition of time; a visual echo of our own archaic consciousness.[76]

But these are fleeting images of limited temporal and geographic concern, for no sooner had the ice caps melted and the forests closed than the seas swamped the land bridge connecting Tasmania to the mainland. The loss of the Bassian Plain halved the land area of the great southern cape from which Tasmania then evolved. The rainforest had already taken part of the country and the invading sea took more: in this case an area of land equal in size to that which remains. The rising sea flooded at least 65,000 square kilometres of open plain.[77] Some of the people living there must have headed north, others south. Many who stayed on the islands of Bass Strait soon fled, and those who stayed behind died. Population pressure must have been high in the small isle for a period of time at the beginning of the Holocene.

Colin Hughes and Richard Cosgrove in one of the caves at Rocky Cape, Tasmania. People have been camping and cooking shellfish here for over 8000 years.

It must have been a difficult time for the Tasmanians as the rainforests expelled people and the flooding plain washed them to high ground. But they coped and adapted with rapidity and intensity. One advantage of the encroaching seas was the creation of a multitude of embayments and estuaries: a rugged indented coastline of infinite opportunity. The ratio of coastline to country in Tasmania is six times greater than that of mainland Australia,[78] so, it might be supposed, what the Tasmanians lost in land they gained in coast. The trade may not have been entirely even but it was workable nonetheless. The consequence was a cultural heritage of sheer volume, antiquity and diversity. There are huge complex middens, scattered artefacts, quarries, stone arrangements and art sites all along the coast. Individual middens extend for kilometres. They line the estuaries for thousands of square kilometres and encompass complex villages and massive open scatters of artefacts. Site densities peak at around

80 sites per kilometre, and densities of 30 sites per kilometre are common. The average density sits comfortably between five and 15 sites along each kilometre of the coast. On the windswept northwest coast each kilometre of the shore contains around 420 cubic metres of midden material; there is, in sum, over 78,000 tonnes of midden material on Tasmania's northwest coast. There is nothing like it in the rest of Australia. The numbers are impressive even though most of the coast remains to be surveyed: over 2400 sites are currently known and there are probably over 7000 still to find.[79]

Even before the last people left the Bassian Plain, people were settled on and exploiting the evolving Tasmanian shores. They were living in a cave at Rocky Cape, for example (with new sea views across Bass Strait), over 8000 years ago. People were also camping on the southern end of the island at Carlton Beach 9000 years ago, overlooking the inundation that would form the Derwent estuary—indicating, if nothing else, considerable antiquity of the new coastal economies of the Tasmanian people and their ready adaptation to their new island.

The situation repeats itself around the island. At Temma there is a complex of over 1000 sites covering 5000 hectares. Other locations are just as impressive, with the sites at Sundown Point covering 132 hectares, Nelson Bay 800 hectares, Greens Creek 315 hectares, and so on. The area has one of the greatest concentrations of archaeological material in the world. The antiquities are substantial, the content diverse. There are associated stone pathways and alignments, mounds, cairns and hunting hides, as well as engravings of mysterious symmetry and artistic appeal, though of more recent antiquity (less than 2000 years). Interestingly, the symbols in the engravings were also seen on the scarified bodies of the people themselves, where they were said to represent the sun and the moon. On the east coast there is a sacred pathway. It was overlain with midden material and remained unused for 800 years before another pathway was built over it. The physical proximity of the alignments is incongruous given the great time that separates them: what was the pervasive belief that linked the construction of both paths across such a long period of time? The adjacent beach is covered with pits, piles and track-ways that continue for several kilometres; what is their connection?[80]

A lot that was happening on the Tasmanian coast and the lives of the people themselves can be vibrantly seen in a secret chamber at Rocky Cape. Here there is a section of the cave that was sealed off 6800 years ago by the volume of food refuse deposited within it. Behind the blockage is a camp of the old people who once lived there, untouched and unseen for almost 7000 years. Abalone shells were piled around the walls of the cave, the centre swept clean for comfort around a fire. Five hearths had been placed near the cave wall to maximise reflected heat. Remains of meals were left on the ground: seals, birds, small marsupials, shellfish and fish from the rocky shores. The people ate bracken ferns, lily tubers and grass tree stems: a balanced diet of protein, fat and carbohydrate. Stone scrapers lay where they were left and a stone mortar was put near the wall, the pestle neatly placed on top—waiting for the occupants to return.[81]

This window in time is absorbed in the multitude of similar moments in history reaching back 8000 years. That history sees people living from the seas and the land, with increased exploitation of land animals after 3500 years ago—as Holocene climates became more variable and the weather became drier and more difficult. The change in subsistence follows the timeframe that saw the end of settlement on Flinders Island to the northeast. It was a time of adjustment; people sought shelter in the cave less frequently and targeted additional and optional resources more regularly. Women appear to have commenced skin diving for abalone and crayfish. Raw materials were acquired over greater distances: presumably traded or carried as people turned to the land as well as the sea to meet their increasing subsistence needs.

They returned, for example, to Warragarra rock shelter in the highlands at about this time—3400 years ago. The site was used in the same way it appears to have been used when first occupied 11,000 years ago—as a sheltered hunting base, as evidenced by the consumption of Bennett's wallabies, kangaroos, possums, bettongs and wombats. Visitation was infrequent in the later Holocene, although occupation increased as time moved on. The same pattern is seen across the valley, at about the same time, at Parmerpar Meethaner Cave. People were using the forested country but with much less frequency than in the Pleistocene (although, again, regional exploitation increased as the Holocene progressed).[82]

One of the most curious changes in subsistence at that time was the removal of fish from the nomadic diet (and the removal of bone implements possibly used to catch them). The change happened about 3500 years ago, after which there is no record of Tasmanians eating marine fish again.[83] The timing coincides with a period of climatic aridity and unpredictability in the later Holocene and might be explained by it. But there are many possible explanations for the mysterious dietary change: a loss of the technique, resulting from prolonged isolation and cultural impoverishment; a cultural taboo within an otherwise adaptive economy; a result of climatic change that led to a preference for fatty foods (seals); fish not being an important part of the diet anyway; a cultural response motivated by an ecological squeeze; a response to algal growth and mass poisoning; a narrowing and balancing of the subsistence base; an intellectual choice of little consequence; a result of prohibition and restructured gender relationships, and so on.[84] My own view is that it was a cultural choice embedded in religious belief. There is no direct evidence for that view, but it seems to be the only scenario that explains the sustained prohibition: if the ability to fish had simply been lost, it would have been remembered again and people would not have been averse to eating fish when offered it in the colonial period; if the reason was dietary, economic or technical, people would hardly have seen fish as abhorrent, as was recorded ethno-historically, and fish bones would surely have turned up occasionally in the thousands of sites occupied by thousands of people living there over the last 3000 years (not one fish bone has been found); if the reason was environmental then it could hardly have been terminal, as fish were astonishingly abundant in the historic period (as they continue to be today). The absence of fish in the diets of thousands of people over thousands of years could only have been sustained through cultural proscription. The Tasmanians were, I suspect, the first to define fish in a religious context (as Christians were subsequently to do), and were among the first of the great peoples of the earth to engage in food avoidance and food taboos—the avoidance of pork by people of the Middle East, Jewish prohibition on shellfish and crustaceans, and Hindu prohibition on killing cows being other eminent examples.

Notions and explanations of cultural impoverishment in the Tasmanian community emerged in part through historic records of their small tool kit and also because of modernist assumptions about technological sophistication and material possession. It was apparent, for example, through the historic era that the Tasmanians had fewer tools than their mainland relations and that their tools were less sophisticated. Notions of material assets and sophistication as indicators of social worth are relative and, as is apparent today (thanks to the proliferation of American culture in the modern world), have little bearing on cultural development, intellectual capacity, social happiness and individual wellbeing. It might also be something of an oversimplification to compare tool kits and conclude culture.

So, for example, while it is true the Tasmanians did not have spear-throwers, it is also true that their spears were much longer, substantially heavier and thrown with much greater velocity than mainland spears. Spear-throwers were also impractical in the forested environments in which the people lived. It is difficult to imagine anyone running through dense undergrowth in thick Tasmanian forest while also attaching a spear to a spear-thrower, and getting a clear shot at the intended prey. The technology and technique works in the wide open spaces of the desert but is hardly of use in the Tasmanian bush. Much easier to pick up a spear and throw it. This, of course, is what the Tasmanians did, with great skill. The ethnography is full of commentary about the deadly accuracy of Tasmanian spear throwers. They were recorded throwing spears

100 metres in distance: the world record javelin throw currently stands at 98.48 metres, set in 1996.[85] Spears were vastly more efficient in the colonial war than British guns—a war that was being won by the Tasmanians until they ran out of men (to keep fighting) and antibodies (to fight introduced disease). Similarly, the lack of a boomerang was unlikely to have been a problem—any more than it was a problem in the late Holocene for people living in Arnhem Land. Tasmanian throwing sticks were thrown in the same whirling action and with just as much deadly accuracy.[86]

With or without fish, bone points, spear-throwers and boomerangs, Tasmanian culture maintained its vitality and force. The coastal economy appears to have been strong, and in the last millennia the Tasmanians lived in established villages along the length of the western and southern coast of the island. These villages remain as clustered ring-shaped depressions today, ideally situated on grassy beaches adjacent to freshwater rivers and wide coastal platforms. These villages were permanent and composed of dome-shaped huts—long before dome-shaped tents were recognised as the ideal form for habitation in cold, blustery conditions. These villages take us away from the desolate image of southern discomfort: cold, naked natives, impoverished, huddled around smoky fires on the windswept Tasmanian coast. Instead we must see them in cozy villages, near freshwater streams, surrounded by picturesque forest and an abundance of seafood.

The huts were circular, with a semi-circular entrance, and constructed over a cavity dug into the ground. Tea-tree (*Leptospermum*) and melaleuca saplings were cut, dug into the ground and bent over to form the dome. The roofs were then thatched with grass and covered by bark. The inside of the huts was further insulated with duck, magpie, cockatoo and crow feathers. Kangaroo skins draped the inside creating comfort and warmth. A small fire was located near the entrance.[87]

The remains of the circular huts are testament to established community, sedentism and successful subsistence economies. They seem to have been a recent development—or at least the remains seen today are comparatively recent (from about 2000 years ago).

They reveal an incredible level of coastal exploitation. At one location at West Point, the local village housed 40–50 people and was occupied for about 500 years, between 1800 and 1300 years ago. The excavated portion of the site contained 20,000 bones and 30,000 artefacts: ample evidence of intense occupation.

Coastal settlement in this area was intense—there are over 274 sites in just 9 kilometres of coast. Many people lived and died there. Those that died appear to have been cremated, their remains placed in small pits. One of these pits contains a shell necklace and what appears to have been a pendant made from a duckbill. The density of sites and the elements of cremation allow us to picture a creative, industrious and consolidated community. Their diet was both wide and narrow. They liked abalone, which constituted 10 per cent of the food they ate. But they also hunted sea birds, marsupials and reptiles (25 per cent of the food remains). But the primary reason for village settlement was the taste of the villagers for elephant seals, then living on the wide rocky shoreline. These constituted 65 per cent of the people's diet. Skeletal and dental evidence shows the primary predation was of young seals (including foetal young) and females, which indicates the exploitation of the colony during the summer breeding season. If anyone has ever seen a male elephant seal they would know the reason why the hunters targeted females. The males weigh between 2 and 4 tonnes, and are aggressive—putting *Diprotodon* hunting by the ancients into some kind of perspective. Females are less than half the size and are rather more docile (they were described as an easy target during the era of sealing). There are no elephant seal colonies on the Tasmanian coast today, and the possibility exists that the village people hunted local colonies to extinction after which the people moved away. The 500-year window of settlement at West Point alludes to that possibility: settlement, exploitation, extinction and abandonment. However, the predation rates at West Point are unknown, and even in the unlikely event that every elephant seal bone at West Point represented an individual seal, then predation over the 500 years of occupation suggests the death of just one animal every 14 days (probably sufficient for a village of 40 people). Consistent predation of juveniles and females may have led to over-exploitation in the long term, but the hypothetical scale of predation seems modest, at least in comparison to historic sealing. In the historic equivalent sealers are recorded as killing 20 elephant seals in half an hour, and a small party of sealers could kill and skin up to 10,000 in a few weeks. The traditional hunting strategy was clearly better managed, even if the colonies eventually expired through imperceptible over-predation.[88]

The Tasmanians also travelled to, and hunted seals on, offshore islands they accessed by canoes made from bundles of stringy eucalyptus bark. The canoes looked rather precarious, as if they were unlikely to stay afloat for long or be very navigable. But people went far on them—the furthest being castaways washed and blown from the coast to King Island, 80 kilometres away. This happened on at least two occasions, 2500 and 1100 years ago. The canoes clearly floated—that journey must have taken at least three uncomfortable days to complete. The stone tools and middens of the survivors suggested they lived there for a time, but it must have been a disheartening, lonely existence.

There are 11 other islands with evidence of human occupation dating from 2500 years ago—indicating the period over which the canoes were in use. The closest is Diamond Island, 300 metres from the shore, and the most distant are Schouten and Lachlan islands, and Ile des Phoques, over 11 kilometres from shore—a long way to paddle a bark canoe. The most dangerous was Tasman Island—arguably the most frightening island in southern Australia. The island is a block of igneous rock, lashed by gales and huge swells. It is only 1 kilometre from the coast but required a 4-kilometre paddle along the base of the most precipitous cliffs in Australia to get there. People visited Tasman Island and some died there, their journey and conquest suggesting great skill, seamanship and courage in pursuit of seals.[89]

The occupation and use of the Tasmanian islands takes us to the physical limits of human colonisation of Australia during the

32. Jawoyn Elder Margaret Katherine at the Gabarnmang rock shelter in Arnhem Land. Some 36 stone pillars support the ceiling, which has been modified to expose flat rock on which a gallery of art has been painted.

33. The extraordinary site of Nawarla Gabarnmang has been enlarged from a natural shelter through the removal of stone to create a henge covering some 1500 square metres. The site is a staggering 45,000 years old.

34. Aboriginal Heritage Officer Colin Hughes entering Wargata Mina Cave, Tasmania. The cave contains hand stencils in ochre and blood that resonate with deep ritual and the mysteries of life in the rainforests long ago.

35. People had settled as far south as the Tasmanian highlands 44,000 years ago. The uplands were glacial, the climate sub-Antarctic and people hunted wallabies in the valleys kept open through fire.

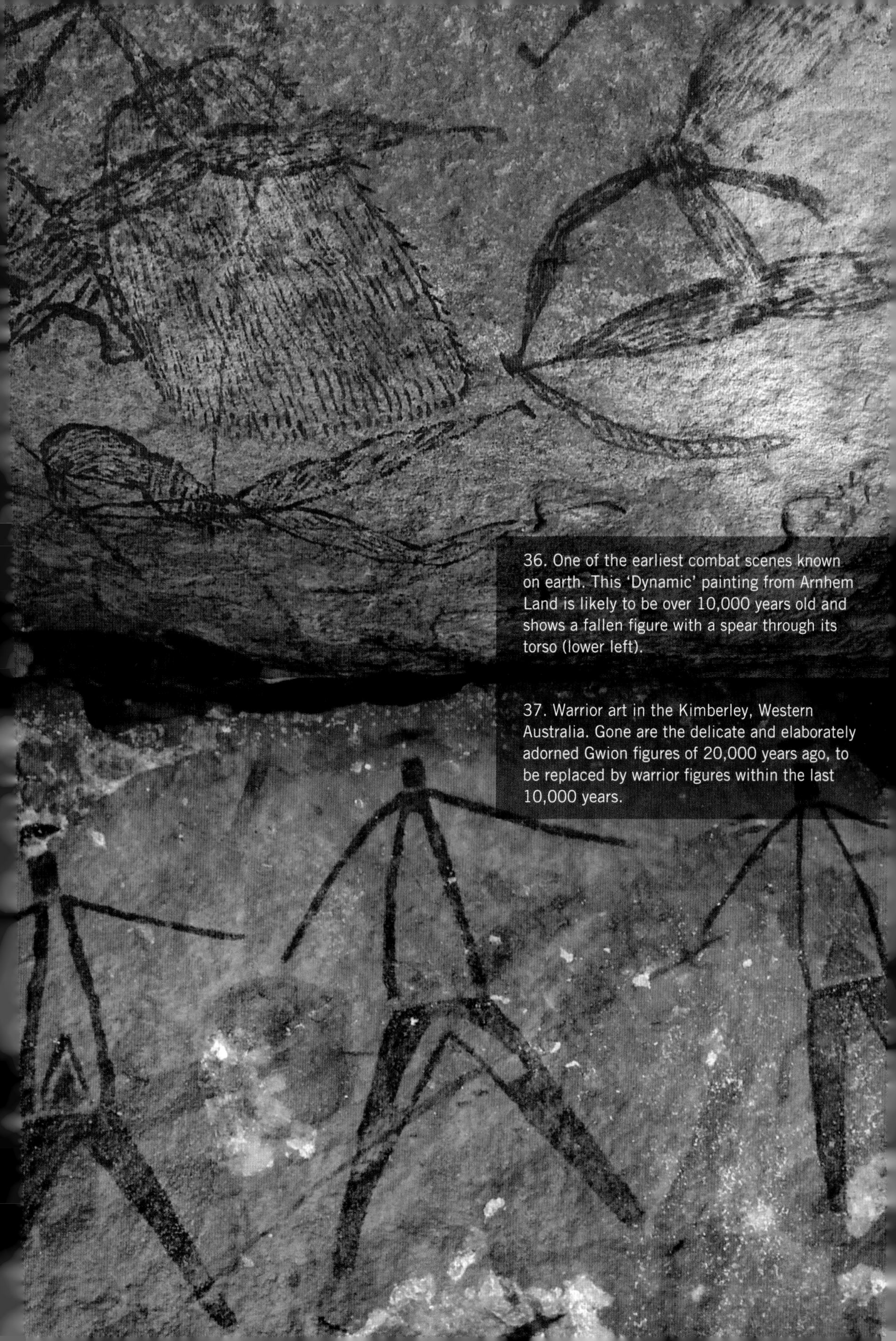

36. One of the earliest combat scenes known on earth. This 'Dynamic' painting from Arnhem Land is likely to be over 10,000 years old and shows a fallen figure with a spear through its torso (lower left).

37. Warrior art in the Kimberley, Western Australia. Gone are the delicate and elaborately adorned Gwion figures of 20,000 years ago, to be replaced by warrior figures within the last 10,000 years.

38. The largest number of battle scenes are found in Arnhem Land dating from about 6000 years ago. Warriors are seen fighting, wounded and dying. Here warriors are shown holding spears, hooked clubs and hafted axes.

39. The Wanjina figures, or creation beings, of the Kimberley region in Western Australia emerged quite recently, after the Gwion figures and the Warrior art of the region.

40. Known as 'Narrabeen Man', this skeleton was found in northern Sydney. He had been speared in the stomach and back and hit over the head with an axe about 3200 years ago—as sea levels reached their highest.

41. Competition for land and resources was great at this time. A spear barb (indicated by the pointer) is lodged in Narrabeen Man's spine; the spear was probably thrown at close range.

42. Coastal people retreated to the larger islands as sea levels rose around 9000 years ago. Colin Groves and Dr Richard Cosgrove investigate ancient hearths on Flinders Island, Bass Strait, abandoned around 7000 years ago.

43. Sedentary village life emerged throughout eastern and southern Australia over the last 2500 years. Villages of stone and thatch houses were likely to have been occupied by several thousand people.

44. Gunditjmara Elder Ken Saunders explains eel traps to Professor Ian McNiven, with replicas of the wicker traps used to capture eels within the artificial channels—the earliest evidence of aquaculture in the world.

45. A 19th-century map of a Gunditjmara eel trap, Victoria. Floodwaters spread across the plains via the channels, and then retreated back up them as the water subsided. Traps were placed in weirs across the channels.

46. Martu Elder Timmy Patterson fire farming in the Western Desert. Fire was the most natural and efficient means for improving productivity in landscapes across Australia and was widely used.

47. Large ceremonial gatherings were common across Australia for the purposes of trade, marriage, and social and political advancement. The population of Australia before white settlement was probably 1.5 million.

Holocene. These are the final destinations of the great nomads after 60,000 years of sweeping social history and extraordinary environmental change—after the seas had risen and the climate had warmed, when coast lands submerged, temperate lands reforested, deserts dried, savannahs flooded, estuaries filled, and distant shores fragmented into the 8222 islands that surround the mainland today. This was the appearance of the Australian shores in the most recent millennia of nomadic settlement. It was also the form of the Great South Land of European imagination at the time of 'discovery'. To the Europeans, *temperata antipodum nobis incognita*, or 'temperate lands on the opposite side of the world that are unknown to us', as it was described on woodcut maps of the 16th century, was a country of maritime mystery and territorial opportunity. It was a country already found yet still searched for: paradise lay, after all, to the southeast of the known world.[90]

Three cheers

One might reflect on this great human narrative as the people themselves might have lived it: tentatively, compassionately, ingeniously, enduringly and communally. One might also see these people in these great landscapes and imagine what they saw: the mega-animals and reptiles that roamed the land, the giant and luxuriant lakes of Carpentaria, Willandra and Bass, the endless untouched savannahs, the expansive, unoccupied deserts, the vast drowned coastal plains. And one might visualise people living in cooler and more open environments in a new world where they ground ochre and painted images that would last forever. Where they collected shellfish on ancient coasts and netted fish in extinct lakes, buried their dead in long-forgotten lakeshores, felled trees in tropical forests, sewed furs in cold temperate forests, hunted wallabies on frigid moorlands and traded ochre across dry desert plains. These are images of real people who lived almost unimaginable lives an almost unimaginably long time ago.

The faithful artistic tradition of Arnhem Land painters 40,000 years ago continued into the recent past. Here they have painted an early vision of a gaff-rigged schooner, complete with sails eased out, revealing the wind on the rear starboard quarter.

A replica of the *Duyfken* or 'Little Dove', that arrived like a raptor on the northern Australian coast in 1606.

Astonishingly, they left records of their lives that we can see, touch and comprehend. Their archaeological legacy is proof of their existence, their accomplishment and their metaphysical reflection, which, it is probably fair to say, few people would believe was possible so long ago. The first Australians were, in so many respects, ahead of their time, and left a material testimony to prove it. Theirs is a record of diversified subsistence and settlement, of society and social networks, of technical innovation and artistic achievement, domesticity and spirituality, evident everywhere—in the tropical rainforests and savannahs, in the arid deserts and coasts, across the ancient lake systems, and in the glaciated mountains of the remote south. The people who had made the first footprints had covered the continent and made it their great estate. These were people who had, with fire in their hands and family at their side, ventured through and lived in an unknown and untamed land, painted a country with religious design and etched it with communal abode, across an ice age and through a global flood. And, as the Tasmanians sat on their remote shores, and other coastal people around Australia sat on theirs, there came a time when they looked out to sea and saw, with their unusually keen eyesight, something different on the horizon.

In the north, people sitting near huge piles of cockleshells might have seen the sails of the Portuguese in the early 16th century. If they did not then their descendants certainly met the Dutch in the 17th century, when Captain Janszoon sailed the *Duyfken* to Cape Keerweer ('Keerweer' meaning 'turn-away') in the Gulf of Carpentaria in 1606. There is a sizeable vision here—proportional, at least, to the significance of its historic implications. It is reasonable to imagine the large sailboat anchored in the lee of the low tropical shore, its baby dinghy full of light-skinned people rowing towards land. It is possible to appreciate the mixed emotions of the local inhabitants—fear and fascination, tension and curiosity—as the dinghy came closer. It ended badly: spears thrown, a sailor killed and who knows how many locals shot.[91]

Another Dutch vessel called the *Pera* visited the same shores 17 years later. The locals were now perhaps more watchful, less anxious than afraid. They would have been wise to be so, for in that meeting two of their kin were kidnapped and three were shot and killed. In that same year the descendants of the ancient inhabitants of Malakunanja and Nauwalabila rock shelters camped on the shores of Arnhem Land and saw the Dutch vessel *Arnhem* surveying their coast. Their country would be named after it.

On the far western coast, the descendants of those who once lived on the glacial plains surrounding the Montebello Islands may have seen the distant sails of the English trader *Trial* in 1622, before the vision miraculously disappeared from view. The ship struck an unmarked reef out to sea. Perhaps nothing was seen and nothing was known of the ship's passing until some of the bodies of the 93 men who died there washed up, decomposing, along the shore.

It is also likely that the people living on the plains of Swan River saw the *Amsterdam* as she sailed past in 1616. The descendants of the cave dwellers at Devil's Lair most surely watched in amazement as the *Leeuwin* nearly shipwrecked on their shores. The nomads of the eastern Nullarbor perhaps recall the *Gulden Zeepaert* when she anchored there in 1627. They describe 'a great white bird' that came out of the sky and was 'tied to the land so it could not get away'. If they did not mythologise that historic experience then Europeans certainly did: the anchor point becoming the exemplar of 'the most remote nations of the world' in the last and most bizarre satirical adventure of *Gulliver's Travels.*

Bizarre adventures continued to the south. The Tasmanians saw Abel Tasman arriving in 1642, and hid as his landing party of six musketeers and six rowers 'all furnished with pikes and side arms' walked into a small camp. The expedition heard the Tasmanians sounding warnings through the forest, but none were to be seen. They observed, instead, local trees over 20 metres high with notches cut up their trunks. The notches were almost 2 metres apart, leading the seamen to conclude the Tasmanians were giants.[92]

At about the same time, Macassan fishermen began visiting the northern coast of Australia—perhaps after the Dutch captured

A Macassan prau, painted on Groote Eylandt, showing the details of a foreign visitation: high numbers on board, a fish being harpooned, a broad square sail, a high bow and stern for making headway through the strong trade winds, and a long dual rudder.

A tranquil image of trepang fishers attending to business at Raffles Bay, Northern Territory, indicating the mechanics of business: stone hearths near the water, flat iron cauldrons, drying racks and smoke houses. Dugout canoes line the shore.

Makassar in 1667. They came to collect sea slugs called trepang, which they traded (as an aphrodisiac) with the Chinese. The trade in trepang led to a substantial commercial fishery across the north of Australia in the 1700s. In 1803, for example, a fishing fleet of 60 praus was recorded with an estimated 6 million slugs, equalling 300 tonnes of dried flesh. The boats carried as many as 2000 sailors. This is a large number of men, but relationships were peaceful and profitable. There are hundreds of Macassan sites along the north coast: stone walls, tamarind trees, ceramics and the remains of smoke houses. The locals captured the arrival of the Indonesians in art and absorbed aspects of their culture. They painted images of praus in caves, and created pictures in stone of their boats and processing factories. They took up the idea of dugout canoes and the sail, and traded metal tools, enhancing the efficiency of local marine subsistence. People took to smoking a long-stemmed pipe. Macassan words were adopted and mythologies shared and created. Macassan liquor bottles were sculpted in wood as symbols of totemic significance. People cohabited and travelled to Indonesia. They returned and painted their experiences in the ancient galleries of Arnhem Land: women wearing matted skirts, and strange animals—one painting depicts monkeys in a tree.[93]

The English arrived in that same century. William Dampier was the first. He landed in the Kimberley in 1699, spoke to some of the people, invited them on board and recorded some of their language. He was the first foreigner to poke into one of their midden sites—the first coastal dig in Australia. Captain Cook arrived in 1770 and sailed along the east coast. People watched him and met him. Relations were good. He stopped on a small island in the Torres Strait before leaving, built a cairn, raised the British flag, fired three volleys and said three cheers. It is unlikely that the Kaurareg islanders understood the meaning of the short ceremony. They may have inspected the small monument and felt the flag left behind: perhaps they took the colours of red, white and blue to mean the colours of ochre, the new arrivals and the ocean they came from. It is less likely they understood the meaning of the associated ritual, or that King George III had 'taken possession of the whole east coast . . . together with all the bays, harbours, rivers and islands'.[94] English settlement followed in 1788.

The nomads whose ancestors started their journey some 60,000 years ago on northern Australian shores thus confronted a new social and environmental challenge. It is tempting to write that, with the arrival of the Europeans, everyone lived happily ever after, but it is the sad truth that many nomads neither lived nor lived happily. Those who survived have a new story to tell. Their story is the most recent chapter in a narrative 2500 generations long. Their story belongs to the last nine generations: a short story that is as intense as the story that preceded it is long. It is a story that engages with a new era of dramatic social and geographic change, and one that has been endured with an unaffected tenacity learnt from their ancestors.

The short story starts with English settlement. Initially intentions were good. The inclusive social traditions of the resident population were accepting of the new people. Open conflict was neither intended nor immediate, but unintended violence filled the air and determined conflict fell from it. The original aggression was passive and unseen, as nomads began to die from diseases they did not know existed, spread by people they had not yet met. The first victims were children, as smallpox spread invisibly across the temperate coasts and along its endless river systems.[95] Children were the most vulnerable and, without immunity, every second child died within a matter of weeks. Adults were more resilient, but the consequence of survival was cruel: death pervading, small bodies buried in haste, the care of dying children and afflicted family, all stricken and near death, unable to gather or eat food with tongues and mouths swollen with lesions, and feet and hands drastically pained and damaged by pustules—sickness compounded by starvation in a pandemic that probably took the lives of over 250,000 people.[96]

The diseases of settlement and contact followed the tsunami of smallpox: exposure to influenza, whooping cough, mumps, measles, pneumonia, tuberculosis and venereal disease took their horrifying toll. And as settlement expanded and the nomads confronted the nightmare that had descended, killing and cruelty were massed upon them. Stories of massacre and atrocity are replete across Australia, as colonisation expanded in the 1800s. Violence of every imaginable kind was acceptable, the accounts as upsetting as they were real—visualise settlers using the amputated fingers of children as pipe stoppers and the amputated breasts of women as tobacco pouches, as the true horror of life at the time rises from the dead.

Within 60 years of European settlement the possession by King George had become the death and dispossession of hundreds of thousands of people. The social dislocation is repeated across the continent, and can be imagined without history's record:[97] women and children killed, families massacred, society ruptured, homelands taken, religions desecrated. The great nomads of Australia had been reduced to people on a broken fringe: minimised and marginalised, unrecognised and irrelevant in the country they had occupied for 60,000 years. Charitable sentiments emerged in the wake of dispossession with piteous compassion and grasping waves of evangelising assimilation resulting in greater alienation from ancestry and country—with no particular plan or opportunity to fill the cultural void. The 'passing' of the 'Aborigines' was predictably seen, but the prediction was of a passing kind, and as the people and the policies attributing it passed, the Aboriginal people remained.

In 2002 I was on my way to the funeral of my old friend and brother Tjantjanu, the man who had walked alone, handcuffed, from the Kimberley to the desert so many years before. He died beside his wife as she made him damper for lunch. I was driving to the 'sorry' camp to share my grief with his family, and had taken an unmarked track through the western half of Australia's arid core. The journey was a sentimental one for I also wanted to visit the last camp of a family of nomads who had left the desert a few years before. Tjantjanu's death affected me and I wanted to reflect on times past and the long era to which he and his nomadic kindred belonged.

The journey to the camp was difficult and the location disappointing, the camp somewhere around a small soak in a swale surrounded by mulga trees. The country was dry, the swale uninteresting—there was no sign of any camp in the adjacent dunes: no physical remains I could see, touch and so reflect romantically upon. Walking around the swale I noticed a small sandstone ridge through the trees. It was low, perhaps not more than 3 metres high, with a small shelter eroded into its base. The shelter invited investigation, but inside there was nothing to suggest any occupation: still nothing that would feed my sentimental desire to connect this historic place with ancient history.

I sat on the grey silt floor of the shelter, the ceilings low so I had to lean back on my elbows to see out. I looked across the swale below and imagined that I looked out as others had done before me. As I did so I noticed a small charcoal drawing on an inner facet of the shelter. The drawing was of a camel, a miniature, perhaps 3 centimetres high, perfectly proportioned. The image grabbed me, for through it I could see the artist similarly seated, sheltering from light drizzle, looking over the swale, taken by the sight of a camel standing among the mulga. The camel, the charcoal drawing implied, was a novel sight and drove the observer to capture the moment as an expression of his natural curiosity. Thus the past echoed loudly, for as the modern artist sketched this extraordinary animal, so too had ancient nomads drawn extraordinary animals over 40,000 years ago. And, in sentimental symmetry, it occurred to me that the image had been captured in charcoal just as the oldest picture in Australia was also drawn in charcoal at Nawarla Gabarnmang untold generations ago.

So, as I sat and observed in 2002, the person before me had sat and observed, just as others had sat and observed for an Australian eternity. My vision was his and his vision was that of his ancestors. So much had changed in that great sweep of time and yet so much remained the same.

There is historical symmetry here, reinforced by enduring ancestry that captures the present and ensures the future. The few hundred years of historic settlement pale against the tens of thousands of years of human settlement that preceded it. The historical experience of shock and horror balances against the history of ages old as an infinitesimal window of pain in an epoch of stoicism and peace. From this perspective the wounds of history are seen to heal on a body that is made from stronger stuff—forged, it might be said, from the hardened genetic, social and psychological legacy of the past. The orthodoxy of ancestry gives rise to a sense of sacred purpose: the adaptive requirements of survival across past climates and in diverse environments engender an adaptive genius for accommodating the inevitability of change in a pervasive ideology of non-change. Life continues, sometimes checked but generally unabated, as the meretricious attraction of modernity overwhelms and adjustments are made for satisfaction in accordance with existing notions of traditional order and permanence.[98]

And it is a fact that, as modern society rushes forward, life goes on according to staid and established principles. And, while it is true that the last nomads were recorded as having left the deserts late last century, it is also true that nomadic life continues there sequestered in the remotest places, surrounded by countrymen who balance the institutional demands of the present with the institutional conventions of the past. The significance of cultural continuity is not lost on any of us, as the traditions of the first people who settled and occupied Australia 60,000 years ago continue nowhere forgotten.

The descendants of Australia's first people now number about 550,000—less than half of the late Holocene population, but growing. That population amounts to just 2 per cent of the total population in Australia, but it is a population that carries political clout and emotive representation far in excess of its numerical expression. It is the political voice of the first people who, through their resilient orthodoxy and extraordinary history, now have legal title to over 2.3 million square kilometres of country: 30 per cent of the total landmass of Australia and some 80 per cent of its northern coastline. The northern shores are reoccupied, the desert re-owned and ancestral connection to the rest unquestioned. Great history repeats itself, the processes of endurance, resilience and adaptability continue as of old: recolonisation of ancestral country continues apace.[99]

About the Author

Scott Cane is an independent consultant.

He completed his PhD at Australian National University, then co-authored a monograph, *Land Use and Resources in Desert Homelands*, for the Northern Australian Research Unit (ANU), before running the social and environmental consulting wing of the Australian National University (ANUtech). Dr Cane then established his own archaeological and anthropological consulting company—the first of its kind in Australia—and has since conducted a vast amount of fieldwork, written over 150 reports and published over 30 papers. He is also the author of *Pila Nguru: The Spinifex People*, an account of the first native title determination on mainland Australia. Dr Cane has worked throughout the Australian deserts and has provided expert opinion to the Federal Court of Australia in relation to 14 native title claims, among which nine have been determined across more than 400,000 square kilometres of land.

Scott Cane has five daughters. He lives near Port Lincoln in South Australia with his second wife, Annie, and their two young daughters.

Acknowledgements

I would like to thank a number of people who gave me unqualified assistance while writing this book. There are those who helped read drafts of the book to assess its basic readability (Dirk Hoffman, Callan Hardy, Rob Paton, Kate Rogers, Emily and Sophie Beresford-Cane), as well as those who provided advice, criticism and generous access to their published materials (Amy Roberts, Steve Webb, Michael Wright, Bruno David, Paul Taçon, Scott Hucknell, Bert Roberts and Mac Jensen). Isabel Cane provided invaluable research assistance, and Annie Cane assisted with every aspect of researching, writing, proofing, reflection and production. Janet Hunt prepared the attractive, readable maps presented in the book.

The book would not exist without the inspiration of Bentley Dean and Martin Butler, who not only invited me to take part in their wonderful TV documentary, but also asked me to write a companion book to go with it. I owe them a debt of gratitude.

I would also like to thank Elizabeth Weiss, Angela Handley, Catherine Taylor and Clare James for their patient and particular editing, and the production of this book.

PHOTO CREDITS

Page i: Charles Mountford Collection. Courtesy of State Library of South Australia (PRG 1218/34/1127X) and Ara Irititja.
Page ii: Courtesy of South Australian Museum (AA338/5/9/76) and Ara Irititja.
Page 5: Photo by Charles Duguid. Courtesy of Ara Irititja.
Pages 6–7: Courtesy of South Australian Museum (AA338/5/1/109).
Page 18: Photo by Alfred Haddon, 1888. Courtesy of Cambridge University Museum of Archaeology and Anthropology (N22899ACH2).
Page 27: Artist's impression, *First Footprints* documentary.
Page 30: Photo by Scott Cane.
Pages 32–3: Courtesy of National Library of Australia.
Page 39: Photo by Scott Cane.
Page 40: Photo by Scott Cane.
Page 52: Photo by Frank Hall, 1948. Courtesy of Ara Irititja.
Page 59: Photo by Scott Cane.
Page 60: Photo by Scott Cane.
Page 64: Photo by John Kramer/Duguid Family Collection. Courtesy of Ara Irititja.
Page 70: Courtesy of South Australian Museum (AA 346/9/10/35).
Page 76: Photograph by Frank Hall, 1948. Courtesy of Ara Irititja.
Page 78: Photo by Scott Cane.
Page 85: Charles Mountford Collection. Courtesy of State Library of South Australia (PRG 1218/34/1127T) and Ara Irititja.
Page 86: Photo by Charles Duguid. Courtesy of National Library of Australia.
Page 91: Charles Mountford Collection. Courtesy of State Library of South Australia (PRG 1218/11/1 p. 104) and Ara Irititja.
Page 94: Courtesy of State Library of Western Australia (BA891/707).
Pages 100–1: Photo by Norman Tindale. Courtesy of South Australian Museum (AA338/5/9/77) and Ara Irititja.
Page 108: *First Footprints* documentary.
Page 109: Courtesy of New Norcia Benedictine Community.
Page 119: *First Footprints* documentary.
Page 129: Photo by Henry King. Courtesy of State Library of New South Wales (PXE 434/10).
Page 144: Charles Mountford Collection. Courtesy of State Library of South Australia (PRG 1218/11/1 p. 216) and Ara Irititja.
Page 153: Photo by Samuel Sweet. Courtesy of National Library of Australia and Raukkan Community Council.
Page 162: Charles Mountford Collection. Courtesy of State Library of South Australia (PRG 1218/34/1308D) and Ara Irititja.
Page 177: Charles Mountford Collection. Courtesy of State Library of South Australia (PRG 1218/34/1284A) and Ara Irititja.
Page 178: Photo by Scott Cane.
Page 185: Duguid Family Collection. Courtesy of Ara Irititja.
Pages 188–9: Photo by Norman Tindale, 1933. Courtesy of South Australian Museum (AA338/5/9/25) and Ara Irititja.
Page 202: Charles Mountford Collection. Courtesy of State Library of South Australia (PRG 1218/34/1229B) and Ara Irititja.
Page 207 top: Charles Mountford Collection. Courtesy of State Library of South Australia (PRG 1218/34/1029B) and Ara Irititja.
Page 207 bottom: Charles Mountford Collection. Courtesy of State Library of South Australia (PRG 1218/34/1029E) and Ara Irititja.
Page 209: *First Footprints* documentary.
Page 214: Charles Mountford Collection. Courtesy of State Library of South Australia (PRG 1218/34/1302B) and Ara Irititja.
Page 223: *First Footprints* documentary.
Page 227: Photo by A.A. White, 1904, taken on Archibald Meston's Bellenden-Ker expedition. Courtesy of Cairns Historical Society.
Page 230: Courtesy of State Library of South Australia (PRG 1218/34/1449H).
Page 239: *First Footprints* documentary.
Page 248 top: *First Footprints* documentary.
Page 248 bottom: Courtesy of Firelight.
Page 251 top: Photo by Annie Clarke. Courtesy of Wanindilyakwa People, Groote Eylandt.

Page 251 bottom: Lithograph by E. Lasalle, 1846, of trepang fishers, Raffles Bay, Northern Territory.

Photo sections

All colour plates are from the *First Footprints* documentary, unless noted below. Plates 1, 2, 11, 14, 17, 35, 43 and 45 are artist's impressions created for the documentary.

Plate 3: Courtesy of CAAMA Productions and Earthbound Consultants.

Plates 30 and 31: Photos by Scott Cane.

Plate 38: Photo by Paul Taçon.

Plate 41: Photo by Jo McDonald.

Plate 45: Based on a sketch by surveyor Alexander Ingram, 1883.

Plate 47: Painting by colonial artist Joseph Lycett, c. 1820, of a corroboree at Newcastle. Courtesy of State Library of New South Wales.

NOTES

Introduction

1 The remarkable story of 20 women and children who remained alone in the Australian desert during the Blue Streak rocket tests in 1964. The film was awarded, among 13 other awards, best feature documentary by the Australian Film Institute.

Chapter 1: Near Extinction

1 Ninkovich et al. (1978), Rampino et al. (1988), Rose and Chesner (1990), Ambrose (1998).
2 Special Issue of *Quaternary International* (2012, vol. 258), and Story et al. (2012).
3 *Indonesia Pilot* (1983, p. 10). The eruption of Krakatoa: Australian Government, Bureau of Meteorology (2012).
4 Although more recent estimates suggest as much as 2000 cubic km of ash (Williams, 2012a, p. 23).
5 Williams (2012b).
6 Fagan (2011, p. 98), although there is emerging evidence that regional environmental refuges survived, within which human populations could have survived—see Jones (2012).
7 Ninkovich et al. (1978), Rampino et al. (1988), Rose and Chesner (1990), Oppenheimer (2002, p. 1604), Webb (2006), Williams et al. (2009; 2010).
8 Rampino et al. (1988, p. 90); also Ambrose (1998), Williams et al. (2009; 2010), Fagan (2011, p. 98).
9 Williams et al. (2009; 2010), Ambrose (2003).
10 Rampino and Ambrose (2000), Ambrose (1998; 2003), Williams et al. (2009; 2010), Fagan (2011), Jones (2012), and Petraglia et al. (2012a; 2012b): with evidence of modern humans in India between 77,000 and 38,000 years ago.
11 Ambrose (2003; 1998, p. 645), Williams et al. (2010) and Fagan (2011, pp. 98 and 99), Oppenheimer (2002; 2012a and b), Gathorne-Hardy and Harcourt-Smith (2003), Haslam and Petraglia (2010), and see a dedicated issue of *Quaternary International* (2012).
12 In Kalimantan, Java and central Sumatra and the Mentawai Islands (Gathorne-Hardy and Harcourt-Smith, 2003; Ambrose, 2003; Louys, 2012), and possibly other refuge areas elsewhere in the blast zone (Petraglia et al., 2012b; Jones, 2012).
13 Swisher et al. (1994), Grun et al. (1997), Wolpoff et al. (2001), Morwood et al. (1998), Brumm et al. (2010), summarised in Webb (2006), Fagan (2011, p. 107).
14 Morwood et al. (2004), also Brown et al. (2004). Morwood et al. (2004, p. 1089) also note stone artefacts 'produced by much heavier percussion' at 102,000 years but 'do not know which hominid species manufactured them'. *Homo floresiensis* is described as a descendant of *H. erectus*, or perhaps an older human ancestor, *H. habilis*, at least 1.8 million years ago (Argue et al., 2009; Jungers et al., 2009).
15 Denisovans are so named from the remains of an ancient skeleton found in Denisova Cave in southern Siberia (see Reich et al., 2010; Reich et al., 2011; Rasmussen et al., 2011).
16 Human tooth in Westaway et al. (2007), artefacts discussed in Oppenheimer (2012a and b). There is also a modern human skull in southern China that is thought to be either 68,000 or between 110,000 to 140,000 years old. There is companion evidence that 'hints' at modern humans in the Indian subcontinent 128,000–108,000 years ago but may be more realistically between 85,000 and 57,000 years old (Petraglia et al., 2012a and b). Also see Storm et al. (2005) and Oppenheimer (2012a and b), and summarised with qualification in Oppenheimer (2009). There is also human fossil evidence in the Philippines with a minimum age of 67,000 years (Mijares et al., 2010) and artefacts thought to be the products of *Homo sapiens* in Malaysia dated to about 70,000 years (Oppenheimer, 2009, p. 9; also Storey et al., 2012). Interestingly, evidence of modern humans only arrives at the site containing *Homo floresiensis* in the Holocene (from 10,000 years ago), when the food remains of monkey, deer, pig and

porcupine appear (Morwood et al., 2004). See O'Connor (2007) and O'Connor et al. (2010) for occupation in Timor 42,000 years ago.

17 See also Hiscock (2008, p. 25).

18 http://tectonics.caltech.edu/sumatra/index.html and www.gps.caltech.edu/%7Edeligne/results/location.html reveal, for example, over 1000 earthquakes over a 4-month period between May and August 2005.

19 Sieh (2007), Bilek et al. (2007).

20 In a comparative example, slightly outside the geographic area relevant to this story, archaeological evidence from Buka Island, in the Solomon Islands, reveals that people travelled 128 km from the nearest land to settle the island 28,000 years ago (Wickler and Spriggs, 1988). Clearly long distances over water could be travelled a long time ago.

21 Chappell (1993).

22 Summarised in Webb (2006, p. 34).

23 In Australia there are 'records of water rafts and bark canoes travelling 27 km and there is a record of a 32-kilometre journey in a sewn bark canoe and castaways from the Tasmanian mainland appear to have survived journeys of over 80 km to King Island within the last 2500 years (Jones, 1976; Bowdler, 1984; Mulvaney and Kamminga, 1999).

24 *Indonesia Pilot* (1983, vol. II, p. 16).

25 Australian Maritime Safety Authority (1993).

26 Australian Maritime Safety Authority (1993).

27 Recorded since 1920: *Indonesia Pilot.*

28 Morwood et al. (1998).

29 Calaby (1976) notes that other animals also made water crossings as well—cuscus, primates, civets, rats, squirrels, pigs and small antelopes—although O'Connor (2007) observes a number of these were introduced between 9000 and 1000 years ago.

30 Calaby (1976).

31 Webb (2006).

32 Siddall et al. (2003).

33 Harris et al. (2005).

34 Dortch and Muir (1980), and note that a large bushfire in Australia can easily be seen from 60–100 km away. It is possible on occasions, for example, to see the volcanic peaks of mainland Sumatra at dawn from the Mentawai Islands, 120 km away. You can also see large Sumatran thunderheads across and adjacent to the larger Mentawai Islands on clear afternoons from the Sumatran mainland. Reference to dust in the Timor Sea in Cornell (1998, p. 483).

35 Allen and O'Connell (2008, p. 37).

36 *Alocasia* rhizomes, and *Panguim* nuts are recorded as foodstuffs in Borneo 40,000–48,000 years ago (Barton and Paz, 2007). Lontar Palms (*Borassus*, Palm sugar) also grow in the southern Indonesian archipelago.

37 Lower sea levels created a vast embayment, with little through (westerly) current as a consequence of the land bridge where Torres Strait now lies, between New Guinea and northern Australia.

38 Australian Maritime Safety Authority (1993).

39 O'Connor et al. (2011).

40 Dwyer (2000).

41 Birdsell (1977), Chappell (1993), Webb (2006), Allen and O'Connell (2008), O'Connell and Allen (2012).

42 Siddall et al. (2003).

43 O'Connell and Allen (2012).

44 Moore (2001), Forster (2004), Merriwether et al. (2005), Hudjashov et al. (2007); also see Hiscock (2008), O'Connell and Allen (2012).

45 See Hiscock (2008) and O'Connell and Allen (2012).

46 In Hiscock (2008, p. 25).

47 Hiscock (2008, pp. 25 and 26), Oppenheimer (2009), Fagan (2011). van Holst Pellekaan et al. (1998) estimate between 60,000 and 119,000, and have 95 per cent confidence in the interval of 36,000–82,600 years (van Holst Pellekaan et al., 2006). Ingman and Gyllensten (2003, p. 1600) identify 40,000–60,000 as well as 40,000–70,000, and note an alternative 'expansion date of from 51,000–85,000 years ago for Australian Aborigines'. Kumar et al. (2009), Oppenheimer (2009), also Forster (2004) estimate 60,000–80,000 years ago. Macaulay et al. (2005) estimate 60,000–75,000, Hudjashov et al. (2007), Kumar et al. (2009) and Atkinson et al. (2008) estimate 50,000–70,000 years ago. Rasmussen et al. (2011) suggest 62,000–75,000 years ago. See Chapter 2 for further

discussion of the antiquity of colonisation.
48 Oppenheimer (2009; 2012a and b), Endicott et al. (2009), Storey et al. (2012).
49 Rasmussen et al. (2011), Fagan (2011, p. 104).
50 Ingman and Gyllensten (2003), Forster (2004), Macaulay et al. (2005), Hudjashov et al. (2007), Oppenheimer (2009), Kumar et al. (2009), Atkinson et al. (2008). A general chronology for the colonisation of modern humans sees them first in Africa 150,000 years ago, in Israel 120,000 years ago and termination of that population around 90,000 years ago, in India 75,000 years ago, Mount Toba eruption 74,000 years ago, then humans in Arabia 72,000 years ago, crossing through southeast Asia and to Australia 60,000–50,000 years ago, entering Europe 50,000–45,000 years ago, travelling towards and in Central Asia 40,000–20,000 years ago, in North America by 19,000–15,000 years ago and in South America 12,000 years ago (Oppenheimer, 2012a and b; Endicott et al., 2009; also Fagan, 2011).
51 Forster (2004), Macaulay et al. (2005), Kumar et al. (2009), Atkinson et al. (2008), O'Connell and Allen (2012, p. 7), see also Hiscock (2008, p. 56) with a rate of 1–4 km per year.
52 See Moore (2001) for modelling that reveals the vagaries of successful colonisation.
53 Foley and Gamble (2009); see also Balme et al. (2009).
54 Fagan (2011, p. 99).
55 Cane (2002).
56 Atkinson et al. (2008), Foley and Gamble (2009), Fagan (2011, p. 98), O'Connell and Allen (2012, p. 8).
57 Barker et al. (2007), Higham et al. (2009).
58 O'Connor (2002; 2007), O'Connor et al. (2002; 2010). There are other ancient archaeological sites in Indonesia but these are comparatively recent. Even the evidence for modern humans in Flores, where *Homo floresiensis* was found, appears to date to the Holocene: the last 10,000 years (it consists of the remains of monkey, deer, pig and porcupine).
59 Including New Guinea and its remote islands (New Britain and New Ireland), see next chapter, also O'Connell and Allen (2012): two sites in New Ireland dated 39,000–41,000, and 42,000–44,000, and two sites in New Britain dated 35,000–45,000, and 39,000–42,000 years ago.

Chapter 2: Super-Nomads

1 Commonwealth of Australia (2002).
2 Woinarski et al. (2007).
3 Flinders (1814, p. 169).
4 See Wroe and Field (2006) for a discussion of ancient marsupials and naivety. My own experience suggests that such innocence is unlikely to have lasted many generations after first settlement, as local animals learnt when to run and when to hide. But as colonisers spread into new lands and met new populations of naive resources the hunting must have remained good and easy for centuries if not thousands of years.
5 Wallace (2010).
6 O'Connor (2007).
7 Roberts et al. (2001), Koch and Barnosky (2006), Webb (2013).
8 Composite accounts may be found in Jones (1968), Horton (1984), Flannery (1990; 1994), Roberts et al. (2001), as well as Mulvaney and Kamminga (1999), Flood (2000), Webb (2006), Hiscock (2008).
9 Flannery (1999), Mulvaney and Kamminga (1999), Flood (2000), Murray and Vickers-Rich (2004), Gillespie and Brook (2006), Gunn et al. (2011), Webb (2013).
10 Prideaux et al. (2009).
11 Murray and Chaloupka (1984), Flannery (1994; 1999), Roberts and Jacobs (2008).
12 Flannery (1994).
13 Murray and Chaloupka (1984), Roberts and Jacobs (2008); see also Mackness (2009).
14 Webb (2006).
15 Our saltwater crocodile is the largest reptile living on earth today.
16 Some 246 crocodiles were removed from Darwin Harbour last year, by way of comparative example.
17 Flannery (1994).
18 Modern-day crocodiles run at speeds of up to about 15 km/h for short periods of time. The fastest human (Jamaican Usain Bolt) topped 43 km/h, so it is likely that a fit hunter-gatherer—in fact most fit people—could outrun a crocodile reasonably easily.

19 Flannery (1994).
20 Webb (2006, p. 143). There is also an engraving of a crocodile-like head in the Olary region of South Australia. The engraving is accurate in proportion, scale and detail: elongated triangular head, eye position, rounded snout and scale patterns. It looks more like a crocodile head than anything else. The petroglyph points to the coexistence of crocodiles and humans during a wet phase in this now arid part of Australia, although the youngest dated remains for terrestrial crocodiles is over 75,000 years (Mountford and Edwards, 1962; Flood, 2000, p. 180).
21 Flannery (1994).
22 Flannery (1990; 1994), Webb (2006). The difference in morphological and ecological accounts suggests to me the possibility that there were different species of giant snake, living in different environments and killing in different ways.
23 Flannery (1994).
24 Hocknull et al. (2009).
25 Montgomery et al. (2002), Cheater (2003), Fry et al. (2006), Webb (2006).
26 Molnar (2004), Webb (2006).
27 In Murray and Chaloupka (1984).
28 The artistic revolution of the Upper Palaeolithic in Europe is conventionally thought to have commenced 35,000 years ago with the earliest securely dated art located at Grotte Chauvet in France being 34,000 years old (see Fagan, 2011; Brener, 2000). There is, more recently, an antiquity of 40,000 years for a red disk at El Castillo in Spain and there are engravings that date to 75,000 years in South Africa (see David et al., 2013).
29 Chaloupka (1999); see also Taçon et al. (2010).
30 Chaloupka (1999, p. 97). Historically, thylacine were recorded rearing just two or three young.
31 Chaloupka (1999, pp. 96–9), Beresford and Bailey (1981), Johnson and Wroe (2003), Gunn et al. (2011, p. 9).
32 Gunn et al. (2011).
33 Chaloupka (1999, p. 99).
34 Akerman (2009).
35 Taken from Murray and Chaloupka (1984); also Flood (1990), Morwood (2002), Mackness (2009).
36 Chaloupka (1999, pp. 45–7 and introductory quote).
37 Isaacs (1984), Jacob (1991), Chaloupka (1999), Webb (2006), and see the opening quote to this chapter.
38 See Crossan (1992).
39 Chaloupka (1999, p. 47).
40 Taçon et al. (1996).
41 Wallace and Wallace (1970); also Cane (2006b).
42 Quoted in Webb (2006, p. 134).
43 Tindale (1974, p. 119), Flood (2000, p. 174).
44 Ouzman et al. (2002).
45 Mulvaney and Kamminga (1999, p. 124) think, perhaps wisely, that it is a link too far, saying that 'assertions that Aboriginal myths reflect ancient "race memories" of particular extinct animals are speculative and we give them little credibility'.
46 Siddall et al. (2003), Hiscock (2008).
47 Such as the Mitchell, McArthur and Flinders flowing north and the Fly and Strickland rivers flowing south from New Guinea. Today there are over 60 major rivers across northern Australia, flowing directly into the sea and carrying nearly two-thirds of all Australia's fresh water away with them.
48 Torgersen et al. (1983), Jones and Torgersen (1988), Harris et al. (2005).
49 Jones and Torgensen (1988, p. 11), Voris (2000).
50 Torgersen et al. (1988).
51 Mulvaney (1961), Webb (2006).
52 Flood (2000, p. 87).
53 Yokoyama et al. (2001), Webb (2006).
54 Cane (2006a).
55 Cane (2006a).
56 Moore (2001).
57 The nomads I met in the remote desert of Australia in the mid 1980s had infants with them and younger married couples who were from the same family. The necessity for established marriage customs and regulated social systems need not have been an obligatory requirement in the early stages of colonisation.
58 See the following references for further understanding of settlement, colonisation,

socialisation and territoriality in Australia: Caspari (2013), Caspari and Lee (2004; 2006), O'Connell et al. (1999), Hawkes (2003), Hamilton (1982), Myers (1986), Cane (2002; 2006a and b), Peterson and Long (1986, p. 58), Peterson and Long (1986, p. 58), Birdsell (1977), Rhindos and Webb (1992), O'Connell and Allen (2012).

59 Webb and Rhindos (1997), O'Connell and Allen (2012), but see Webb (2006) for much slower figures of population growth in the Upper Pleistocene. Also note that this calculation is approximate—generalised from an estimated 'clan' size of 20 people in an average clan estate of 3.5 sq. km: giving a population density of approximately one person per 0.18 sq. km. This is consistent with the density figures along coastal Arnhem Land, but higher than population density inland, where again figures vary, but may have averaged about one person per 20 sq. km (see Peterson and Long, 1986, pp. 41 and 42).

60 Roberts et al. (1990a), Roberts et al. (1998).

61 Malakunanja was then occupied consistently and continually until the historic period.

62 Roberts et al. (1990b).

63 Malakunanja is such an important site that its antiquity has been the source of considerable archaeological debate. The researchers believe their estimated chronology of 50,000–60,000 years to be 'within one random uncertainty of the 95 per cent confidence limits' between the depth of the date and the date itself. Thus the 'one in three' probability that the date is 10,000 years older or younger accords with a statistical uncertainty at sigma 1 and the overall age/depth regression gives a 95 per cent and 99 per cent in that antiquity. An age of 40,000 years or less for the site is highly improbable (Roberts et al., 1990a, p. 127, Roberts, personal communication, 2013). There is both general acceptance of this antiquity—Flood (2000), Erlandson (2012, p. 18), Keegan (2012), Hiscock (2008; 2012)—and particular criticism of it—Allen (1994), O'Connell and Allen (1998), Mulvaney and Kamminga (1999), Allen and O'Connell (2003), O'Connell and Allen (2012)—and discussion either way, with a curiously implicit and seemingly intuitive acceptance of an antiquity of 50,000 years or more for first settlement that is clearly inferred from the older antiquity and implying, if not necessitating, an acceptance of it (see Bowdler, 1990, vs Roberts et al., 1990b, and Roberts et al., 1993, cf. Hiscock, 2006, Allen and O'Connell, 2003, vs Bird et al., 2002, vs Allen and Holdaway, 1995. Also, for a final word, Roberts et al., 1998).

64 Roberts et al. (1990b) and mentioned in Flood (2000).

65 Chlorite is related to talc, which is softer and feels soapier.

66 See also Taçon and Brockwell (1995), Flood (2000).

67 Roberts et al. (1993), Roberts et al. (1994), Jones (1999), Flood (2000), Fifield et al. (2001).

68 David et al. (2011).

69 Delannoy et al. (2012).

70 Hope et al. (2004), Fairbairn et al. (2006), Summerhayes et al. (2010).

71 Groube (1989).

72 Groube (1986), O'Connell and Allen (2004).

73 White et al. (1970), Summerhayes et al. (2010); see also Fairbairn et al. (2006).

74 Groube (1989).

75 Summerhayes et al. (2010).

76 Hope et al. (2004).

77 Slack et al. (2004).

78 David (1993), David et al. (1997).

79 O'Connor (1995), McConnell and O'Connor (1997), Fifield et al. (2001): the statistical variance on the determined antiquity of 39,700 years indicates the site could have been occupied 43,000–46,500 years ago. O'Connor subsequently dates the site at 42,800 years with a possible deviation of 40,950–44,650 years ago. This also appears to be the view of O'Connell and Allen (2012), who identify the median range as 43,100–45,600 with a mean of 44,000 years, and Hiscock (2008), who identifies the site as 43,000–46,500 years old.

80 O'Connor (1995), Frawley and O'Connor (2010).

81 See Pitman and Wallis (2012) for an overview.

82 The experiments were part of a thesis by G. Sheridan (1979).

83 O'Connor and Fankhauser (2001).
84 Balme (2000) presents an antiquity of 41,000 before present while O'Connell and Allen (2012) record 43,300–46,300 years and Hiscock (2008) presents 44,000–47,500 years ago.
85 And meaning 'Milkwater' because of its pastel colour during flood (Cane, 2001a).
86 Floodwaters from monsoonal rains flow from that catchment into the desert lake system at about 2 km/h. It takes about eight days for rain falling in the Kimberley to pass Sturt Creek Station (Carnegie, 1898, p. 362) and about ten days to reach Paraku (Lake Gregory) (Cane, 2006a).
87 After severe floods in 1993, see Bowler et al. (2001).
88 Compare observations of Bowler et al. (2001, p. 77) and Veth et al. (2009, p. 4).
89 Cane (1984).
90 Veth et al. (2009).
91 van der Kaars (1991), Wallis (2001), Hiscock and Wallis (2005).
92 Elkin (1938; p. 424), Hiatt (1976), Tonkinson (1978), Sutton (1991), Myers (1986), Stanner (1987, p. 226), Cane (2002).
93 Cane (2002; 2012).
94 Cane (1984; 1996a), see also O'Connell and Hawkes (1981), O'Connell et al. (1983), Yen (1989), Latz (1995).
95 Smith (1987; 1989; 2013, p. 89), Smith et al. (1997). Another cave called Kulpi Mara (meaning Cave Hand) is located near the Palmer River, to the east. This site is about 30,000 years old (Thorley, 1998).
96 The only other source of equivalent quality I am aware of comes from a small mine near Kings Canyon, 75 km southeast from Puritjarra (Cane and Stanley, 1985, p. 101).
97 Smith (1989), Rosenfeld and Smith (2002), Thorley (2004).
98 See Hiscock and Wallis (2005) and Hiscock (2008) for elaboration of desert transformations, Smith (1996) for regional desert occupation, and Cane (2012) for western desert society.
99 Turney et al. (2001).
100 Roberts et al. (1996), Cane (1995; 2001b), Turney et al. (2001). Allen's Cave was named after Allen Stewart who found it. He was the last Mirning man living permanently on the Nullarbor Plain. He was removed from his shack at Mundrabilla by the local station owner after the determination of Native Title by the High Court of Australia (*Mabo v. Queensland (No. 2)* (1992) 175 CLR 1) and went to live at Norseman.
101 Cane (1995).
102 Walshe (2012).
103 van der Kaars et al. (2006).
104 Sydney Harbour holding 560 gigalitres, by comparison.
105 Law et al. (2010), Przywolnik (2005). There is also a probable antiquity for settlement in the Chichester Range that is around 45,000 years old, recorded in an unpublished report by Hook, Sinclair and Wright, quoted in Smith (2013).
106 Morse (1988; 1993), Przywolnik (2005).
107 Western Australian Fisheries (2006).
108 Hesp et al. (1999).
109 Pearce and Barbetti (1981), Flood (2000), O'Connell and Allen (2012).
110 Dortch and Dortch (1996), Fifield et al. (2001).
111 Dortch (1984).
112 Bowler (1998), Bowler et al. (1970), Bowler et al. (2003), Webb (1989), Shawcross (1998) and see Flood (2000), Mulvaney and Kamminga (1999) and Hiscock (2008) for general discussion.
113 Webb (2013).
114 Balme (1995), Johnston (1993), Loy (1990), Flood (2000).
115 Turney et al. (2008).
116 Harris et al. (2005).
117 Colhoun (2000).
118 There is a tentative date for human settlement of 39,500 years ago in the Derwent River, near Hobart, although secondary dating offers an alternative antiquity of 26,000 years (Paton pers. com.).
119 Colhoun et al. (1999), Colhoun and Barrows (2011).
120 Cosgrove (1999), O'Connell and Allen (2004; 2012), also Turney et al. (2008).
121 Pike-Tay and Cosgrove (2002), Pike-Tay et al. (2008).
122 Cosgrove et al. (1990), Cosgrove (1999).
123 Cosgrove and Pike-Tay (2004).

124 Cosgrove and Allen (2001), Pike-Tay et al. (2008).
125 See also Cosgrove (1999).

Chapter 3: The Great Drought

1 See White (1967), Peterson (1968; 1973), Schrire (1982), Jones (1985).
2 Hope et al. (1985), Jones (1985).
3 Jones and Johnson (1985).
4 Jones and Johnson (1985), White (1967).
5 Geneste et al. (2010; 2012). Axes of similar age are also found in Japan (see Takashi, 2012).
6 Stone axes would be utilised throughout the world until about 2500 years ago, when axes made of iron finally replaced them (first used in southwestern Asia).
7 Kamminga and Allen (1973), Jones and Johnson (1985).
8 Brener (2000, p. 4).
9 David et al. (2012).
10 Taçon and Chippendale (1994), and see Chapter 4.
11 Chaloupka (1999, p. 123), Luebbers (1975), and see Chapter 4.
12 Chaloupka (1999), Jones (1985).
13 Roberts et al. (1997), Morwood (2002, p. 135).
14 Watchman (1993), Morwood (2002, pp. 268 and 270); see also Taylor (2005b).
15 The oldest shell beads occur in the eastern Mediterranean—they are found associated with a burial and are 92,000 years old. There are also perforated estuarine shells in a site in South Africa dated from 76,000 years ago, in Tanzania from 37,000 years ago, and elsewhere in the Levant from around 40,000 years ago. The oldest shell beads in Europe are located in Bulgaria and are 43,000 years old (summarised in Balme and Morse, 2006).
16 Balme and Morse (2006).
17 Morse (1988; 1993), Balme and Morse (2006): there is also a fragment of baler shell at Widgingarri Shelter near the Kimberley coast and a fragment of pearl shell, dated to 28,000 and 19,000 respectively—when the sea was nearby and subsequently over 200 km away, indicative of either massive levels of mobility or coastal trade networks (see O'Connor, 1996).
18 Summarised in Flood (1990).
19 Marine animals are the most frequent animals portrayed and include stingrays, bream, flounder, groper, leather jackets, sharks, turtles (with eggs and laying eggs), dolphins and whales (Vinnicombe, 1987).
20 Lorblanchet (1983).
21 Elkin (1931), Berndt (1959), Cane (2012).
22 So named because of the station at which it was first described in the historic era. Panaramitee Station is located in northeastern South Australia (Basedow, 1914; Mountford and Edwards, 1963).
23 The contemporary imagery contained in dot painting is not necessarily true to pure desert artistic tradition. That tradition is part dot (in so far as people recreate traditions of sand painting which feature that symbolism), part cave painting (which occasionally features these symbols), but they are largely absent from sacred artistic representations expressed on wood, sacred paraphernalia carved into hardwoods, and consist of closely incised lines, rather than tracks and circles found in contemporary dot paintings and ancient Panaramitee art.
24 Clegg (1987), see Smith (2013).
25 General summaries in Mulvaney and Kamminga (1999), Flood (2000), Morwood (2002). Detailed analysis by Edwards (1966; 1971), Maynard (1977; 1979), Rosenfeld (1982), Franklin (1991; 1996; 2011).
26 Smith (2013).
27 Clegg (1987).
28 Mulvaney (1975), Rosenfeld et al. (1981). Morwood (2002)—at Sandy Creek 1 and reported in Flood (1990, p. 118) as associated with occupational material 32,000 years old.
29 Nobbs and Dorn (1988), Flood (2000, pp. 157–61), Bednarik (2002), Morwood (2002, p. 78).
30 See McGilchrist (2009).
31 There is one human face from central Europe dated between 28,000 and 32,000 years ago but its preservation is poor and its features approximate. It was buried with a man in a grave and may have once been a life-like, naturalistic face. But it is one of few until 12,000 years ago. Then there is a unique collection of engraved faces in a small cave

called La Marche near the French town of Lussac-les-Châteaux. The cave was thought to have been occupied by a small family, and the 115 portraits engraved on smooth slabs of limestone transported to the cave. The engravings are difficult to decipher, but the faces are there, nonetheless—a unique treasure in an otherwise undifferentiated human past over the next 10,000 years (Brener, 2000).

32 Gamble (1982).
33 Brener (2000); see also Gamble (1982) on Venus figurines.
34 McDonald (2005), Mulvaney quoted in Smith (2013, p. 243).
35 See the facial representations in Dix (1977), Flood (2000, p. 154), McDonald (2005, p. 129).
36 McDonald (2005); see also Brady and Carson (2012).
37 White et al. (1970), Haberle (1993), Fairbairn et al. (2006), Hope (2009).
38 Cosgrove and Pike-Tay (2004), Pike-Tay et al. (2008): Typical densities of bone are in the order of 250,000 pieces of bone and 20,000 artefacts every cubic metre of deposit. Archaeologists have examined over 640,000 fragments of bone so far (Cosgrove and Allen, 2001); see also Allen et al. (1989), Webb and Allen (1990), Stern and Marshall (1993), Thomas (1993), Sheppard (1997).
39 But despite the vast quantities of bone subjected to analysis there is no evidence for the exploitation of now extinct giant marsupials.
40 The source of this rare volcanic glass is called Darwin's Crater, inland from Macquarie Harbour. The crater was only 'found' 30 years ago but had clearly been in the geographic vocabulary of the Tasmanians for a very long time.
41 In the Blue Mountains at or before 22,930 (Stockton and Holland, 1974), at Kenniff Cave in the Queensland central highlands at 18,800 years (Mulvaney and Joyce, 1965), and Cloggs Cave and Birrigai at 21,000 (Flood, 1980; Flood et al., 1987).
42 See Singh and Geissler (1985) and Wright (1986).
43 Flood et al. (1987).
44 Smith (2013, pp. 70 and 106).
45 Bowler (1998), van der Kaars (1991), Wallis (2001), Smith (2005), Smith (2013), Hiscock and Wallis (2005).
46 O'Connor et al. (1998), Slack et al. (2009), Law et al. (2010), Smith (2013 p. 79–80).
47 O'Connor et al. (1998), Slack et al. (2009), Law et al. (2010).
48 Thorley (1998).
49 The low numbers of artefacts indicate low intensity of cave usage, and can be compared to occupation in caves in Tasmania and Arnhem Land at the same time, where people left 12,000 artefacts and 20,000 artefacts per cubic metre of deposit respectively (Kiernan et al., 1983; Smith, 1989; Cane, 1995; Thorley, 1998).
50 See also Nicholson and Cane (1991b).
51 Such weathered holes—called blowholes because of the wind that surges in and out of them with changing atmospheric conditions—are so abundant across the Nullarbor that it is dangerous to walk or drive away from known tracks at night. They are easy to fall into and impossible to get out of without help.
52 Ward (2004).
53 Quoted in Smith (2013).
54 Balme and Hope (1990), Balme (1995).
55 Bowler et al. (2003), updating previous hydrologic characterisations in 1998.
56 Balme (1995).
57 Flood (2000, p. 51).
58 Bowler et al. (1970), Allen (1974), Balme (1995), Balme and Hope (1990), Loy (1990), Johnston (1993), Walshe (1998).
59 Barbetti and McElhinny (1972), Bowler et al. (2003).
60 Webb (1989).
61 See chronological summary in Smith and Sharp (1993), Flood (2000, Appendix 1); also Hiscock (2008), and in Chapter 2.
62 Mooney et al. (2011). The increase in firing from the earliest time of colonisation is striking but also correlates with broader climatic trends: there are more fires in wetter, warmer periods (when, presumably, there was more fuel to burn) and fewer fires in colder, drier periods (when there was less to burn).
63 Fairbairn et al. (2006), Hope (2009).

64 Jones and Johnson (1985), Hope et al. (1985), Jones (1985); see also Hughes and Sullivan (1981) in the context of the Holocene.

65 Kershaw (1986; 1994), Moss and Kershaw (2000), Kershaw and Whitlock (2000). See also Longmore and Heijnis (1999), who report an extreme fire on Fraser Island (Queensland) 70,000 years ago.

66 The original estimation for burning at Lake George is 125,000 years ago—similar to the timing of the first major evidence for charcoal at Lynch's Crater in Cape York and in oceanic cores in the Lombok Ridge in the Indian Ocean and the Coral Sea (185,000 years and 130,000 years ago respectively). These results raise the intriguing possibility that human colonisation of Australia is much older than even the oldest dates suggest it to be. The early date for burning at Lake George has been reassessed at around 60,000 years ago—the antiquity that is most frequently accepted by archaeologists—but there is little commentary about the implied antiquity of colonisation at the other locations (see Singh and Geissler, 1985; Wright, 1986; Kershaw et al., 1994, 2003, 2010; Wang et al., 1999; Hope et al., 2004).

67 Hiatt (1967), Cosgrove (1999), Colhoun et al. (1999), McIntosh (2010).

68 Wang et al. (1999).

69 Changes in the carbon isotopes in fossilised emu and *Genyornis* egg shell indicates a shift from plants (consumed by the birds who laid the eggs) characteristic of hot climates with summer rainfall to grasses and chenopod shrubs typical of colder drier climates: i.e. from a seasonal wet to a semi-dry climate (Miller et al., 1999; 2005).

70 Miller et al. (1999; 2005), Johnson et al. (1999), Magee and Miller (1998), Kershaw et al. (2003), Magee et al. (2004), Murphy et al. (2012), Smith (2009; 2013).

71 Horton (1982), Head (1989), Bowman (1988), Smith (2013).

72 Peron (1809), Jones (1968), also Jones (1969).

73 Ash Wednesday across southeastern Australia in 1983 and Black Saturday in Victoria in 2009.

74 See any number of publications on this subject: Burbidge (1943), Jones (1969), Hallam (1975), Gould (1980), O'Connell and Hawkes (1981), Kimber (1983), Cane and Stanley (1985), Cane (1996b), Latz (1995), Bird et al. (2008), Gammage (2011) and Chapter 4.

75 Cane and Stanley (1985).

76 Roberts et al. (2001), Johnson (2005), Koch et al. (2006), Roberts and Brook (2010c).

77 Flannery (1999), Roberts and Brook (2010b), Koch et al. (2006).

78 Roberts et al. (2001).

79 Jones (1968), Horton (1984), Flannery (1990; 1999), Miller et al. (1999; 2005), Roberts et al. (2001), Pate et al. (2002), Bird et al. (2003), Brook and Bowman (2004), Johnson (2005), Wroe and Field (2006), Wroe et al. (2006), Cupper and Duncan (2006), Hiscock (2008), Roberts and Brook (2010a; 2010b; 2010c), Prideaux et al. (2010), Grun et al. (2010), Gillespie et al. (2012), Surovell and Grund (2012), Webb (2013).

80 Webb (2008), Smith (2013).

81 Roberts and Jacobs (2008), Turney et al. (2008), Gillespie et al. (2012), McIntosh (2010); see also Cosgrove et al. (2010).

82 These sites are summarised in Johnson (2005), also Roberts et al. (2001), and include: *NSW*—Mooki River at 42,000, Lake George at 28,700, Lake Tandou at 29,600, Lake Menindee at 31,000 and Lime Springs at 24,000; *VIC*—Cloggs Cave at 28,900 (also Flood, 2000); *SA*—Seton Site at 20,000; *WA*—Tight Entrance Cave at 33,000; *TAS*—Main Cave, Montagu at 13,000; *PNG*—Nombe rock shelter at 14,500 years.

83 See Gillespie and Brook (2006), Grun et al. (2010), Fillios et al. (2010) and Smith (2013) compared to original investigations by Dodson et al. (1993), Field and Dodson (1999), Field et al. (2001), Field et al. (2008), Trueman et al. (2005).

84 Gillespie et al. (1978), Horton and Wright (1981), van Huet et al. (1998), Mulvaney and Kamminga (1999), Johnson (2005), Hiscock (2008).

85 Hucknell in *First Footprints*, Episode 2, and personal communication (2013).

86 See Horton (1986): Cosgrove and Allen (2001, p. 425) believe it is difficult to believe otherwise, and Wroe and Field (2006, p. 2017) think it inconceivable.

87 Hughes et al. (2011).
88 Flannery et al. (1983), Gillieson and Mountain (1983), Hope et al. (1993), Fairbairn et al. (2006).
89 Archer et al. (1980).
90 Balme (1980), Dortch (1984).
91 Tindale (1955), Tedford (1967), Hope et al. (1983).
92 Cupper and Duncan (2006): the old hearth is 45,000 years old and appears to have been dug into bone deposits, although why this would be done is difficult to determine unless it was an oven.
93 Walshe (2012).
94 Webb (2013).
95 Hope et al. (1977).
96 Vanderwal and Fullagar (1989).
97 Gorecki et al. (1984).
98 Dodson et al. (1993), Furby et al. (1993), and see Smith (2013), Fillios et al. (2010).
99 Gillespie et al. (1978).
100 The marks look decidedly man-made but have been interpreted by Horton and Wright (1981) as being made by the teeth of marsupial lions (*Thylacoleo*).
101 See McCarthy (1979, pp. 33–5).
102 By Kim Akerman and a group of people from Balgo community.
103 Ngarta et al. (2004, pp. 62–4). A number of other people were also rumoured to still be living in the desert at this time. Yawa may have travelled with a man called Pitjri, whose camp and tracks we also encountered in 1989.
104 See, for example, Prideaux et al. (2009) in relation to the water needs of the giant kangaroo *Procoptodon goliah*, and note that camels have a slow turnover of water and a low metabolic rate. They do not sweat until it is over 38°C, their faeces contain less than 50 per cent water, and they can partition water so as to be able to drink large quantities without urinating. The hump of a camel stores enough food for 6 months (Newman, 1983).
105 Brook and Johnson (2006), Roberts and Brook (2010a), Surovell and Grund (2012).
106 Smith (2013).
107 See Chaloupka (1999, Ch. 2), Taçon et al. (1996), David (2002).
108 Trueman et al. (2005), Wroe et al. (2006; 2013), Webb (2013).
109 Bowler et al. (2012), but note variations on that theme in Bowler (1998) and Bowler et al. (2003).
110 van der Kaars (1991), van der Kaars et al. (2006), Nanson et al. (1992), O'Connor (1995), Magee and Miller (1998), English et al. (2001), Bowler et al. (2001; 2003 but cf. Bowler 1998), Wallis (2001), van der Kaars and De Deckker (2002), Smith (2005; 2013), Hiscock and Wallis (2005), Ayliffe et al. (2008), Prideaux et al. (2007), Veth et al. (2009), Roberts and Brook (2010a), Cohen et al. (2012).
111 Lambeck et al. (2002).
112 Voris (2000), Lambeck et al. (2002), Barrows et al. (2002), Petherik et al. (2008; 2013), Clark et al. (2009).
113 Petherik et al. (2008), Clark et al. (2009).
114 Harris et al. (2005).
115 Webb (2013).
116 De Deckker (2001), van der Kaars and De Deckker (2002), van der Kaars et al. (2006), Hesse et al. (2004).
117 Hesse et al. (2004), Lambeck et al. (2002), Petherik et al. (2013).
118 Hiscock and Wallis (2005), Frawley and O'Conner (2010, p. 318).
119 van der Kaars et al. (2006), Hesse et al. (2004).
120 Chivas et al. (2001), Hope et al. (2004).
121 Torgersen et al. (1983; 1988), Jones and Torgersen (1988), De Deckker (2001), Chivas et al. (2001), Reeves et al. (2008).
122 Smith (2013).
123 Hope et al. (2004), Fairbairn et al. (2006).
124 Hope et al. (2004), Petherik et al. (2013).
125 Page et al. (1994), Nanson et al. (2008).
126 Barrows et al. (2001), Hesse et al. (2004), Petherik et al. (2013).
127 Bowler and Magee (1978), Page et al. (1994), Hesse et al. (2004), Bowler et al. (2012)—presenting a modified model of Pleistocene hydrology from previous models in Bowler (1998) and Bowler et al. (2003).
128 Petherik et al. (2013).
129 Note that estimates vary wildly regarding the size of these ice caps—from 5000 sq. km (De Deckker, 2001) to 108 sq. km (Petherik et al., 2013).
130 De Deckker (2001), Colhoun and Barrows (2011), Barrows et al. (2002; 2004), Shulmeister et al. (2004), Mooney et al. (2011).

131 Turney et al. (2001).
132 Hesse et al. (2004).
133 Magee and Miller (1998), Magee et al. (2004), Bowler (1998, p. 149), Miller et al. (1999), Luly (2001), Smith (2013).
134 van der Kaars and De Deckker (2002).
135 Wallis (2001, p. 112), Frawley and O'Connor (2010).
136 Smith et al. (1995).
137 Nanson et al. (1992; 2008), English et al. (2001).
138 Page et al. (1994), Nanson et al. (2008).
139 Williams et al. (2001), Glasby et al. (2010).
140 Page et al. (1994), Hesse et al. (2004): in the Murray–Darling Basin, for example, evaporation dropped to about 1000 mm per year in the peak glacial period, compared with about 1800 mm per year today. Carbon dioxide levels fell by as much as 40 per cent (compared with today), thus limiting plant growth and reducing its ability to recover from fire.
141 McKenzie and Kershaw (2000), Luly (2001), Hesse et al. (2004), Petherik et al. (2013).
142 In Chapters 1 and 2.
143 Cane (1990).
144 Something also noticed by the explorer Carnegie when he crossed it in the 1890s (Carnegie, 1898).
145 Elkin (1931), Cane (2006b).
146 Cane (1984; 1989; 1990; 2006a; 2008).
147 Brockwell et al. (1989).
148 Cane (1990; 1993; 2002).
149 See Veth (1989) for a model (barrier and refuge) of population dispersal and contraction, and Smith (2013) for a model (point to point) of consolidation.
150 See Sutton (1991), David (2002), Cane (2002).
151 Cane (1996b).
152 Cane (2012). A similar account of desertification elsewhere in the desert is told by Mountford, quoted in Flood (2000, p. 21).
153 Cane (2002).
154 On the northern desert margin at Carpenter's Gap, there is evidence for decreased site usage, although at Carpenter's Gap 3 nearby there is preliminary evidence for a peak in occupation at the peak of glacial aridity (O'Connor, 1995; Wallis, 2001; O'Connor and Veth, 2006). At Mandu Mandu rock shelter in the northwest there is occupation at 39,000–23,000 years ago (Morse, 1993). In the Pilbara occupation is seen at Juukan (2), Mesa JJ24 and Milly's Cave between 28,000 and 17,000 years ago (Slack et al., 2009; Hughes et al., 2011; Marwick, 2002). In the Little Sandy Desert, Serpents Glen reveals occupation at 28,000 years ago, and in central Australia, Puritjarra sees people there at 35,000 and 24,000–8000 years ago (Veth et al., 2008; Smith, 2013). In the Lake Eyre Basin, Pleistocene occupation is seen at 18,400 years at Cuckadoo Shelter in the north and at 22,000 at Madigan Gulf 4 on the lake (Davidson et al., 1993; Magee and Miller, 1998). There is evidence for occupation at Hookina Creek in the Flinders Ranges at 26,000 years ago (Smith, 2013, p. 129). The Nullarbor Plain sees people at Koonalda Cave and Allen's Cave at 26,000–16,000 and 22,000 years ago respectively (Wright, 1971; Sharpe and Sharpe, 1976; Cane, 1995); and see summary in Smith (2013).
155 Smith et al. (1998), Smith and Fankhauser (2009), Smith (2013).
156 Wright (1971), Maynard and Edwards (1971).
157 Webb (2006; 2007).
158 Average Indonesian males are 162 cm, and females 151 cm; average African males are 168 cm, and females 158 cm; average Australian males are 178 cm, and females 164 cm.
159 Thomson (1975), Cane (2006a).
160 See Smith (2013), Bowler (1998), Bowler et al. (2003), Bowler et al. (2012).
161 Wright (1994), Rhode et al. (2006), Fagan (2011).
162 See David (2002) and Smith (2013).
163 Allen (1974). Smith (1988) notes that these artefacts are not seed-grinding implements per se, but are, in my experience, the remnants of original seed-grinding implements. Balme (1990) notes that some of the described pieces are not in situ and may be younger than 15,000 years, and Bowler (1998) cites a number of examples that support the notion of late Pleistocene seed grinding.
164 Cane (1989).
165 Cane (1989).

166 Bowler (1998), McConnell and O'Connor (1997), McConnell (1998), Fullagar and Field (1997).
167 Cane (1989; 1996a).
168 Hiscock (2008), Smith (2013).
169 Jones (1985), David et al. (2011), and summarised in Lourandos (1997) and Flood (2000).
170 Cape York: Morwood (2002), Morwood and Hobbs (1995), David (2002); Great Dividing Range: Mulvaney (1975); Alps: Flood (1980), Flood et al. (1987).
171 Allen (1996), Holdaway and Porch (1996), Cosgrove (1999), Cosgrove and Allen (2001).
172 Morse (1988).
173 Bowdler (1990).
174 O'Connor (1996).
175 Quoted in Smith (2013).
176 Neal and Stock (1986).
177 Lampert (1971).
178 Hanckel (1985).
179 Bowdler (1984). There are also recent dates of settlement at least 30,000, perhaps 35,000 years ago on the very northern margin of the Bassian Plain, southeast of present-day Melbourne (Hewitt and Allen, 2010).
180 Sim (1994).
181 Sim and Thorne (1990).

Chapter 4: The Great Flood

1 Dodson and Wright (1989), Hope et al. (2004), Hesse et al. (2004), Mooney et al. (2011), Petherik et al. (2013).
2 Woodroffe et al. (1988), Ross et al. (1992), Wallis (2001), Hope et al. (2004), van der Kaars et al. (2006).
3 Kershaw et al. (2007), Black et al. (2008), Fitzsimmons and Barrows (2010), Mooney et al. (2011), Fletcher and Moreno (2011; 2012), Petherik et al. (2013).
4 Woodroffe et al. (1988), Hope et al. (2004), van der Kaars et al. (2006), Smith and Ross (2008), Marx et al. (2009), Smith (2009), Fitzsimmons and Barrows (2010), Mooney et al. (2011), Fletcher and Moreno (2012), Petherik et al. (2013), Smith (2013).
5 Chappell and Thom (1977), Chappell and Polach (1991), Yokoyama et al. (2000), Lambeck et al. (2002), Belperio et al. (2002), Haworth et al. (2002), Cann et al. (2006), Murray-Wallace (2007), Smith (2013). The high stand peaked 1 m above current levels about 6400 years ago across the southern coast of the Great Australian Bight (Belperio et al., 2002), and was as high as 1–3 m above present levels in the Gulf of Carpentaria and Cape York 6000–5000 years ago (Haworth et al., 2002; Faulkner, 2009).
6 Dortch and Morse (1984), Murray-Wallace (2007), Reeves et al. (2008), Smith (2013). Torres Strait: Lawrence and Lawrence (2004); Kangaroo Island: Lampert (1981). The Recherche Archipelago between 9000 and 11,000 years ago, Rottnest islands 8000–7000 years ago, the Houtman Abrolhos Islands 12,000–11,000, and the Montebello and Barrow islands 9000 years ago.
7 Barker (1991; 1996), Lamb and Barker (2001).
8 Rowland (1980).
9 Veth et al. (2007) quoted in Smith (2013); Dortch and Morse (1984).
10 Bowdler (1984). A similar situation is revealed on King Island (Sim, 1994). The last evidence for the people is about 12,000 years ago. However, there are signs of more recent occupation on both Hunter and King islands within the last 2000 years. People returned to the islands, but it seems as lonesome castaways rather than intended visitors: people blown, washed by the tide—lucky to have found land and unlucky enough to have been left there alone to die. Also note that Jones (1979) reports a site on King Island that is 7600 years old, suggesting a relict population may also have survived on this island for a time.
11 Sim (1994).
12 Harrington (2012).
13 Lampert (1981), Clark and Lampert (1981), also Draper (1987): the island was unoccupied at contact, the coastal Aboriginal people referring to it as a sacred island for the spirits of the dead (see Flood, 2000, p. 140).
14 See Wright (1971), Mulvaney (1975), Flood (2000), Cane (2001b).
15 Oppenheimer (1998).
16 Mulvaney (1975), Flood (1990; 2000), Dixon (1972), Isaacs (1984), Berndt (1940), Tindale

(1987), Dortch and Morse (1984), Cane (2002).

17 Summarised in Flood (1999); also Isaacs (1984), Dortch and Morse (1984).

18 Cane (2002), and Chapter 3.

19 Marun (1969), Akerman (1989), Nicholson (1994), Walshe (1994), Cane (1995; 2001b), Turney et al. (2001), Smith (2013).

20 Cane (1995), Turney et al. (2001), Smith (2013).

21 Seton site: Lampert (1981); Cheetup Site: Smith (1993; 1996); Tunnel Cave: Dortch (1994); Devil's Lair: Balme et al. (1978), Dortch (1984, p. 81), Mulvaney and Kamminga (1999).

22 Generalised in Lourandos (1997), Hiscock (2008) and David (2002, p. 121). Magnificent Gallery: Morwood and Jung (1995), Morwood (2002, p. 131).

23 Cane (1984).

24 Taçon and Chippendale (1994); also Taçon (1994), Chaloupka (1999).

25 Luebbers (1975), Jones (2004).

26 Where they were also used as musical implements—two being aligned and used as clapping sticks. Normally smaller, lighter, symmetrical boomerangs were designed and used for this purpose.

27 See Mulvaney and Kamminga (1999), Hiscock (2006; 2008).

28 They first appear in China about 25,000 years ago (Fagan 2011, p. 119).

29 Slack et al. (2004), Hiscock and Attenbrow (1998).

30 Robertson et al. (2009).

31 McDonald et al. (2007); also Pardoe (1988), Webb (1989; 1995).

32 Cane (2006a).

33 See also Bellwood (1997), Gray and Jordan (2000).

34 Martins et al. (2012).

35 Savolainen et al. (2004), Johnson and Wroe (2003).

36 Kailola et al. (1993), Cane (1997).

37 Starling (1971), Lampert (1971), Bailey (1975), Coutts (1981; 1984), McBryde (1982), Bowdler (1977; 1982), Sullivan (1984), Marshall (1988), Godfrey (1989), Aiken et al. (1992), Colley (1992): summarised in Cane (1997).

38 Bailey (1975) and McBryde (1982) summarised in Cane (1997).

39 Campbell (1969), Starling (1971) and Connah (1974) summarised in Cane (1997).

40 Dyall (1982) summarised in Cane (1997).

41 Lampert (1971).

42 Lampert (1981), Luebbers (1982), Dortch et al. (1984), Bowdler (1990), O'Connor (1992), O'Connor and Sullivan (1994), Nicholson and Cane (1991a), Smith (1993) and Nicholson (1994) summarised in Cane (1997; 2001b).

43 Nicholson (1994).

44 Kailola et al. (1993).

45 Morse (1988), O'Connor (1987; 1992; 1994; 1996), Bowdler (1999), Przywolnik (2005) and summary in Cane (1997).

46 Lorblanchet (1977; 1992), O'Connor (1999), Veitch (1999), Przywolnik (2005), Wells and Lali (2003) quoted in Smith (2013), Clune and Harrison (2009).

47 O'Connor and Sullivan (1994), Benterrak et al. (1984).

48 Meehan (1982), Beaton (1985), Rowland (1987; 1988), Hall and Hiscock (1988), Woodroffe et al. (1988), Mowat (1995), Cane (1997), Chaloupka (1999), Hiscock (2008), Faulkner (2009).

49 The antiquity of spear-throwers may predate the Holocene with evidence from dated art in the Kimberley pointing to as early as 17,000 years ago for this invention (Walsh and Morwood, 1999).

50 Chaloupka (1999).

51 Taçon (1993; 1994). See Peterson and Long (1986), Sutton (2003).

52 See Morwood (2002), David (2002).

53 McDonald (1999).

54 Mulvaney (1976), McBryde (1984).

55 Johnston (1993), see Ross (1985).

56 Lourandos (1997)—Cane (1989) for seed grinding; David (2002), Lourandos (1997) and Smith (2013) for antiquity (also Chapter 3).

57 Williams (1985; 1987), Lourandos (1997).

58 Balme and Beck (1996).

59 Lourandos (1997).

60 Coutts et al. (1978), Head (1989); also Lourandos (1997).

61 Jones (1968; 1969), Hallam (1975), Gott (1982), Lourandos (1997), Gammage (2011).

62 Brown (1987), Pardoe (1988), Butlin (1983; 1993), Webb (1995), Littelton and Allen (2007), and summary in Mulvaney and Kamminga (1999).
63 Barker (1975), Pretty (1986), Mulvaney and Kamminga (1999).
64 Gould (1969), Tindale (1977), O'Connell and Hawkes (1981), Cane (1984; 1990; 1996a; 2002), Cane and Stanley (1985), Latz (1995), Smith (2013).
65 Marun (1969), Cane (1995), Walshe (1994), quoted in and also see Smith (2013).
66 Aiston (1937), Mulvaney (1976).
67 Mulvaney (1976), Flood (2000), Jones (2004).
68 McBryde (1997), Mulvaney (1997) quoted in Smith (2013).
69 Davidson (1952), Clarke (1976), Baynes (1984), Smith (2013).
70 Munn (1970), Cane (2012).
71 Elkin (1940), Berndt and Berndt (1943), Meggitt (1962), Myers (1986), McConvell (1997), Cane (2012).
72 Kiernan et al. (1983).
73 Cosgrove (1999), Allen (1996), Pike-Tay and Cosgrove (2002).
74 Noetling (1910), Plomley (1966), Hiatt (1967), Jones (1971), Cane et al. (1979).
75 See Jones (1974).
76 Lourandos (1983; 1997), Cosgrove (1985).
77 Harris et al. (2005).
78 There is 194 sq. km of land for every kilometre of coast on the mainland, and 29 sq. km of land for every kilometre of coast in Tasmania.
79 Stockton (1983), Cane (1997).
80 Reber (1965), Jones (1971), Vanderwal (1977), Gaffney and Stockton (1980), Cosgrove (1985), Cane (1997). Art: Robinson in Plomley (1966). Stone alignments: Jones (1965), Cane (1980).
81 Jones (1980).
82 Lourandos (1997), Cosgrove (1995), and compare Allen and Porch (1996), Hiscock (2008).
83 But see Taylor (2007).
84 Jones (1971; 1977; 1978), Vanderwal (1978), Allen (1979), Horton (1979), Bowdler (1980), Walters (1981), White and O'Connell (1982), Dunnett (1993), Colley and Jones (1987), Lourandos (1997), Cane (1997), Mulvaney and Kamminga (1999), Hiscock (2008).
85 Records made by Robinson (in Plomley, 1966), 27 January 1834 and 20 October 1830; also Jones (1971, p. 461).
86 See Ling Roth (1899).
87 Robinson in Plomley (1966).
88 Jones (1966; 1967; 1981; 1984), Stockton (1982), Lourandos (1988), Mulvaney and Kamminga (1999), summary Cane (1997): historic sealing, Day (2012, pp. 26 and 34). The last breeding colony of elephant seals was exterminated on King Island in the 1800s. Apart from the birth of two pups on the west coast of Tasmania in 1958 and 1957, no breeding has taken place in Australia since that time (Bryden, 1983). There is also evidence for imperceptible over-predation in the accumulation of abalone shells at West Point, where the shellfish people ate became smaller and smaller through time.
89 See Jones (1976). King Island: Jones (1976), Murray et al. (1982), Sim (1990; 1994), Bowdler (1984); islands generally: Brown (1991); Tasman Island: Harris (1984), Gaughwin (1985), Brown (1991), Cane (1997).
90 Suarez (1999).
91 Mulvaney (1989, p. 8).
92 Tasmania: Giblin (1928, p. 12); North West Shelf: Green (1986), www.museum.gov.au/maritime-archaeology-db/wrecks; South Australia: Tindale (1986, p. 265) and *Gulliver's Travels*, Swift (1986); Northern Territory: Mulvaney and Kamminga (1999, p. 423) and www.voc.linet.net.au/voages.html.
93 Macknight (1969), Macknight and Gray (1970), Baker (1992), Mitchell (1994), Chaloupka (1999), Mulvaney and Kamminga (1999) (site summary in Cane, 1997).
94 Native title was recognised over the island in 2001 (*Kaurareg People v Queensland* [2001] FCA 657).
95 Butlin (1993).
96 Reported by George Augustus Robinson in his journal of northwestern Tasmania, edited by Plomley (1966).
97 But see Reynolds (1981), Flood (2006), Perkins and Langton (2008), Sutton (2011), Bottoms (2013).

98 See discussion in Stanner (1966; 1984), Tonkinson (1978) and Cane (2002).

99 This figure includes 50 per cent of the Northern Territory and 85 per cent of its coastline: and consists of a total of 1,581,000 sq. km of native title determination, and 755,564 sq. km as land rights. Rights to land across Cape York are either determined through native title or land-use agreement: population, see Taylor (2005a).

BIBLIOGRAPHY

Aiken, G., Nicholson, A.F. and Cane, S.B. (1992) North Coast middens—A report on the distribution, type and representation of middens in northern NSW and south east Queensland. Report to the Australian Heritage Commission, Canberra.

Aiston, G. (1937) The Aboriginal narcotic pitcheri. *Oceania* 7:372–7.

Akerman, K. (1989) Report on a shell pendant from Allen's Cave. Unpublished report.

Akerman, K. (2009) Interaction between humans and megafauna depicted in Australian rock art. *Antiquity* 83(322):319.

Allen, H. (1974) The Bagundji of the lower Darling Basin: Cereal gatherers in an uncertain environment. *World Archaeology* 5:309–22.

Allen, H. (1979) Left out in the cold: Why the Tasmanians stopped eating fish. *The Artefact* 4:1–10.

Allen, H. (1998) Reinterpreting the 1969–1972 Willandra Lakes archaeological surveys. *Archaeology in Oceania* 33(3):207–20.

Allen, J. (1994) Radiocarbon determinations, luminescence dating and Australian archaeology. *Antiquity* 68:339–43.

Allen, J. (ed.) (1996) *Report on the Southern Forests Project: Site descriptions, stratigraphies and chronologies.* Melbourne: School of Archaeology, La Trobe University.

Allen, J. and Holdaway, S. (1995) The contamination of Pleistocene radiocarbon determinations in Australia. *Antiquity* 69:101–12.

Allen, J., Marshall, B. and Ranson, D. (1989) A note on excavations at the Maxwell River Site, M86/2, South West Tasmania. *Australian Archaeology* 29:3–9.

Allen, J. and O'Connell, J.F. (2003) The long and the short of it: Archaeological approaches to determining when humans first colonised Australia and New Guinea. *Australian Archaeology* 57:5–19.

Allen, J. and O'Connell, J.F. (2008) Getting from Sunda to Sahul. In S. O'Connor, G. Clarke and F. Leach (eds) *Islands of Inquiry: Colonisation, seafaring and the archaeology of maritime landscapes*, pp. 31–46. Terra Australis 29. Canberra: ANU E Press.

Allen, J. and Porch, N. (1996) Warragarra rockshelter. In J. Allen (ed.) *Report on the Southern Forests Project: Site descriptions, stratigraphies and chronologies*, pp. 195–218. Melbourne: School of Archaeology, La Trobe University.

Ambrose, S.H. (1998) Late Pleistocene human population bottlenecks, volcanic winter, and differentiation of modern humans. *Journal of Human Evolution* 34:623–51.

Ambrose, S.H. (2003) Did the super-eruption of Toba cause a human population bottleneck? Reply to Gathorne-Hardy and Harcourt-Smith. *Journal of Human Evolution* 45:231–7.

Archer, M., Crawford, I.M. and Merrilees, D. (1980) Incisions, breakages and charring, some probably man-made, in fossil bones from Mammoth Cave, Western Australia. *Alcheringa* 4(2):115–31.

Argue, D., Morwood, M.J., Sutikna, T., Jatmiko and Saptomo, E.W. (2009) *Homo floresiensis*: A cladistic analysis. *Journal of Human Evolution* 57:623–39.

Arnold, J.E. (1995) Transportation, innovation and social complexity amongst hunter-gatherer societies. *American Anthropologist* 97:733–47.

Atkinson, Q.D., Gray, R.D. and Drummond, A.J. (2008) mtDNA variation predicts population size in humans and reveals a major southern Asian chapter in human history. *Molecular Biology and Evolution* 25(2):468–74.

Australian Government, Bureau of Meteorology (2012), www.bom.gov.au/tsunami/history/1883.shtml.

Australian Maritime Safety Authority (1993) *Survival at Sea: A training and instruction manual.* Canberra: AGPS.

Ayliffe, L.K., Prideaux, G.J., Bird, M.I., Grun, R., Roberts, R.G. et al. (2008) Age constraints on Pleistocene megafauna at Tight Entrance Cave in southwestern Australia. *Quaternary Science Reviews* 27:1784–8.

Bailey, G.N. (1975) The role of molluscs in coastal economies: The results of midden analysis in Australia. *Journal of Archaeological Science* 2:45–62.

Baker, R. (1992) Macassan site survey and bibliography. Unpublished report. Darwin: Museum and Art Galley of the Northern Territory.

Balme, J. (1980) An analysis of charred bone from Devil's Lair, Western Australia. *Archaeology and Physical Anthropology in Oceania* 15(2):81–6.

Balme, J. (1990) The antiquity of grinding stones in semi arid western New South Wales. *Australian Archaeology* 32:3–9.

Balme, J. (1995) 30,000 years of fishery in western New South Wales. *Archaeology in Oceania* 30:1–21.

Balme, J. (2000) Excavations revealing 40,000 years of occupation at Mimbi Caves, south central Kimberley, Western Australia. *Australian Archaeology* 51:1–5.

Balme, J. and Beck, W. (1996) Earth mounds in southeastern Australia. *Australian Archaeology* 42:39–51.

Balme, J., Davidson, I., McDonald, J., Stern, N. and Veth, P. (2009) Symbolic behaviour and the peopling of the southern arc route to Australia. *Quaternary International* 202:59–68.

Balme, J. and Hope, J. (1990) Radiocarbon dates from midden sites in the Lower Darling River area of western New South Wales. *Archaeology in Oceania* 25:85–101.

Balme, J., Merrilees, D. and Porter, J.K. (1978) Late Quaternary mammal remains, spanning about 30,000 years from excavations in Devil's Lair, Western Australia. *Journal of the Royal Society of Western Australia* 61:33–65.

Balme, J. and Morse, K. (2006) Shell beads and social behaviour in Pleistocene Australia. *Antiquity* 80(310):799–811.

Barbetti, M. and McElhinny, M. (1972) Evidence of a geomagnetic excursion 30,000 yr BP. *Nature* 239:327–30.

Barker, B.C. (1975) Peridontal disease and tooth dislocation in Aboriginal remains from Lake Nitchie (NSW), West Point (Tasmania) and Limestone Creek (Victoria). *Archaeology and Physical Anthropology in Oceania* 10:185–217.

Barker, B.C. (1991) Nara Inlet 1: Coastal resource and the Holocene marine transgression in the Whitsunday Islands, Central Queensland. *Archaeology in Oceania* 26(3):102–9.

Barker, B.C. (1996) Maritime hunter-gatherers on the tropical coast: A social model for change. In S. Ulm, I. Lilley and A. Ross (eds) *Australian Archaeology '95*. Tempus 6:31–44.

Barker, G., Barton, H., Bird, M., Daly, P., Datan, I. et al. (2007) The 'human revolution' in lowland tropical Southeast Asia: The antiquity and behaviour of anatomically modern humans at Niah Cave, Sarawak, Borneo. *Journal of Human Evolution* 52:243–61.

Barrows, T.T., Stone, J.O. and Fifield, L.K. (2004) Exposure ages for Pleistocene periglacial deposits in Australia. *Quaternary Science Reviews* 23:697–708.

Barrows, T.T., Stone, J.O., Fifield, L.K. and Cresswell, R.G. (2001) Late Pleistocene glaciation of the Kosciusko massif, Snowy Mountains, Australia. *Quaternary Research* 55:179–89.

Barrows, T.T., Stone, J.O., Fifield, L.K. and Cresswell, R.G. (2002) The timing of the Late Glacial Maximum in Australia. *Quaternary Science Reviews* 21:159–73.

Barton, H. and Paz, V. (2007) Subterranean diets in the tropical rainforests of Sarawak, Malaysia. In T.P. Denham, J. Iriarte and L. Vrydaghs (eds) *Rethinking Agriculture: Archaeological and ethnographic perspectives*, pp. 5–77. One World Archaeology. California: Left Coast Press Inc.

Basedow, H. (1914) Aboriginal rock carvings of great antiquity in South Australia. *Journal of the Royal Anthropological Institute* 44:195–211.

Baynes, A. (1984) Native mammal remains from Wilgie Mia Aboriginal ochre mine: Evidence on the pre-European fauna of the western arid zone. *Records of the Western Australian Museum* 11:297–310.

Beaton, J.M. (1985) Evidence for a coastal occupational time lag at Princess Charlotte Bay (north Queensland). *Archaeology in Oceania* 20(1):1–20.

Bednarik, R. (2002) The dating of rock art: A critique. *Journal of Archaeological Science* 29:1213–33.

Bellwood, P. (1997) *The Prehistory of the Indo-Malaysian Archipelago*. Honolulu: University of Hawaii Press.

Bellwood, P. (2009) The dispersals of established food-producing populations. *Current Anthropology* 50(5):621–6.

Belperio, A.P., Harvey, N. and Bourman, R.P. (2002) Spatial and temporal variability in the Holocene sea-level record of the South Australian coastline. *Sedimentary Geology* 150:153–69.

Benterrak, K., Muecke, S. and Roe, P. (1984) *Reading the Country*. Perth: Fremantle Arts Centre Press.

Beresford, B. and Bailey, G. (1981) *Search for the Tasmanian Tiger*. Hobart: Blubberhead Press.

Berndt, R.M. (1940) Some aspects of Jaralde culture, South Australia. *Oceania* 11:164–8.

Berndt, R.M. (1959) The concept of 'The Tribe' in the Western Desert of Australia. *Oceania* 30(2):81–107.

Berndt, R.M. and Berndt, C.H. (1943) A preliminary report. *Oceania* 13(3):243–80; 13(4):362–75; 14(1):30–66; 14(2):24–58.

Bilek, S.L., Satake, K. and Sieh, K. (2007) Introduction to the special issue on the 2004 Sumatra-Andaman earthquake and the Indian Ocean tsunami. *Bulletin of the Seismological Society of America* 97(1A):S1–S5.

Bird, M.I., Hope, G. and Taylor, D. (2004) Populating PEP II: The dispersal of humans and agriculture through Austral-Asia and Oceania. *Quaternary International* 118–19:145–63.

Bird, M.I., Turney, C.S.M., Fifield, L.K., Jones, R., Ayliffe, L.K. et al. (2002) Radiocarbon analysis of the early archaeological site of Nauwalabila I, Arnhem Land, Australia: Implications for sample suitability and stratigraphic integrity. *Quaternary Science Reviews* 21:1061–75.

Bird, M.I., Turney, C.S.M., Fifield, L.K., Smith, M.A., Miller, G.H. et al. (2003) Radiocarbon dating of organic and carbonate carbon in *Genyornis* and *Dromaius* eggshell using stepped combustion and added acidification. *Quaternary Science Reviews* 22:1805–12.

Bird, R. Bliege, Bird, D.W., Codding, B.F., Parker, C.H. and Jones, J.H. (2008) The 'fire stick farming' hypothesis: Australian Aboriginal foraging strategies, biodiversity, and anthropogenic fire mosaics. *Proceedings of the National Academy of Sciences of the USA* 105(39):14796–801.

Birdsell, J.B. (1977) The recalibration of a paradigm for the first peopling of greater Australia. In J. Allen, J. Golson and R. Jones (eds) *Sunda and Sahul: Prehistoric studies in Southeast Asia, Melanesia and Australia*, pp. 113–67. London: Academic Press.

Black, M.P., Mooney, S.D. and Attenbrow, V. (2008) Implications of a 14,200 year contiguous fire record for understanding human–climate relationships at Goochs Swamp, New South Wales, Australia. *The Holocene* 18(3):437–47.

Blinkorn, J. (2012) Uncovering a landscape buried by the super-eruption of Toba, 74,000 years ago: A multi-proxy environmental reconstruction of landscape heterogeneity in the Jurreru Valley, south India. *Quaternary International* 258:135–47.

Bohte, A. and Kershaw, P. (1999) Taphonomic influences on the interpretation of the palaeological record from Lynch's Crater, northeastern Australia. *Quaternary International* 57–8:49–59.

Bottoms, T. (2013) *Conspiracy of Silence*. Sydney: Allen & Unwin.

Bowdler, S. (1977) The coastal colonisation of Australia. In J. Allen, J. Golson and R. Jones (eds) *Sunda and Sahul: Prehistoric studies in Southeast Asia, Melanesia and Australia*, pp. 205–46. London: Academic Press.

Bowdler, S. (1980) Fish and culture: A Tasmanian polemic. *Mankind* 12(4):334–40.

Bowdler, S. (1982) *Coastal Archaeology in Eastern Australia*. Canberra: Department of Prehistory, R.S.Pac.S., Australian National University.

Bowdler, S. (1984) *Hunter Hill, Hunter Island*. Terra Australis 8. Canberra: Australian National University.

Bowdler, S. (1990) 50,000 year old site in Australia: Is it really that old? *Australian Archaeology* 31:93.

Bowdler, S. (1990) The Silver Dollar Site, Shark Bay: An interim report. *Journal of the Australian Institute of Aboriginal Studies* 2:60–3.

Bowdler, S. (1999) Research at Shark Bay, WA and the nature of coastal adaptations in Australia.

In J. Hall and I.J. McNiven (eds) *Australian Coastal Archaeology*, pp. 79–84. Research Papers in Archaeology and Natural History 31. Canberra: ANH Publications, Australian National University.

Bowler, J.M. (1998) Willandra Lakes revisited: Environmental framework for human occupation. *Archaeology in Oceania* 33:120–55.

Bowler, J.M., Gillespie, R., Johnston, H. and Boljkovac, K. (2012) Wind v water: Glacial maximum records from the Willandra Lakes. In S. Haberle and B. David (eds) *Peopled Landscapes: Archaeological and biogeographical approaches to landscapes*, pp. 271–96. Terra Australis 34. Canberra: ANU E Press.

Bowler, J.M., Johnston, H., Olley, J.M., Prescott, J.R., Roberts, R.G. et al. (2003) New ages for human occupation and climatic change at Lake Mungo, Australia. *Nature* 421:837–40.

Bowler, J.M., Jones, R.M., Allen, H. and Thorne, A.G. (1970) Pleistocene human remains from Australia: A living site and human cremation from Lake Mungo, western New South Wales. *World Archaeology* 2:39–60.

Bowler, J.M. and Magee, J.W. (1978) Geomorphology of the Mallee region in semi-arid northern Victoria and western New South Wales. *Proceedings of the Royal Society of Victoria* 90:5–20.

Bowler, J.M., Wyrwoll, K. and Li, Y. (2001) Variations of the northwest Australian summer monsoon over the last 300,000 years: The palaeohydrological record of the Gregory (Mulan) Lakes System. *Quaternary International* 83–5:63–80.

Bowman, D.M.J.S. (1998) Tansley Review 101: The impact of Aboriginal landscape burning on the Australian biota. *New Phytologist* 140(3):385–410.

Brady, L.M. and Carson, A. (2012) An archaic face from the Woodstock Adydos Protected Reserve, north western Australia. *Australian Archaeology* 74:98–102.

Brener, M. (2000) *Faces: The changing look of humankind*. New York: University Press of America.

Brockwell, S., Gara, T., Colley, S. and Cane, S.B. (1989) The anthropology and archaeology of Ooldea Soak and Mission. *Australian Archaeology* 28:55–78.

Brook, B.W. and Johnson, C.N. (2006) Selective hunting of juveniles as a cause of the imperceptible overkill of the Australian Pleistocene megafauna. *Alcheringa* 30:39–48.

Brooke, B.W. and Bowman, D.M.J.S. (2004) The uncertain blitzkrieg of Pleistocene megafauna. *Journal of Biogeography* 31:517–23.

Brown, P. (1987) Pleistocene homogeneity and Holocene size reduction: The Australian human skeletal evidence. *Archaeology in Oceania* 22:41–67.

Brown, P., Sutikan, T., Morwood, M.J., Soejono, R.P., Jatmiko et al. (2004) A new small-bodied hominin from the Late Pleistocene of Flores, Indonesia. *Nature* 431:1055–61.

Brown, S. (1991) Aboriginal archaeological sites in eastern Tasmania: A cultural resource management strategy. *Occasional Papers Series 3*. Hobart: Department of Parks, Wildlife and Heritage.

Brumm, A., Jensen, G.M., van den Bergh, G.D., Morwood, M.J., Kurniawan, I. et al. (2010) Hominins on Flores, Indonesia, by one million years ago. *Nature* 464:748–53.

Bryden, M.M. (1983) Earless or 'true' seals. In R. Strathan (ed.) *The Australian Museum Complete Book of Australian Mammals*, pp. 466–8. Sydney: Angus & Robertson.

Builth, H., Kershaw, A.P., White, C., Roach, A., Hartney, L. et al. (2008) Environmental and cultural change on the Mt Eccles lava-flow landscapes of southwest Victoria, Australia. *The Holocene* 18(3):413–24.

Bulbeck, D. and O'Connor, S. (2011) The Watinglo mandible: A second terminal Pleistocene *Homo sapiens* fossil from tropical Sahul with a test on existing models for the human settlement of the region. *Journal of Comparative Human Biology* 62:1–29.

Burbidge, J. (1943) Ecological succession observed during regeneration of *Triodia pungens* after burning. *Journal of the Royal Society of Western Australia* 28:149–56.

Bureau of Resource Science and the Fisheries Development Corporation (1993) *Australian Fisheries Resources*. Brisbane: Imprint Limited.

Burney, D.A. and Flannery, T.F. (2005) Fifty millennia of catastrophic extinctions after human contact. *Trends in Ecology and Evolution* 20(7):395–401.

Burrows, N.D., Burbidge, A.A., Fuller, P.F. and Behn, G. (2006) Evidence of altered fire regions in the Western Desert region of Australia. *Conservation Science* 5(3):272–84.

Butlin, N.G. (1983) *Our Original Aggression: Aboriginal populations of south-eastern Australia 1788–1850.* Sydney: Allen & Unwin.

Butlin, N.G. (1989) The palaeoeconomic history of Aboriginal migration. *Australian Economic History Review* 29:3–57.

Butlin, N.G. (1993) *Economics and the Dreamtime: A hypothetical history.* Cambridge: Cambridge University Press.

Calaby, J. (1976) Some biogeographic factors relevant to the Pleistocene movement of man in Australasia. In R.L. Kirk and A.G. Thorne (eds) *The Origin of the Australians*, pp. 23–8. Canberra: Institute of Aboriginal and Torres Strait Islander Studies.

Campbell, V.M. (1969) A field survey of shell middens of the lower Macleay Valley, with reference to their potential and possible methods of investigation. Unpublished BA (Hons) thesis. Armidale: University of New England.

Cane, S.B. (1980) Stone features in Tasmania. Unpublished MA Qual. thesis, Department of Prehistory and Anthropology, Canberra: Australian National University.

Cane, S.B. (1984) Desert Camps. PhD thesis, Department of Prehistory, R.S.Pac.S. Canberra: Australian National University.

Cane, S.B. (1989) Australian Aboriginal seed grinding and its archaeological record: A case study from the Western Desert. In D.R. Harris and G.C. Hillman (eds) *Foraging and Farming: The evolution of plant exploitation*, pp. 99–118. London: Unwin Hyman.

Cane, S.B. (1990) Desert demography: A case study of pre-contact Aboriginal densities. In B. Meehan and N. White (eds) *Hunter-Gatherer Demography: Past and present*, pp. 149–60. Sydney: University of Sydney Press.

Cane, S.B. (1993) Seismic survey on the Maralinga Lands. Report to Maralinga Tjarutja, South Australia.

Cane, S.B. (1995) Excavation report for Allen's Cave, Nullarbor Plain. Department of Aboriginal Heritage, South Australian Government.

Cane, S.B. (1996a) Australian Aboriginal subsistence in the Western Desert. In D.G. Bates and S.H. Lees (eds) *Case Studies in Human Ecology*, pp. 14–54. New York: Plenum Press.

Cane, S.B. (1996b) Spinifex Stories: Myth lines and the Great Victoria Desert and Nullarbor Plain. Report to the Australian Heritage Commission, Canberra.

Cane, S.B. (1997) A coastal heritage. Unpublished report to the Australian Heritage Commission, Canberra.

Cane, S.B. (2001a) Milkwater and honey: Aboriginal associations with the Tjurabalan claim area WC95/074. A draft report to Ngaanyatjarra Council, Crown Solicitors Office and the Office of the Premier and Cabinet, Western Australia.

Cane, S.B. (2001b) The Great Flood: Eustatic change and cultural change in Australia during the late Pleistocene and Holocene. In A. Anderson, S. O'Connor and I. Lilley (eds) *Histories of Old Ages: Essays in honour of Rhys Jones*, pp. 141–66. Canberra: Coombs Academic Publishing, Australian National University.

Cane, S.B. (2002) *Pila Nguru: The Spinifex People.* Perth: Fremantle Arts Press.

Cane, S.B. (2006a) Countrymen: Ethnography for the Ngurara Native Title Claim. Report to Ngaanyatjarra Council and the Federal Court of Australia, Perth.

Cane, S.B. (2006b) Yankunytjatjara/Antakirinja Native Title Claim. Report to the Federal Court of Australia, South Australian Registry, for the Native Title Unit, Aboriginal Legal Rights Movement, South Australia.

Cane, S.B. (2008) Wati and Wilyaru: A contextual ethnography of the Kokatha, Kuyani and Barngarla overlap area. Report to SANTS and the Federal Court of Australia.

Cane, S.B. (2012) Yilka and the Western Desert: Expert opinion regarding Western Desert society and the Yilka Native Title Claim. Adelaide: Federal Court of Australia.

Cane, S.B. and Stanley, O. (1985) *Land Use and Resources in Desert Homelands.* Darwin: Northern Australian Research Unit, Australian National University.

Cane, S.B., Stockton, J. and Vallance, A. (1979) A note on the diet of the Tasmanian Aborigines. *Australian Archaeology* 9:77–81.

Cann, J.H., Murray-Wallace, C.V., Riggs, N.J. and Belperio, A.P. (2006) Successive foraminiferal faunas and inferred palaeoenvironments associated with the postglacial (Holocene) marine transgression, Gulf St Vincent, South Australia. *The Holocene* 16(2):224–34.

Carnegie, D.W. (1898) *Spinifex and Sand.* London: Pearson.

Caspari, R. (2013) The evolution of grandparents. *Scientific American* 22:38–43.

Caspari, R. and Lee, S.-H. (2004) Older age becomes common late in human evolution. *Proceedings of the National Academy of Sciences of the USA* 101(30):10895–900.

Caspari, R. and Lee, S.-H. (2006) Is human longevity a consequence of cultural change or modern biology? *American Journal of Physical Anthropology* 129:512–17.

Chaloupka, G. (1999) *Journey in time: The 50,000 year story of the Australian Aboriginal rock art of Arnhem Land.* Sydney: Reed New Holland.

Chappell, J. (1993) Late Pleistocene coasts and human origins in the Austral region. In M. Spriggs, D.E. Yen, W. Ambrose, R. Jones, A. Thorne et al. (eds) *A Community of Culture: The people and prehistory of the Pacific*, pp. 43–8. Occasional Papers in Prehistory 21, Canberra: Australian National University.

Chappell, J., Omura, A., Esat, T., McCulloch, M., Pandolfi, J. et al. (1996) Reconciliation of late Quaternary sea levels derived from coral terraces at Huon Peninsula with deep sea oxygen isotope records. *Earth and Planetary Science Letters* 141:227–36.

Chappell, J. and Polach, H. (1991) Post-glacial sea-level rise from a coral reef at Huon Peninsula, Papua New Guinea. *Nature* 349:147–9.

Chappell, J. and Thom, B.G. (1977) Sea levels and coasts. In J. Allen, J. Golson and R. Jones (eds) *Sunda and Sahul: Prehistoric studies in Southeast Asia, Melanesia and Australia*, pp. 175–291. London: Academic Press.

Cheater, M. (2003) Chasing the magic dragon. *National Wildlife Magazine* (National Wildlife Federation) 41(5).

Chesner, C.A. (2012) The Toba caldera complex. *Quaternary International* 258:5–18.

Chivas, A.R., Garcia, A., van der Kaars, S., Couapel, M.J.J., Holt, S. et al. (2001) Sea-level and environmental changes since the last interglacial in the Gulf of Carpentaria, Australia: An overview. *Quaternary International* 83–5:19–46.

Clark, P. (2000) Ashmore Reef: Archaeological evidence of past visitation. *The Bulletin of the Australian Institute of Maritime Archaeology* 24:1–8.

Clark, P.U., Dyke, A.S., Shakun, J.D., Carlson, A.E., Clark, J. et al. (2009) The last glacial maximum. *Science* 325:710–14.

Clark, R.L. and Lampert, R.J. (1981) Past changes in burning regime as markers of man's activity on Kangaroo Island, South Australia. In R. Lampert *The Great Kartan Mystery.* Terra Australis 5, Appendix I, pp. 186–9. Canberra: Department of Prehistory, Australian National University.

Clarke, L. (1976) Two Aboriginal rock pigments from Western Australia: Their properties, use and distribution. *Studies in Conservation* 21:143–52.

Clarkson, C., Jones, S. and Harris, C. (2012) Continuity and change in the lithic industries of the Jurreru Valley, India, before and after the Toba eruption. *Quaternary International* 258:165–79.

Clegg, J. (1987) Style and tradition at Sturt's Meadow. *World Archaeology* 19:236–55.

Clune, G. and Harrison, R. (2009) Coastal shell middens of the Abydos Plain, Western Australia. *Archaeology in Oceania* 44(Supplement):70–80.

Cogger, H.G. (1979) *Reptiles and Amphibians of Australia.* Sydney: Reed.

Cohen, T.J., Nanson, G.C., Jansen, J.D., Jones, B.G., Jacobs, Z. et al. (2012) Late Quaternary mega-lakes fed by the northern and southern river systems of central Australia: Varying moisture sources and increased continental aridity. *Palaeogeography, Palaeoclimatology, Palaeoecology* 356–357:89–108.

Colhoun, E.A. (2000) Vegetation and climate change during the last interglacial-glacial cycle in western Tasmania, Australia. *Palaeogeography, Palaeoclimatology, Palaeoecology* 155:195–209.

Colhoun, E.A. and Barrows, T.T. (2011) The glaciation of Australia. In J. Ehlers, P.L. Gibbard and P.D. Hughes (eds) *Quaternary Glaciations—Extent and chronology: A closer look*, pp. 1037–45. Developments in Quaternary Science, Vol. 15. Amsterdam: Elsevier.

Colhoun, E.A., Pola, J.S., Barton, C.E. and Heijnis, H. (1999) Late Pleistocene vegetation and climatic history of Lake Selina, western Tasmania. *Quaternary International* 57–8:5–23.

Colhoun, E.A., van de Geer, G. and Mook, W.G. (1982) Stratigraphy, pollen analysis, and paleoclimatic interpretation of Pulbeena Swamp, Northern Tasmania. *Quaternary Research* 18:108–26.

Colley, S.M. (1992) Archaeological evidence for abalone fishing by Aboriginal people on the New South Wales south coast. Report to Blake Dawson Waldron Solicitors on behalf of the New South Wales Land Council.

Colley, S.M. and Jones, R. (1987) New fish bone data from Rocky Cape, North West Tasmania. *Archaeology in Oceania* 22(2):67–71.

Commonwealth of Australia (2002) *Ashmore Reef National Nature Reserve and Cartier Island Marine Reserve: Management plan*. Canberra: Environment Australia.

Connah, G. (1974) Report to the National Parks and Wildlife Service, New South Wales, on the archaeological work in the Lower Macleay River area 1972–74.

Cornell, J. (1998) *World Cruising Routes*. London: Adlard Coles Nautical.

Cosgrove, R. (1985) New evidence for early Holocene Aboriginal occupation in northeast Tasmania. *Australian Archaeology* 21:19–36.

Cosgrove, R. (1989) Thirty thousand years of human colonization in Tasmania: New Pleistocene dates. *Science* 243(4899):1706–8.

Cosgrove, R. (1995) Late Pleistocene behavioural variation and time trends: The case from Tasmania. *Archaeology in Oceania* 30(3):83–104.

Cosgrove, R. (1999) Forty-two degrees south: The archaeology of Late Pleistocene Tasmania. *Journal of World Prehistory* 13(4):357–402.

Cosgrove, R. and Allen, J. (2001) Prey choice and hunting strategies in the Late Pleistocene: Evidence from south west Tasmania. In A. Anderson, S. O'Connor and I. Lilley (eds) *Histories of Old Ages: Essays in honour of Rhys Jones*, pp. 397–429. Canberra: Coombs Academic Publishing, Australian National University.

Cosgrove, R., Allen, J. and Marshall, B. (1990) Palaeo-ecology and Pleistocene human occupation in south central Tasmania. *Antiquity* 64:59–78.

Cosgrove, R., Field, J., Garvey, J., Brenner-Coltrain, J., Goede, A. et al. (2010) Overdone overkill: The archaeological perspective on Tasmanian megafaunal extinctions. *Journal of Archaeological Science* 37:2486–503.

Cosgrove, R. and Pike-Tay, A. (2004) The Middle Palaeolithic and Late Pleistocene Tasmania hunting behaviour: A reconstruction of the attributes of modern human behaviour. *International Journal of Osteoarchaeology* 14:321–32.

Coutts, P.J.F. (1981) Coastal archaeology in Victoria part 1: The morphology of coastal archaeological sites. *Proceedings of the Royal Society of Victoria* 92(1):67–80.

Coutts, P.J.F. (1984) Coastal archaeology in south-eastern Victoria. *Records of the Victorian Archaeological Survey* 14.

Coutts, P.J.F., Frank, P.K. and Hughes, P.J. (1978) Aboriginal engineers of the Western District, Victoria. *Records of the Victorian Archaeological Survey* 7.

Croke, J.C., Magee, J.W. and Wallensky, E.P. (1999) The role of the Australian monsoon in the western catchment of Lake Eyre, central Australia, during the last interglacial. *Quaternary International* 57–8:71–80.

Crossan, J.D. (1992) *The Historical Jesus: The life of a Mediterranean Jewish peasant*. New York: Harper One.

Cupper, M. and Duncan, J. (2006) Last glacial megafaunal death assemblage and early human occupation at Lake Menindee, southeastern Australia. *Quaternary Research* 66:332–41.

David, B. (1993) Nurrabullgin cave: Preliminary results from a pre-37,000 year old rockshelter, North Queensland. *Archaeology in Oceania* 28:50–4.

David, B. (2002) *Landscapes, Rock-Art and the Dreaming: An archaeology of preunderstanding.* Leicester: Leicester University Press.

David, B., Barker, B., Petchey, F., Delannoy, J.-J., Geneste, J.-M. et al. (2012) A 28,000 year old excavated painted rock from Nawarla Gabarnmang, northern Australia. *Journal of Archaeological Science* 30:1–9.

David, B., Geneste, J.-M., Petchey, F., Delannoy, J.-J., Barker, B. et al. (2013) How old are Australia's pictographs? A review of rock art dating. *Journal of Archaeological Science* 40:3–10.

David, B., Geneste, J.-M, Whear, R.L., Delannoy, J.-J., Katherine, M. et al. (2011) Nawarla Gabarnmang, a 45,180+/–910 cal BP site in Jawoyn Country, southwest Arnhem Land plateau. *Australian Archaeology* 73:73–7.

David, B., Roberts, R., Tuniz, C., Jones, R. and Head, J. (1997) New optical and radiocarbon dates from Ngarrabullgan Cave, a Pleistocene archaeological site in Australia: Implications for the comparability of time clocks and for human colonisation of Australia. *Antiquity* 71:183–8.

Davidson, D.S. (1952) Notes on pictographs and petroglyphs of Western Australia and a discussion of their affinities with appearances elsewhere on the continent. *Proceedings of the American Philosophical Society* 96:76–117.

Davidson, I., Sutton, S.A. and Gale, S.J. (1993) The human occupation of Cuckadoo 1 Rockshelter, north western central Queensland. In M.A. Smith, M. Spriggs and B. Fankhauser (eds) *Sahul in Review: Pleistocene archaeology in Australia, New Guinea and island Melanesia.* Occasional Papers in Prehistory 24, pp. 164–72. Canberra: Research School of Pacific Studies. Australian National University.

Day, D. (2012) *Antarctica: A biography.* Sydney: Knopf.

De Deckker, P. (2001) Late Quaternary cyclic aridity in tropical Australia. *Palaeogeography, Palaeoclimatology, Palaeoecology* 170:1–9.

Delannoy, J.-J., David, B., Geneste, J.-M., Katherine, M., Barker, B. et al. (2012) The social construction of caves and rockshelters: Chauvet Cave (France) and Nawarla Gabarnmang (Australia). *Antiquity* 87:1–18.

Denham, T., Fullagar, R. and Head, L. (2009) Plant exploitation on Sahul: From colonisation to the emergence of regional specialisation during the Holocene. *Quaternary International* 202:29–40.

Dix, W. (1977) Facial expressions in Pilbara rock engravings. In P.J. Ucko (ed.) *Form in Indigenous Art: Schematisation in the art of Aboriginal Australia and prehistoric Europe,* pp. 277–85. Canberra: Australian Institute of Aboriginal Studies.

Dixon, R.M. (1972) *The Dyirbal Language of North Queensland.* Cambridge: Cambridge University Press.

Dodson, J. (1977) Late Quaternary Palaeoecology of Wyrie Swamp, southeastern South Australia. *Quaternary Research* 8:97–114.

Dodson, J., Fullagar, R., Furby, J. and Prosser, I. (1993) Humans and megafauna in a late Pleistocene environment from Cuddie Springs, north western New South Wales. *Archaeology in Oceania* 28:94–9.

Dodson, J. and Wright, R.V.S. (1989) Humid to arid to subhumid vegetation shift on Pilliga Sandstone, Ulungra Springs: New South Wales. *Quaternary Research* 32:182–92.

Dortch, C.E. (1984) *Devil's Lair: A study in prehistory.* Perth: Western Australian Museum.

Dortch, C.E. and Dortch, J. (1996) Review of Devil's Lair artefact classification and radiocarbon chronology. *Australian Archaeology* 43:28–31.

Dortch, C.E. and Morse, K. (1984) Prehistoric stone artefacts on some offshore islands in Western Australia. *Australian Archaeology* 19:31–47.

Dortch, C.E., Kendrick, G.W. and Morse, K. (1984) Aboriginal mollusc exploitation in south-west Australia. *Archaeology in Oceania* 19:81–104.

Dortch, C.E. and Muir, B.G. (1980) Long range sightings of bushfires as possible incentive for Pleistocene voyagers to Greater Australia. *Western Australian Naturalist* 14:194–8.

Dortch, J. (1994) Pleistocene carbon dates from Tunnel Cave, south western Australia. *Australian Archaeology* 38:45–57.

Draper, N. (1987) Context for the Kartan: A preliminary report on excavations at Cape du Couedic, Kangaroo Island. *Archaeology in Oceania* 22(1):1–8.

Dunnett, G. (1993) Diving for dinner: Some implications from Holocene middens for the role of coasts in the late Pleistocene. In M.A. Smith, M. Spriggs and B. Fankhauser (eds) *Sahul in Review: Pleistocene archaeology in Australia, New Guinea and island Melanesia.* Occasional Papers in Prehistory 24:247–57. Canberra: Research School of Pacific Studies. Australian National University.

Dwyer, D. (2000) Disaster and recovery: A Rotenese discovery tale for Ashmore Reef (Pulau Pasir), North Australia. *The Bulletin of the Australian Institute of Maritime Archaeology* 24:115–18.

Dyall, L.K. (1982) Aboriginal fishing stations on the Newcastle coastline, NSW. In S. Bowdler (ed.) *Coastal Archaeology in Eastern Australia,* pp. 52–62. Canberra: ANU Press.

Edwards, R. (1966) Comparative study of rock engravings in south and central Australia. *Proceedings of the Royal Society of South Australia* 90:33–8.

Edwards, R. (1971) Art and Aboriginal prehistory. In D.J. Mulvaney and J. Golson (eds) *Aboriginal Man and Environment,* pp. 356–67. Canberra: ANU Press.

Elkin, A.P. (1931) The social organisation of South Australian tribes. *Oceania* 2:44–73.

Elkin, A.P. (1938) Kinship in South Australia. *Oceania* 8(2):419–52.

Elkin, A.P. (1940) Kinship in South Australia. *Oceania* 10(3):295–349, (4)369–88.

Endicott, P., Ho, S.Y.W., Metspalu, M. and Stringer, C. (2009) Evaluating the mitochondrial timescale of human evolution. *Trends in Ecology and Evolution* 24(9):515–21.

English, P., Spooner, N.A., Chappell, J., Questiaux, D.G. and Hill, N.G. (2001) Lake Lewis basin, central Australia: Environmental evolution and OSL chronology. *Quaternary International* 83–5:81–101.

Erlandson, J.M. (2012) On a fast track: Human discovery, exploration and settlement. *Australian Archaeology* 74:17–18.

Fagan, B.M. (2011) *World Prehistory: A brief introduction.* Prentice Hall: Boston.

Fairbairn, A.S., Hope, G.S. and Summerhayes, G.R. (2006) Pleistocene occupation of New Guinea's Highland and subalpine environments. *World Archaeology* 38(3):371–86.

Faulkner, P. (2009) Focused, intense and long-term: Evidence for granular ark (*Anadara granosa*) exploitation from late Holocene shell mounds of Blue Mud Bay, northern Australia. *Journal of Archaeological Science* 36:821–34.

Feldmuller, M., Gee, P., Pitt, J. and Feuerherdt, L. (2012) *Best Practice Camel Book: An illustrated guide to the 2012 Australian Standard, Model Code of Practice and Standard Operating Procedures relevant to the humane control of feral camels.* Edition 1. Prepared for the South Australian State Feral Camel Management Project. Adelaide: Rural Solutions.

Field, J. and Dodson, J. (1999) Late Pleistocene megafauna and human occupation at Cuddie Springs, Southern Australia. *Proceedings of the Prehistoric Society* 65:275–301.

Field, J., Fillios, M. and Wroe, S. (2008) Chronological overlap between humans and megafauna in Sahul (Pleistocene Australia-New Guinea): A review of the evidence. *Earth-Science Reviews* 89:97–115.

Field, J., Fullagar, R. and Lord, G. (2001) A large area excavation at Cuddie Springs. *Antiquity* 75:696–702.

Fifield, L.K., Bird, M.I., Turney, C.S.M., Hausladen, P.A., Santos, G.M. et al. (2001) Radiocarbon dating of the human occupation of Australia prior to 40 ka BP—Successes and pitfalls. *Radiocarbon* 43:1139–45.

Fillios, M., Field, J. and Charles, B. (2010) Investigating human and megafauna co-occurrence in Australian prehistory: Mode and causality in fossil accumulations at Cuddie Springs. *Quaternary International* 211:123–43.

Fitzsimmons, K.E. and Barrows, T.T. (2010) Holocene hydrological variability in temperate southeastern Australia: An example from Lake George, New South Wales. *The Holocene* 20(4):585–97.

Fitzsimmons, K.E., Bowler, J.M., Rhodes, E.J. and Magee, J.M. (2007) Relationships between desert dunes during the late Quaternary in the Lake Frome region, Strzelecki Desert, Australia. *Journal of Quaternary Science* 22(5):549–58.

Flannery, T.F. (1990) Pleistocene faunal loss: Implications of the aftershock for Australia's past and future. *Archaeology in Oceania* 55(2):45– 63.

Flannery, T.F. (1994) *The Future Eaters.* Sydney: Reed Books.

Flannery, T.F. (1999) Debating extinction. *American Association for the Advancement of Science* 283(5399):182–3.

Flannery, T.F., Mountain, J. and Aplin, K. (1983) Quaternary kangaroos from Nombe rock shelter, Papua New Guinea, with comments on the nature of megafaunal extinction in the New Guinea Highlands. *Proceedings of the Linnean Society of NSW* 107(2):75–9.

Fletcher, M.-S. and Moreno, P.I. (2011) Zonally symmetric changes in the strength and position of the southern westerlies drove atmospheric CO_2 variations over the past 14 k.y. *Geology* 39:419–22.

Fletcher, M.-S. and Moreno, P.I. (2012) Have the southern westerlies changed in a zonally symmetric manner over the last 14,000 years? A hemisphere-wide take on a controversial problem. *Quaternary International* 253:32–46.

Flinders, M. (1814) *Voyage to Terra Australis.* London: Bulmer and Cleveland-Row.

Flood, J. (1980) *The Moth Hunters: Aboriginal prehistory of the Australian Alps.* Canberra: Australian Institute of Aboriginal Studies.

Flood, J. (1990) *The Riches of Ancient Australia.* Brisbane: University of Queensland Press.

Flood, J. (2000) *Archaeology of the Dreamtime: The story of prehistoric Australia and its people.* Sydney: Angus & Robertson.

Flood, J. (2006) *The Original Australians: Story of the Aboriginal people.* Sydney: Allen & Unwin.

Flood, J., David, B., Magee, J., and English, B. (1987) Birrigai: A Pleistocene site in the south eastern highlands. *Archaeology in Oceania* 22(1):9–26.

Foley, R. and Gamble, C. (2009) The ecology of social transitions in human evolution. *Philosophical Transactions of the Royal Society Biological Sciences* 364:3267–79.

Forster, P. (2004) Ice ages and the mitochondrial DNA chronology of human dispersals: A review. *Philosophical Transactions of the Royal Society of London* 359:255–64.

Franklin, N.R. (1991) Explorations of the Panaramitee style. In P. Bahn and A. Rosenfeld (eds) *Rock Art and Prehistory: Papers presented to the Symposium G of AURA Congress, Darwin 1988*, pp. 120–35. Oxford: Oxbow Books.

Franklin, N.R. (1996) An analysis of rock engravings in the Mt Isa region northwest Queensland. *Tempus* 4:137–49.

Franklin, N.R. (2011) Rock art in South Australia: Analysis of Panaramitee tradition engravings and paintings. In A. Roberts and K. Walshe (eds) *Issues in South Australian Aboriginal Archaeology. Journal of the Anthropological Society of South Australia.* Special edition 34:56–89.

Frawley, S. and O'Conner, S. (2010) A 40,000 year wood charcoal record from Carpenter's Gap 1: New Insights into palaeovegetation change and indigenous foraging strategies in the Kimberley, Western Australia. In S. Haberle, J. Stevenson and M. Prebble (eds) *Altered Ecologies: Fire, climate and human influence on terrestrial landscapes.* Terra Australis 32, pp. 299–321. Canberra: ANU Press.

Fry, B.G., Vidal, N., Norman, J.A., Vonk, F.J., Scheib, H. et al. (2006) Early evolution of the venom system in lizards and snakes. *Nature* 439(7076):584–8.

Fullagar, R. and Field, J. (1997) Pleistocene seed-grinding implements from the Australian arid zone. *Antiquity* 71:300–7.

Furby, J.H., Fullagar, R., Dodson, J.R. and Prosser, I. (1993) The Cuddie Springs bone bed revisited, 1991. In M.A. Smith, M. Spriggs and B. Fankhauser (eds) *Sahul in Review: Pleistocene archaeology in Australia, New Guinea and island Melanesia.* Occasional Papers in Prehistory 24:204–10. Canberra: Research School of Pacific Studies, Australian National University.

Gaffney, L. and Stockton, J. (1980) Results of the Jordan River midden excavation. *Australian Archaeology* 10:68–78.

Gamble, C. (1982) Interaction and alliance in Palaeolithic society. *Man* 17:92–107.

Gammage, B. (2011) *The Biggest Estate on Earth. How Aborigines made Australia.* Sydney: Allen & Unwin.

Gathorne-Hardy, F.J. and Harcourt-Smith, W.E.H. (2003) The super-eruption of Toba: Did it cause a human bottleneck? *Journal of Human Evolution* 45:227–30.

Gaughwin, D. (1985) Archaeological reconnaissance survey of the Tasman Peninsula. *Australian Archaeology* 20:38–57.

Geneste, J.-M., David, B., Plisson, H., Clarkson, C., Delannoy, J.-J. et al. (2010) Earliest evidence for ground-edge axes: 35,400 ⁺/-410 cal BP from Jawoyn Country, Arnhem Land. *Australian Archaeology* 71:66–9.

Geneste, J.-M., David, B., Plisson, H., Delannoy, J.-J. and Petchey, F. (2012) The origins of ground-edge axes: New findings from Nawarla Gabarnmang, Arnhem Land (Australia) and global implications for the evolution of fully modern humans. *Cambridge Archaeological Journal* 22(1):1–17.

Giblin, R.W. (1928) *The Early History of Tasmania.* London: Methuen and Co.

Gillespie, R. and Brook, B.W. (2006) Is there a Pleistocene archaeological site at Cuddie Springs? *Archaeology in Oceania* 41(1):1–11.

Gillespie, R., Camens, A.B., Worthy, T.H., Rawlence, N.J., Reid, C. et al. (2012) Man and megafauna in Tasmania: Closing the gap. *Quaternary Science Reviews* 37:38–47.

Gillespie, R., Horton, D.R., Ladd, P., Macumber, P.G., Rich, T.H. et al. (1978) Lancefield Swamp and the extinction of the Australian megafauna. *Science*, New Series, 200(4345):1044–8.

Gillieson, D. and Mountain, M.J. (1983) Environmental history of Nombe rockshelter, Papua New Guinea. *Archaeology in Oceania* 18:53–62.

Glasby, P., O'Flaherty, A. and Williams, M.A.J. (2010) A geospatial visualisation and chronological study of a late Pleistocene fluvial wetland surface in the semi-arid Flinders Ranges, South Australia. *Geomorphology* 118:130–51.

Godfrey, M.C.S. (1989) Shell midden chronology in southwestern Victoria: Reflections of change in prehistoric population and subsistence. *Archaeology in Oceania* 24(2):65–9.

Gorecki, P.P., Horton, D.R., Stern, N. and Wright, R.V.S. (1984) Coexistence of humans and megafauna in Australia: Improved stratigraphic evidence. *Archaeology in Oceania* 19:117–19.

Gott, B. (1982) Ecology of plant use by the Aborigines of southern Australia. *Archaeology in Oceania* 17:59–66.

Gould, R.A. (1969) Subsistence behaviour among the Western Desert Aborigines of Australia. *Oceania* 39(4):253–74.

Gould, R.A. (1980) *Living Archaeology.* Cambridge: Cambridge University Press.

Gray, R.D. and Jordan, F.M. (2000) Language trees support the express-train sequence of Austronesian expansion. *Nature* 405:1052–5.

Green, J.N. (1986) The survey and identification of the English East India Company ship, *Trial* (1622). *International Journal of Nautical Archaeology* 15(3):195–202.

Groube, L. (1986) A 40,000 year-old human occupation site at Huon Peninsula, Papua New Guinea. *Nature* 324:453–5.

Groube, L. (1989) The taming of the rain forests: A model for Late Pleistocene forest exploitation in New Guinea. In D.R. Harris and C.C. Hillman (eds) *Foraging and Farming: The evolution of plant exploitation*, pp. 292–302. One World Archaeology 13. London: Unwin Hyman.

Grun, R., Eggins, S., Aubert, M., Spooner, N., Pike, A.W.G. et al. (2010) ESR and U-series analysis of faunal material from Cuddie Springs, NSW, Australia: Implications for the timing of the extinction of the Australian megafauna. *Quaternary Science Reviews* 29:596–610.

Grun, R., Thorne, A., Swisher III, C.C., Rink, J., Schwarcz, H.P. et al. (1997) Dating the Ngandong humans. *Science*, New Series 276(5318):1575–6.

Gunn, R.G., Douglas, L.C. and Whear, R.L. (2011) What bird is that? Identifying a probable painting of *Genyornis newtoni* in Western Arnhem Land. *Australian Archaeology* 73:1–12.

Haberle, S. (1993) Pleistocene vegetation change and early human occupation of a tropical mountainous environment. In M.A. Smith, M. Spriggs and B. Fankhauser (eds) *Sahul in Review: Pleistocene archaeology in Australia, New Guinea and island Melanesia.* Occasional Papers in Prehistory 24:109–23. Canberra: Research School of Pacific Studies, Australian National University.

Haberle, S. and David, B. (eds) (2012) *Peopled Landscapes: Archaeological and biogeographical approaches to landscapes.* Terra Australis 34. Canberra: ANU E Press.

Haberle, S., Stevenson, J. and Prebble, M. (eds) (2010) *Altered Ecologies: Fire, climate and human influence on terrestrial landscapes.* Terra Australis 32. Canberra: ANU Press.

Hall, J. and Hiscock, P. (1988) Excavations of the new Brisbane Airport site (LB:C69): Evidence for early mid Holocene coastal occupation in Moreton Bay, SE Queensland. *Queensland Archaeological Research* 1:85–94.

Hallam, S.J. (1975) *Fire and Hearth.* Canberra: Australian Institute of Aboriginal Studies.

Hamilton, A. (1982) Descended from Father, belonging to Country: Rights to land in the Australian Western Desert. In E. Leacock and R. Lee (eds) *Politics and History in Band Societies*, pp. 85–108. Cambridge: Cambridge University Press.

Hanckel, M. (1985) Hot Rocks: Heat treatment at Burrill Lake and Currarong, New South Wales. *Archaeology in Oceania* 20:98–103.

Harle, K., Heijnis, H., Chisari, R., Kershaw, A.P., Zoppi, U. et al. (2002) A chronology for the long pollen record from Lake Wangoom, western Victoria (Australia) as derived from uranium/thorium disequilibrium dating. *Journal of Quaternary Science* 17(7):707–20.

Harle, K., Kershaw, A.P. and Heijnis, H. (1999) The contributions of uranium/thorium and marine palynology to the dating of the Lake Wangoom pollen record, western plains of Victoria, Australia. *Quaternary International* 57–8:25–34.

Harrington, P. (2012) *Flinders Island Sustainability Plan: Renewable energy consultation paper.* Prepared for the Flinders Council.

Harris, P., Heap, A., Passlow, V., Sbaffi, L., Fellows, M. et al. (2005) *Geomorphic Features of the Continental Margin of Australia.* Geoscience Australia, Record 2003/30, p. 142. Canberra: Australian Government.

Harris, S. (1984) Seal hunters on Tasman Island. *Australian Archaeology* 19:8–14.

Haslam, M. (2012) A southern Indian Middle Palaeolithic occupation surface sealed by the 74 ka Toba eruption: Further evidence from Jwalapuram Locality 22. *Quaternary International* 258:148–64.

Haslam, M. (2012) Dhaba: An initial report on an Acheulean, Middle Palaeolithic and microlithic locality in the Middle Son Valley, north-central India. *Quaternary International* 258:191–9.

Haslam, M. and Petraglia, M. (2010) Comment on 'Environmental impact of the 73 ka Toba super-eruption in South Asia' by M.A.J. Williams, S.H. Ambrose, S. van der Kaars, C. Ruehlemann, U. Chattopadhyaya et al. [Palaeogeography, Palaeoclimatology, Palaeoecology 284 (2009):295–314]. *Palaeogeography, Palaeoclimatology, Palaeoecology* 296:199–203.

Hawkes, K. (2003) Grandmothers and the evolution of human longevity. *American Journal of Human Biology* 15:380–400.

Haworth, R.J., Baker, R.G.V. and Flood, P.G. (2002) Predicted and observed Holocene sea-levels on the Australian coast: What do they indicate about hydro-isostatic models in far-field sites? *Journal of Quaternary Science* 17(5–6):581–91.

Head, L. (1989) Using palaeoecology to date Aboriginal fishtraps in Lake Condah, Victoria. *Archaeology in Oceania* 24:110–15.

Hesp, P., Murray-Wallace, C. and Dortch, C.E. (1999) Aboriginal occupation on Rottnest Island, Western Australia, provisionally dated by aspartic acid racemization assay of land snails to greater than 50ka. *Australian Archaeology* 49:7–13.

Hesse, P.P., Magee, J.W. and van der Kaars, S. (2004) Late Quaternary climates of the Australian arid zone: A review. *Quaternary International* 118–19:87–102.

Hewitt, G. and Allen, J. (2010) Site distribution and archaeological integrity: The case of Bend Road, an open site in Melbourne spanning pre-LGM Pleistocene to late Holocene periods. *Australian Archaeology* 70(1):1–16.

Hiatt, B. (1967) The food quest and economy of the Tasmanian Aborigines. *Oceania* 38:99–133,190–219.

Hiatt, L.R. (1976) Introduction. In L.R. Hiatt (ed.) *Australian Aboriginal Mythology: Essays in honour of W.E.H. Stanner.* Canberra: Australian Institute of Aboriginal Studies.

Higham, T.F.G., Barton, H., Turney, C.S.M., Barker, G., Ramsey, C.B. et al. (2009) Radiocarbon dating of charcoal from tropical sequences: Results from the Niah Great Cave, Sarawak, and their broader implications. *Journal of Quaternary Science* 24(2):187–97.

Hiscock, P. (1990) How old are the artefacts at Malakunanja II? *Archaeology in Oceania* 25(3):122–4.

Hiscock, P. (2006) Blunt and to the point: Changing technological strategies in Holocene Australia. In I. Lilley (ed.) *Archaeology of Oceania: Australia and the Pacific Islands*, pp. 69–95. Oxford: Blackwell.

Hiscock, P. (2008) *Archaeology of Ancient Australia*. London: Routledge.

Hiscock, P. (2012) Dancing on pins: Tension between clever theory and material records in Australian archaeology. *Australian Archaeology* 74:25–6.

Hiscock, P. and Attenbrow, V. (1998) Early Holocene backed blade artefacts from Australia. *Archaeology in Oceania* 33:49–63.

Hiscock, P. and Wallis, L. (2005) Pleistocene settlement of deserts from an Australian perspective. In P. Veth, M.A. Smith and P. Hiscock (eds) *Desert Peoples: Archaeological perspectives*, pp. 34–57. Melbourne: Blackwell.

Hocknull, S.A., Piper, P.J., van den Bergh, G.D., Due, R.A., Moorwood, M.J. et al. (2009) Dragon's Paradise Lost: Palaeobiogeography, evolution and extinction of the largest-ever terrestrial lizards (*Varanidae*). *PLoS ONE* 4(9):e7241.

Holdaway, S. and Fanning, P. (2010) Geoarchaeology in Australia: Understanding human–environmental interactions. *Geological Society*, Special Publications 346:71–85.

Holdaway, S., Fanning, P. and Rhodes, E. (2008) Challenging intensification: Human–environmental interactions in the Holocene geoarchaeological record from western New South Wales, Australia. *The Holocene* 18(3):403–12.

Holdaway, S. and Porch, N. (1996) Dates as data: An alternative approach to the construction of chronologies for Pleistocene sites in southwest Tasmania. In J. Allen (ed.) *Report on the Southern Forests Project: Site descriptions, stratigraphies and chronologies*, pp. 252–77. Melbourne: School of Archaeology, La Trobe University.

Hope, G. (2009) Environmental change and fire in the Owen Stanley Range, Papua New Guinea. *Quaternary Science Reviews* 28:2261–76.

Hope, G., Flannery, T. and Boeardi (1993) A preliminary report of changing Quaternary mammal faunas in subalpine New Guinea. *Quaternary Research* 40:117–26.

Hope, G., Hughes, P.J. and Russell-Smith, J. (1985) Geomorphological fieldwork and the evolution of the landscape of Kakadu National Park. In R. Jones (ed.) *Archaeological Research in Kakadu National Park*, Special Publication 13, pp. 229–40. Canberra: Australian National Parks and Wildlife Service.

Hope, G., Kershaw, A.P., van der Kaars, S., Xiangjun, S., Liew, P.-M. et al. (2004) History of vegetation and habitat change in the Austral-Asian region. *Quaternary International* 118–19:103–26.

Hope, G. and Tulip, J. (1994) A long vegetation history from lowland Irian Jaya, Indonesia. *Palaeogeography, Palaeoclimatology, Palaeoecology* 109:385–98.

Hope, J.H., Dare-Edwards, A. and McIntire, M. (1983) Middens and megafauna: Stratigraphy and dating of Lake Tandou lunette, western NSW. *Archaeology in Oceania* 18:45–53.

Hope, J.H., Lampert, R.J., Edmondson, E., Smith, M.J. and van Tets, G.F. (1977) Late Pleistocene faunal remains from Seton Rock Shelter, Kangaroo Island, South Australia. *Journal of Biogeography* 4(4):363–85.

Horton, D. (1979) Tasmanian adaptation. *Mankind* 12:28–34.

Horton, D. (1982) The burning question: Aborigines fire and Australian ecosystems. *Mankind*, 13:237–51.

Horton, D. (1984) Red kangaroos, the last of the mega-fauna. In P.S. Martin and R.G. Klein (eds) *Quaternary Extinctions: A prehistoric revolution*, pp. 639–79. Tucson: University of Arizona Press.

Horton, D. (1986) Seasons of repose: Environment and culture in the late Pleistocene of Australia. In A. Aspimon (ed.) *Pleistocene Perspectives*, Vol. 2, pp. 1–14. Sydney: Allen & Unwin.

Horton, D.R. and Wright, R.V.S. (1981) Cuts on Lancefield bones: Carnivores, not humans the cause. *Archaeology in Oceania* 16:73–80.

Hough, R. (1994) *Captain James Cook: A biography*. London: Hodder and Stoughton.

Hudjashov, G., Kivisild, T., Underhill, P.A., Endicott, P., Sanchez, J.J. et al. (2007) Revealing the prehistoric settlement of Australia by Y chromosome and mtDNA analysis. *Proceedings of the National Academy of Sciences of the USA* 104(21):8726–30.

Hughes, P., Hiscock, P., Sullivan, M. and Marwick, B. (2011) Archaeological investigations at Olympic Dam in arid northeast South Australia. In A. Roberts and K. Walshe (eds) *Issues in South Australian Aboriginal Archaeology, Journal of the Anthropological Society of South Australia.* Special edition 34:21–37.

Hughes, P.H. and Sullivan, M.E. (1981) Aboriginal burning and late Holocene geomorphic events in eastern NSW. *Search* 12:227–78.

Indonesia Pilot (1983) Admiralty Charts Hydrographer of the Navy, Volume II. England.

Ingman, M. and Gyllensten, U. (2003) Mitochondrial genome variation and evolutionary history of Australian and New Guinean Aborigines. *Genome Research* 13:1600–6.

Ingman, M., Kaessmann, H., Paabo, S. and Gyllensten, U. (2000) Mitochondrial genome variation and the origin of modern humans. *Nature* 408:708–13.

Isaacs, J. (ed.) (1984) *Australian Dreaming: 40,000 years of Aboriginal history.* Sydney: Lansdowne Press.

Jacob, T.K. (ed.) (1991) *In the Beginning: A perspective on traditional Aboriginal societies.* Perth: Western Australia Ministry of Education.

Jacobs, Z. and Roberts, R. (2011) Dating duo illuminates Modern Humans' journey. *Science* 332:658–61.

Johnson, B.J., Miller, G.H., Fogel, M.L., Magee, J.W., Gagan, M.K. et al. (1999) 65,000 years of vegetation change in central Australia and the Australian summer monsoon. *Science,* New Series, 284(54170):1150–2.

Johnson, C.N. (2002) Determinants of loss of mammal species during the late Quaternary 'megafauna' extinctions: Life history and ecology, but not body size. *Proceedings of the Royal Society Biological Sciences* 269:2221–7.

Johnson, C.N. (2005) What can data on late survival of Australian megafauna tell us about the cause of their extinction? *Quaternary Science Reviews* 24:2167–72.

Johnson, C.N. and Wroe, S. (2003) Causes of extinction of vertebrates during the Holocene of mainland Australia: Arrival of the dingo, or human impact? *The Holocene* 13(6):941–8.

Johnston, H. (1993) Pleistocene sites in the central Murray–Darling basin. In M.A. Smith, M. Spriggs and B. Fankauser (eds) *Sahul in Review: Pleistocene archaeology in Australia, New Guinea and island Melanesia.* Occasional Papers in Prehistory 24:183–96. Canberra: ANU Press.

Jones, M.R. and Torgersen, T. (1988) Late Quaternary evolution of Lake Carpentaria on the Australia-New Guinea continental shelf. *Australian Journal of Earth Sciences* 35(3):313–24.

Jones, P. (2004) *Boomerang: Behind an Australian icon.* Adelaide: Wakefield Press.

Jones, R.M. (1965) Archaeological reconnaissance in Tasmania. *Oceania* 35:191–201.

Jones, R.M. (1965) Excavations of a stone arrangement in Tasmania. *Man* 62:78.

Jones, R.M. (1966) A speculative archaeological sequence for north west Tasmania. *Records of the Queen Victoria Museum, Launceston* 25:1–12.

Jones, R.M. (1967) Middens and man in Tasmania. *Australian Natural History* 18:359–64.

Jones, R.M. (1968) The geographical background to the arrival of man in Australia and Tasmania. *Archaeology in Oceania* 3:186–215.

Jones, R.M. (1969) Fire stick farming. *Australian Natural History* 16:224–8.

Jones, R.M. (1971) Rocky Cape and the problem of the Tasmanians. Unpublished PhD thesis, Canberra: Australian National University.

Jones, R.M. (1974) Tasmanian tribes. In N.B. Tindale, *Tribes and Boundaries in Australia,* Appendix, pp. 319–56. Berkeley: University of California Press.

Jones, R.M. (1976) Tasmania: Aquatic machines and offshore islands. In G. de Sieveking, I.H. Longworth and K.E. Wilson (eds) *Problems in Economic and Social Anthropology,* pp. 235–63. London: Duckworth.

Jones, R.M. (1977) The Tasmanian paradox. In R.V.S. Wright (ed.) *Stone Tools as Cultural Markers,* pp. 189–204. Prehistory and Material Culture Series 12. Canberra: Australian Institute of Aboriginal Studies.

Jones, R.M. (1978) Why did the Tasmanians stop eating fish? In R.A. Gould (ed.) *Explorations in Ethno-archaeology*, pp. 11–47. Albuquerque: University of New Mexico Press; Santa Fe: School of American Research.

Jones, R.M. (1979) A note on the discovery of stone tools and a stratified prehistoric site on King Island, Bass Strait. *Australian Archaeology* 9:87–95.

Jones, R.M. (1980) Different strokes for different folks: Sites, scales and strategy. In I. Johnson (ed.) *Holier Than Thou: Proceedings of the Kiola Conference on Australian prehistory*, pp. 151–71. Canberra: Department of Prehistory, Australian National University.

Jones, R.M. (1981) Rocky Cape, West Point and Mount Cameron West, north-west Tasmania. In Australian Heritage Commission *The Heritage of Australia: The illustrated register of the national estate.* Melbourne: Macmillan.

Jones, R.M. (1984) Hunters and history: A case study from western Tasmania. In C. Schrire (ed.) *Past and Present in Hunter Gatherer Studies.* Sydney: Academic Press.

Jones, R.M. (1985) *Archaeological Research in Kakadu National Park.* Special Publication 13. Canberra: Australian National Parks and Wildlife Service.

Jones, R.M. (1985) Archaeological conclusions. In R. Jones (ed.) *Archaeological Research in Kakadu National Park*, pp. 291–8. Special Publication 13. Canberra: Australian National Parks and Wildlife Service.

Jones, R.M. (1999) Dating the human colonisation of Australia: Radiocarbon and luminescence revolutions. *Proceedings of the British Academy* 99:37–65.

Jones, R.M. and Johnson, I. (1985) Deaf Adder Gorge: Linder Site, Nauwalabila 1. In R. Jones (ed.) *Archaeological Research in Kakadu National Park*, pp. 165–227. Special Publication 13. Canberra: Australian National Parks and Wildlife Service.

Jones, R.M. and Negerevich, T. (1985) A review of previous archaeological work. In R. Jones (ed.) *Archaeological Research in Kakadu National Park*, pp. 1–15. Special Publication 13. Canberra: Australian National Parks and Wildlife Service.

Jones, S.C. (2012) Local and regional scale impacts of the 74ka Toba supervolcanic eruption on hominid populations and habitat in India. *Quaternary International* 258:100–18.

Jungers, W.L., Harcourt-Smith, W.E.H., Wunderlich, R.E., Tocheri, M.W., Larson, S.G. et al. (2009) The foot of *Homo floresiensis*. *Nature* 459:81–4.

Kailola, P.J., Williams, M.J., Stewart, P.C., Reichelt, R.E., McNee, A. et al. (1993) *Australian Fisheries Resources.* Canberra: Bureau of Resource Sciences, Department of Industries and Energy, and the Fisheries Research and Development Corporation.

Kamminga, J. and Allen, H. (1973) Report of the archaeological survey. Alligator Rivers, Environmental fact-finding study. Canberra.

Keegan, W. (2012) Now bring me that horizon. *Australian Archaeology* 74:22–3.

Keen, I. (2004) *Aboriginal Economy and Society: Australia at the threshold of colonisation.* Oxford: Oxford University Press.

Kershaw, A.P. (1986) Climatic change and Aboriginal burning in north-east Australia during the last two glacial/interglacial cycles. *Nature* 322:47–9.

Kershaw, A.P. (1994) Pleistocene vegetation of the humid tropics of northeastern Queensland, Australia. *Palaeogeography, Palaeoclimatolgy, Palaeoecology* 109:399–412.

Kershaw, A.P., Bulman, D. and Busby, J.R. (1994) An examination of modern and pre-European settlement pollen samples from southeastern Australia—Assessment of their application to quantitative reconstruction of past vegetation and climate. *Review of Palaeobotany and Palynology* 82:83–96.

Kershaw, A.P., McKenzie, G.M., Brown, J., Roberts, R.G. and van der Kaars, S. (2010) Beneath the peat: A refined pollen record from an interstadial at Caledonia Fen, highland eastern Victoria, Australia. In S. Haberle, J. Stevenson and M. Prebble (eds) *Altered Ecologies: Fire, climate and human influence on terrestrial landscapes.* Terra Australis 32, pp. 33–48. Canberra: ANU Press.

Kershaw, A.P., McKenzie, G.M., Porch, N., Roberts, R.G., Brown, J. et al. (2007) A high-resolution record of vegetation and climate through the last glacial cycle from Caledonia Fen, southeastern highlands of Australia. *Journal of Quaternary Science* 22(5):481–500.

Kershaw, A.P., Moss, P. and van der Kaars, S. (2003) Causes and consequences of long-term climatic variability on the Australian continent. *Freshwater Biology* 48:1274–83.

Kershaw, A.P., van der Kaars, S. and Moss, P.T. (2003) Late Quaternary Milankovitch-scale climatic change and variability and its impact on monsoonal Australasia. *Marine Geology* 201:81–95.

Kershaw, A.P. and Whitlock, C. (2000) Palaeoecological records of the last glacial-interglacial cycle: Patterns and causes of change. *Palaeogeography, Palaeoclimatology, Palaeoecology* 155:1–5.

Kiernan, K., Jones, R.M. and Ranson, D. (1983) New evidence from Fraser Cave for glacial age man in south-west Tasmania. *Nature* 301:28–32.

Kimber, R. (1983) Black lightning: Aborigines and fire in the Central Australian and Western Desert. *Archaeology in Oceania* 18(1):38–45.

Koch, P.L. and Barnosky, A.D. (2006) Late Quaternary extinctions: State of the debate. *Annual Review of Ecology, Evolution, and Systemics* 37:215–50.

Kumar, S., Ravuri, R.R., Koneru, P., Urade, B.P., Sarkar, B.N. et al. (2009) Reconstructing Indian–Australian phylogenic link. *BioMed Central Evolutionary Biology* 9(173):1–5.

Lahr, M.M. and Foley, R. (1994) Multiple dispersals and modern human origins. *Evolutionary Anthropology* 3:48–60.

Lahr, M.M. and Foley, R.A. (1998) Towards a theory of modern human origins: Geography, demography, and diversity in recent human evolution. *Yearbook of Physical Anthropology* 41:137–76.

Lamb, L. and Barker, B. (2001) Evidence for early Holocene change in the Whitsunday Islands: A new radiocarbon determination from Nara Inlet 1, *Australian Archaeology* 51:42–3.

Lambeck, K., Yokoyama, Y. and Purcell, T. (2002) Into and out of the last Glacial Maximum: Sea-level change during Oxygen Isotope Stages 3 and 2. *Quaternary Science Reviews* 21:343–60.

Lampert, R.L. (1971) *Burrill Lake and Currarong: Coastal sites in southern New South Wales.* Terra Australis 1. Canberra: Department of Prehistory, Australian National University.

Lampert, R.L. (1981) *The Great Kartan Mystery.* Terra Australis 5. Canberra: Department of Prehistory, Australian National University.

Langley, M.C., Clarkson, C. and Ulm, S. (2011) From small holes to grand narratives: The impact of taphonomy and sample size on the modernity debate in Australia and New Guinea. *Journal of Human Evolution* 61:197–208.

Latz, P. (1995) *Bushfires and Bushtucker: Aboriginal plant use in Central Australia.* Alice Springs: Institute of Aboriginal Development.

Law, W.B., Cropper, D.N. and Petchey, F. (2010) Djadjiling Rockshelter: 35,000 ^{14}C years of Aboriginal occupation in the Pilbara, Western Australia. *Australian Archaeology* 70:68–72.

Lawrence, D. and Lawrence, H.R. (2004) Torres Strait: The region and its people. In R. Davis (ed.) *Woven Histories, Dancing Lives*, pp. 15–21. Canberra: Aboriginal Studies Press.

Lewis, L. (2012) Grain size distribution analyisis of sediments containing Younger Toba tephra from Ghoghara, Middle Son Valley, India. *Quaternary International* 258:180–90.

Ling Roth, H. (1899) *The Aborigines of Tasmania* (facsimile of second edition). Hobart: Fullers.

Littleton, J. and Allen, H. (2007) Hunter-gatherer burials and the creation of persistent places in southeastern Australia. *Journal of Anthropological Archaeology* 26:283–98.

Longmore, M.E. and Heijnis, H. (1999) Aridity in Australia: Pleistocene records of palaeohydrological and palaeoecological change from the perched lake sediments of Fraser Island, Queensland, Australia. *Quaternary International* 57–8:35–47.

Lorblanchet, M. (1977) Summer report of fieldwork, Dampier, WA. *Australian Institute of Aboriginal Studies Newsletter* 7:36–40.

Lorblanchet, M. (1983) Chronology of the rock engravings of Gum Tree Valley and Skew Valley near Dampier, W.A. In M. Smith (ed.) *Archaeology at ANZAAS.* Perth: Western Australian Museum.

Lorblanchet, M. (1992) The rock engravings of Gum Tree Valley and Skew Valley, Dampier, Western Australia: Chronology and function of the sites. In J. McDonald and I.P. Haskovic (eds) *State of the Art: Regional rock art studies in Australia and Melanesia*, pp. 39–59. Occasional AURA Publication 6. Melbourne: Australian Rock Art Research Association.

Lourandos, H. (1983) 10,000 years in the Tasmanian highlands. *Australian Archaeology* 16:39–47.

Lourandos, H. (1988) Seals, sedentism and change in Bass Strait. In B. Meehan and R. Jones (eds) *Archaeology with Ethnography: An Australian perspective*, pp. 277–85. Canberra: Department of Prehistory, RSPacS, Australian National University.

Lourandos, H. (1997) *Continent of Hunter-gatherers: New perspectives in Australian prehistory*. Cambridge: Cambridge University Press.

Louys, J. (2012) Mammal community structure of Sundanese fossil assemblages from the Late Pleistocene, and a discussion on the ecological effects of the Toba eruption. *Quaternary International* 258:80–7.

Loy, T.H. (1990) Getting blood from a stone. *Australian Natural History* 32(6):470–9.

Loy, T.H., Jones, R., Nelson, D.E., Meehan, B., Vogel, J. et al. (1990) Accelerator radiocarbon dating of human blood proteins in pigments from Late Pleistocene art sites in Australia. *Antiquity* 64:110–16.

Luebbers, R.A. (1975) Ancient boomerangs discovered in South Australia. *Nature* 253:39.

Luebbers, R.A. (1982) The Coorong report: An archaeological survey of the northern Coorong. Department of Environment and Planning, South Australian Government.

Luly, J.G. (2001) On the equivocal fate of Late Pleistocene *Callitris* Vent. (*Cupressaceae*) woodlands in arid South Australia. *Quaternary International* 83–5:155–68.

Macaulay, V., Hill, C., Achilli, A., Rengo, C., Clarke, D. et al. (2005) Single, rapid coastal settlement of Asia revealed by analysis of complete mitochondrial genomes. *Science*, New Series, 308(5724):1034–6.

McBryde, I. (1982) *Coast and Estuary: Archaeological investigations on the north coast of New South Wales at Wombah and Schnapper Point*. Canberra: Australian Institute of Aboriginal Studies.

McBryde, I. (1984) Kulin greenstone quarries: The social contexts of production and distribution for the Mt William site. *World Archaeology* 16(2):267–85.

McBryde, I. (1997) The landscape is a series of stories: Grindstones, quarries and exchange in Aboriginal Australia: A Lake Eyre case study. In A. Ramos-Millan and A. Bustillo (eds) *Siliceous Rocks and Culture*, pp. 587–607. Granada: University of Granada.

McCarthy, F.D. (1979) *Australian Stone Tool Implements*. Sydney: Australian Museum.

McConnell, K. (1998) The prehistoric use of Chenopodiaceae in Australia: Evidence from Carpenter's Gap shelter I in the Kimberley, Australia. *Vegetation History and Archaeobotany* 7:179–88.

McConnell, K. and O'Connor, S. (1997) 40,000 year record of plant foods in the southern Kimberley Ranges, Western Australia. *Australian Archaeology* 45:20–31.

McConvell, P. (1997) Long lost relations: Pama-Nyungan and northern kinship. In P. McConvell and N. Evans (eds) *Archaeology and Linguistics*, pp. 207–35. Aboriginal Australia in Global Perspective. Melbourne: Oxford University Press.

McDonald, J. (1999) Bedrock notions and isochrestic choice: Evidence for localised stylistic patterning in the engravings of the Sydney region. *Archaeology in Oceania, Making a Mark: Papers on rock art for Andre Rosenfeld* 34(3):145–60.

McDonald, J. (2005) Archaic faces to headdresses: The changing role of rock art across the arid zone. In P. Veth, M. Smith and P. Hiscock (eds) *Desert Peoples: Archaeological perspectives*, pp. 116–41. Oxford: Blackwell Publishers.

McDonald, J., Donlan, D., Field, J.H., Fullagar, R.L.K., Coltrain, J.B. et al. (2007) The first archaeological evidence for death by spearing in Australia. *Antiquity* 81(314):877–85.

McGilchrist, I. (2009) *The Master and His Emissary: The divided brain and the making of the Western world*. New Haven and London: Yale University Press.

McIntosh, P.D. (2010) Fire, erosion and the end of the megafauna. *Australasian Science* 31(7):27–9.

McKenzie, G.M. and Kershaw, A.P. (2000) The last glacial cycle from Wyelangta, the Otway region of Victoria, Australia. *Palaeogeography, Palaeoclimatology, Palaeoecology* 155:177–93.

Mackness, B.S. (2009) Reconstructing *Palorchestes* (*Marsupialia: Palorchestidae*)—from giant kangaroo to marsupial tapir. *Proceedings of the Linnean Society of NSW* 130:21–36.

Macknight, C.C. (1969) The Macassans: A study of the early trepang industry along the Northern Territory coast. Unpublished PhD thesis. Canberra: Australian National University.

Macknight, C.C. and Gray, W.J. (1970) *Aboriginal Stone Pictures in Eastern Arnhem Land.* Canberra: Australian Institute of Aboriginal Studies.

McNiven, I.J. (2008) Inclusions, exclusions and transitions: Torres Strait Islander constructed landscapes over the past 4000 years, northeast Australia. *The Holocene* 18(3):449–62.

Macphail, M.K. (1979) Vegetation and climates in southern Tasmania since the last glaciation. *Quaternary Research* 11:306–41.

Magee, J.W. and Miller, G.H. (1998) Lake Eyre palaeohydrology from 60 ka to the present: Beach ridges and glacial maximum aridity. *Palaeogeography, Palaeoclimatology, Palaeoecology* 144:307–29.

Magee, J.W., Miller, G.H., Spooner, N.A. and Questiaux, D. (2004) A continuous 150ky monsoon record from Lake Eyre, Australia: Insolation-forcing implications and unexpected Holocene failure. *Geology* 32:885–8.

Marshall, H. (1988) Variability in coastal archaeological sites in the Port Fairy area, Victoria. Unpublished BA (Hons) thesis. Canberra: Australia National University.

Martins, S., Soong, B.-W., Wong, V.C.N., Giunti, P., Stevanin, G. et al. (eds) (2012) Mutational origin of Machado-Joseph disease in the Australian Aboriginal communities of Groote Eylandt and Yirrkala. *American Medical Association Online* 20 February: E1–E6.

Marun, L.H. (1969) Progress report on 'Nullarbor Project 1969' (Doc. 69/879) to the Australian Institute of Aboriginal Studies.

Marwick, B. (2002) Milly's Cave: Evidence for human occupation of the inland Pilbara during the last glacial maximum. *Tempus* 7:21–33.

Marx, S.K., McGowan, H.A. and Kamber, B.S. (2009) Long-range dust transport from eastern Australia: A proxy for Holocene aridity and ENSO-type climate variability. *Earth and Planetary Science Letters* 282:167–77.

Matthews, N.E. (2012) Ultra-distal tephra deposits from super-eruptions: Examples from Toba, Indonesia and Taupo Volcanic Zone, New Zealand. *Quaternary International* 258:54–79.

May, S.K., Taçon, P.C., Wesley, D. and Travers, M. (2010) Painting history: Indigenous observations and depictions of the 'Other' in northwestern Arnhem Land, Australia. *Australian Archaeology* 71:57–65.

Maynard, L. (1977) Classification and terminology in Australian rock art. In P.J. Ucko (ed.) *Form in Indigenous Art: Schematisation in the art of Aboriginal Australia and prehistoric Europe*, pp. 387–403. Canberra: Australian Institute of Aboriginal Studies.

Maynard, L. (1979) The archaeology of Australian Aboriginal art. In S.M. Mead (ed.) *Exploring the Visual Arts of Oceania*, pp. 83–110. Honolulu: University of Hawaii Press.

Maynard, L. and Edwards, E. (1971) Wall markings. In R.V.S. Wright (ed.) *Archaeology of the Gallus Site, Koonalda Cave.* Australian Aboriginal Studies 26, pp. 61–83. Canberra: Australian Institute of Aboriginal Studies.

Meehan, B. (1982) *Shell Bed to Shell Midden.* Canberra: Australian Institute of Aboriginal Studies Press.

Meggitt, M.J. (1962) *Desert People.* Chicago: Chicago University Press.

Merriwether, D.A., Hodgson, J.A., Friedlaender, F.R., Allaby, R., Cerchio, S. et al. (2005) Ancient mitochondrial M haplogroups identified in the southwest Pacific. *Proceedings of the National Academy of Sciences of the USA* 102(37):13034–9.

Mijares, A.S., Detroit, F., Piper, P., Grun, R., Bellwood, P. et al. (2010) New evidence for a 67,000-year-old human presence at Callao Cave, Luzon, Philippines. *Journal of Human Evolution* 59:123–32.

Miller, G.H., Magee, J.W., Johnson, B.J., Fogal, M.L., Spooner, N.A. et al. (1999) Pleistocene extinction of *Genyornis newtoni*: Human impact on Australian megafauna. *Science*, New Series 283(5399):205–8.

Miller, G., Mangan, J., Pollard, D., Thompson, S., Felzer, B. et al. (2005) Sensitivity of the Australian monsoon to insolation and vegetation: Implications for human impact on continental moisture balance. *Geology* 33:65–8.

Mitchell, S. (1994) Stone exchange network in northern Australia: A case study from Croker Island, northwestern Arnhem Land. In M. Sullivan, S. Brockwell and A. Webb (eds) *Archaeology in the North*, pp. 188–200. Darwin: Northern Australian Research Unit, Australian National University.

Molnar, R.E. (2004) *Dragons in the Dust: The palaeobiology of the Giant Monitor Lizard Megalania.* Indiana: Indiana University Press.

Montgomery, J.M., Gillespie, D., Sastrawan, P., Fredeking, T.M. and Stewart, G.L. (2002) Aerobic salivary bacteria in wild and captive Komodo dragons. *Journal of Wildlife Diseases* 38(3):545–51.

Mooney, S.D., Harrison, S.P., Bartlein, P.J., Daniau, A.-L., Stevenson, J. et al. (2011) Late Quaternary fire regimes of Australasia. *Quaternary Science Reviews* 30:28–46.

Moore, J.H. (2001) Evaluating five models of human colonization. *American Anthropologist* 103(2):395–408.

Morse, K. (1988) Mandu Mandu rockshelter: Pleistocene human coastal occupation of North West Cape, Western Australia. *Archaeology in Oceania* 23:81–8.

Morse, K. (1993) New radiocarbon dates from North West Cape, Western Australia. Preliminary report. In M.A. Smith, M. Spriggs and B. Fankauser (eds) *Sahul in Review: Pleistocene archaeology in Australia, New Guinea and island Melanesia.* Occasional Papers in Prehistory 24:155–3. Canberra: Australian National University.

Morwood, M. (2002) *Visions of the Past: The archaeology of Australian Aboriginal art.* Sydney: Allen & Unwin.

Morwood, M. and Hobbs, D.R. (eds) (1995) *Quinkan Prehistory: The archaeology of Aboriginal art in S.E. Cape York Peninsula, Australia.* Tempus 3, Anthropology Museum, St Lucia: University of Queensland.

Morwood, M.J. and Jung, S. (1995) Excavations at Magnificent Gallery. In M.J. Morwood and D.R. Hobbs (eds) *Quinkan Prehistory: The archaeology of Aboriginal art in S.E. Cape York Peninsula, Australia*, pp. 93–100. Tempus 3, Anthropology Museum, St Lucia: University of Queensland.

Morwood, M.J., O'Sullivan, P.B., Aziz, F. and Raza, A. (1998) Fission-track ages of stone tools and fossils on the east Indonesian island of Flores. *Nature* 392:173–6.

Morwood, M.J., Soejono, R.P., Roberts, R.G., Sutikna, T., Turney, C.S.M. et al. (2004) Archaeology and the age of a new hominid from Flores in eastern Indonesia. *Nature* 431(7012):1087–91.

Moss, P.T. and Kershaw, A.P. (2000) The last glacial cycle from the humid tropics of northeastern Australia: Comparison of a terrestrial and a marine record. *Palaeogeography, Palaeoclimatology, Palaeoecology* 155:155–76.

Mountford, C.P. and Edwards, R. (1963) Rock engravings of Panaramitee Station. *Transactions of the Royal Society of South Australia* 86:131–46.

Mowat, F.M. (1995) Variability in western Arnhem Land shell midden deposits. BA (Hons) thesis. Canberra: Australian National University.

Mulvaney, D.J. (1961) The Stone Age of Australia. *Proceedings of the Prehistoric Society* 27:56–107.

Mulvaney, D.J. (1975) *The Prehistory of Australia.* Melbourne: Penguin.

Mulvaney, D.J. (1976) The chain of connection: The material evidence. In N. Peterson (ed.) *Tribes and Boundaries in Australia*, pp. 72–94. Canberra: Australian Institute of Aboriginal Studies.

Mulvaney, D.J. (1989) *Encounters in Place: Outsiders and Aboriginal Australians 1606–1985.* St Lucia: University of Queensland Press.

Mulvaney, D.J. and Joyce, E.B. (1965) Archaeological and geomorphological investigations at Mt Moffat Station, Queensland, Australia. *Proceedings of the Prehistoric Society* 31:147–212.

Mulvaney, D.J. and Kamminga, J. (1999) *Prehistory of Australia.* Sydney: Allen & Unwin.

Mulvaney, K. (2003) Transformations—Rock walls to canvas: Representations of the totemic geography in Aboriginal Australia. *Before Farming* 2(5):1–13.

Munn, N. (1970) The transformation of subjects into objects in Walbiri and Pitjantjatjara myth. In R.M. Berndt (ed.) *Australian Aboriginal Anthropology*, pp. 141–63. Canberra: Australian Institute of Aboriginal Studies.

Murphy, B.P., Williamson, G.J. and Bowman, D.M.J.S. (2012) Did central Australian megafaunal extinction coincide with abrupt ecosystem collapse or gradual climatic change? *Global Ecology and Biogeography* 21:142–51.

Murray, A.S. and Roberts, R.G. (1997) Determining the burial time of single grain quartz using optically stimulated luminescence. *Earth and Planetary Science Letters* 152:163–80.

Murray, J., Wallace, A. and Geode, A. (1982) Prehistoric human remains from an islet in Bass Strait. *Archaeology in Oceania* 17(2):82–9.

Murray, P. and Chaloupka, G. (1984) The Dreamtime animals: Extinct megafauna in Arnhem Land rock art. *Archaeology in Oceania* 19(3):105–16.

Murray, P. and Vickers-Rich, P. (2004) *Magnificent Mihirungs: The colossal flightless bird of the Dreamtime.* Bloomington: Indiana University Press.

Murray-Wallace, C.V. (2007) Eustatic sea-level changes since the last glaciation. In S.A. Elias, *Encyclopedia of Quaternary Science*, pp. 3034–43. Amsterdam: Elsevier.

Myers, F. (1986) *Pintupi Country Pintupi Self: Sentiment, place and politics among Western Desert Aborigines.* Washington/Canberra: Smithsonian Institute Press/Australian Institute of Aboriginal Studies.

Nanson, G.C., Chen, X.Y. and Price, D.M. (1995) Aeolian and fluvial evidence of changing climate and wind patterns during the past 100 ka in the western Simpson Desert, Australia. *Palaeogeography, Palaeoclimatology, Palaeoecology* 113:87–102.

Nanson, G.C., Price, D.M., Jones, B.G., Maroulis, J.C., Coleman, M. et al. (2008) Alluvial evidence for major climate and flow regime changes during the middle and late Quaternary in eastern central Australia. *Geomorphology* 101:109–29.

Nanson, G.C., Price, D.M. and Short, S.A. (1992) Wetting and drying of Australia over the past 300 ka. *Geology* 20:791–4.

Neal, R. and Stock, E. (1986) Pleistocene occupation in the south-east Queensland coastal region. *Nature* 323:618–21.

Newman, D.M.R. (1983) Camels. In R. Strahan (ed.) *The Australian Museum Complete Book of Australian Mammals*, pp. 496–9. Sydney: Angus & Robertson.

Ngarta, J.B., Jukuna, M.C., Lawe, P. and Eirlys, R. (2004) *Two Sisters Ngarta and Jukuna.* Perth: Fremantle Arts Press.

Nicholson, A. (1994) Archaeology on an arid coast: Environment and material cultural influences on subsistence economies on the west coast of South Australia. MA thesis. Canberra: Australian National University.

Nicholson, A.F. and Cane, S.B. (1991a) Archaeology on the Anxious Coast. *Australian Archaeology* 33:3–13.

Nicholson, A.F. and Cane, S.B. (1991b) Desert camps: Analysis of Australian Aboriginal proto-historic campsites. In C.S. Gamble and W.A. Boismier (eds) *Ethnoarchaeological Approaches to Mobile Campsites: Hunter-gatherer and pastoralist case studies*, pp. 263–355. International Monographs in Prehistory, Ethnoarchaeological Series 1. Michigan: Ann Arbor.

Ninkovich, D., Sparks, R.S.J. and Ledbetter, M.T. (1978) The exceptional magnitude and intensity of the Toba eruption, Sumatra: An example of the use of deep-sea tephra layers as a geological tool. *Bulletin of Volcanology* 41(3):286–98.

Nobbs, M.F. and Dorn, R.I. (1988) Age determinations for rock varnish formations with petroglyphs: Cation-ratio dating of 24 motifs from the Olary region, South Australia. *Rock Art Research* 5(2):108–46.

Noetling, F. (1910) The food of the Tasmanian Aborigines. *Papers and Proceedings of the Royal Society of Tasmania* 279–305.

O'Connell, J.F. and Allen, J. (1998) When did humans first arrive in Greater Australia and why is it important to know? *Evolutionary Anthropology* 6:132–46.

O'Connell, J.F. and Allen, J. (2004) Dating the colonization of Sahul (Pleistocene Australia-New Guinea): A review of recent research. *Journal of Archaeological Science* 31:835–53.

O'Connell, J.F. and Allen, J. (2012) The restaurant at the end of the universe: Modeling the colonisation of Sahul. *Australian Archaeology* 75:5–17.

O'Connell, J.F., and Hawkes, K. (1981) Alyawara plant use and optimal foraging theory. In B. Winterhalder and E.A. Smith (eds) *Hunter-gatherer Foraging Strategies: Ethnographic and archaeological analyses.* Chicago: University of Chicago Press.

O'Connell, J.F., Hawkes, K. and Blurton Jones, N.G. (1999) Grandmothering and the evolution of *Homo erectus. Journal of Human Evolution* 36:461–85.

O'Connell, J.F., Latz, P.K. and Barnett, P. (1983) Traditional and modern plant use among the Alyawara of Central Australia. *Economic Botany* 37(1):80–109.

O'Connor, S. (1987) The stone house structures of High Cliffy Island, north west Kimberley, WA. *Australian Archaeology* 25:30–9.

O'Connor, S. (1992) The timing and nature of prehistoric land use in northern Australia. *Archaeology in Oceania* 27(2):49–60.

O'Connor, S. (1994) A 6700 BP Date for Island Use in the West Kimberley, Western Australia: New evidence from High Cliffy Island. *Australian Archaeology* 39:102–7.

O'Connor, S. (1995) Carpenter's Gap Rockshelter 1: 40,000 years of Aboriginal occupation in the Napier Ranges, Kimberley, WA. *Australian Archaeology* 40:58–9.

O'Connor, S. (1996) Thirty thousand years in the Kimberley: Results of excavation of three rockshelters in the coastal west Kimberley, WA. In P. Veth and P. Hiscock (eds) *Archaeology of Northern Australia: Regional perspectives.* Tempus 4. St Lucia: Anthropology Museum, University of Queensland.

O'Connor, S. (1999) A diversity of coastal economies: Shell mounds in the Kimberley region in the Holocene. In J. Hall and I.J. McNiven (eds) *Australian Coastal Archaeology*, pp. 37–50. Research Papers in Archaeology and Natural History 31. Canberra: ANH Publications, Australian National University.

O'Connor, S. (2002) Pleistocene Timor: Further corrections, a reply to Bednarik. *Australian Archaeology* 54:46–51.

O'Connor, S. (2007) New evidence from East Timor contributes to our understanding of earliest modern human colonisation east of Sunda Shelf. *Antiquity* 81(313):523–35.

O'Connor, S. and Arrow, S. (2008) Boat images in the rock art of northern Australia with particular reference to the Kimberley, Western Australia. In G. Clarke, F. Leach and S. O'Conner (eds) *Islands of Inquiry: Colonisation, seafaring and the archaeology of maritime landscapes*, pp. 397–409. Terra Australis 29. Canberra: ANU Press.

O'Connor, S., Barham, A., Spriggs, M., Veth, P., Aplin, K. et al. (2010) Cave archaeology and sampling issues in the tropics: A case study from Lene Hara Cave, a 42,000 year old occupation site in East Timor. *Australian Archaeology* (71):29–40.

O'Connor, S. and Fankhauser, B. (2001) One step closer: An ochre covered rock from Carpenter's Gap Shelter 1, Kimberley Region, WA. In A. Anderson, S. O'Connor and I. Lilley (eds) *Histories of Old Ages: Essays in honour of Rhys Jones*, pp. 287–300. Canberra: Coombs Academic Publishing, Australian National University.

O'Connor, S., Ono, R. and Clarkson, C. (2011) Pelagic fishing at 42,000 years before the present and the maritime skills of Modern Humans. *Science* 334(6059):1117–21.

O'Connor, S., Spriggs, M. and Veth, P. (2002) Excavations at Lene Hara establishes occupation in East Timor at least 30,000–35,000 years on: Results of recent field work. *Antiquity* 76:45–50.

O'Connor, S. and Sullivan, M. (1994) Distinguishing middens and cheniers: A case study from the southern Kimberley, WA. *Archaeology in Oceania* 29(1):16–28.

O'Connor, S. and Veth, P. (2006) Revisiting the past: Changed interpretations of Pleistocene settlement, subsistence and demography in northern Australia. In I. Lilley (ed.)

Archaeology of Oceania, Australia and the Pacific Islands, pp. 31–47. Oxford: Blackwell.

O'Connor, S., Veth, P. and Campbell, C. (1998) Serpent's Glen Rockshelter: Report of the first Pleistocene-aged occupation sequence from the Western Desert. *Australian Archaeology* 46:12–22.

Oppenheimer, S. (1998) *East of Eden—The drowned continent of southeast Asia.* London: Weidenfeld & Nicolson.

Oppenheimer, S. (2002) Limited global change due to the largest known Quaternary eruption, Toba ~74 kyr BP? *Quaternary Science Reviews* 21:1593–609.

Oppenheimer, S. (2009) The great arc of dispersal of modern humans: Africa to Australia. *Quaternary International* 202:2–13.

Oppenheimer, S. (2012a) A single southern exit of modern humans from Africa: Before or after Toba? *Quaternary International* 258:88–99.

Oppenheimer, S. (2012b) Out-of-Africa, the peopling of continents and islands: Tracing uniparental gene trees across the map. *Philosophical Transactions of the Royal Society Biological Sciences* 367:770–84.

Ouzman, S., Taçon, P.S.C., Mulvaney, K. and Fullagar, R. (2002) Extraordinary engraved bird track from north Australia: Extinct fauna, Dreaming being and/or aesthetic masterpiece? *Cambridge Archaeological Journal* 12(1):103–12.

Page, K., Dare-Edwards, A., Nanson, G. and Price, D. (1994) Late Quaternary evolution of Lake Urana, New South Wales, Australia. *Journal of Quaternary Science* 9(1):47–57.

Pardoe, C. (1988) The cemetery as symbol: The distribution of prehistoric Aboriginal burial grounds in south eastern Australia. *Archaeology in Oceania* 23(1):1–16.

Pate, D.F., McDowell, M.C., Wells, T. and Smith, M.A. (2002) Last recorded evidence for megafauna at Wet Cave, Naracoorte, South Australia, 45,000 years ago. *Australian Archaeology* 54:53–4.

Pearce, R.H. and Barbetti, M. (1981) A 3800-year-old archaeological site at Upper Swan, Western Australia. *Archaeology in Oceania* 16(3):173–8.

Perkins, R. and Langton, M. (2008) *First Australians: An illustrated history.* Melbourne: Miegunyah Press.

Peron, M.F. (1809) *A Voyage of Discovery of the Southern Hemisphere.* London: Phillips (translated from the French) (facsimile of 1975 edition). Melbourne: Marsh Walsh.

Peterson, N. (1968) The pestle and mortar: An ethnographic analogy for archaeology in Arnhem Land. *Mankind* 6:567–70.

Peterson, N. (1973) Camp site location amongst Australian hunter-gatherers. *Archaeology and Physical Anthropology in Oceania* 8:173–93.

Peterson, N. with Long, J. (1986) *Australian Territorial Organisation.* Oceania Monograph 30. Sydney: University of Sydney.

Petherick, L., Bostock, H., Cohen, T.J., Fitzsimmons, K., Tibby, J. et al. (2013) Climatic records over the past 30 ka from temperate Australia—A synthesis from the Oz-INTIMATE workgroup. *Quaternary Science Reviews* 30:1–20.

Petherick, L., McGowan, H. and Moss, P. (2008) Climate variability during the last glacial maximum in eastern Australia: Evidence of two stadials? *Journal of Quaternary Science* 23(8):787–802.

Petraglia, M.D., Korisettar, R. and Pal, J.N. (2012a) The Toba volcanic super-eruption of 74,000 years ago: Climate change, environments and evolving humans. *Quaternary International* 258:1–4.

Petraglia, M.D., Ditchfield, P., Jones, S. et al. (2012b) The Toba volcanic super-eruption, environmental change, and hominin occupation history in India over the last 140,000 years. *Quaternary International* 258:119–34.

Pike-Tay, A. and Cosgrove, R. (2002) From reindeer to wallaby: Recovering patterns of seasonality, mobility, and prey selection in the Palaeolithic Old World. *Journal of Archaeological Method and Theory* 9(2):101–46.

Pike-Tay, A., Cosgrove, R. and Garvey, J. (2008) Systematic seasonal land use by the late Pleistocene Tasmanian Aborigines. *Journal of Archaeological Science* 35:2532–44.

Pitman, H.T. and Wallis, L.A. (2012) The point of spinifex: Aboriginal uses of spinifex grasses in Australia. *Ethnobotany Research and Applications* 10:109–31.

Plomley, N.J.B. (ed.) (1966) *Friendly Mission: The Tasmanian journals and papers of George Augustus Robinson, 1829–1834.* Hobart: Tasmanian Historical Research Association.

Prentice, M.L., Hope, G.S., Maryunani, K. and Peterson, J.A. (2005) An evaluation of snowline data across New Guinea during the last major glaciation, and area-based glacier snowlines in the Mt Jaya region of Papua, Indonesia, during the last glacial maximum. *Quaternary International* 138–9:93–117.

Pretty, G.L. (1986) Australian history at Roonka. *Journal of the Historical Society of South Australia* 14:107–32.

Prideaux, G.J., Ayliffe, L.K., DeSantis, L.R.G., Schubert, B.W., Murray, P.F. et al. (2009) Extinction implications of a Chenopod browse diet for a giant Pleistocene kangaroo. *Proceedings of the National Academy of Sciences of the USA* 106(28):11646–50.

Prideaux, G.J., Gully, G.A., Couzens, A.M.C., Ayliffe, L.K., Jankowski, N.R. et al. (2010) Timing and dynamics of late Pleistocene mammal extinctions in southwestern Australia. *Proceedings of the National Academy of Sciences of the USA* 107(51):22157–62.

Prideaux, G.J., Roberts, R.G., Megirian, D., Westaway, K.E., Hellstrom, J.C. et al. (2007) Mammalian responses to Pleistocene climate change in southeastern Australia. *Geology* 35:33–6.

Przywolnik, K. (2005) Long-term transitions in hunter-gatherers of coastal northwestern Australia. In P. Veth, M. Smith and P. Hiscock (eds) *Desert Peoples: Archaeological perspectives*, pp. 177–205. Oxford: Blackwell Publishing.

Quaternary International (2012). Special issue. The Toba Volcanic Super-eruption of 74,000 years ago: Climate change, environment and evolving humans, 258:1–200.

Rampino, M.R. and Ambrose, S. (2000) Volcanic winter in the garden of Eden: The Toba super-eruption and Late Pleistocene human population crash. *Geological Society of America*, Special paper 345:71–82.

Rampino, M.R. and Self, S. (1992) Volcanic winter and accelerated glaciation following the Toba super-eruption. *Nature* 359:50–2.

Rampino, M.R. and Self, S. (1993) Climate-volcanism feedback and the Toba eruption of ~74,000 years ago. *Quaternary Research* 40:269–80.

Rampino, M.R., Self., S. and Stothers, R.B. (1988) Volcanic winters. *Annual Reviews of Earth Planetary Science* 16:73–99.

Rasmussen, M., Guo, X., Wang, Y., Lohmueller, K.E., Rasmussen, S. et al. (2011) An Australian Aboriginal genome reveals separate human dispersals into Asia. *Science* 333:94–8.

Reber, G. (1965) Aboriginal carbon dates from Tasmania. *Mankind* 6:264–8.

Reeves, J.M., Chivas, A.R., Garcia, A., Holt, S., Couapel, M.J.J. et al. (2008) The sedimentary record of palaeoenvironments and sea-level change in the Gulf of Carpentaria, Australia, through the last glacial cycle. *Quaternary International* 183:3–22.

Reich, D., Green, R.E., Kircher, M., Krause, J., Patterson, N. et al. (2010) Genetic history of an archaic hominin group from Denisova Cave in Siberia. *Nature* 468:1053–60.

Reich, D., Patterson, N., Kircher, M., Delfin, F., Nandineni, M.R. et al. (2011) Denisova admixture and the first Modern Human dispersals into Southeast Asia and Oceania. *The American Journal of Human Genetics* 89:516–28.

Reynolds, H. (1981) *The Other Side of the Frontier.* Melbourne: Penguin.

Rhindos, D. and Webb, E. (1992) Modeling the initial colonisation of Australia: Perfect adaptation, cultural variability and cultural change. *Proceedings of the Australasian Society for Human Biology* 5:441–54.

Rhode, D., Madsen, D.B. and Jones, K.T. (2006) Antiquity of early Holocene small-seed consumption and processing at Danger Cave. *Antiquity* 80(308):328–39.

Roberts, R., Walsh, G., Murray, A., Olley, J., Jones, R. et al. (1997) Luminescence dating of rock art and past environments using mud-wasp nests in northern Australia. *Nature* 387:696–9.

Roberts, R.G. and Brook, B. (2010a) And then there were none? *Science* 327:420–2.

Roberts, R.G. and Brook, B. (2010b) The biggest losers. *Australian Science* July/August:14–17.

Roberts, R.G. and Brook, B. (2010c) Turning back the clock on the extinction of megafauna in Australia. *Quaternary Science Reviews* 29:593–5.

Roberts, R.G., Flannery, T.F., Ayliffe, L.K., Yoshida, H., Olley, J.M. et al. (2001) New ages for the last Australian megafauna: Continent-wide extinction about 46,000 years ago. *Science*, New Series 292(5523):1888–92.

Roberts, R.G. and Jacobs, Z. (2008) The lost giants of Tasmania. *Australian Science* Oct:14–17.

Roberts, R.G., Jones, R. and Smith, M.A. (1990a) Thermoluminescence dating of a 50,000-year-old human occupation site in northern Australia. *Nature* 345(6271):153–6.

Roberts, R.G., Jones, R. and Smith, M.A. (1990b) Stratigraphy and statistics at Malakunanja II: Reply to Hiscock. *Archaeology in Oceania* 25(3):122–5.

Roberts, R.G., Jones, R. and Smith, M.A. (1990c) Early dates from Malakunanja II, a reply to Bowdler. *Australian Archaeology* 31:94.

Roberts, R.G., Jones, R. and Smith, M.A. (1993) Optical dating at Deaf Adder Gorge, Northern Territory, indicates human occupation between 53,000 and 60,000 years ago. *Australian Archaeology* 37:58–9.

Roberts, R.G., Jones, R. and Smith, M.A. (1994) Beyond the radiocarbon barrier in Australian prehistory. *Antiquity* 68:611–16.

Roberts, R.G., Jones, R., Spooner, N.A., Head, M.J., Murray, A.S. et al. (1994) The human colonisation of Australia: Optical dates of 53,000 and 60,000 years bracket human arrival at Deaf Adder Gorge, Northern Territory. *Quaternary Geochronology (Quaternary Science Reviews)* 13:575–83.

Roberts, R.G., Spooner, N.A., Jones, R., Cane, S., Olley, J.M. et al. (1996) Preliminary luminescence dates for archaeological sediments on the Nullarbor Plain, South Australia. *Australian Archaeology* 42:7–16.

Roberts, R.G., Yoshida, H., Galbraith, R., Laslett, G., Jones, R. et al. (1998) Single-aliquot and single-grain optical dating confirm thermoluminescence age estimates at Malakunanja II rock shelter in northern Australia. *Ancient TL* 16(1):19–24.

Robertson, G., Attenbrow, V. and Hiscock, P. (2009) Multiple uses for Australian backed artefacts. *Antiquity* 83(320):296–308.

Rose, W.I. and Chesner, C.A. (1990) Worldwide dispersal of ash and gases from the earth's largest known eruption: Toba, Sumatra, 75 ka. *Palaeogeography, Palaeoclimatology, Palaeoecology* (Global and Planetary Change section) 89:269–75.

Rosenfeld, A. (1982) Style and meaning in Laura art: A case study in the formal analysis of style in prehistoric art. *Mankind* 13(3):199–217.

Rosenfeld, A., Horton, D. and Winter, J. (1981) *Early Man in north Queensland.* Terra Australis 6. Canberra: Department of Prehistory, Australian National University.

Rosenfeld, A. and Smith, M.A. (2002) Rock art and the history of Puritjarra rock shelter, Clelend Hills, central Australia. *Proceedings of the Prehistoric Society* 68:102–24.

Ross, A. (1985) Archaeological evidence for population change in the middle to late Holocene in southeastern Australia. *Archaeology in Oceania* 20(3):81–9.

Ross, A., Donnelly, T. and Wasson, R. (1992) The peopling of the arid zone: Human environmental interaction. In J. Dodson (ed.) *The Naïve Lands: Prehistory and environmental change in Australia and the Southwest Pacific*, pp. 76–114. Melbourne: Longman Cheshire.

Rowland, M.J. (1980) The Keppel Islands—Preliminary investigations. *Australian Archaeology* 11:1–17.

Rowland, M.J. (1987) Preliminary archaeological survey of the coastal areas of Bundaberg 1:250,000 sheet (KE). Unpublished report. Department of Environment and Heritage, Brisbane.

Rowland, M.J. (1988) The Whitsunday Islands: Initial historical and archaeological observations and implications for future research. *Queensland Archaeological Research* 3:72–87.

Savolainen, P., Leitner, T., Wilton, A.N., Matisoo-Smith, E., Lundeberg, J. et al. (2004) A detailed picture of the origin of the Australian dingo, obtained from the study of mitachondrial DNA. *Proceedings of the National Academy of Sciences of the USA* 101(33):12387–90.

Schrire, C. (1982) *The Alligator Rivers: Prehistory and ecology in western Arnhem Land.* Terra Australia 7. Canberra: Department of Prehistory, Research School of Pacific Studies, Australian National University.

Sharpe, C.E. and Sharpe, K.J. (1976) A preliminary survey of engraved boulders in the art sanctuary of Koonalda Cave, South Australia. *Mankind* 10:125–30.

Shawcross, W. (1998) Archaeological excavations at Mungo. *Archaeology in Oceania* 33:183–200.

Sheppard, P.J. (1997) Characterisation of cherts from sites in southwest Tasmania. *Archaeology in Oceania* 32:47–53.

Sheridan, G. (1979) Tulas and triodia: A multidisciplinary investigation of the mechanics and antecedents of the konndi tula and their implications for prehistory. MA (Qualifying) thesis. Department of Prehistory and Anthropology. Canberra: Australian National University.

Shulmeister, J., Goodwin, I., Renwick, J., Harle, K., Armand, L. et al. (2004) The southern hemisphere westerlies in the Australasian sector over the last glacial cycle: A synthesis. *Quaternary International* 118–19:23–53.

Siddall, M., Rohling, E.J., Almogi-Labin, A., Hemleben, C., Meischner, D. et al. (2003) Sea-level fluctuations during the last glacial cycle. *Nature* 423:853–8.

Sieh, K. (2007) The Sunda megathrust—Past, present and future. *Journal of Earthquake and Tsunami* 1(1):1–19.

Sim, R. (1990) Prehistoric sites on King Island in the Bass Strait: Results of an archaeological survey. *Australian Archaeology* 31:33–4.

Sim, R. (1994) Prehistoric human occupation in the King and Furneaux Group Islands Regions, Bass Strait. In M. Sullivan, S. Brockwell and A. Webb (eds). *Archaeology in the North*, pp. 358–74. Darwin: Northern Australian Research Unit.

Sim, R. and Thorne, A. (1990) Pleistocene human remains from King Island, south eastern Australia. *Australian Archaeology* 31:44–51.

Singh, G. and Geissler, E.A. (1985) Late Cainozoic history of vegetation, fire, lake levels and climate at Lake George, NSW. *Philosophical Transactions of the Royal Society of London B* 311:379–447.

Slack, M., Fillios, M. and Fullagar, R. (2009) Aboriginal settlement during the LGM in Brockman, Pilbara region, Western Australia. *Archaeology in Oceania* 44 (supplement):32–9.

Slack, M.J., Fullagar, R.L.K., Field, J. and Border, A. (2004) New Pleistocene ages for backed artifact technology in Australia. *Archaeology in Oceania* 39:131–7.

Smith, M.A. (1987) Pleistocene occupation in arid Central Australia. *Nature* 328:710.

Smith, M.A. (1988) Central Australian seed grinding implements and Pleistocene grindstones. In B. Meehan and R.M. Jones (eds) *Archaeology with Ethnography: An Australian perspective*, pp. 94–109. Canberra: Department of Prehistory, Australian National University.

Smith, M.A. (1989) The case for a resident human population in the Central Australian ranges during full glacial aridity. *Archaeology in Oceania* 24(3):93–105.

Smith, M.A. (2005) Desert archaeology, linguistic stratigraphy and the spread of the Western Desert language. In P. Veth, M. Smith and P. Hiscock (eds) *Desert Peoples: Archaeological perspectives*, pp. 168–86. Oxford: Blackwell Publishing.

Smith, M.A. (2009) Late Quaternary landscapes in Central Australia: Sedimentary history and palaeoecology of Puritjarra rock shelter. *Journal of Quaternary Science* 24(7):747–60.

Smith, M.A. (2013) *The Archaeology of Australia's Deserts*. Cambridge World Archaeology Series. Cambridge: Cambridge University Press.

Smith, M.A., Bird, M.A., Turney, C.M.S., Fifield, L.K., Santos, G.M. et al. (2001) New ABOX AMS ^{14}C Ages remove dating anomalies at Puritjarra rock shelter. *Australian Archaeology* 53:45–6.

Smith, M.A. and Fankhauser, B. (2009) Geochemistry and identification of Australian red ochre deposits. *Palaeoworks Technical Paper 9*. Canberra: National Museum of Australia and Centre for Archaeological Research, Australian National University.

Smith, M.A., Fankhauser, B. and Jercher, M. (1998) The changing provenance of red ochre at Puritjara rock shelter, central Australia: Late Pleistocene to the present. *Proceedings of the Prehistoric Society* 64:275–92.

Smith, M.A., Prescott, J.R. and Head, M.J. (1997) Comparison of ^{14}C and luminescence chronologies at Puritjarra rock shelter, Central Australia. *Quaternary Science Reviews (Quaternary Geochronology)* 16:299–320.

Smith, M.A. and Ross, J. (2008) What happened at 1500–1000 cal. BP in Central Australia? Timing, impact and archaeological signatures. *The Holocene* 18(3):379–88.

Smith, M.A. and Sharp, N.D. (1993) Pleistocene sites in Australia, New Guinea and Island Melanesia: Geographic and temporal structure of the archaeological record. In M.A. Smith, M. Spriggs and B. Fankauser (eds) *Sahul in Review: Pleistocene archaeology in Australia, New Guinea and island Melanesia.* Occasional Papers in Prehistory 24:37–59. Canberra: ANU Press.

Smith, M.A., Vellen, L. and Pask, J. (1995) Vegetation history from archaeological charcoals in central Australia: The late Quaternary record from Puritjarra rock shelter. *Vegetation History and Archaeobotany* 4:171–7.

Smith, M.A., Williams, A.N., Turney, C.S.M. and Cupper, M.L. (2008) Human–environment interactions in Australian drylands: Exploratory time-series analysis of archaeological records. *The Holocene* 18(3):389–401.

Smith, M.V. (1993) Research a L'Esperance: A prehistory of the Esperance region of south western Australia. Unpublished PhD thesis. Perth: University of Western Australia.

Smith, M.V. (1996) South western Australian coastal economies: A new review. Unpublished paper presented to the Australian Coastal Archaeology Symposium, 1994.

Stacey, N. (2000) Pearlers, planes and people of the sea: Early Bajo voyages to the north Australian region. *Bulletin of the Australian Institute of Maritime Archaeology* 24:41–50.

Stanner, W.E.H. (1966) *On Aboriginal Religion.* Oceania Monograph 11. Sydney: University of Sydney.

Stanner, W.E.H. (1984) Religion, totemism and symbolism. In M. Charlesworth, H. Morphy, D. Bell and K. Maddock (eds) *Religion in Aboriginal Australia: Essays on Aboriginal spirituality*, pp. 1–23. Cambridge: Cambridge University Press.

Stanner, W.E.H. (1987) The Dreaming. In W.H. Edwards (ed.) *Traditional Aboriginal Society.* Melbourne: Macmillan.

Starling, J.A. (1971) Aboriginal sites in the Sim Committee areas. A report to the Australian Institute of Aboriginal Studies, Canberra.

Stern, N. and Marshall, B. (1993) Excavations at Mackintosh 90/1 in Western Tasmania: A discussion of stratigraphy, chronology and site formation. *Archaeology in Oceania* 28(1):1–8.

Stockton, E.D., and Holland, W. (1974) Cultural sites and their environment in the Blue Mountains. *Archaeology and Physical Anthropology in Oceania* 9:36–65.

Stockton, J. (1982) Seals in Tasmanian prehistory. *Proceedings of the Royal Society of Victoria* 94(2):53–60.

Stockton, J. (1983) The prehistoric population of north west Tasmania. *Australian Archaeology* 17:67–78.

Storey, M., Roberts, R.G. and Saidin, M. (2012) Astronomically calibrated 40Ar/39Ar age for the Toba supereruption and global synchronization of late Quaternary records. *Proceedings of the National Academy of Sciences of the USA* 109(46):18684–8.

Storm, P., Aziz, F., de Vos, J., Kosasih, D., Baskoro, S. et al. (2005) Late Pleistocene *Homo sapiens* in a tropical rainforest fauna in East Java. *Journal of Human Evolution* 49:536–45.

Strahan, R. (ed.) (1983) *The Australian Museum Complete Book of Australian Mammals.* Sydney: Angus & Robertson.

Suarez, T. (1999) *Early Mapping of Southeast Asia.* Singapore: Periplus.

Sullivan, M.E. (1984) A shell midden excavated at Pambula Lake on the far south coast of NSW. *Archaeology in Oceania* 19(1):1–15.

Summerhayes, G.R., Leavesley, M., Fairbairn, A., Mandui, H., Field, J. et al. (2010) Human adaption and plant use in Highland New Guinea 49,000 to 44,000 years ago. *Science* 330:78–81.

Surovell, T.A. and Grund, B.S. (2012) The associational critique of Quaternary overkill and why it is largely irrelevant to the extinction debate. *American Antiquity* 77(4):673–8.

Sutton, P. (1991) Myth as history, history as myth. In I. Keen (ed.) *Being Black: Aboriginal cultures in 'settled' Australia*, pp. 251–68. Canberra: Aboriginal Studies Press.

Sutton, P. (2003) *Native Title in Australia: An ethnographic perspective.* Cambridge: Cambridge University Press.

Sutton, P. (2011) *The Politics of Suffering: Indigenous Australia and the end of the liberal consensus.* Melbourne: Melbourne University Press.

Swift, J. (1986) *Gulliver's Travels.* London: Penguin Classics.

Swisher III, C.C., Curtis, G.H., Jacob, T., Gatty, A.G. and Suprijo Widiasmoro, A. (1994) Age of the earliest known hominids in Java. *Science* 263:1118–21.

Taçon, P. (1993) Regionalism in the recent rock art of western Arnhem Land, Northern Territory. *Archaeology in Oceania* 28:112–20.

Taçon, P. (1994) Socialising landscapes: The long-term implications of signs, symbols and marks on the land. *Archaeology in Oceania* 29(3):117–29.

Taçon, P. (2011) Reading the rocks. *Archaeology* January/February:32–7, 68.

Taçon, P., Brennan, W. and Lamilami, R. (2011) Rare and curious Thylacine depictions from Wollemi National Park, New South Wales and Arnhem Land, Northern Territory. In J. Specht and R. Torrence (eds) *Changing Perspectives in Australian Archaeology*, Part XI., *Technical Reports of the Australian Museum* 23:165–74.

Taçon, P. and Brockwell, S. (1995) Arnhem Land prehistory in landscape, stone and paint. *Antiquity* 69:676–95.

Taçon, P. and Chippendale, C. (1994) Australia's ancient warriors: Changing depictions of fighting in the rock art of Arnhem Land, N.T. *Cambridge Archaeological Journal* 4(2):211–48.

Taçon, P., Langley, M., May, S.M., Lamilami, R., Brennan, W. et al. (2010) Ancient bird stencils discovered in Arnhem Land, Northern Territory, Australia. *Antiquity* 84:416–27.

Taçon, P., May, S.K., Fallon, S.J., Travers, M., Wesley, D. et al. (2010) A minimum age for early depictions of southeastern Asian praus in the rock art of Arnhem Land, Northern Territory. *Australian Archaeology* 71:1–10.

Taçon, P., Wilson, M. and Chippendale, C. (1996) Birth of the Rainbow Serpent in Arnhem Land rock art and oral history. *Archaeology in Oceania* 31:103–24.

Takashi, T. (2012) MIS3 edge-ground axes and the arrival of the first *Homo sapiens* in the Japanese archipelago. *Quaternary International* 248:70–8.

Taylor, J. (2005a) Population and patterns of residence. In B. Arthur and F. Morphy (eds) *Macquarie Atlas of Indigenous Australia: Culture and society through space and time*, pp. 66–77. Sydney: Macquarie Library.

Taylor, L. (2005b) The visual arts. In B. Arthur and F. Morphy (eds) *Macquarie Atlas of Indigenous Australia: Culture and society through space and time*, pp. 114–25. Sydney: Macquarie Library.

Taylor, R. (2007) The polemics of eating fish in Tasmania: The historical evidence revisited. *Aboriginal History* 31:1–26.

Tedford, R.H. (1967) The fossil Macropodidae from Lake Menindee, New South Wales. *University of California Publications in Geological Sciences* 64:1–165.

Thomas, I. (1993) Late Pleistocene environments and Aboriginal settlement patterns in Tasmania. *Australian Archaeology* 36:1–12.

Thomson, D. (1975) *Bindibu Country.* Melbourne: Nelson.

Thorley, P.B. (1998) Pleistocene settlement in the Australian arid zone: Occupation of an inland riverine landscape in the central Australasian ranges. *Antiquity* 72:34–45.

Thorley, P.B. (2004) Rock art and the archaeological record of Indigenous settlement in Central Australia. *Australian Aboriginal Studies* 1:79–89.

Thorne, A., Grun, R., Mortimer, G., Spooner, N.A., Simpson, J.J. et al. (1999) Australia's oldest human remains: Age of the Lake Mungo 3 skeleton. *Journal of Human Evolution* 36:591–612.

Timmreck, C., Graf, H.-F., Zanchettin, D., Hagemann, S., Kleinen, T. et al. (2012) Climatic response to the Toba super-eruption: Regional changes. *Quaternary International* 258:30–44.

Tindale, N.B. (1955) Archaeological site at Lake Menindee, New South Wales. *Records of the South Australian Museum* 11:296–8.

Tindale, N.B. (1974) *Tribes and Boundaries in Australia.* Berkeley: University of California Press.

Tindale, N.B. (1977) Adaptive significance of the Panara or grass seed culture of Australia. In R.V.S. Wright (ed.) *Stone Tools and Cultural Markers: Change, evolution and complexity*, pp. 340–9. Canberra: Australian Institute of Aboriginal Studies Press.

Tindale, N.B. (1986) Anthropology. In C.R. Twidale, M.J. Tyler and J. Davies (eds) *Ideas and Endeavours: The natural sciences in South Australia*, p. 235. Adelaide: Royal Society of South Australia.

Tindale, N.B. (1987) The wandering of Tjirbruki: A tale of the Kaurna People. *Records of the South Australian Museum* 20:5–13.

Tonkinson, R. (1978) *The Mardudjara Aborigines: Living the dream in Australia's deserts.* New York: Holt Rinehart and Winston.

Torgersen, T., Hutchinson, M.F., Searle, D.E. and Nix, H.A. (1983) General bathymetry of the Gulf of Carpentaria and the Quaternary physiography of Lake Carpentaria. *Palaeogeography, Palaeoclimatology, Palaeoecology* 41:207–25.

Torgersen, T., Luly, J., De Deckker, P., Jones, M.R., Searle, D.E. et al. (1988) Late Quaternary environments of the Carpentaria Basin, Australia. *Palaeogeography, Palaeoclimatology, Palaeoecology* 67:245–61.

Trueman, C.N.G., Field, J.H., Dortch, J.M, Charles, B. and Wroe, S. (2005) Prolonged coexistence of humans and megafauna in Pleistocene Australia. *Proceedings of the National Academy of Sciences of the USA* 102(23):8381–5.

Turney, C.S.M., Bird, M.I. and Roberts, R.G. (2001) Elemental ^{13}C at Allen's Cave, Nullarbor Plain, Australia: Assessing post-depositional disturbance and reconstructing past environments. *Journal of Quaternary Science* 16:779–84.

Turney, C.S.M., Flannery, T.F., Roberts, R.G., Reid, C., Fifield, L.K. et al. (2008) Late-surviving megafauna in Tasmania, Australia, implicate human involvement in their extinction. *Proceedings of the National Academy of Sciences of the USA* 105(34):12150–3.

van der Kaars, S.A. (1991) Palynology of eastern Indonesian marine piston-cores: A late Quaternary vegetation and climate record for Australasia. *Palaeogeography, Paleoclimatology, Palaeoecology* 85:239–302.

van der Kaars, S.A. (2012) The influence of the 73 ka Toba super-eruption on the ecosystems of northern Sumatra as recorded in marine core BAR94-25. *Quaternary International* 258:43–53.

van der Kaars, S.A. and De Deckker, P. (2002) A late Quaternary pollen record from deep-sea core Fr10/95, GC17 offshore Cape Range Peninsula, northwestern Western Australia. *Review of Palaeobotany and Palynology* 120:17–39.

van der Kaars, S.A., De Deckker, P. and Gingele, F.X. (2006) A 100,000–year record of annual and seasonal rainfall and temperature for northwestern Australia based on a pollen record obtained offshore. *Journal of Quaternary Science* 21(8):879–89.

van der Kaars, S.A., Williams, M.A.J., Bassinot, F., Guichard, F., Moreno, E. et al. (2012) The influence of the ~73 ka Toba super-eruption on the ecosystems of northern Sumatra as recorded in marine core BAR94-25. *Quaternary International* 258:45–53.

van Holst Pellekaan, S.M., Frommer, M., Sved, J.A. and Boettcher, B. (1998) Mitochondrial control region sequence variation in Aboriginal Australians. *American Journal of Human Genetics* 62:435–49.

van Holst Pellekaan, S.M., Ingman, M., Toberts-Thomson, J. and Harding, R.M. (2006) Mitochondrial genomics identifies major haplogroups in Aboriginal Australians. *American Journal of Physical Anthropology* 131:282–94.

van Huet, S., Grun, R., Murray-Wallace, C.V., Redvers-Newton, N. and White, J.P. (1998) Age of the Lancefield megafauna: A reappraisal. *Australian Archaeology* 46:5–11.

Vanderwal, R.I. (1977) The Shag Bay rockshelter, Tasmania. *The Artefact* 2:161–70.

Vanderwal, R.I. (1978) Adaptive technology in southwest Tasmania. *Australian Archaeology* 8:107–27.

Vanderwal R.I. and Fullagar, R. (1989) Engraved *Diprotodon* tooth from the Spring Creek locality, Victoria. *Archaeology in Oceania* 24(1):13–16.

Veitch, B. (1999) Shell middens from the Mitchell Plateau: A reflection of a wider phenomenon? In J. Hall and I.J. McNiven (eds) *Australian Coastal Archaeology*, pp. 51–64. Research Papers in Archaeology and Natural History 31. Canberra: ANH Publications, Australian National University.

Veth, P. (1989) Islands in the interior: A model for the colonisation of Australia's arid zone. *Archaeology in Oceania* 24(3):81–92.

Veth, P. (1993) The Aboriginal occupation of the Montebello Islands, northwest Australia. *Australian Aboriginal Studies* 2:39–50.

Veth, P., Aplin, K., Wallis, L., Manne, T., Pulsford, T. et al. (2007) *The Archaeology of Montebello Islands, North Western Australia: Late Quaternary foragers on an arid coastline.* British Archaeological Reports International Series, 1668. Oxford: Archaeopress.

Veth, P., McDonald, J. and White, B. (2008) Dating of Bush Turkey Rockshelter 3 in the Calvert Ranges establishes early Holocene occupation of the Little Sandy Desert. *Australian Archaeology* 66:33–44.

Veth, P., Smith, M., Bowler, J., Fitzsimmons, K., Williams, A. et al. (2009) Excavations at Parnkupirti, Lake Gregory, Great Sandy Desert: OSL ages for occupation before the last glacial maximum. *Australian Archaeology* 69:1–10.

Veth, P., Smith, M. and Hiscock, P. (eds) (2005) *Desert Peoples: Archaeological perspectives.* Oxford: Blackwell Publishing.

Vinnicombe, P. (1987) *Dampier Archaeological Project: Resource document, survey and salvage of Aboriginal sites, Burrup Peninsula, WA.* Perth: Woodside Petroleum/Department of Aboriginal Sites, Western Australian Museum.

Voris, H.K. (2000) Maps of Pleistocene sea levels in Southeast Asia: Shorelines, river systems and time durations. *Journal of Biogeography* 27:1153–67.

Wallace, A.R. (2010) *The Malay Archipelago* (facsimile of original 1869 edition). Oxford: Beaufoy Books.

Wallace, N. (1977) Change in spiritual and ritual life in Pitjantjatjara society, 1966–1973. In R.M. Berndt (ed.) *Aborigines and Change: Australia in the 1970s*, pp. 74–89. Social Anthropology Series 11. Canberra/New Jersey: Australian Institute of Aboriginal Studies/Humanities Press.

Wallace, N.M. and Wallace, P.H. (1970) Australian Institute of Aboriginal Studies—Field Report, 1970. Canberra: Australian Institute of Aboriginal Studies.

Wallis, L.A. (2001) Environmental history of northwest Australia based on phytolith analysis at Carpenter's Gap 1. *Quaternary International* 83–5:103–17.

Walsh, G.L. and Morwood, M.J. (1999) Spear and spear thrower evolution in the Kimberley region, N.W. Australia. *Archaeology in Oceania* 34:45–58.

Walshe, K. (1994) A taphonomic analysis of the vertebrate material from Allen's Cave: Implications for Australian arid zone archaeology. Unpublished PhD thesis. Canberra: Australian National University.

Walshe, K. (1998) Taphonomy of Mungo B assemblage: Indicators for subsistence and occupation of Lake Mungo. *Archaeology in Oceania* 33:201–6.

Walshe, K. (2012) Port Augusta hearth site dated to 40,000 years. *Australian Archaeology* 74:106–9.

Walters, I. (1981) Why the Tasmanians stopped eating fish: A theoretical consideration. *The Artefact* 6(1 and 2):71–7.

Wang, X., van der Kaars, S., Kershaw, P., Bird, M. and Jansen, F. (1999) A record of fire, vegetation and climate through the last three glacial cycles from Lombok Ridge core G6-4 Indian Ocean, Indonesia. *Palaeogeography, Palaeoclimatology, Palaeoecology* 147:241–56.

Ward, I. (2004) Comparative records of occupation in the Keep River region of the eastern Kimberly, north western Australia. *Australian Archaeology* 59:1–9.

Watchman, A. (1993) Evidence of a 25,000-year-old pictograph in northern Australia. *Geoarchaeology* 8(6):465–73.

Watson, P. (2005) *Ideas: A history from fire to Freud.* London: Weidenfeld & Nicolson.

Webb, C. and Allen, J. (1990) A functional analysis of Pleistocene bone tools from two sites in southwest Tasmania. *Archaeology in Oceania* 255(2):75–9.

Webb, R.E. and Rhindos, D.J. (1997) The mode and tempo of the initial human colonisation of empty landmasses: Sahul and the Americas compared. *Archaeological Papers of the American Anthropological Association* 7(1):233–50.

Webb, S.G. (1987) A palaeodemographic model of late Holocene Central Murray Aboriginal society, Australia. *Human Evolution* 2:385–406.

Webb, S.G. (1989) *The Willandra Lakes Hominids.* Canberra: Department of Prehistory, Research School of Pacific Studies, Australian National University.

Webb, S.G. (1995) *Palaeopathology of Aboriginal Australians: Health and disease across a hunter-gatherer continent.* Cambridge: Cambridge University Press.

Webb, S.G. (2006) *The First Boat People.* Cambridge Studies in Biological and Evolutionary Anthropology 47. Cambridge: Cambridge University Press.

Webb, S.G. (2007) Further research of the Willandra Lakes fossil footprint site, southeastern Australia. *Journal of Human Evolution* 52:711–15.

Webb, S.G. (2008) Late Quaternary distribution and biogeography of the southern Lake Eyre basin (SLEB) megafauna, South Australia. *Boreas* 38:25–38.

Webb, S.G. (2013) *Corridors to Extinction and the Australian Mega-fauna.* Amsterdam: Elsevier.

Webb, S.G., Cupper, M.L. and Robins, R. (2006) Pleistocene human footprints from the Willandra Lakes, south eastern Australia. *Journal of Human Evolution* 50:405–13.

Westaway, K.E., Morwood, M.J., Roberts, R.G., Rokus, A.D., Zhao, J.-X. et al. (2007) Age and biostratigraphic significance of the Punung rainforest fauna, East Java, Indonesia, and implications for *Pongo* and *Homo*. *Journal of Human Evolution* 53:709–17.

Western Australian Fisheries (2006) Deep mysteries of the Perth Canyon. *Western Fisheries* July:28–31.

White, C. (1967) Early stone axes in Arnhem Land. *Antiquity* 41:49–52.

White, J.P., Crook, K.A.W. and Ruxton, B.P. (1970) Kosipe: A late Pleistocene site in the Papuan highlands. *Proceedings of the Prehistoric Society* 36:152–70.

White, J.P. and O'Connell, J. (1982) *A Prehistory of Australia, New Guinea and Sahul.* Sydney: Academic Press.

Wickler, S. and Spriggs, M. (1988) Pleistocene human occupation of the Solomon Islands, Melanesia. *Antiquity* 72:703–6.

Williams, E. (1985) Estimation of prehistoric populations of archaeological sites in south western Victoria: Some problems. *Archaeology in Oceania* 20(3):73–80.

Williams, E. (1987) Complex hunter-gatherers: A view from Australia. *Antiquity* 61:310–21.

Williams, M. (2012a) Did the 73 ka Toba super-eruption have an enduring effect? Insights from genetics, prehistoric archaeology, pollen analysis, stable isotope geochemistry, geomorphology, ice cores, and climate models. *Quaternary International* 269:87–93.

Williams, M. (2012b) The ~73 ka Toba super-eruption and its impact: History of a debate. *Quaternary International* 258:19–29.

Williams, M.A.J., Ambrose, S.H., van der Kaars, S., Ruehlemann, C., Chattopadhyaya, U. et al. (2009) Environmental impact of the 73 ka Toba super-eruption in South Asia. *Palaeogeography, Palaeoclimatology, Palaeoecology* 284:295–314.

Williams, M.A.J., Ambrose, S.H., van der Kaars, S., Ruehlemann, C., Chattopadhyaya, U. et al. (2010) Reply to the comment on 'Environmental impact of the 73 ka Toba super-eruption in South Asia' by M.A.J. Williams, S.H. Ambrose, S. van der Kaars, C. Ruehlemann, U. Chattopadhyaya et al. [*Palaeogeography, Palaeoclimatology, Palaeoecology* 284 (2009):295–314]. *Palaeogeography, Palaeoclimatology, Palaeoecology* 296:204–11.

Williams, M.A.J., Prescott, J.R., Chappell, J., Adamson, D., Cock, B. et al. (2001) The enigma of a late Pleistocene wetland in the Flinders Ranges, South Australia. *Quaternary International* 83–5:129–44.

Woinarski, J., Mackey, B., Nix, H. and Traill, B. (2007) *The Nature of Northern Australia: Natural values, ecological processes and future prospects.* Canberra: ANU E Press.

Wolpoff, M.H., Hawkes, J., Frayer, D.W. and Hunley, K. (2001) Modern human ancestry at the peripheries: A test of the replacement theory. *Science* 291:293–7.

Woodroffe, C., Chappell, J. and Thom, B.G. (1988) Shell middens in the context of estuarine development, South Alligator River, Northern Territory. *Archaeology in Oceania* 23:95–103.

Wright, K.I. (1994) Ground-stone tools and hunter-gatherer subsistence in southwest Asia: Implications for the transition to farming. *Society for American Archaeology* 59(2):238–63.

Wright, R.V.S. (1986) How old is Zone F at Lake George? *Archaeology in Oceania* 21:138–9.

Wright, R.V.S. (ed.) (1971) *Archaeology of the Gallus Site, Koonalda Cave.* Australian Aboriginal Studies 26. Canberra: Australian Institute of Aboriginal Studies.

Wroe, S. and Field, J. (2006) A review of the evidence for a human role in the extinction of Australian megafauna and an alternative explanation. *Quaternary Science* 25:2692–703.

Wroe, S., Field, J., Archer, M., Grayson, D.K., Price, G.J. et al. (2013) Climate change frames debate over the extinction of megafauna in Sahul (Pleistocene Australia-New Guinea). *Proceedings of the National Academy of Sciences of the USA* 110(22):8777–81.

Wroe, S., Field, J. and Grayson, D.K. (2006) Megafaunal extinction: Climate, humans and assumptions. *Trends in Ecology and Evolution* 21(2):61–2.

Yen, D.E. (1989) The domestication of environment. In D.R. Harris and G.C. Hillman (eds) *Foraging and Farming: The evolution of plant exploitation*, pp. 55–72. One World Archaeology. London: Unwin Hyman.

Yokoyama, Y., Lambeck, K., De Deckker, P., Johnston, J. and Fifield, L.K. (2000) Timing of the last glacial maximum from observed sea-level minima. *Nature* 406:713–16.

Yokoyama, Y., Purcell, A., Lambeck, K. and Johnston, P. (2001) Shore-line reconstruction around Australia during the last glacial maximum and late glacial stage. *Quaternary International* 83–5:9–18.

INDEX

In this index, page numbers in **bold** indicate illustrations. Page numbers followed by 'cap' indicate text in a caption.